Otto Fuchs was born on May 13th 1978 in Mariazell, Styria/Austria. He discovered a deep passion for rock & roll while still in his early teens. At fourteen years old, he becomes the youngest writer for the German "Rock & Roll Music Magazine". From 2000–2004 he hosted "The Rocket 88 Show" for KRKT 99.1 FM Rock It Radio, Ventura, California. Numerous interviews with 1950s Rock & Roll Legends such as Billy Lee Riley, Marvin Rainwater, Gene Vincent Blue Cap Drummer Dickie "Be Bop" Harrell, Bill Haley's Comets members Marshall Lytle, Joey Welz and Bill Turner are led & recorded by Fuchs for this show. During that period he also places various articles in the German "Dynamite— The World Of Rock & Roll" magazine. In 2005, he began to contribute reviews and interviews for German jive, swing & rockabilly magazine "Slam Bam". Bob Timmers of the Rockabilly Hall Of Fame recruited him as columnist for the Tennessee-based Rockabilly Hall Of Fame. While Otto Fuchs continued to write in German for the "Stompin' News" magazine, the column for the Rockabilly Hall Of Fame was the first medium requiring him to write in his second language, English. During a trip to his former home, London (where he lived from 1997–1999), Otto Fuchs met John Howard. Soon the two men came to the agreement that "UK Rock" (whose editor John Howard was, at that time) will publish his work as well. Otto Fuchs currently hosts the Internet Radio Programme "Rockabilly Rules OK" on Rockabilly Radio (www.rockabillyradio.net). He also hosted the "Rockin' The Juke Joint Show" from 2015 until 2020, the final year of KRKT 99.1FM Post Falls, Idaho, being active. Otto Fuchs also authored two books on Bill Haley, for Books On Demand: The Father of Rock & Roll,

The Rise of Bill Haley and Rock & Roll and The Father Of Rock & Roll, The Rock & Roll Revival Years and Bill Haley's Legacy. His third book is the one you are reading now—"Elvis Presley".

Left to right: Otto Fuchs, Terry Blackwood and His Imperials Minoriten Cathedral in Vienna (2019). Thanks again for the invitation to the great singer, Dennis Jale, from Austria who is neither a soundalike nor an impersonator, but just a great performer who suits all the songs Elvis Presley was meant to sing! In closing the inspiration and decision to write on Elvis Presley after having authored a Bill Haley Biography is still rooted in the USA and my youth then. It is for many a dream to go to the US. Especially to those who love Rockabilly music.

Most of it comes from the south. Blueprint-givers Hank Williams and Hardrock Gunther from the South, Bill Haley from the north, but influenced by his Kentucky born mandolin playing father. Elvis Presley a Memphian. For a long time the southern flag, as music symbol and display of being rebellious with a Rebel flag, it is part of the Rockin' scene for more than forty years.

My dad allowed me, I was 14 to choose all destinations of our 14 days trip. Not a long time, so I tried to squeeze in as much as I could. That meant seventeen airplane flights, two of these transatlantic. In 1993, we repeated it and were three weeks in the US, with a short breakaway to Mexico. I saw Detroit in Michigan, New York, Memphis in Tennessee, Tupelo in Mississippi, Lubbock and

Harlingen in Texas, Lancaster, Philadelphia, Boothwyn and Chester in Pennsylvania, Los Angeles in California and the capital of Mexico: Mexico City. From all the places, I loved the ones in Dixie the most. Elvis' Graceland was magnificent, I visited twice, many of the older fans approached me with "Oh, we have got a little Elvis here."

I did not ever in my life like to be compared to or called Elvis. It changed over the years; now middle-aged, I am glad that there is still some Presleyesqueness around me. Tupelo, Elvis' birthplace, was sweet. Lubbock, Buddy Holly's hometown and burial site seemed very quiet. Buddy still remembered, with a statue, including a Walk of Fame for other Texan musicians. On the two occasions I have been there, the town had something about the day after, the music died. After the return in 1993, from the States I wrote a travel essay about it. This was published in a Rock and Roll dedicated music magazine, EST. Since 1977.

For the love of my life, Nicole Fuchs and our daughters Lucienne Laura and Vivienne Marleen Fuchs.
I shall dedicate this book to all who cared and still care for Elvis.

In 1996, while serving National Service for the Austrian army—I even got to see him live at the Pyramid in Vösendorf, near Vienna. Two years later I learned about his tragic death, when pump gunning youngsters tried to rob him, and killed him—Jimmy "Orion" Ellis and his partner Elaine Thompson … a third female person in the shop survived. This was not the first time Jimmy Ellis was shot at, once asking for directions, some criminals most likely drug dealers, thought him to be an undercover agent and shot him. He survived that attack in the 1980s.

A good Elvis Early Years Performer I got to see and speak was Travis Le Doyt at the Wildest Cats in Town Rock and Roll Weekender Festival in Pakefield, England. He had such a resemblance to young Elvis, that many of the females turned into red tomato faces while posing for pictures with him. He also had an interesting album with him, on which he sang Elvis classics to a contemporary backing band arrangement.

Table of Contents

Introduction

Elvis Aron Presley was born on 8 January 1935 in Tupelo/Mississippi. His twin brother Jesse Garon Presley died at birth. Elvis showed musical talent at an early age. Singing along gospels in the Assembly of God Church. Elvis had the choice for his birthday, to either get a bicycle or a guitar. His choice was the bicycle. Though his mum, ever worried about him, chose a guitar. Elvis surely learned to love the guitar. In the mid-1940s, the family moved to Memphis/Tennessee, flat broke with a Ford T model. After graduating from Humes High School, Elvis started employment at Crown Electrics, driving a truck. His first acetate was "My Happiness" at the Memphis Recording Service.

The slogan of the soon to be famous SUN Studio was: "We record anything—everywhere"—and so Elvis cut his first professional disc, self-produced for the sum of a quarter Dollar. A year later, on 6 July 1954, the 29th birthday of the then reigning King of Rock and Roll—Bill Haley: "That's Allright" b/w "Blue Moon Of Kentucky" was recorded. The first song being a Blues song by Arthur Big Boy Crudup, dating back to the 1920s, the flipside a Bluegrass hit for Bill Monroe. Like in a movie, legends history tells us that Elvis was in the cinema, watching Marlon Brando in "The Wild One", when Dewey Phillips the local DJ Star played "That's Alright" on his "Red, Hot, 'n' Blue" Show. Getting so much positive feedback, that he wanted to interview young Elvis.

His parents picked him up in the cinema, supposedly bringing him over to Dewey Philips' studio. Dewey had no relation to Sam Phillips ... The breakthrough for Elvis came, when RCA Records bought him out of his SUN contract for the sum of 35,000 Dollars, including the purchase of all of Elvis' SUN songs. Almost simultaneously with Colonel Tom Parker overtaking Elvis' management from Bob Neale. (Also, a Memphis DJ). The Elvis Presley produced fusion of Hillbilly, Rhythm and Blues and Gospel—so to say "Rockabilly" music, was officially born. Blueprint being laid by Hank Williams triggers all sorts of fantasies and imaginations, a lot of them are true, a lot of them are not true."

(Larry)

In my opinion, Elvis was always Elvis, he did not have to compete for any King of Rock and Roll title. Yet, people earn for a King … He was a genuine human being, and a most versatile artist. The Rock and Roll of his career span was Rockabilly, Rock and Roll, partially Rhythm and Blues, Gospel, Rock and Roll Love Songs, Ballads, Doo-Wop, Novelty Songs—Elvis had all of this described sub-niches of Rock and Roll in his repertory—does that make him The King?

(Author Otto Fuchs)

Just Kings of Rock and Roll Vs The King of Rock and Roll

Is it "The King of Rock and Roll" or is it "Just Kings of Rock and Roll"—still a hot topic, going back to the late 1980s …

The lighter film material, which so many critics point a finger on, are actually far-ahead to other Rock and Roll singers' B-movies. Actually, in a time where there was no MTV (Music Television Programmer's with music videos aimed at young audiences)—it was pretty sharp to record albums—enter a "good feel movie" around it, and make 1,000,000 USD per movie for Elvis plus royalties of the Soundtrack albums. Colonel Tom Parker is easily painted as the "snake in the garden of Elvis", but he brought Elvis to a new height of stardom—his contemporaries should they not have been killed in airplane crashes (Buddy Holly, Ritchie Valens and The Big Bopper), car crashes (Eddie Cochran, Chuck Willis), Russian roulette (Johnny Ace) or just flee south of the border for tax debts like Bill Haley … Would they have reached a greater stardom under Tom Parker's management?

Tommy Sands was managed by the Colonel for a while, but fell out with Frank Sinatra after he—Tommy Sands—divorced Frank's daughter Nancy Sinatra. The rumour that Sinatra Senior intentionally damaged or hurt the career of Sands, is still not out of this world … The most and longest established music magazine from Germany specialised into the first era or Rock and Roll which roughly lasted from 1954 until 1963—went even further, the Editor in Chief asked his readers whom they considered as "King of Rock and Roll". This is what Claus D. Röglin wrote about the subject, getting his readers into the right discussion mood. Back in time—to the year 1989 and edition 68 and 69 of "Rock and Roll" (www.rocknroll-magazin.de)

For discussion:

What I recognised …

As I was sorting my MC (music cassettes) collection, and heard some of these for the first time, I noticed, how often at live-shows or radio shows of concerts Little Richard always presented as "King of Rock and Roll". The same, goes for Bill Haley and Elvis Presley. Whereas Elvis was announced the most as "True King". Also, other artists, some from our own country—Ted Herold. ("German Elvis, German King of Rock and Roll!) In the beginning I didn't pay much thought to the terminology of "King of Rock and Roll". But when I started to research for our upcoming Rock and Roll-lexicon (while studying a lot of literature) I often was confronted with an artist and his title as being "The King of". It seemed not to be the fair judgement or title giving.

To give the title, or alone to the terminology to an artist whose contribution is manifested in covering Rock and Roll Songs of original artists. Whereas an artist like Chuck Berry has all the necessary attributes to be labelled as "King of Rock and Roll", so is that title-giving a very unethical and unfair action: Absolutely unfair towards Chuck Berry.

It appears to me, that it is unfair, not to announce Chuck Berry as King of Rock and Roll. Chuck Berry had many talents, he was not only great in his vocal delivery, but also a great songwriter. He had a special talent, not to forget the guitar playing what he was capable of in that direction was immense. He is also a great writer, not only because of his songs. But of his self-written Autobiography. You could throw in now, that Chuck Berry never had a NR.1 hit, with the exception of "My Ding A Ling" at the beginning of the 1970s. Why then great performer?

John Lennon the intellectual head of The Beatles was stated saying about Chuck Berry: "If you tried to give rock and roll another name, you might call it 'Chuck Berry'." I think that in this quote with a deep meaning, everything is said. Those who know about the past 35 years Pop and Rock-History, including artists who performed in that time frame, that Rock-History would be most definitely, different, than it is. Alone musically speaking how would The Beatles have sounded, The Rolling Stones and all the other groups. What would have become off them, without Chuck Berry?

Would these groups have existed? Paul McCartney was once quoted in reply to that question—a simple "No"!

Chuck Berry was always into the things his audience was in, he never missed out in addressing their hopes, feelings. Humour, fear … He was the voice of the youth of, "that generation". His songs include the lifestyle and the history of a whole generation. He manifested that young generation (1950s–1960s) in his songs. Also, the rhythms suited it. With songs like "School Days", "Sweet Little

Sixteen", "Roll Over Beethoven", "Johnny B. Goode", "Memphis, Tennessee", "Nadine", "You Never Can Tell" and all the others he might have not the greatest hit (when he performed these songs himself at first). How many? Hundreds of performers and groups? Had their first taste of success with a cover or a revived Chuck Berry tune.

Chuck Berry stayed faithful to Rock and Roll for over 30 years, he never jumped on any bandwagon that was trendy. Contrary to the 1950s, when our music, Rock and Roll was invading the world, todays music is industrial produced, exchangeable mass consumption. Produced for mentally bankrupt people. Today's stars have the charm of Shop Window-Dolls.

Chuck Berry (with likeness to all other Rock and Roll Greats) had his success foremostly through the primitive basic power of Rock and Roll and through the incomparable charisma of his person. Un-influenced by the musical trend continues: A real Rock and Roll Fan is as a Rock and Roll Fan after 10, 20 and more years, the same Rock and Roll Fan that he always had been.

To me, the terminology "King of Rock and Roll" is meant firstly to Chuck Berry, because if we stay honest, what would have become out of the already late great, former Rock and Roll—Stars today? Elvis Presley like Buddy Holly (who was a great artist anyway) would be a second Frank Sinatra by today's standards. And Roy Orbison had cut more Pop-Ballads, so called Mini-Operas, more than Rockabilly or Rock and Roll. But I do not want to make a secret out of the fact that he is a great singer to me, and also an equally talented songwriter. I like to listen to him and his songs very much indeed.

In 1977, it was in Münster (Germany), I had the chance of seeing Chuck Berry ("Live") onstage, and I was fortunate enough to have small talk with him. I asked for a definition of his about Rock and Roll. His reply was as follows: "Rock and Roll? I cannot explain that to you straight to the point. You know it is more of a lifestyle and somehow a way how you look at your life. When thinking of my songs, which I still bring onto the stage. Then things like Dancing, Girls, Cars, Coca-Cola, Pony Tails, about the first girlfriend of mine—generally mostly about the life in the 1950s. With all its daily major problems and minor problems.

Man, that is Rock and Roll, to me, and I believe, that is transformed into my songs. I cannot phrase the meaning of Rock and Roll to you in better words, that'll be the job given from me to those always better-knowing types who write fat-pages books about Rock and Roll, and who basically always lie wrong with their research and outcome.

Rock and Roll cannot be explained in solely writing about it, you must play it, sing it and you must live it. Understand, 'Life', you've got to live Rock and Roll, simply living it, yeah!"

If Chuck Berry should go one day the way of all created on earth, I will send a garland over to the States on which you will read "The Greatest Rock and Roll Singer and Writer In The World Will Never Stop Singing!"

To me Chuck Berry is the "King of Rock and Roll", in so we are back at the beginning of this article. To find a moral and an endpoint on all of this: "Chuck Berry has done more with his music for the understanding what the USA stand for, more for world peace than all US-Presidents after World War II" altogether.

Claus-D. Röglin, Chief-Editor/July 1989—"Rock and Roll Musik Magazin Edition 68/13th year since being founded."

A lot of readers the "Rock and Roll Musik Magazin" (Est. 1977) reacted in the following edition Nr. 69, published in the year 1989—via the Post Box—the place given to readers to give feedback in open letters, in that case the Chief Editor Claus D. Röglin brought up the discussion who "The King of Rock and Roll" is. Arguably maybe laughable for an Elvis Presley, who modestly argued that there is only one King—The Saviour!

"Hello Claus! Gratefulness for Edition 69, which arrived on Thursday, October 5th. As I am currently sick with influenza, I had time, to work myself through your booklet. As soon as I started with it, I felt attracted by your story on 'The King of Rock and Roll'. I would like to make clear before I go any further, that I do not have a Rock and Roll dedicated library, with the exception of the ROCK-Lexica, Rowel-Publishing Reinbeck, First Edition, December 1973 and the analysis of Elvis Presley feature 'Let me be your teddy bear' by Mike Rodgers, at that time over the station NDR 2, which was broadcast in 11 episodes. There is not much to add to your analysis. The main thing was brought by you to paper. But maybe some personal thoughts from my side: The terminology 'King of Rock and Roll' is more of, firstly actually a term for the Public Relations Offices.

Also, a marketing strategy of the singer/performer in question, like an Elvis Presley, Little Richard, Bill Haley or Jerry Lee Lewis. Maybe the reason why Chuck Berry never was labelled as 'King of Rock and Roll', that in the old times he was not marketed very well. He didn't see much of his royalties or fees. This did not change until 1966 (source Rock Lexica). Maybe for that reason he was not interested in star-allures, contrary to Little Richard. Both artists are Afro-American, so they had hard times until the mid-1950s, it must have been quite a challenge to make a stand in the community and certainly also in show-business. While Little Richard in 1957 gave up on his career, Chuck Berry, due to the Brit-Invasion/Beat era came out once more out as a big star, whereas Little Richard was almost forgotten by then. Elvis Presley was marketed endlessly until his pre-mature death. Maybe you see a point to this subject through my perception, also.

With rocking regards-keep on rocking"

Werner Thal, Rostock, DDR (East Germany).

Dear Claus-D. Röglin,

First of all, I find it is legitimate that every Rock and Roll fan chooses his own personal favourite performer, and in so his own personal "King of Rock and Roll". My favourite—without dubbing him now "King" would be Eddie Cochran.

Rock historic-wise there is no doubt, that Chuck Berry has had an influence to the following performers, in a way hard to analyse, especially to Rock-guitarists. On the other hand, I find it not necessary, what would have been without Chuck Berry. What if we would not have had an Elvis Presley, what if not a Bill Haley, Buddy Holly or Alan Freed? Would the Beatles have been formed without an Elvis Presley? I believe, Rock and Roll would have come through, sooner or later, if not with the aforementioned artists, then with others. All of this legendary Rock and Rollers (and many others) were a stylistically influence to Rock and Roll music. But all of these legendary Rock and Rollers (and many others) influenced stylistically Rock and Roll, and helped to popularise it.

Should there be now an award be given with the title "King of Rock and Roll", then in my opinion I would only give artists the chance to get the credit, who were active in the years 1955 until 1959. So, to say the years of the original and real Rock and Roll era. The discussion or the example of Rock and Rollers who started their careers after 1959:

1. I do not find relevant, as the ones who were too young to die (Buddy Holly, Eddie Cochran) in an unfortunate and unfair position.
2. Rock and Roll (in its original form) did not have from 1960 on the same position like in the years when the youth was rebelling, it changed to dance music or was used as nostalgic entertainment.
3. You could also argue who, after the end of the Rock and Roll era, did the most to somehow continue it. Chuck Berry composed songs until the mid-1960s, some good Rock and Roll titles (though he copied himself), but then took it back to only perform his old songs and perform these worse, without excitement (despite rare occasions when he showed his old form). Elvis on the other hand recorded a lot of garbage during his movie years and truly very few Rock and Roll songs. But in 1968 with his attention-winning Stage Comeback one of the instigators of a new Rock and Roll Boom. The argument "He stayed not faithful to Rock and Roll" has not a lot of relevance, in my opinion. But who brought Rock and Roll forward and into the mainstream, during the formative years of the 1950s?

The argument that an artist stayed faithful until today is not of any relevance. But who was it who popularised Rock and Roll in the 50s the most? Who influenced the most musicians? No doubt Chuck Berry influenced following generations through his (guitar) sound and his power in composing songs. Nevertheless, I remain with my opinion that Elvis Presley had more influence. His expressive black-sounding singing voice mixed Country and Rhythm and Blues elements in an ideal way. Sam Phillips was the first one to note that. It was Elvis, who popularised Rock and Roll worldwide, the reason for having the most hits. His advantage was surely, that he was younger than Bill Haley and whiter than Chuck Berry, so for most of the white kids a better identification figure, he certainly was.

Numerous well-known musicians first came in touch with music through Elvis. His Live-concerts gave many the ideal kick, to try music out themselves. I would also like to cite John Lennon here: "It was Elvis made me addicted to the Big Beat. I listened to 'Heartbreak Hotel' and thought—this is it! I began to grow sideburns and all wear all other gear." (John Lennon—*In His Own Words*, 1981, page 17):

Bill Haley and Chuck Berry are seen through my eyes as the Great Grandfathers of Rock and Roll. Bill in the white Country influenced niche, Chuck in the black of the R&B coming influencing sounds for Rock and Roll. But it was Elvis who made the perfect synthesis between black and white music. To me he is the King of Rock and Roll (even though he was a performer, not a songwriter). The thesis that Elvis or Buddy Holly without Chuck would be like a second Sinatra been, I definitely deny. Elvis did not become attracted to Rock and Roll through listening to Chuck Berry. It was more so that he grew up under the influence in Tupelo/Mississippi. There were many Afro-American Blues and Gospel singers which influenced Elvis from childhood. In Memphis, he listened to B.B. King and learned more about the white artists with a Country background (Ernest Tubb, Bob Willis, Roy Acuff) and others.

One must acknowledge that Elvis' influence on following Rock-Generations was the one of style, the way of singing and partially his strange show He was the most successful R&R singer worldwide.

You could give following artists the title "King of Rock and Roll", specially split between the artists:

Chuck Berry is the King of Rock and Roll of guitarists and songwriters.

Elvis Presley is the King of Rock and Roll of the singers.

Bill Haley is the King of Country-Rock and Roll or the first hour in rock music's King of Rock and Roll

Jerry Lee Lewis is the King of Rock and Roll for piano players.

Little Richard is the King of the Rock and Roll—Shouters.

This can be continued—so anyone should be finding satisfaction …

(Martin Wörner)

I find the discussion about who is The King of Rock and Roll tiring. There never was never a King of Rock and Roll, as Rock and Roll never existed at all.

Today Rock and Roll is so versatile that for each niche a master can be found. Today you can say that in their entire output of work people like Elvis, Little Richard—maybe the best onstage, Carl Perkins likewise Buddy Holly are the artists were who influenced the following generation musically the most.

I prefer Chuck Berry among all others, as he is possibly the most versatile artist of all that ever were. In his work you'll find Blues, Rhythm and Blues, Ballads, Rockers, Novelty, Jazz and many more.

No matter what Chuck Berry-Record you spin, except the "Greatest Hits" compilations, these recordings are versatile, you'll never get bored listening through them. Chuck Berry is for me not only "Reelin' and Rockin'" or "School Days". Chuck Berry is also "It Hurts Me Too", "Dear Dad", "Ramblin' Rose" or "Flying Home". That's the reason why Chuck Berry is so listenable today and why he found so many copy-cats. Opinions from 1989 by the then in Chief-Editor Position sitting Claus D. Röglin, 1989, with feedback by engaged readers. A fine discussion on who is "The (undisputed) King of Rock and Roll". The magazine "Rock and Roll Musik Magazin" (www.rocknroll-magazin.de) est. 1977, stood brave against the Zeitgeist and with enthusiastic music journalists who wrote without payment, but out of labour of love about "Rock and Roll"/"Rockabilly", "Classic Rhythm and Blues", "Neo-Rockabilly", "Psychobilly", "Country" and "Teddy Boy Rock and Roll" … It stopped publication with its May edition of 2021, after 44 years.

Chapter One
A Living Superstar

Elvis Aron Presley was born on 8 January 1935, as son of Gladys Love (nee Smith; 1912–1958) and Vernon Elvis Presley (1916–1979). Elvis is one of the most significant cultural icons of the 20th century. He is still referred to as "King of Rock and Roll" or simply "the King".

Elvis was born in a two-room one floor house, built by his father Vernon in preparation for the birth. Jesse Garon Presley, his identical twin brother, was delivered stillborn 35 minutes before the birth of Elvis. Jesse was buried in an unmarked grave, at Princeville Cemetery in Tupelo/Mississippi. After Elvis hit stardom, he asked people on several occasions to try to find the whereabouts of Jesse's grave but to no avail, as no papers marked the spot.

Elvis was very close to his parents, forming a special bond with his mother Gladys. The family attended the Assembly of God church, hear Elvis found his musical inspiration. Although he came into conflict with the Pentecostal church in later years, he never officially left it. Reverend Rex Humbard officiating at Elvis Presley's funeral, stated that Elvis was an admirer of Humbard's ministry.

His ancestry can be found in a Western European mix, including German, Scots-Irish, Scottish, with French Norman. Gladys would often tell the family that before the Civil War, her great-great-grandmother, Morning Dove White, was a "full-blooded Cherokee Indian", although some genealogists doubt the claim.

Elaine Dundy in her book *Elvis and Gladys*, claims that Elvis Presley's great-great-grandmother Nancy Burdine Tackett was Jewish, citing a third cousin of Presley's, Oscar Tackett. It seems though, that this belief was not widespread in the Presley family. Also, columnist Nate Bloom challenged the claim, called the cousins, to which the reference "tall tale" came up. Nevertheless, Elvis had a necklace with a Christian cross and a David star, which he carried among the TCB emblem (Taking Care of Business).

Gladys was regarded by relatives and friends as the dominant member of the small family. Vernon moving from one odd job to another, with little ambition. The Presleys often relied on help from neighbours and government food assistance. They were also among the survivors of the Tupelo-Gainesville tornado outbreak in 1936. Losing their home in 1938, as Vernon was found guilty of kiting a check written by the landowner, Orville S. Bean, the dairy farmer and cattle-and-hog broker for whom he then worked. He was jailed for eight months, Gladys and Elvis moving in with relatives.

In September 1941, Elvis entered first grade at East Tupelo Consolidated. His teachers rating him as average. Encouraged to enter a singing contest, after having impressed one of his teachers with a rendition of Red Foley's country song "Old Shep", during morning prayers, he entered it:

Dressed as cowboy, the ten-year-old Elvis Presley stood on a chair to reach the microphone to sing "Old Shep" coming at a respectable fifth. The contest being held on 3 October 1945.

A few months later, Elvis was presented with his first guitar for his birthday, though he had hoped for either a bicycle or a rifle. In 1946, he received basic guitar lessons from two of his uncles and the new pastor at the family's church. He later recalled: "I took the guitar, and I watched people, and I learned to play a little but I would never sing in public. I was very shy about it."

Entering the new school, Miliam, for sixth grade in September the same year, he was seen by his classmates as a loner. In the following year, he began bringing his guitar into school on a daily basis, playing and singing during lunchtime. At times being teased as "trash kid who played hillbilly music". The Presleys were then living in a largely African-American neighbourhood.

A devotee of Mississippi Slim's radio show on Tupelo's WELO, Elvis, was described as "crazy about music" by Mississippi Slim's younger brother, who was a classmate of Elvis. The younger brother would take him to the station. Soon Slim supplemented Elvis's guitar tuition, demonstrating him chord techniques. When his protegee was 12 years old, Slim scheduled him for two on the air performances. At the first Elvis was overcome by stage fright, succeeding in performing the following week.

In November 1948, the family moved to Memphis/Tennessee, where after living for nearly a year in rooming houses, they finally landed them a two-bedroom apartment in the social housing complex Lauderdale Courts. Enrolled at L.C. Humes High School, Elvis Presley gained only a C in music in his eighth grade. His music teacher telling him he had no aptitude for singing. He challenged that with bringing in his guitar, the very next day, to sing the recent hit "Keep Them Cold Icy Fingers Off Me". A classmate later recalled, stating the teacher to say: "I agree that Elvis was right, when he said that I didn't appreciate his kind of singing."

Elvis was at that time still shy to perform openly, as he was occasionally being bullied by classmates, which viewed him as a "mama's boy". In 1950 he began practicing guitar more regularly. He was then tutored by Jesse Lee Denson, a neighbour two and a half years older than Elvis. A loos musical collective was formed between Jesse Lee Denson, Elvis Presley, Dorsey and Johnny Burnette, playing frequently around Lauderdale Courts. Elvis soon started his first jobs, such as at Loew's State Theatre, Precision Tool and MARL Metal Products.

In his junior year, Elvis began standing out more of his classmates. He had changed in appearance: Long sideburns, a Tony Curtis like pomaded hairstyle, sharp clothes he had purchased at Beale Street's famous Lansky Brothers, which he was wearing by his senior year.

Elvis soon overcame his fear of performing outside of Lauderdale Courts, competing even in Humes' Annual "Minstrel" show in April of 1953. He sang and accompanied himself on guitar to "Til I Waltz Again With You" which at that time, was a current hit for Teresa Brewer. It did a lot for him. He recalled: "I wasn't popular in school ... I failed music—only thing I ever failed—then they entered me in this talent show ... when I came onstage, I heard people kind of rumbling and whispering and so forth, 'cause nobody knew even I sang. It was amazing how popular I became after that." Elvis who never received formal music training or learned to read music, studied and played by ear. He frequented record stores with jukeboxes and listening booths. He knew all of Hank Snow's songs, also liking the output of the likes of Roy Acuff, Ernest Tubb, Ted Daffan, Jimmie Rodgers, Jimmie Davis and Bob Wills.

The Southern gospel singer Jake Hess, one of his favourite performers, was a significant influence on Elvis' ballad singing style. Elvis Presley being a regular at the monthly All Singings in downtown Memphis. Many white gospel artists performed there, reflecting the influence the African-American spiritual music had on them and the United States. Elvis also adored the music of black gospel singer Sister Rosetta Tharpe.

Like some of his peers, Elvis might have attended blues venues, in the then still segregated South, only on nights for exclusively white audiences. Most likely also popped into some clubs in Beale Street. He certainly listened to the regional radio stations, such as WDIA-AM, which played "race music": spirituals, blues, and the modern, backbeat jump blues and Rhythm and Blues.

Many of his later songs would be inspired by local Afro-American musicians and singers, such as Big Boy Arthur Crudup and Rufus Thoms. B.B. King recalled that he had known Elvis Presley before he was popular. When both frequented Beale Street. By the time Elvis had graduated from high school, he already had signed out music for his future.

In 1953, Elvis walked into the offices of Sun Records, intending to pay for a few minutes of studio time at the "Memphis Recording Service", to record a two-sided acetate: "My Happiness" and "That's When Your Heartaches Begin". Later he pointed out, that he intended to record it as a gift for his mother, and that he merely was interested in what he "sounded like". There would have been a much cheaper, amateur record-making service at a nearby general store. Elvis certainly also impressed his girlfriend Dixie with the recording.

Elvis Presley Biographer and Rock Historian Peter Guralnick thinks that Elvis Presley chose Sun in the hope of being discovered. Asked by receptionist Marion Keisker what kind of singer he was, Elvis replied: "I sing all kinds." When she pressed him on who he sounded like, he repeatedly answered, "I don't sound like nobody." After he had recorded, Sun Records President Sam Phillips asked Keisker to note down the young man's name, which she did. She added her own commentary—"Good ballad singer. Hold."

In January 1954, Elvis showed up at Sun for a second acetate. This time tackling "I'll Never Stand In Your Way" and "It Wouldn't Be The Same Without You"—but for now, nothing more came out of it.

Not long after, he failed the audition for the local vocal quartet, the Songfellows, saying to his father Vernon, "The told me I couldn't sing". Songfellow Jim Hamill later stated that Elvis was turned down because he did not demonstrate an ear for harmony at the time.

In April of '54 Elvis began working for the Crown Electric Company, as a truck driver. A friend, Ronnie Smith, suggested, after playing locally with him, that he should contact Eddie Bond. The band leader of Smith's professional band, which had an opening for a vocalist. Eddie Bond recited Elvis, the ladder Rockabilly Sun Recording Artist Eddie Bond saying to Elvis Presley: "Stick to truck driving, because you're never going to make it as a singer."

Sam Phillips was still looking for a singer to bring the sounds of black artists to a broader white audience. As Keisker said: "Over and over I remember Sam saying, 'If I could find a white man who had the Negro sound and the Negro feel, I could make a billion dollars.'

In June, Sam acquired the demo for the ballad 'Without You', which he thought would suit teenage singer Elvis Presley. But Sam though the output by Elvis did not do the ballad justice. So he asked Elvis to sing as many numbers as he knew, he was impressed enough to book musicians Scotty Moore (lead guitar) and Bill Black (bass) in, to provide Elvis with a backing band. The session commenced on the evening of July 5th 1954 at 706 Union Avenue based Sun Records. But not much came out of it, just when they were about to give up, Elvis in an last attempt took his guitar and launched into the blues number 'That's Allright' originally recorded by Arthur 'Big Boy' Crudup."

Scotty Moore recalled: "All of a sudden, Elvis just started singing this song, jumping around, acting the fool then Bill picked up his bass, starting acting the fool, too, and I started playing with them. Sam, I think, had the door to the control booth open … he stuck his head out and said, 'What are you doing?' And we said, 'We don't know. We'll back up,' he said, 'try to find a place to start, and do it again.'"

Sam Phillips began taping, because this was the sound he had been looking for, so long. Elvis delivered. Three days later, popular Memphis DJ, Dewey Phillips played "That's Allright" on his Red, Hot, and Blue Show. Rockabilly by Elvis Presley and The Blue Moon Boys was on its way.

Listeners began phoning in, eager trying to find out who the singer was. The interest was such that Dewey Phillips played the song "That's Allright" repeatedly during the last two hours of his show. Interviewing Elvis on air. He asked the young talent what high school he attended, to clarify his colour for the many callers who had assumed he was black. During the next few days, the trio recorded the Bill Monroe Bluegrass number "Blue Moon Of Kentucky". Again in their distinctive style, employing a jury-rigged echo effect that Sam Phillips dubbed "slapback". A single was pressed, with "That's Allright" on the 'A' side and "Blue Moon of Kentucky" on the 'B' side. Being released on Sun Records in 1954.

One of their first public engagements came to be on July 17th 1954, at the Bon Air Club—Elvis still playing his child-sized guitar.

At the end of the month, appearing at the Overton Park Shell, with Slim Whitman headlining. A combination of nervousness, response to rhythm, plus performing for a large audience, as well as inserting something he had seen with R&B singers, emphasising his movements—made young women and girls in the audience scream.

Scotty Moore recalled: "During the instrumental parts, he would back off from the mike and be playing and shaking, and the crowd would just go wild." Bill Black, also a natural showman, whooped and rode his bass, hitting double licks that Elvis would later remember as "really a wild sound, like a jungle drum or something."

A short while afterwards, Scotty and Bill quit their old band to play with Elvis regularly. DJ and promotor Bob Neal becoming the trio's manager. From August through October, Elvis, Scotty and Bill played regularly at the Eagle's Nest club in Memphis, returning to Sun studio for more recording sessions. Elvis, quickly gaining more and more confidence on the stage.

"His movement was a natural thing, but he was also very conscious of what got a reaction." Remembered Scotty Moore and added: "He'd do something one time and when he would expand it real quick." Elvis Presley and his band then billed as The Blue Moon Boys made one only appearance at the Grand Ole Opry in Nashville/Tennessee on 2 October 1954. He received a polite response, but it was Opry manager Jim Denny who told Sam Phillips: "Not bad, but did not suit the program."

Already two weeks later, Elvis and his boys were booked on the major rival to the Opry, the Louisiana Hayride. This show as much more adventurous and would bring in many of the Rock and Roll and Rockabilly artists following the path of Elvis in, later. It was being broadcast to 198 radio stations in 28 states. Elvis Presley had another attack of nerves during his first set, receiving a muted reaction by the audience. Second appearance was already more composed and with a more energetic sound, which gave them an enthusiastic reception by the crowd.

Soon house drummer DJ Fontana brought in a new element, complementing Elvis Presley's movements with accented beats, which he had originally mastered in strip clubs.

Soon Elvis Presley was a well-established star from Tennessee to West Texas. In January 1955, he had signed a formal management contract with Bob Neal, which in return had brought him to attention of Colonel Tom Parker. Parker having successfully managed Country star Eddy Arnold, at that time looking after as manager for Hank Snow, would book Presley on Snow's February tour. In Odessa/Texas a 19 year old Roy Orbison saw the show and said about it later: "His energy was incredible, his instinct was just amazing … I just didn't know what to make of it. There was no reference point in the culture to compare it."

Elvis Presley made his television debut on March 3rd 1955 on the KSLA TV broadcast of Louisiana Hayride, failing an audition for Arthur Godfrey's Talent Scouts, on the CBS television network. By August of 1955, Sun had released ten sides to "Elvis Presley, Scotty and Bill", the trio being joined for their newest recordings by a drummer.

"That's Allright" had been described by a Memphis journalist as the "R&B idiom of negro field jazz", "Blue Moon Of Kentucky" as "more in the country field." But it was the blending of the two, which like for Bill Haley before, made it difficult for Elvis Presley to get airplay. Bob Neal stated, that white stations would not touch it, because he sounded too black, while black stations thought he sounded too white. At the time Elvis Presley was billed as "The King of Western Bop", "The Hillbilly Cat" and "The Memphis Flash".

In 1955, Elvis renewed his contract with Bob Neal, assigning Colonel Tom Parker as his special adviser. An extensive touring schedule was held. Bob Neal noted: "It was almost frightening, the reaction that came to Elvis from the teenaged boys. So many of them, through some sort of jealousy, would practically hate him. There were occasions in some towns in Texas, when we'd have to be sure to have a police guard, because somebody'd always try to take a crack at him. They'd get a gang and try to waylay him or something."

With DJ Fontana, their regular drummer, now as a quartet they joined Bill Haley and His Comets in mid-October 1955, playing support to the King of Rock and Roll Bill Haley. Which Elvis Presley would soon dethrone. Haley's "Rock Around The Clock" had been a Nr.1 hit, and was still riding the charts, with other Haley hits like "Shake, Rattle and Roll" and "Dim Dim The Lights" riding high also. Bill Haley observed that Elvis Presley had a natural feel for rhythm, advising him to sing fewer ballads.

Elvis was voted as the year's most promising male artist at the Disc Jockey Convention in November of 1955. Three major record companies made offers of up to $25,000, Parker and Phillips striking a deal with RCA Victor on November 21st 1955 to acquire Elvis Presley's Sun contract for an unprecedented $40,000.

As Elvis, with 20, was still a minor, his father signed the contract on his behalf.

Colonel Tom Parker also arranged a deal with the owners of Hill and Range music Publishing, Jean and Julian Aberbach, creating Elvis Presley and Gladys music. Handling all new material by Elvis. Songwriters were obliged to forgo one third of their customary royalties, in exchange for Elvis having perform their compositions. By December, RCA had begun to promote its new singer heavily. Having reissued also many of his SUN recordings.

On 10 January 1956, just having turned 21, Elvis Presley made his first recordings for RCA Records in Nashville. His backup band was augmented with studio musicians and singers—Floyd Cramer (piano), Chet Atkins (guitar) the background singers The Jordanaires as led by Gordon Stoker, filling out the sound. The unusual, almost suicidal, moody "Heartbreak Hotel" with a lot of RCA duplicated slapback echo was produced for Elvis first single. Colonel Tom Parker booked Elvis on the CBS Stage Show for six appearances over two months. This programme, produced in New York being hosted on alternating weeks by big band leaders, brothers Tommy and Jimmy Dorsey. After his first appearance on 28 January 1956, introduced by disc jockey Bill Randle, Elvis stayed for two week long sessions at RCA's New York studios.

The sessions in New York brought the music world, a rendition of Carl Perkins' Rockabilly anthem "Blue Suede Shoes". In February, Elvis Presley's "I Forgot To Remember To Forget", recorded at Sun, initially released the previous August, became a Top 10 Billboard Country hit. Bob Neal's managing contract was terminated, with Colonel Tom Parker becoming Elvis Presley's manager until the stars untimely death on 16 August 1977. On 12 March 1956, Elvis purchased a one-story ranch style house, with a two-car attached garage in a quiet residential neighbourhood, on Audubon Street in Memphis. The home was profiled in national magazines, soon becoming a focal point for fans, media and celebrities to visit. Elvis living there with is parents for a year, outgrowing the quietness, which he disturbed unintentionally. Staying there from March 1956 until March 1957.

RCA Victor released his debut album "Elvis Presley" on 23 March 1956, featuring a varied selection of five previously unreleased Sun recordings plus seven newly recorded songs, two being Country styled and one a bouncy pop-like Rock and Roll tune. Some songs defined the evolving sound of Rock and Roll: "Blue Suede Shoes" plus other covers of Little Richard, Ray Charles and The Drifters. Robert Hilburn, a music critic, noted: "These were the most revealing of all. Unlike many white artists … who watered down the gritty edges of the original R&B versions of songs in the '50s, Presley reshaped them. He not only injected the tunes with is vocal character but also made guitar, not piano, the lead instrument in all three cases." The album containing the songs:

"Blue Suede Shoes", "I'm Counting On Your", "I Got A Woman", "One Sided Love Affair", "I Love You Because", "Just Because", "Tutti Frutti", "Trying To Get To You", "I'm Gonna Sit Down and Cry (Over You)", "I'll Never Let You Go" (Little Darlin'), "Blue Moon" and "Money Honey". It became the first Rock and Roll album to top the Billboard chart, a position held for 10 weeks!

The cover inspired cultural historian Gilbert B. Rodman to note that the artwork "of Elvis having the time of his life on stage with a guitar … as the instrument that best captured the style and spirit of this new music."

After Elvis Presley's first two appearances on the Milton Berle Show on NBC, on 3 April 1956, on the deck of the USS Hancock in San Diego, prompting cheers from sailors and screams from their dates, a shaky flight almost killed Elvis and his band en flight to Nashville. An engine of the plane died in the air, with the plane almost going down over Arkansas.

Twelve weeks after its initial release Elvis Presley and "Heartbreak Hotel" made Nr. 1 in the US charts. Shortly after Elvis had signed with RCA Carl Perkins crossed into the Top 10 of the Country, R&B and Pop charts with his self-penned Sun records released Rock and Roll song "Blue Suede Shoes", some nervous RCA managers unfamiliar with Rock and Roll on a more detailed scale, wondered if they had bought the right artist from Sam Phillips.

Less successful was Elvis' first ever engagement to Las Vegas/Nevada. It was in late April of 1956, when he began his two-week residency at the New Frontier Hotel and Casino, on the famous Las Vegas strip.

The shows were poorly received by the conservative, middle-aged hotel guests—"like a jug of corn liquor at a champagne party," as Newsweek noted.

Elvis would sign his seven year contract with Paramount Pictures, began a tour of the Midwest in mid-May, taking 15 cities in 15 days. In Vegas he had attended shows by the Northern Rock and Roll band Freddie Bell and The Bell Boys, he was so struck by their cover of "Hound Dog", penned by songwriters

Jerry Lieber and Mike Stoller, and having been an R&B hit for Big Mama Thornton, that the song became the closing set of his own set.

After a show in La Crosse/Wisconsin, an urgent message was sent to FBI director J. Edgar Hoover, by the local Catholic diocese's newspaper warning that "Presley is a definite danger to the security of the United States. ... His actions and motions, were such to rouse the sexual passions of teenaged youth ... After the show, more than 1000 teenagers tried to gang into Presley's room at the auditorium ... Indications of the harm Presley did just in La Crosse, where the two high school girls ... whose abdomen and thighs had Presley's autograph."

The second Milton Berle Show came on 5 June 1956 at NBC's Hollywood studio, on hectic schedule—Milton Berle advised Elvis Presley to leave his guitar backstage: "Let them see you, son." During the performance Elvis abruptly halted the temp of "Hound Dog", waving his arm, launching into a slow, griding version, accentuating the energy of the song, with exaggerating the body movements.

His gyrations created a storm of controversy. Newspaper and even mild-mannered TV critics were outraged. Jack Gould of the New York Times wrote: "Mr Presley has no discernible singing ability. ... His phrasing, it can be called that, consists of stereotyped variations that go with a beginner's aria in a bathtub ... His one speciality, is an accented movement of the body ... primarily identified with the repertoire of the blond bombshells of the burlesque runway."

Ben Gross of the New York Daily News opined that popular music "has reached its lowest depths, in the grunt and groin antics of one Elvis Presley. ... Elvis, who rotates his pelvis ... gave an exhibition that was suggestive and vulgar, tinged with the kind of animalism that should be confined to dives and bordellos."

Ed Sullivan, host of the Toast of Town variety show ruled out that Elvis Presley would ever perform on the nation's most popular TV show, declaring Elvis as "unfit for family viewing". Elvis soon found himself named "Elvis The Pelvis" to which he replied:

"One of the most childish expressions I ever heard, coming from an adult."

Nevertheless as the Berle shows received such high ratings it was Steve Allen, who invited Elvis to perform on his show, as he did later with Jerry Lee Lewis. Who, ever grateful to Steve Allen, named one of his sons Steve Allen ...

Allen later wrote: "I found Elvis Presley's strange, gangly, country-bop charisma, his hard-to-define-cuteness, and his charming eccentricity intriguing."

Elvis sang, dressed in a Tuxedo, but with "Blue Suede Shoes".

"Hound Dog" to a basset dog. Later that night Elvis was also seen on Hy Gardner calling, Pressed on whether he had "learned" anything from the criticism, he replied, quite rightfully and naturally: "No, I haven't, I don't feel like I'm doing anything wrong … I don't see how any type of music would have any bad influence on people, when it's only music … I mean, how would Rock and Roll music make anyone rebel against their parents?"

The next day Elvis recorded "Hound Dog", "Any Way You Want Me" and "Don't Be Cruel". With the Jordanaires bringing in harmony singing, they would work with Elvis way into the 1960s.

An outdoor concert appearance in Memphis, his hometown followed, he announced it with: "You know, those people in New York are not gonna change me none. I'm gonna sow you what the real Elvis is like tonight."

But in August of 1956 a judge in Jacksonville/Florida ordered Elvis Presley to tame his act, so throughout the following performance, he largely kept still, except for wiggling his little finger in protest. The single "Don't Be Cruel" b/w "Hound Dog" hit the top of the charts for 11 weeks—a mark that would not be surpassed for 36 years.

In the first week of September Elvis Presley's second album was produced in Hollywood. Jerry Leiber and Mike Stoller, contributed "Love Me". Steve Allen's show with Elvis and thanks to Elvis, had for the first time beaten CBS's Ed Sullivan Show. Despite his June announcement Elvis was booked for three performances on the ladder show for $50,000. The first, on September 9th 1956 was seen by 60,000,000 viewers, a 82.6 percent of the television audience. Actor Charles Laughton hosted the show, filling in for Ed Sullivan, who recovered from a car accident. Elvis appeared in two segments, broadcast from CBS Television City in Los Angeles. Presumably Elvis Presley was filmed from the waist up only.

Ed Sullivan told the paper TV Guide: "As for his gyrations, the whole thing can be controlled with camera shots." The performance on "Tost of Town" resulted in a record breaking advance order total of 1 million. Guaranteeing a gold record, before relesae. More than any other event it was The Ed Sullivan Show that made Elvis Presley a national celebrety of superstardom in 1956.

A cultural shift had taken place, it was Elvis musicially, maybe even more than Bill Haley, as Elvis was possibly more likely more accessible for teenagers to identify themselves with him (boys) and to be adored by (girls)—he gave the young a belief in themselves, as a distinct and somehow unified generation. The first in America, ever to feel the power of an integrated youth culture.

His live performances guaranteed frenzied responses wherever he performed, Scotty Moore recalled: "He'd start out, 'You ain't nothin' but a Hound Dog, and they'd just go to pieces. They'd always react the same way. There'd be a riot every time.' So for his two Mississippi Alabama Fair and Dairy Show, 50 National Guardsmen were added to the police security, preventing trouble within the crowd."

His second album "Elvis" was released in October of '56, quickly occupying the Nr. 1 slot of the album charts.

The LP included "Old Shep", first sung by him publicly at a talent show in 1945. It was the first time he played piano on an RCA session. Peter Guralnick, rock historian and Elvis biographer, noted: "in the halting chords and somewhat stumbling rhythm, both the unmistakable emotion and the equally unmistakable valuing of emotion over technique." Accessing Elvis first body of work, such as "That's Allright", rock critic Dave Morsh assessed: "these records, more than any others, contain the seeds of what Rock and Roll was, has been and most likely what it may foreseeably become."

The album contained the following titles:

"Rip It Up", "Love Me", "When My Blue Moon Turns To Gold Again", "Long Tall Sally", "First In Line", "Paralysed", "So Glad You're Mine", "Old Shep", "Ready Teddy", "Anyplace Is Paradise", "How's The World Treating You", "How Do You Think I Feel".

Elvis Presley returned to the Ed Sullivan Show, this time hosted by Mr Sullivan himself, on 28 October 1956. His first motion picture, "Love Me Tender", was released on 21 November 1956. Though originially produced as a non-musical Western entitled "The Reno Brothers", the title was changed to "Love Me Tender" and four musical numbers were added. By the time the movie was relesed, "Love Me Tender" topped the single charts. Critics did not receive Elvis acting abilities well, considering that he never went to an acting school, he was a natural. It seems, that most critics just did not want to leave a good word on Elvis, still so controversial over his TV and stage performances. Also Rock and Roll was still a hot topic in the US, every Rock and Roll Star, be it Bill Haley, Eddie Cochran, Gene Vincent or Chuck Berry walking a thin line, between success and controversy. Always careful not loosing their careers.

The film "Love Me Tender" naturally did very well at the box-office, as the bad critics of back then, nowadays read as approval of Elvis rebelliousness and new approach leading to a musical revolution, it must have read back in the 1950s to the Teenagers.

On 4 December 1956, Elvis Presley dropped by at the Sun Studio in Memphis, where Carl Perkins was having a recording session. Also Jerry Lee Lewis was on hand, Johnny Cash came by for a short visit with his wife Vivian, before doing Christmas shopping. Sam Phillips knew what to do, he ordered a journalist and photographer of the Memphis Press Scimitar, for a memorial shot. The four jammed for a while, on many Rock and Roll songs, but naturally on spirituals also, though not able to release anything, as Elvis was exclusively signed to RCA, Phillips led the tapes rolling on the jams session, to become known as recordings by The Million Dollar Quartet.

The year 1956 ended with a front-page story in The Wall Street Journal, which reported that Elvis Presley merchandise had grossed $22,000,000, on top of his record sales. Billboard magazine declared that he had placed more songs in the Hot 100, than any other artist since records were noted in charts. In his first full year at RCA Records, Elvis Presley had accounted for over 50% of the label's singles sales.

Elvis Presley's third and final appearance on the Ed Sullivan Show took place on 6 January 1957—he was at this time, solely filmed above the waist. His hair falling in his face, he played around, also with the make-up artist, as looking a little like Rudolpho Valentino in his famous role of "The Sheik". He closed the show with the spiritual "Peace In The Valley". At the end, Ed Sullivan declared that Elvis is "a real decent, fine boy" shaking hands with the young man. Two days later, the Memphis draft board announced that Elvis was classified 1-A, after medical tests, he would serve the US Army at some time.

Three singles by Elvis, released in the first half of 1957, went to number one: "Too Much", "All Shook Up" and "Teddy Bear". He even caused headlines in the prestigious New York times, as "Presley Records a Craze in Soviet", like other Rock and Roll recordings, his, were also distributed secretly or not so secretly for high prices, on X-ray plates, in Leningrad.

In 1957, he purchased his beloved mansion "Graceland", with 18 rooms, eight miles south of downtown Memphis, in Whitehaven. The Technicolor movie "Loving You" was released in July, as the make-up artist suggested, that he would photograph so well with black hair, Elvis dyed it that way. The soundtrack album "Loving You", went to Nr. 1. It contained these Elvis songs:

"Mean Women Blues", "(Let Me Be Your) Teddy Bear", "Loving You", "Got A Lot Of Livin To Do", "Lonesome Cowboy", "Hot Dog", "(Let's Have A) Party", "Blueberry Hill", "True Love", "Don't Leave Me Now", "Have I Told You Lately That I Love You", "I Need You So".

The title track was written by Leiber and Stoller, who were then asked to write four of the six songs recorded at the sessions for "Jailhouse Rock", the forthcoming motion picture starring Elvis Presley. They developed a close working relationship with Elvis, he in return saw them as his good luck charm.

Leiber remembered thinking of Elvis at first as being "not authentic", concluding on his first-judgement that "after all, he was a white singer, and my standards were black." According to Stoller, the songwriting duo were "surprised at the kind of knowledge that he had about black music. We figured that he had these remarkable pipes and all that, but we didn't realise that he knew so much about the blues. We were quite surprised to find out he knew as much about it as we did. He certainly knew a lot more than we did about country and gospel music." Leiber adding: "He was fast. Any demo you gave him he knew by heart in ten minutes." Stoller recalled: "Elvis Presley was protected by his manager and entourage. He was removed. … They kept him separate."

Frank Sinatra, who was a teenager heart-throb in the 1940s, and inspired swooning teenage girls, in that decade, condemned Rock and Roll by saying: "Rock and Roll is a brutal, ugly, degenerate, vicious … it fosters almost totally negative and destructive reactions in young people. It smells phoney and false. It is sung, played and written, for the most part, by cretinous goons. … This rancid-smelling aphrodisiac I deplore." Asked for a response Elvis Presley was quoted as saying: "I admire the man. He has a right to say what he wants to say. He is a great success and a fine actor, but I think he shouldn't have said it. This is a trend, just the same as he faced when he started years ago."

Elvis also undertook three brief tours in 1957. With continuous rapport by the audiences. A Detroit newspaper suggested that the "trouble with going to see Elvis Presley is that you're liable to get killed."

But Villanova students pelted him with eggs in Philadelphia, in Vancouver, Canada, there were riots at the end of the show, which led to the stage being destroyed.

The year for Elvis ended musically with a Christmas album. Jerry Leiber and Mike Stoller were there with Elvis in the studio. Towards the end of the session, they wrote a song on the spot on Elvis Presley's request—"Santa Clause Is Back In Town". The holiday release, contained the following songs:

"Santa Claus Is Back In Town", "White Christmas", "Here Comes Santa Claus", "I'll Be Home For Christmas", "Blue Christmas", "Santa Bring My Baby Back (To Me)", "O Little Town O'Bethlehem", "Silent Night", "Peace In The Valley", "Take My Hand (Precious Lord)", "It Is No Secret (What God Can Do)".

The album also become a Nr. 1 hit. Stretching his Number One albums to four, so far.

After the sessions, Scotty Moore (lead guitar) and Bill Black (bass) quit working for Elvis, over a salary dispute. But they were brought back, on Elvis insisting, that he continuously wanted to work with them.

But they were no longer part of Elvis' inner circle anymore. On 20 December 1957, Elvis Presley was drafted, the drafting board, allowing him to finish the forthcoming movie "King Creole", in which $350,000 were already been invested by Paramount's producer Hal Wallis. With the love song "Don't" penned again by the songwriting efforts of Jerry Leiber and Mike Stoller, he had his tenth million Nr. 1 seller in the singles charts.

In January 1958 recording sessions for the album accompanying the upcoming movie "King Creole" directed by Austrian director Michael Curtiz, who had directed "Casablanca" with Humphrey Bogart, were held. Three songs coming from Leiber and Stoller. A studio session on February 1st 1958, was to be the final one with bassman Bill Black.

Bill Black sadly dying in 1965.

The LP "King Creole" contained the movie's songs:

"King Creole", "As Long As I Have You", "Hard Headed Woman", "Trouble", "Dixieland Rock", "Don't Ask Me Why", "Lover Doll", "Crawfish", "Young Dreams", "Steadfast, Loyal And True", "New Orleans".

24 March 1958: Elvis Presley conscripted into the United States Army, as a private at Fort Chafee, near Fort Smith/Arkansas. The arrival of Private Presley as he stepped from the bus, was a major media event, with many photographers accompanying him into the fort. Elvis announced that he was looking forward to his military stint, stating he did not expect nor wanted to be treated like anyone else: "The Army can do anything it wants with me."

He then commenced with basic training at Fort Hood/Texas. In early August, his mother Gladys was diagnose with hepatitis, with her condition rapidly worsening. Elvis was granted special leave to fly out to Memphis, visiting his mum at the hospital. He reached her two days before she died, aged 46. Elvis was devastated, as their relationship was a very close and special one.

After training, Elvis joined the 3rd Armoured Division in Friedberg, Germany. (1 October 1958). He was greeted by 1000 German fans at his arrival in Bremerhaven. Introduced to amphetamines by a sergeant while being on manoeuvres—he became evangelical about their positive benefits for energy, strength, weight loss—he would later offer them to friends, who joined him, in taking them.

In the Army, he was also introduced to karate, which he studied seriously over the years, including some of karate's movements into his stage performances.

Elvis in the Army was as generous as ever, donating TV sets for the base, buying extra set of fatigues for everyone in his outfit plus donating his Army pay to charity. While in Germany, he met the then 14-year-old Priscilla Beaulieu. From the moment they met, they had a special connection a bond that would last in different relation their entire life time, and for Priscilla beyond Elvis Presley's lifetime. Today she thinks, her meaning in life is to protect and cherish Elvis memory for future generations. At home RCA Records was very well equipped to keep Elvis career going in the charts, he would score ten Top 40 Singles, while serving in the Army, at home: "Wear My Ring Around Your Neck", "Hard Headed Woman", "One Night" (1958), "A Fool Such As I" and "A Big Hunk O' Love" (1959) as top-sellers. With the album "Elvis' Golden Records" (1958), hitting number three on the LP charts.

It contained the following hits:

"Hound Dog", "Loving You", "All Shook Up", "Heartbreak Hotel", "Jailhouse Rock", "Love Me", "Too Much", "Don't Be Cruel", "That's When Your Heartaches Begin", "Teddy Bear", "Love Me Tender", "Treat Me Nice", "Anyway You Want Me", "I Want You, I Need You, I Love You".

Elvis returned to USA on 2 March 1960. He was honourably discharged with the rank of sergeant on March the 5th. The train that he had boarded from New Jersey to Tennessee was mobbed all the way. Elvis being called upon to appear for adoring fans at scheduled stops. On the night of March 20th, he recorded at RCA's Nashville studio to begin work on a new album. Resulting also with a new hit single, namely "Stuck On You", which swiftly became another Presley Nr. 1 hit. Two weeks later he recorded the ballads "It's Now Or Never" and "Are You Lonesome Tonight?", along with the rest of the songs for the long play "Elvis Is Back".

"Make Me Know It", "Fever", "The Girl Of My Best Friend", "I Will Be Home Again", "Dirty, Dirty Feeling", "Thrill Of Your Love", "Soldier Boy", "Such A Night", "It Feels So Right", "Girl Next Door-Went-A-Walking", "Like A Baby", "Reconsider Baby" were the songs of the album.

Music historian John Robertson summed the album up, as follows: "A flirtatious teenage idol, with a heart of gold; a tempestuous, dangerous lover; a gutbucket blues singer; a sophisticated nightclub entertainer; a raucous rocker". It was all on "Elvis Is Back".

A TV Special took place on 12 May 1960, Elvis being welcomed home by none less than Frank Sinatra—the eight minutes segment with Elvis Presley and Frank Sinatra, for which Colonel Tom Parker secured for his client Elvis $125,000, drew enormous viewing ratings. Both Sinatra and Elvis sang hits from one and another, in a duet, with Mr Sinatra commenting on the show: "We work the same ways, only in different areas."

It finally put an end to the hostility the Entertainer Frank Sinatra had towards Rock and Roll artists, who admired him. Another life-long Sinatra fan was none other than the Father of Rock and Roll Bill Haley.

"G.I. Blues" the soundtrack to Elvis Presley's first movie, since he left the army, reached number one in October 1960.

The LP containing the songs: "Tonight Is So Right For Love", "What's She Really Like", "Frankfurt Special", "Wooden Heart", "G.I. Blues", "Pocketful Of Rainbows", "Shoppin' Around", "Big Boots", "Didja Ever", "Blue Suede Shoes", "Doin' The Best I Can".

His first album of sacred material, very dear to his heart, reaching number 13 on the US pop chart and number 3 in the UK, remarkable figures for an album of spiritual music.

Songs: "His Hand In Mine", "I'm Gonna Walk Them Golden Stairs", "In My Father's House (There Are Many Mansions), "Milky White Way", "Known Only To Him", I Believe In The Man In The Sky", "Joshua Fit The Battle", "Jesus Knows What I Need", "Down Sweet Chariot", "Mansion Over The Hilltop", "If We Never Meet Again", Working On The Building".

In February of 1961/Elvis Presley performed two benefit shows in Memphis, on behalf of 24 local charities. Before at a luncheon, he was presented by RCA with a plaque, certifying worldwide sales of over 75 million records. A marathon 12-hour session produced nearly all of the outcome for his new album "Something's For Everybody". The album becoming another number 1 seller. John Robertson described it as: "A pleasant, unthreatening pastiche of music that had once been Elvis's birth right".

"There's Always Me", "Give Me The Right", "It's A Sin", Sentimental Me", "Starting Today", "Gently", "I'm Coming Home", "In Your Arms", "Put The Blame On Me", "Judy", "I Want You With Me", "I Slipped, I Stumbled, I Fell".

On 25 March 1961, Elvis played a benefit show in Hawaii for a Pearl Harbour Memorial, it was to be his last public performance in concert for seven years.

Two films, in the dramatic vein "Flaming Star" and "Wild In The Country" were released, doing good at the box-office but not as much the lighter "G.I. Blues" had done. So Elvis agreed on non-dramatic roles for the future, with some exceptions, in movie-acting, though.

Producer Hal Wallis, who was responsible for nine of Elvis Presley's films remarked: "A Presley picture is the only sure thing in Hollywood."

Starring in three movies a year, the scripts, movies and soundtracks would not be as of the same quality, as they had been before. Jerry Leiber noted, that even before, in the 1950s the soundtracks had the same formula: "Three ballads, one medium-tempo, and one break blues boogie."

Julie Parish who appeared with Elvis in "Paradise, Hawaiian Style" (1966) said that he hated many of the sogs chosen for the movie. Gordon Stoker from The Jordanaires recalled that Elvis Presley would retreat from the studio microphone: "The material was so bad that he felt like he couldn't sing it."

But many of the soundtracks also featured a song or two by another respectable writing team Doc Pomus and Mort Shuman. In the first half of the decade of the 1960s, three of Elvis Presley's soundtrack albums hit the top of the charts, a few of his all-time-favourite songs coming from films, such as "Can't Help Falling In Love" (1961) and "Return To Sender" (1962). "Viva Las Vegas", the title track of the 1964 film, was a minor hit, but became a Presley favourite over the years. From 1964 until 1968, Elvis had only one-top-ten hit "Crying In The Chapel" (1965), a gospel like pop-tune, which had been recorded in 1960.

The only non-film LP released at the time being "How Great Thou Art" (1967), this Gospel album winning him his first Grammy Award for "Best Sacred Performance". Dave Marsh noted about Elvis, that he was "arguably the greatest white gospel singer of his time, really the last Rock and Roll artist to make gospel a vital a component of his music personality, as his secular songs."

"How Great Thou Art", "In The Garden", "Somebody Bigger Than You And I", "Farther Along", "Stand By Me", "Without Him", "So High", "Where Could I Go But To The Lord", "By And By", "If The Lord Wasn't Walking By My Side", "Run On", "Where No One Stands Alone", "Crying In The Chapel".

During Christmas season 1966, over seven years after they had first met, Elvis proposed to Priscilla. Married on 1 May 1967 in Las Vegas/Nevada at the Aladdin Hotel, they would have an on-and-off marriage, caused by the flow of formulaic movies and later, many stage engagements by Elvis Presley. In 1967 when "Clambake", the soundtrack to yet another Elvis movie, did poor, RCA recognised an issue, but the damage to the career of Elvis had already been done.

Elvis' only child, his daughter Lisa Marie Presley, was born on 1 February 1968.

Of the eight Elvis Presley singles released between January 1967 and May 1968, two charted in the Top 40, though not higher than number 28. The soundtrack album to "Speedway" peaking at 82. Colonel Tom Parker was getting ready to re-launch Elvis' career via Television, which was crucial in making a household name, back in the 1950s. He had a Christmas special in mind. Recorded in late June 1968 in Burbank/California, the TV Special simply titled "Elvis", aired on 3 December 1968. Thanks to its visionary producer Steve Binder, who had Elvis revisit his roots with Scotty Moore and DJ Fontana, integrated some acted scenes, reminiscent of the good Elvis films of the '50s, as well as new songs into it, having Elvis appear in black leather designed by Bill Belew.

Having him not singing Christmas carols, but the timeless "If I Can Dream", inspired by Dr Martin Luther's famous civil rights speech—Elvis had re-invented himself. For Steve Binder he was "the man who wrote the book on being a Rockstar"—that story was told with the ELVIS Special, later to be nicknamed "68 Comeback Special". A term Elvis did not like, as he thought he had a continuous career, and wasn't remote of his fans, until that TV Special.

The show, NBC's highest rated that season, captured 42% of the total viewing audience.

Eye Magazine's writer Joe Landau wrote: "There is something magical about watching a man who has lost himself, find his way back home. He sang with the kind of power people no longer expect of Rock and Roll singers. He moved his body with a lack of pretension and effort that must have made Jim Morrison green with envy." By January 1969, the single "IF I Can Dream", written for the Special, reached number 12 in the US Charts. With the soundtrack album cracking into the Top 10. Elvis' friend Jerry Schilling said the special was about what "he had not been able to do for years, being able to choose the people; being able to choose the songs and not being told what had to be on the soundtrack … He was out of prison, man". Steve Binder said of Elvis Presley's reaction: "I played Elvis the 60 minute show, and he told me in the screening room, 'Steve it's the greatest thing I've ever done in my life. I give you my word I will never sing a song I don't believe in.'"

Elvis now also wanted to reinvent himself in the studio, engaging in a series of recording sessions at the American Sound Studio, in Memphis. This leading to the acclaimed album "From Elvis in Memphis". Released in June 1969, it was his first non-spiritual nor non-soundtrack long play, incorporating a dedicated period in the studio, in eight years. Dave Marsh summed it up with his review: "a masterpiece, in which Presley immediately catches up with pop music trends that had seemed to pass him by during the movie years. He sings country songs, soul songs and rockers with real conviction, a stunning achievement."

Songs "From Elvis In Memphis": "After Loving You", "I'm Moving On", "True Love Travels On A Gravel Road", "Only The Strong Survive", "Long Black Limousine", "Any Day Now", "Power Of My Love", "In The Ghetto", "Gentle On My Mind", "It Keeps Right On-A-Hurtin'", "Wearin' That Loved On Look", "Mama Liked The Roses", "I'll Hold You In My Heart", "Kentucky Rain", "Hey Jude", "Inherit The Wind".

Elvis was keen to commence with live performing, offers came in from all around the world. The London Palladium offering Parker $28,000 for a one-week engagement. The Colonel responded "That's fine for me, how much can you get for Elvis?" When the International Hotel in Las Vegas opened in May, boasting the largest showroom in the city, it was also about to announce that it had booked Elvis Presley. 57 shows over four weeks, a very demanding schedule for Elvis who had not done live shows in years. Elvis also had to look for a band, as the Jordanaires, also Scotty Moore and DJ Fontana did not want to lose out on lucrative session work in Nashville.

Elvis assembled a top-notch new accompaniment, led by guitarist who had worked with Ricky Nelson, plus including two gospel groups—The Imperials and The Sweet Inspirations. But Elvis was most nervous, it was his first engagement onstage in years, plus it was Vegs, where he had bombed in 1956.

Elvis also researched, visiting several shows in Sin City, seeing and meeting Tom Jones—both becoming friends. Still studying Karate, he recruited Bill Belew to design a karate inspired suit for his premiere. This would become the proto-type of his stage wear during his later years.

Hotel owner Kirk Kerkorian sent out a plane to New York, to fly in all big name rock journalists for Elvis Presley's debut.

Elvis took the stage without introduction, the audience of 2200 giving him a standing ovation, many celebrities in the audience, and that before he even sang a note. A third standing ovation followed with the encore of "Can't Help Falling In Love". At the press conference after the show, a journalist referred to him as "The King" to which Elvis gestured towards Fats Domino, who was present also: "No, that's the real King of Rock and Roll". At the next day, the Colonel worked out a five year contract for Elvis to perform each February and August at the International, for an annual salary of $1 million.

Newsweek commented: "There are several unbelievable things about Elvis, the most incredible is his staying power, in a world where meteoric careers fade like shooting stars." Rolling Stone concluded that Elvis Presley was a "supernatural, his own resurrection". In November 1969 his final non-concert film, "Change of Habit" opened in cinemas.

The double LP "From Memphis To Vegas/From Vegas To Memphis", was released the same month. The first album set consisted of live recordings from the International Hotel in Las Vegas, while the second more cuts from the American Sound Sessions.

Songs: "Blue Suede Shoes", "Johnny B. Goode", "All Shook Up", "Are You Lonesome Tonight", "Hound Dog", "I Can't Stop Loving You", "My Babe", "Mystery Train/Tiger Man", "Words", "In The Ghetto", "Suspicious Minds", "Can't Help Falling In Love", "Inherit The Wind", "This Is The Story", "Stranger In My Own Home Town", "A Little Bit Of Green", "And The Grass Won't Pay No Mind".

Cassandra Peterson, the later TV's Elvira, met Elvis Presley during this period in Las Vegas, working as a showgirl: "He was so anti-drug when I met him. I mentioned to him that I smoked marijuana, and he was just appalled. He said, "Don't ever do that again." Elvis was not only opposed to drunk, also to alcohol, as some family members had been alcoholics, he rarely drank.

In 1970, he produced the album "On Stage" at the International, performing two show's a night, for a two-month long engagement.

Songs: "CC Rider", "Release Me", "Sweet Caroline", "Runaway", "The Wonder Of You", "Polk Salad Annie", "Yesterday", "Proud Mary", "Walk A Mile In My Shoes", "Let It Be Me".

In April 1970, Elvis enjoyed a Nr. 1 hit with "The Wonder Of You" in the UK Pop Charts and the US Adult Contemporary Charts.

While MGM filmed his first concert movie, the tremendous and critically acclaimed "That's The Way It Is".

During this engagement, there were several serious life threats directed towards him. The FBI took the threat seriously, security being stepped up for his next two shows. Elvis went onstage in a jump suit, with a Derringer in his right boot and a 45 pistol in his waistband, but the concerts passed without incidents.

The album "That's The Way It Is" shifted stylistically with live and studio recordings to a more mature Elvis sound. John Robertson, music critic, stated: "The authority of Presley's singing, helped disguise the fact that the album stepped decisively away from the American-roots inspiration of the Memphis sessions, towards a more middle of the road sound."

Songs on the album are: "I Just Can't Help Believing", "Twenty Days And Twenty Nights", "How The Web Was Woven", "Patch It Up", "Mary In The Morning", "You Don't Have To Say You Love Me", "You've Lost That Lovin' Feeling", "I've Lost You".

A very classy, very clean, white pop album—most suitable to promote Elvis Presley's Las Vegas shows.

On 7 September 1970, following his engagement at the International, a one-week-long concert tour, largely of the South, his first since 1958 followed. This was followed by West Coast tour in November '70.

On 21 December 1970, Elvis Presley master-minded a meeting with US President Richard Nixon. Elvis expressed at the White House his patriotism, his thoughts on the Hippies, the drug culture and counter culture in general. Nixon gave Elvis what he had asked for, a Badge for the Bureau of Narcotics and Dangerous Drugs, making Elvis a DEA Agent.

The U.S. Junior Chamber of Commerce named Elvis one of its Ten Most Outstanding Young Men of the Nation on 16 January 1971. The City of Memphis changing the name of the Highway 51 South, on which Graceland stood, to "Elvis Presley Boulevard". Elvis also receiving a Lifetime Achievement Award known as the Bing Crosby Award, by the National Academy of Recording Arts and Sciences, the Grammy Award organisation.

Three albums were released by Elvis in 1971: "Elvis Country", "Love Letters From Elvis" and "Elvis Sings The Wonderful World Of Christmas". Peter Guralnick saw a "real highlight" in the recordings of "I Will Be True", "It's Still There" and "I'll Take You Home Again, Kathleen"—three songs that Elvis recorded in a rare solo-set, on the piano. Guralnick describes it as "yearning, wistfulness, loneliness, need—all were communicated with a naked lack of adornment that Elvis was seeming to find increasingly difficult to display, in the formal process of recording."

Songs of "Elvis Country": "Snowbird", "Tomorrow Never Comes", "Little Cabin On The Hill", "Whole Lotta Shakin' Goin' On", "Funny How Time Slips Away", "I Really Don't Want To Know", "There Goes My Everything", "It's Your Baby Rock It", "The Fool", "Faded Love", "I Washed My Hands In Muddy Water", "Make The World Go Away".

Love Letters From Elvis: "Love Letters", "When I'm Over You", "If I Were You", "Got My Mojo Working", "Heart Of Rome", "Only Believe", "This Is Our Dance", "Cindy, Cindy", "I'll Never Know", "It Ain't No Big Thing (But It's Growing)", "Life".

Elvis Sings The Wonderful World of Christmas:

"O Come, Ye All Faithful", "The First Noel", "On A Snowy Christmas Night", "Winter Wonderland", "The Wonderful World Of Christmas", "It Won't Seem Like Christmas (Without You)", "I'll Be Home On Christmas Day", "If I Get Home On Christmas Day", "Holly Leaves And Christmas Trees", "Merry Christmas Baby", "Silver Bells".

Another live documentary of Elvis, the performer, was shot by MGM in April of 1972. This time winning a Golden Globe award for the Best Documentary—"Elvis On Tour". His gospel album "He Touched Me", earned him his second Grammy award, for Best Inspirational Performance. A 14-days tour commencing with four consecutive sold out dates at New York's Madison Square Garden, with the evening concert on July 10th 1972 being recorded and issued on LP a few weeks later. "Elvis: As Recorded At Madison Square Garden" became one of the biggest selling albums of Elvis Presley. "Burning Love" was released on single, after the tour, cracking the Top 10.

At the same time, Elvis and Priscilla had grown distant. In 1971, after an affair Elvis had with Joyce Bova, which to some sources resulted in a pregnancy and an abortion, Bova claimed that Elvis wanted her to move in at Graceland, and saw his relation to his wife Priscilla coming to an end.

The Presleys separated on 23 February 1972, after Priscilla disclosed her relationship with Mike Stone, a karate instructor Elvis had recommended her. Five months later Elvis new girlfriend Linda Thompson, a former Miss Tennessee and a songwriter, moved with him, to Graceland. Joe Moscheto of The Imperials said that the failure of his marriage "was a blow from which he never recovered."

In January 1973, Elvis Presley performed two benefit concerts for the Kui Lee Cancer Fund, resulting in the ground-breaking TV Satellite special "Aloha From Hawaii". Two shows were recorded, one as a backup, should technical issues arise. Aired as scheduled on 14 January 1973, the first global concert satellite broadcast, reached millions of viewers live and on tape delay. The accompanying double album, released in February, went to Number One. Selling over five million copies in the United States.

At a midnight show at the same month over exuberant fans stormed the stage, Elvis throwing one intruder off with Karate, fearing that the men had been sent by Mike Stone to kill him.

The divorce of the Presleys taking effect on 9 October 1973. Twice in the same year Elvis overdosed on Barbiturates, spending three days in coma in his hotel suite after the first incident.

His doctor George Nichopolus was quoted as saying: "Elvis Presley felt that by getting drugs from a doctor, he wasn't the common everyday junkie, getting something off the street."

Since the comeback to the stage, Elvis Presley had staged more live shows with each passing year, with 168 concerts in 1973, the busiest schedule. Also in 1974 he continued his busy and intensive touring schedule.

But his health worsened, as members of the TCB band noted. Keyboardist Tony Brown: (At Elvis arrival at the University of Maryland) "He fell out of the limousine, to his knees. People jumped to help, but he pushed them away like, 'Don't help me.' He walked on stage and held onto the mike for the first thirty minutes, like it was a post. Everybody's looking at each other like, is the tour gonna happen?' Guitarist John Wilkinson: "He was all gut. He was slurring. He was so fucked up ... It was obvious he was drugged. It was obvious there was something terribly wrong with his body. It was so bad the words to the songs were barely intelligible. … I remember crying. He could barely get through the introductions." A few days later John Wilkinson found an exhausted Elvis Presley in his dressing room: "I watched him in his dressing room (in Detroit), just draped over a chair, unable to move. So often I thought, *Boss, why don't you just cancel this tour and take a year off…?* I mentioned something in a guarded moment. He patted me on the back and said, 'It'll be all right. Don't you worry about it.'"

Elvis Presley continued to play to sell-out crowds.

On 13 July 1976, Vernon Presley, who had become deeply involved in his son's financial affairs, fired bodyguards Red West, a friend of Elvis Presley since the 1950s, Sonny West and David Hebler on "cut back on expenses". Elvis himself was in Palm Springs at that time, the firing might have also been in the room for some time, since there were many lawsuits because of their rough treatments on people who came to close to Elvis Presley. Others think, that this three members of the Memphis Mafia, were already at that time too outspoken on the prescribed medication habit of Elvis. RCA Records at that time had enjoyed a steady stream of product from Elvis for two decades, but grew anxious, as Elvis Presley's interest in recoding seemed to wane. After a December 1973 session that produced 18 songs, enough for almost two albums, he did not enter the studio in 1974. But the Colonel selling RCA another concert record—"Elvis Recorded Live On Stage In Memphis".

Recorded on 20 March 1974, it included a version of "How Great Thou Art" that would win Elvis his third and final competitive Grammy Award, all three of his wins having been, out of 14 total nominations, for gospel recordings. Elvis returned to the studio in March 1975, another recording session to be held at the end of '75 Elvis turned down. In 1976, RCA sent a mobile studio to Graceland that made two full-scale recording sessions possible. Between July 1973 and October 1976 Elvis recorded content for six studio albums, still label and Manager wanted to get out more of him.

Five of those albums entered the top five of the Country charts, three reaching number one: "Promised Land" (1975), "From Elvis Presley Boulevard, Memphis/Tennessee" (1976) and "Moody Blue" (1977). But none the pop charts. Single wise it looked similar: "My Boy" was a number one adult contemporary chart hit in 1975, with "Moody Blue" topping the country chart and reaching Nr. 2 on the adult contemporary chart in 1976.

Elvis and Linda Thompson split in 1976. Elvis taking up on a new girlfriend Ginger Alden, at that time 21 years of age. He gave her an engagement ring two months later.

At this time, he received some poor reviews by the press for live concerts: "Presley had become a grotesque caricature of his sleek, energetic former self. Hugely overweight, his mind dulled by the pharmacopeia he daily ingested, he was barely able to pull himself through his abbreviated concerts." (Journalist Tony Scherman, early 1977.)

In Alexandria/Louisiana, Elvis was on stage for less than one hour and "was impossible to understand". He cancelled his show in Baton Rouge, with the rest of the tour being cancelled. Despite his failing health, Elvis Presley stuck to most of his touring commitments. In Rapid City/South Dakota, "he was so nervous on stage that he could hardly talk," according to Presley historian Samuel Roy, unable to "perform any significant movement". "Way Down" Elvis Presley's last single was issued on 6 June 1977.

For his next tour, CBS filmed two concerts for a TV Special, "Elvis in Concert", to be aired in October. Elvis Presley's final concert to be held on 26 June 1977 in Indianapolis/Indiana at the Market Square Arena.

On 16 August 1977, the world learned that Elvis Presley died at his home on Elvis Presley Boulevard, Graceland.

Chapter Two
Elvis Alive

"He was a king among men, a country boy with a golden voice, destined to captivate the hearts of millions. From his ramshackle beginnings in the backwoods of Tennessee to the blinding lights of sold-out concert arenas ... soon millions had made him their king, their idol—their prisoner. He needed to escape the merciless clutches of fame—before it squeezed every last drop of life from him!" (From the book "ORION" by Gail Brewer-Giorgio).

"Orion is the novel that began the explosive worldwide Elvis controversy and launched my bestselling book—IS ELVIS ALIVE? ORION is the book that started it all, a book which travelled a bizarre and amazing journey, a book which may have come too close to a startling reality: Did a superstar rock singer hoax his own death? ... ORION—the fiction that may be too close to the truth." (Gail Brewer Giorgio)

A woman named Gail-Brewer-Giorgio wrote a book in 54 days about a singer of fiction, named Orion Darnell, who faked his own death. This started a conspiracy theory: That Elvis Presley did not die on 16 August 1977, but went into a protection programme by the US government, for not being only a key witness to a financial scam, directly related to the Mob ... To which he was not on only a victim, but crucial to the punishment for those involved. His life was in danger, as was the one of fictional Orion. Gail Brewer-Giorgio was seen on Oprah Winfrey, Larry King, David Letterman, USA Today, NBC, ABC, and written about in virtually every newspaper of the USA.

But it had started a little earlier: It was 16 August 1977, so the day, on which the world was about to learn about the death of the "King of Rock and Roll" Elvis Presley. A member of the "Atlanta Journal Constitution" began writing her novel. A novel, about the fictionalised character Orion Darnell. The outstanding part of it, was that the hero of fiction, faked his own death, to escape the limelight and danger. Gail Brewer-Giorgio said she was "inspired by the death" of Elvis Presley to come up with such an idea, plus her intuition told her, this could have been something Elvis Presley might have had done.

In 1978, her intuition seemed to sound true, in more than one way: SUN International Records, owned by Shelby Singleton released the LP "Duets" by Jerry Lee Lewis and Friends. On two songs Jerry Lee Lewis clearly duetted with Charlie Rich, but on the remaining ten it seemed he was having the duets of his life with none less than Elvis Presley. The American columnist James Bacon, tried to find an answer to whose voice, other than the voices of the afore mentioned Charlie Rich and Jerry Lee Lewis belonged to. James Bacon made mention of letters concerning a column about Elvis Presley, released earlier, would not stop. In the column the voice on the album "Duets" was credited to Elvis Presley. James Bacon, also had word from Memphis Mafia and one of Elvis Presley's closest associated Red West, that it was indeed Elvis on this recordings, who gave a hand to an old friend—Jerry Lee Lewis.

Sometimes in the 1960s, at the end of one of the songs, you can hear Jerry Lee Lewis also clearly asking "Man, you're ready for tonight, Elvis?" Jerry Lee Lewis did not comment on the release of "Duets". One letter received, stated that the voice belonged to an impersonator or soundalike named Jimmy Ellis who would soon make some more news. But James Bacon refused to believe, that anyone else except Elvis could sing that way. Plus, he insisted that Jerry Lee Lewis did not need Publicity gags like this. Most likely, Jerry Lee Lewis was not even asked of the enhanced re-release of some of his vintage SUN recording output. Some letters also wrote that it was recorded after 16 August 1977, that Elvis might have faked his death …

In 1979, Gail Brewer-Giorgio which was just awaiting publication of her novel "Orion", received a mysterious phone call. The voice seemed to belong to Elvis Presley, but the man introduced himself as Orion. When Gail insisted that Orion was a work of fiction, the reply on the other line insisted: "I know that I'm Orion, I was born today."

The call had come from Shelby Singleton's offices at SUN Studios in Nashville/Tennessee. It did not belong to a character of fiction, which came to life, but to the mysterious singer on "Duets" whom so many had believed to be Elvis Presley—his name was Jimmy Ellis. But that was kept in secret for now, his LP "Reborn" was awaiting release under the alter-ego Orion.

Jimmy Ellis himself was born in 1945, his parents forenames are to be known as Gladys and Vernon, he was adopted in early childhood. Making recordings as early as 1964 for Dradco Records, he was the literally billed "?" artist on SUN, on the single "That's Allright" b/w "Blue Moon Of Kentucky" in 1972. The "Duet-partner" of Jerry Lee Lewis, which was followed up with a long play named Trio. This album featured him either harmonizing or duetting again with Jerry Lee Lewis, also Carl Perkins, Johnny Cash and Charlie Rich.

In interviews Jimmy Ellis aka Orion, journalists obviously also asked him about his opinion on the subject if Elvis was alive? He stated that he sounded like Elvis, and that even that he is not billed as Elvis, many of his fans believed that as a matter of fact he may be Elvis, and hides behind a mask. A similar hair, a similar height did also part of it. But he did not see himself as an impersonator, the good lord decides on how a man sounds, and Elvis hadn't the monopoly on voices.

Shelby Singleton, President of SUN Records, and producer of Orion's music was quoted as saying: "Orion sings no Elvis songs and he is no impersonator. As a matter of fact he sounds like Elvis, he has the same vocal chords and wears a mask. That's what the stories with having had plastic-surgery and that he is Elvis. That he had intended to escape the limelight, but needed to perform. 90 percent of the people who have seen him live, believe he is Elvis. We promote Orion as Orion, not as Elvis, but we hope to also attract some Elvis fans. He will become a Superstar, not as Elvis or the Beatles, but a Superstar."

In 1981 after placing several singles in the US Country charts, he was voted "Most Promising Male Country Vocalist" by Cashbox, had released three albums released to his artist's name Orion. But he seemed to get tired of the gimmick. The mask, bothered him. But it was in his SUN contract, that he was not due to perform without it, nor appear in public without it.

Even Paparazzi tried to get a priced picture of the singer without the mask.

Shelby Singleton explained: "If he would just wear a mask, we can make him a star. He didn't really want to do it, I had an artist here at the time that I had to transform in some way to make him famous, and he was resisting. But, looking back, I think he didn't like it because he figured none of his friends would know that it was really him."

While Jimmy Ellis, still defended his appearance with a mask in the early 1980s: "The mask is my identity, everyone has one … Johnny Cash his dark-clothes, Crystal her hair, Willie Nelson his bandanas and I the mask."

He finally had enough during a performance on New Year's Eve in 1983—and unveiled himself on stage. Singleton ripped up his contract shortly afterwards. This seemed the end of the story of Orion, and the intuition Gail Brewer-Giorgio had that possibly Elvis Presley might have faked his death. Or was it a cover up to the cover up? Nevertheless, it was topped with "The Elvis Tape" obviously recorded in 1981. As far as for Gail-Brewer-Giorgio is concerned, it is Elvis Presley talking on it. Here's an excerpt transcription of The Elvis Tape, which was included with Gail Brewer-Giorgio's 1988 book "Is Elvis Alive?":

"This interview is being conducted by Legend books, with the author of the novel Orion and a book about the book entitled 'the most incredible Elvis Presley Story ever told.' Hello I'm Jeff Prew and we have with us today author Gail Brewer Giorgio, it's good to have you here today Gail, tell us a little bit about the book Orion. I understand that this is fiction but it's had a very strange Story in real life, tell us how the book started in 1977!"

Gail Brewer-Giorgio: "I guess I was inspired by the death of Elvis Presley. I thought a phenomenon had occurred: Everybody was making an exodus to Memphis. I kept thinking 'my God a president hasn't died ...,' later I decided that I would like to create a contemporary hero and I created a Orion out of a combination of mythology and religion brought it together into a singer. I wrote the book in about 54 days, at least the first draught, you have to remember there were literally no books or biographies out about Elvis Presley so I didn't have anything to copy and I didn't want to copy: If I had wanted to write a biography, I would have basically. I wanted to create a hero of fiction and I wanted that he would hoax his own death. I came up with that idea, well in mythology basically the legend Orion has a derivative which is Arion (A-r-i-o-n). ... it's about a man who sang: He was being penalised for being a great singer, his life was in danger and so in order to save his life, he's out to sing and begs the sailors to sing once more. He jumps to the ocean and is saved by the Dolphins, and is taken to an island and they think he's dead. The whole story actually comes from the mythology Arion and it's amazing how close it may have come to the life of Elvis Presley. I guess that's when my troubles began ... Jeff: "Someone sent you a mystery tape."

Gail Brewer-Giorgio: "Counting several releases, Simon and Schuster pocket books etcetera and then that book mysteriously disappeared about 1981." Jeff: "You mean it just disappeared off the bookshelves?" Gail Brewer-Giorgio: "A lot of things had happened, during that period of course that's why I've written a book about the book." "Last year I was presented with a tape in front of witnesses, there were two ladies actually that presented me with a tape." Jeff: "This is an audio tape or a video tape or?"

Gail Brewer Giorgio: "An audio tape, I was told right up front that the tape had been doctored: The person that the voice is talking to has cut their voice out—deliberately—the voice on the tape had been talking on the telephone to someone who was recording. The women who had given me the tape really didn't want to say too much. There are other reasons for that, their identity, their personal involvement with Elvis Presley and also they believe that Elvis Presley or more than believe they told me he was alive and that they understood why the things happened to my book that did. I was told to get a voiceprint while the voiceprint expert was in Texas and had some Association with Watergate tapes etcetera and they compared it with known interviews with Elvis Presley. The voice print came back 15 December '87 and it came back as positive, meaning that the voice on the mystery tape and that of the known element being Elvis Presley with a reasonable assurance was one in the same. What they were unable to ascertain is when it was actually done."

Jeff: "In other words there's nothing at least, as far as what you've heard on this tape that would absolutely prove that it was made after 16 August 1977." Gail Brewer-Giorgio: "Sense that when you're talking to someone on the phone you say hello so and so today is January 8th 19 such a session. I'm talking to you now. In fact, if it were on the tape I'd be very suspicious, but by the context of the tape I believe it was done after 16 August 1977, because what he says. Jeff: 'With your book and this tape, actually both of your books but certainly the novel Orion we have a situation, perhaps are you saying that this is sort of life imitating art or vice versa?"

Gail Brewer-Giorgio: "Exactly so many of the things that I wrote in Orion began to come true after the fact and I believe, I was penalised for it." Jeff: "Well I'm dying to hear this tape, so let's play some of this tape right now": (The Elvis Tape, unknown voice, identified by a voice expert as Elvis Presley): "People ask me all the time, where I'm living. Naturally I can't say. But it's a good place to hide. I, it actually started when I arrived in Hawaii, I made arrangements with a friend of mine to move out of the state. It was really something, because everything worked, just it was meant to be. I mean, there was an island that I had learned about a long time and ah I guess I always knew, that someday I was probably to have to use it."

"Anyway, I really can't say that I didn't need the rest. Slowly, I started getting myself into shape. I didn't sing much. I needed the rest even more, than more than I knew. But after about a year, I started missing the people and the entertaining. I have been entertaining for the better part of my life. It's very hard stopping doing something that you've been doing that long. But I, I started travelling all over the world. It's been enjoyable, it's been a battle also, … growing beards, and this and that from keeping of being recognised. And I guess, I guess about two years ago I went to Europe, which is something I always wanted to do, something I wanted to do for a long time. I mean, I've been always sorry that I haven't been to Europe before. I guess I could have, but I just didn't take the time."

"Anyway, the first place I wanted to see in Germany was a place called Wiesbaden. I don't know if you've ever seen … Wiesbaden before. But my girlfriend was with me. We went to a place to get something to eat. And uh, a waitress there asked me what I would like to have. And I said, I don't know really, what would you suggest? And she stood still: She just kept staring at me, and I started getting very nervous. At that time, I had a beard, I had lost a few pounds. … Very hard for anyone to recognise me. Then, she asked me if I'd be anytime in Germany in the past. And then, I got more nervous (laughs). … She said: 'You know I never forget a face, and she said I don't know how you did it. And I don't care how you did it, she said I just hope that you are as happy as you made me tonight. You know, that's the type of experience, that I never forget."

Jeff: "That struck me, in this portion of the tape—he says that he was sorry that he didn't go to Europe, as we all know he has been, his military tour of duty back in the 1950s in Germany how do you resolve that?" Gail Brewer-Giorgio: "I think a lot of people that have been in the service do not consider that going to Europe. I have a neighbour who says he would love to go to Europe, my husband and I had gone to Europe and he said I love to go to Europe and then after he said that he told me about the experiences he had in France when he was in the army. So I do believe that that's probably what he was referring to that he didn't perform or tour Europe."

Jeff: "Then he's referring to that woman he was talking to, apparently she says I don't care how you did it how do you interpret that?" Gail Brewer-Giorgio: "There can't be no other interpretation. He is obviously talking about these spot and he says he got more nervous because she said I never forget a face which refers to him being there before I take it to mean that she was recognising him."

Jeff: "Based on what we've heard so far—can you actually tell when this tape was made?' Gail Brewer-Giorgio: "I was told that was made in 1981.' Jeff: 'Alright, that would be four years after the death of Elvis Presley."

Gail Brewer-Giorgio: "He does mention in here that he was growing beards to keep from being recognised getting himself in shape he talks about having gone to Hawaii which I thought was interesting because in Orion ... Orion escapes to Hawaii, of course, I used my Hawaii because of the connotation of the Arion mythology. I've found it very very strange he said Hawaii but Elvis Presley loved Hawaii ..."

(Tape continues): "There's been a lot of times, that I would like to have changes somethings. But I've learned when something has been done, you can't look back. Sometimes it's not good to look back. I think, you know that she means as much to me as life itself. And hopefully, with the good Lord willing, sometimes people be kind to us and I see her again." Jeff: "Now in that portion of the tape, he refers to a she who do you think he means by she?"

Gail Brewer-Giorgio: "I would guess that he was referring to Lisa, keep in mind as we listened to this tape is the person he's talking to must have asked about her and by the description I would think it would be Lisa we also have to keep in mind the person that he's talking to if he is asking her about members of her family she would take that out so sometimes the conversation sounds a little rambling but we have to remember that it is not a monologue he's actually talking to someone so in other words he's responding to someone's question in fact when you listen to the tape and the voice print expert pointed this out there the stops in the starts are a pretty poor job I think of taking your voice out the voice print expert made a point of saying that this was probably about four conversations put together that explains why the subject matter changes perhaps when the phone conversations were being recorded if that's what it was there might have been repetition to of certain things but when it was put together it was put together in such a way that they could get as much on one side all right."

Jeff: "Well, then let's go on to the next portion of the tape: "As far as enjoying life now. I can go to football games, to the movies, but what interests me most, is seeing people in a way, that I hadn't been before. I mean I talked to people and I could help in some way. And for me that has to be the best part of life. And as far, as she is concerned or any part of my family, I don't think it is a good idea right now. I mean, there is no hard feelings or anything, but she always wanted her own life. And it makes me happy, that she is alright. You know, a lotta times, people walk up to me and they say that they are concerned about people finding out. Then they think about it for a while … then they usually say that nobody will believe them anyway."

Jeff: "Now what we just heard there is referring to another she on assuming it's a different person because he's talking about no hard feelings, who do you suppose that she is?" Gail-Brewer-Giorgio: "I would think it could be talking about Priscilla." Jeff: "Any idea where he could go to football games or being large crowds and going to movies and so on and not be recognised?" Gail Brewer-Giorgio: "He probably under normal circumstances would have been recognised, but with the fact nobody would be looking for him since he no longer exists he would have a new identity he says at different points he's growing beards and wearing sunglasses he probably isn't as heavy as he once was I have been told that he has a code name. This person has been recognised and they said well he looks like an older Elvis Presley we would be an older Elvis Presley because it be 53 and not 42." Jeff: "Have you ever imagined what he would look like, as far as the colour of his hair?"

Gail Brewer Giorgio: "As far as his hair-colour, his hair had turned prematurely grey like his father's. If you had seen Vernon his hair was a whitish grey also I understand his mother's hair had turned prematurely grey too and she died it Elvis was known to dye his hair."

"I don't know, I don't know in the first place it would be it would be foolish to walk back into a lifestyle that I just escaped from. But I'm going to continue my music and give people as much of what I can. I had people write letters to me, just fantastic. It's nice to know that there are people, that are truly concerned. … When you have friends like this, when people care about you that much, when you do something. And there's a lot of things I would like to do, there's a lot of music I would like to attempt." Jeff; "On that particular portion of the tape he's talking about how foolish it would be to walk back into a lifestyle it he worked so hard to escape from."

Gail Brewer-Giorgio: "That's a key phrase as far as I'm concerned it explains why he did what he wanted to do he left his lifestyle he didn't just simply go into hiding he said I escaped from it he does talk about still wanting to give people music." Jeff: "How do you think you would be able to do that?" Gail Brewer-Giorgio: "Well we have a lot of speculation without going through my whole book there has been speculation as to using a cover coming out under another name. He would have to come out under another name as the reason being is that if he didn't he would be forced to do the same old music or music that had been copyrighted pre 1977, which really would have boxed him in. By coming out under perhaps another name he would cause a lot of controversy certainly."

Jeff: "He might even be perceived as an Elvis imitator." Gail Brewer-Giorgio: "That's true that's true one of the things about imitator though in order to imitate they need the lights in the costumes and the razzamatazz they don't record, because they don't record like Elvis Presley and a lot of them even lip sync to Elvis music."

"If he is going to do other albums other material he would have to come out under another name he would also have to use that name and be able to disappear whenever he wanted one thing a mysterious singer Orion also came into view about the same time my book did and also disappeared, but by the way the same time the book did. Many people have questioned who's on the album but we can't see a face that's recording and so they could put any face or any name on and that is the question that I delve into in my book and I think I've come up with some pretty good answers."

Jeff: "And also the fact that this voice that's purported to be Elvis Presley's is saying that people are concerned about him and are writing letters to him does that that suggest that there are other people you know in this secret?" Gail Brewer-Giorgio: "Graceland Nr.1, is receiving a tremendous amount of letters Elvis Presley is making more money now quote unquote death than he did in life but there is a Legion of fans a Legion of a legitimate media out there not that we're not but I'm talking about 2020 they actually did a whole hour on the cover of the death of Elvis Presley, but the fans are just legions of fans who believe one that is live or two that there's a major cover up. If there's a major cover up in the question is why a major cover so yes many many letters are coming to Graceland."

"As far as being concerned. I still date. I'm dating a young lady right now, that is very helpful to me, as far as keeping my sanity. She's been good for me, when we, when we first met, she kept telling me how she liked my music. When we first met, she was kinda in shock, when we first met, like most people. She was glad that I was still here. One thing led to another. Now she goes with me, to every place I go. I mean, it's nice, I have a lotta time on my hands now. I am getting a lotta in the sports now, I am still working out. Playing racquetball and karate when I get a chance. This helps me to stay in shape, and a clean living surely can't hurt."

Jeff: "He mentioned in the portion we just heard—a young lady friend down assuming that Elvis is now in is really 50s how young would a young lady be?" Gail Brewer-Giorgio: "Elvis had a wonderful way of speaking about women as young ladies. I thought it was interesting too that he says that she kind of looked at me in shock when we first met like most people but she was glad I was still here again to me that dates it as after 16 August 1977 why would prior to that anyone. Say Jenn, glad you're still here and I'm shocked to see that you are basically that's what he is saying."

Jeff: "Referring to playing racquetball at getting into karate again he stresses clean living how can we square a remark like that against all of these allegations about the drug abuse that have seen the dog his life and certainly his death how do you square those two tape around here he talks about that I have read many biographies on him I think the drug problem if it was a problem was overstated 1970 Elvis was appointed by Richard Nixon as an agent of the Bureau of narcotics and dangerous drugs and in many biographies which people overlook it is stated that Elvis pretended to be whacked out I think he pretended to do this so he could listen in on conversations about him we must also take into consideration that when they talk about the quote drug abuse they're talking about prescribed drugs for medical reasons because autopsy remains had been destroyed according to 2020 and some of the other biographies I believe it was overstated also we want to listen to the next part of the tape he talks about that that."

Jeff: "Alright, I'm curious, I'd like to hear this":

"You know there's one thing, that always gotten to me. There is a lotta people making a lotta money outta the drug thing. If that's what makes them happy, that's fine. But, it is not true. As a fact of matter, is that I haven't even taken a sleeping pill in three years. If I had the chance to do everything again, I probably make the same mistakes, but uh, you grow attached to people. You grow attached to people, that are with you. Then your life, a lotta times, comes more important to the people, that you realise … You try to help as many people as you can, but sometimes, sometimes you can please someone."

"Sometimes you can't please anybody. You know. A lotta times I thought the image hurt me. But I, I always knew there would be a price I would have to pay. There's a lot of people that are lonely, you don't have to be on the poor side of life to be lonely, you don't have to be rich, to be lonely. You can be standing in a group of a 100 people, and you can be lonely. It's a strange thing you know.

Lately, I have been trying to write music, which is something I've always wanted to do. I just never took the time, and I am trying to play the guitar better. I still play the piano. I spent most of my time getting myself back into shape. It is not easy. To get everything done at the same time. There has been a lot of things that have happened. I have got to be very careful. I mean, I met a young lady in a supermarket once and she kept following me."

"Apparently, she said, I almost can't believe, but I think I know who you are. And I said, honey if you don't tell anybody, I won't. And, uh, and there in the supermarket she started crying. And I said, honey don't you cry. And the tears just started falling down her face. And she put her arms around me, and she said, I think I can feel what you have been through. And she said, I will always love you. You know—things like that are experiences you just can't buy. It's very hard to forget anything like that. But, things are like that have been happening to me a lot. (…)" Jeff: "What sort of illnesses did he take drugs for?"

Gail Brewer-Giorgio: "Glaucoma, he took drugs for that he had: problems lot of biographies stayed a lot of medical problems that he did have high blood pressure, but he had a high energy level. Elvis Presley did. I just find it very hard that a man could have stood on his feet and did the gruelling performances he did that last year and be a drug addict. I just do not believe it I don't think it's physically possible (…)" Jeff: "I have not taken a sleeping pill in three years now assuming that this tape was made in 1981 or 1980 that would take it back to approximately 1977." Gail Brewer-Giorgio: "That's right."

Jeff: "He refers also about a young woman in the supermarket now in your book Orion near the end of you refer to Orion being recognised and telling someone if you don't say anything about it I won't be here again we have white imitating art." Gail Brewer Giorgio: "Yeah yeah really is, he does talk about meeting this woman. I find too that when she said I almost can't believe it but I know who you are again when he says 'honey if you don't tell anybody I won't.' I find it very hard to believe that pre 1977 he would have taken the chance of walking around supermarkets etc … I think he felt free to do it after 77 because frankly people weren't looking for him he was supposedly dead.' Jeff: 'One of the things that struck me too is we listen to these clips of this tape has how these people who he claims to have seen him how can they keep this a secret why isn't this out why aren't people running around whispering?'"

Gail Brewer-Giorgio: "Actually, it is out that's the strange part about it Merle Haggard commented to People magazine about the feeling that I was Presley was alive people have reported seeing him but let's face it Jeff if you were sitting on an aeroplane next to someone who looked like Elvis Presley you might look at him and say you know he looks like Elvis Presley or an older Elvis Presley and even if he told you he was. You probably wouldn't believe him #1 #2 if you did believe and there's very few people who believe you that's right so I think that was his cover also is that people just simply aren't going to believe it.' Jeff: 'All right let's move on."

"I don't think. I don't think anybody can tell, or say exactly what's going to happen from one day to the next. But I'm not complete in hiding now. I mean I'm seen by people all the time. As far as, as appearing nationally. I would say it would be silly, to say the least, to get back into something that's been taken me so long, to get out off. But I, I'd like to continue my music. I'd like to do some new things, I'd like to do, some tracks that couldn't be done in the past. But mostly I wanted to continue to entertain people. That's been something that is in my mind. That's something I'd like to get in, not as much as I used to. I'm sure that sometime in the near future, it has to happen. Until that, I am continuing living the most normal life, I possibly can. I don't think anybody could have done the best or do any better, to what happened to me."

"Sometimes I feel like, that's like being on an island, but I'm on an island. It's kind of hard to go through this life, just memories, I presume that's what I have now. I would still like to give a back lot to people, that have given so much to me. I'm hoping that, a lotta people out there are not disappointed with me. I didn't mean to put anybody through pain. It's taken a lot, to do, what I had to do. But, I'm thinking in the long run, it is going to pay off. I believe that doing things that way, has made it a lot easier on me, than everybody else. To find out, what's going exactly on, as far as the music is concerned being able to make things happen, better now. I don't know life is very strange. I have no clue, so many different types of experiences, that I didn't know sometimes where I'm at. But I have learned a lot. I'm always learning more. There is no way that you can stop learning."

"You have to continue to learn. … A lot of movies have come out in the past, in the recent past, which I haven't enjoyed at all. It's an interesting thing, when you are involved in entertainment, you realise that there are a lot of things, like various things. But people try to portray, make you look in a certain way. I think they are doing the same in movies, they want to make things come out in a certain way. If they don't the feel like, they haven't done their job."

Jeff: "I was curious about something he mentioned there about being silly to come out and appear nationally do you think he would ever do i?" Gail Brewer-Giorgio: "He does make mention that he's not completely in hiding and that he seen by people all the time. I have a feeling that a man whose life has been music is not going to completely give it up it wasn't the music that he disliked anyway I think it was his way of life after all Graceland had become a mausoleum for Elvis Presley he had to leave his house hidden in the trunk of a car he couldn't go anyplace but I believe totally believe he's either already producing music and we've heard it and don't realise it or definitely something is in the making 10 years is a long time of course he's only talking here about three or four years I believe he's probably been doing something."

Jeff: "I am curious too as to how he explains about him hoping it a lot of people are disappointed with me how could someone be disappointed with someone who's dead?" Gail Brewer-Giorgio: "From I think he's talking about the fact that people will realise that he still here I'm sure if he's still here that family members are aware of it but the fans at large would be disappointed with him my answer to that is having talked to so many of the fans I can't even tell you how many fans have called me with information and please do this book and please go on with it and tell your Storey they said that they understand I suppose there be a few that will be angry but for the most part I think that Elvis gave them an awful lot I think they do totally understand just like the woman in the supermarket said she does understand and I think she reflects how people feel there's very few of us that could ever have lived total life of being imprisoned by their fame such as Elvis Presley. I do think the fans understand it but he certainly worries about I think he cares about them now."

Jeff: "He also refers to some movies that have come out in the recent past and obviously because he says he doesn't enjoy them he's not referring them to movies that he appeared in himself doesn't sound like it; it sounds like there were some movies right after August 16 1977 documentaries?" Gail Brewer-Giorgio: 'There were documentaries there was movie that was called Elvis produced by Dick Clark it was number one in the ratings when it was on it starred Kurt Russell an I believe there were some other things that were done I didn't see the mall apparently it misrepresented what he was his unflattering or overly flattering but an image is certainly he didn't agree with he says they wish he had asked him, of course, they couldn't have asked him." Jeff: "Alright well then let's move on in the next portion of the tape:

But, it is just like the drug thing I was talking about. Movies, a lot of it, it is something that is not true. And there is not something I can do about it. I wish, they would have asked me about it, before they made the movie, but there isn't a lot I can do right now. I do believe, there is a lot of people that will never forget and that is good. Because, sometimes you feel without any memories. It is nice to know that there are people who have memories on you too. I'm looking forward spending this coming Christmas in a new way. It's always been a very happy time in the year for me. I'm looking forward, to possibly see some people that are going to be shocked. I'm just hoping, that this people that I'm going to see, won't be hurt. I know, they are gonna be shocked. It's gonna be good, because Christmas time is a good time of the year, to make everything ok … If there's ever a time, I could make an appearance, I think Christmas time would be …"

Jeff: "Well, he's referring here to this coming Christmas I guess to use his words that would mean what Christmas of 1980 one 82 probably around that time frame he's really not talking about coming out but about seeing people that are going to be shocked and I should be close friends relatives that didn't know obviously when you say seeing people and they're going to be shocked again that seems to be dated after August 77."

Gail Brewer-Giorgio: "Because he would have not shocked people prior to Christmas the movie for other people keeping the secret and this will keep listening mistake we keep hearing more and more people who he's going to see all these people. Gail Brewer-Giorgio: It may be secret or I wouldn't be here I do believe it falls back again to who would believe me anyway and if you were a close friend you might tell another close friend they might believe you but I don't think if you stood up on some kind of platform and said I've seen him that they would believe you so I think that's what he's probably referring to." Jeff: "Okay we'll play some more of this tape:

I'm looking forward to a lot of new things in the future. I made a lot of new friends, and I think it's gonna be better this time. I can look outta the window now, and I can see a lot more than I ever have. And I think the reason is, I can actually go to the places that I'm looking at. I can be alone. I can be around people, and do the type of things that I like to do. Without having a hundred people there at my side. It's a different experience for me. That's a good experience. I realise that sooner or later that it's gonna end. I hate to see that it's gonna end. I know some time, the secret has got to be let out. If it hadn't been

69

for what I knew and know now, things might have been different. I have to do my music, there is no way of getting around it. … I tell you, so hopefully things will work out better this time. Let's hope, wait and see."

I made a lot of new friends, I just want that done, I think.

Jeff: "He's talking about something going to be better this time how could things be better than the life he lived before?" Gail Brewer-Giorgio: "Well, apparently the life he lived before was not a good life." Jeff: "Not a happy life?" Gail Brewer-Giorgio: "I don't believe it was happy. I believe again that it was a Golden mausoleum, he does talk about the fact that the secret is going to be let out sooner or later. He does realise that something is going to end and I believe something he's talking about is probably being in hiding totally, but he also seems to think or have a plan that when he does come back out assuming he is alive that it will work better."

"Probably, will work better because number one no one will know where Elvis Presley lives he did not have that advantage beforehand. I read a statistic the other day, that there are two houses most recognisable in the world once the White House and the second one is Graceland so with that in mind I think you know what he had to go through however I do not believe outside the White House thousands of fans clinging to the gate to the point that he at one point had hired a look alike the least I read this to leave in one car so that he could escape in the other this might sound fun for a little while for most of us but I do not think it's fun on a daily basis." Jeff: "He keeps referring also to as I have to do my music. I want to do some writing, if he does do music again in what form? Would it be strictly in a recording studio?"

Gail Brewer-Giorgio: "I think probably albums will be one way, perhaps video, performing. One doesn't know if he has not performed again I touched upon this in the book about the book the most incredible Elvis Presley Story ever told, there has been some speculation that he has performed yeah I believe he will. Again I believe his safety and his privacy will be that no one will know where he is once he leaves. But you have to remember Elvis Presley is no longer 42 Elvis Presley's not 33 is not the Adonis we remember him Elvis Presley is a man heading towards his mid-50s one of these days Elvis Presley could be a grandfathering that's going to be very hard for I have reached female so I don't think the performing will certainly be the way it was. But obviously the music's important." Jeff: "Certainly not the voice."

"The voice wouldn't be the same you hear a lot of the great singers and their voices do give out so they have difficulty reaching higher notes to her absolutely alright will move on to the next portion of this very very interesting tape:

"I know that I have been very fortunate. I hope I see that can't be any different. I hope see new things coming. It's gonna be good for everybody. I'd like to finish the book that I have started on my life. As far as what I've been doing. Three or four years, I am working on an album, something that I wanted to do in the last few years. … Returning to people, that have helped me in the past. To help me with the music, and put out, maybe … I don't know if we can get hold of all the people. But that's something we have been working on. I am looking forward to that. I think, a lotta people have given me the chance, to continue, without bringing the tomb out on the open. It took a lot to get me into hiding, it would be a shame if things would just turned around in five seconds."

Jeff: "What we've just heard there he's talking about taking a lot to get him into hiding what sort of things?" Gail Brewer-Giorgio: "Well obviously total hiding the way he supposedly did it, leaving the one life behind and going into another life. He planned it apparently prior even to 16 August 1977, he cleaned house he got rid of the Memphis mafia. They gave the excuse if it wasn't excuse that the payroll was overextended in … lot of those people at very close to Elvis Co so I think it did take a lot it would be very hard just to do what he did to actually do it to be so fed up with the kind of life that's not fed up with the music not fed up with the fans per se because he really he loved the fans but the whole life of not being able to ever go to a football game just the simple things he says you to see people the way he wanted to see them took a lot to get him into hiding and I think he's afraid that if he comes out what would happen is the real wait and see attitude he has right now and I would imagine one day he thinks about it and the next day he it's scared stiff."

Jeff: "And of course that raises a very very basic question who was that in the coffin at Graceland on 17 August 1977 lying in state as hundreds thousands of people passed by the coffin inside." Gail Brewer-Giorgio: "Including you I understand … there's a lot of speculation obviously the majority of the fans have written in their newsletters and periodicals I've had journalists call me I've been a journalist but guess it was a wax dummy there's been questions as to why the coffin weighed 900 pounds some have speculated that it had a cooling unit in it to cool the wax dummy I don't know who was in the closet but that seems to be the number one guess and it seems to be the number one question I think among the lot of the sceptics does it not well a lot of people wonder why Vernon would have even put his son on display it was about protest too much kind of thing when Elvis' mother died, he was very upset and so was Vernon at her funeral turned into a circus it seems very very odd that with great deliberation that this particular viewing and funeral had turned into a circus by invitation so the only thing I can think of is if they had had a very very quiet dignified private kind of funeral people would not have believed he died therefore put the body or whatever on display and again this is all guesswork and it's not simply my guess work on mimicking thousands of fans out there put something on display and say there he is now you can leave him alone go away there's nobody here anymore for you to see I can't come up with another reason."

Jeff: "And I think another question that a lot of people want to know too is that to pull off something like this this grandiose scheme it just seems that too many things could go wrong does it not to you?" Gail Brewer-Giorgio: "Oh absolutely many things went wrong that's what's so funny again I get into the talk about this in my book yeah there's tremendous amount of things that went wrong there so many many questions that if you just took one question alone out of my book you would have enough to speculate as to what happened there's just so much but again we would be perhaps one single thing that sort of jumps out at you in which they appear to have botched while the name on the grave Elvis's middle name was Aron yes and again I go through in my book as to why he was named with a single A had to do with his being born a twin the legal documents that are all with the single a RCA promotion has the single the death certificate which I go through in the book because that raises a lot of questions that I won't get into it right now but the name itself Elvis's middle name was Aron but Vernon only tombstone at Graceland the eternal monumental Elvis Presley has spelled his son's name with the double A."

Jeff: "like in Aaron that's right the bottom of the tombstone it says by Vernon Presley now wouldn't that be an honest mistake?" Gail Brewer-Giorgio: "Though this failure sons name the most famous face in the world there are other things about the grave that raises questions superstition is funny and not only was Elvis very religious and his family religious but I would imagine there were some superstitions allot of people don't buy plots because they're superstitious they don't want to fulfil anything but if we were we wouldn't have our tombstone made it seems to me that it was just a way of saying he's not buried there that's one example."

72

"It has given me a lot of time to do work, where before I had to constantly do things over and over again as far as the music was concerned. It's hard to do something you wanted, change it drastically, if you've been used to it in the past. If you haven't gotten any time, I hadn't any time before, my time had been taken up. But this is different, this really gives me chance to get into something. To do a piece of material the way I wanted to do it, instead of somebody's telling me this or that way. ... I just have to do things this time, the way I want it. I think it will work a lot better. The first album we already released, is something I was doing a few months ago and I enjoyed it."

"But I tell you, but ... if we'd ever release it. There was a lot of memory on the songs, we tried some new songs. I had a lot of fun doing it. But, the next album we put out, I really hope we can get hold of the people from the past. It would be a rewarding experience, to think, that everything would work so smoothly. My whole life has been something like a dream. And I had this happen, I mean to get all the people together that helped me in the past to help with a new album. ... It would have to be the biggest experience in my life, and I am certain it would be good for them too. I am looking forward to it. And I know, many times we despair, then life has something passed us by. But you know dreams can come true."

Jeff: "Okay, it's been a real pleasure talking with you here about this extraordinary tape recording we've just listened to and also learning more about your book entitled the most incredible Elvis Presley story ever told, Gail, do you really think Elvis Presley is still alive, honest now."

Gail Brewer-Giorgio: "I haven't seen him personally so I really don't know there has been times though I've received some very mysterious phone calls and I don't know if I've spoken to him or not mean the calls have come in to this house to this house yes yes and again I talk about it in the book all I can say is that read the book and the people will have to be the judge; they've listened to the tape they can check the evidence; all I can say is they will have to be the judge. Elvis says on the tape nobody would believe it anyway."

Other books next to "Is Elvis Alive?" on the subject, written by Gail Brewer Giorgio are "The Elvis Files" and "Elvis Undercover".

It seemed that "Is Elvis Alive" and the re-publication of Orion, once more inspired Jimmy Ellis, who prepared for a comeback with the song "Down In Mississippi", released under the alias Steven Silver.

The lyrics tell us that Elvis is still here:

73

"I remember down in Mississippi, picking cotton in the sun. And I'd sing with the black folks, when the day was done. I dreamed even then, that the world would be my stage.

And someday, my shoes would shake loose, that Mississippi clay. Then we moved from Tupelo to Memphis just trying to survive. I cut a record for my mama, and almost overnight, the Colonel signed me up.

I was living out my dream, my momma was so proud, when you called me The King. Down In Mississippi, I play my guitar, sing my Rock and Roll songs and dream I'd be a star. I went down from Mississippi to Nashville/Tennessee, but my shoes never shook loose the Mississippi clay.

One day I was no longer a kid in a Cadillac, just an old Rock and Roller tired of coming back. I was a prisoner of my fame, and when my momma died, the lord seemed to say to me, you need to change your life. But I was too big to just turn my back and leave. So I changed the way I look, and now no one knows me, everybody in the world believes the king is gone. but I'm down in Mississippi, and it's good to be back home. Down in Mississippi, not far from Tupelo, near a dusty road, underneath a magnolia tree, I play my guitar and sing my songs, now my blue suede shoes are home at last, in this Mississippi clay, I sure do miss you folks, until we meet again, adios."

For a long time, it was unbeknownst to anyone that it was again Jimmy Ellis fuelling the fire if Elvis was indeed alive. Born in 1945 in Orrville/Alabama he had begun his recording career with the Dradco label in 1964. He first recorded for Shelby Singleton in 1972, when he cut updated versions of Elvis Presley's first two sides—"That's Allright" and "Blue Moon Of Kentucky". The coupling was also released on Sun without artist credit. After recording for some other companies, such as for Boblo Records, where the album "By Request Ellis Sings Elvis" was released at the dawn of the 1970s. He signed with Shelby Singleton for SUN in November of 1978. National recognition was achieved with in early 1979, with his first SUN release, "Save The Last Dance For Me", which featured his voice over-dubbed as artificial duet with Jerry Lee Lewis.

The duet credited to Jerry Lee Lewis and Friend stayed on Billboard's Top 20 charts for weeks and became the subject of the afore mentioned wild speculations. DJ's, club owners and fans alike wondered about the identity of the mystery duet partner of The Killer Jerry Lee Lewis. The single and the following album "Duets" was at first accused of being an illegitimate SUN release of old recordings by Jerry Lee and Elvis. The TV Show "Good Morning America" actually conducted a "scientific voice scan" of the unidentified singer and concluded it belonged to Elvis. It was somewhere around this time that Gail Brewer-Giorgio's book "Orion" fell into the hands of SUN Records—and the fictional character Orion was brought to life.

The single "Ebony Eyes" was released by Sun, then the LP "Reborn", picturing a ghostly singer wearing a Lone Ranger type mask rising from a coffin. (The album was later repackaged with a picture of Jimmy Ellis, with a mask, as his new alter ego Orion.)

SUN International launched a massive promotional campaign on Orion, complete with biographical information: He was born in 1936 in Robbinsville/Tennessee, he attended high school in Nashville, his parents were Jesse and Dixie Darnell, he was married to Danielle Darnell and had a 10 year old daughter named Mele Leilani—all taken as far as Gail Brewer-Giorgio claimed without consent from her book "Orion". In November 1979, Orion stated: "I don't think there's any question about me sounding like Elvis. I'm not billed as Elvis, but, yeah lots of my fans think I'm Elvis, that I never died and that Elvis is playing behind the mask. I have black hair and I'm tall. But I don't copy anything. I'm just Orion. Elvis didn't corner the market on voices. It's whatever the Man upstairs decides."

Jimmy Ellis hated being Orion. Although he was one of the first Elvis impersonators, by 1981, there were hundreds competing with Orion to perform at the same nightclubs and small theatres. Ellis didn't even consider himself an impersonator—he considered himself a real, one-of-a-kind performer who could write and sing his own songs. He asked Singleton if he could record under his own name once again, and drop the mask. Singleton rejected the idea. Why abandon the sure thing they had (with "Orion") and attempt the thing that had failed so many times before (the career of Jimmy Ellis)? Ellis kept asking, and Singleton kept turning him down.

Frustrated by the limitations of his job and unable to express himself musically, Ellis began to suffer something of an identity crisis. Both resenting and worshipping Elvis, he started to believe that he might actually be related to the King. Ellis had been given up for adoption at the age of two. His biological father was listed on his birth certificate only as "Vernon". Elvis's parents, Gladys and Vernon Presley, had according to some, split up for a while in the mid-1940s, and Vernon Presley had reportedly lived near where Ellis was born in Alabama.

For a time, Ellis truly believed that Vernon Presley was his real father, which explained why he had so many uncanny similarities with Elvis.

For New Year's Eve 1983, Ellis-as-Orion had been booked at the Eastern States Exposition in Massachusetts, the biggest headlining gig he'd ever had. At the end of his performance, Ellis tore off the Orion mask in front of a crowd of 5,000 people and announced that he wasn't Orion—he was James Ellis. Photos of the moment ran in newspapers around the country, proving beyond a doubt that the man behind the mask was definitely not the King.

While few people really thought that Orion was Elvis Presley, removing the Orion mask was still career suicide. Not only was the commercial gimmick gone, but Ellis had openly defied Shelby Singleton. In early 1984, Ellis met with Singleton at Sun Records, and all contracts relating to Orion were cancelled. Singleton later said that after Ellis left Orion behind, more than 100 Elvis impersonators approached him, asking if they could step into the Orion persona … and he turned them all down.

Though with or without mask, the controversy continued:

Was Orion a front for Elvis?

Was it Elvis voice on the album's and Orion's face on the covers?

Why was Orion on the same record label that Elvis once was?

Why is Orion's record producer a man named Bobby Smith? Didn't Elvis have a cousin by that name?

Why are the Orion costumes designed by the same man that designed the costumes for Elvis Presley?

Are there two Orions?

Why was Orion seen at Graceland?

Who is the power and the money behind Orion?

Gail Brewer-Giorgio wrote in "Is Elvis Alive?" that she received a late phone call by man identifying himself as Orion:

"I, ah, heard something about you selling your book to, ah, Ballantine. I don't think you should let Ballantine publish ORION, I mean, you said it right. Elvis is like Orion." Brewer-Giorgio replied: "I'm glad you like the book, but it really isn't about Elvis, I never knew Elvis, never was around him. I truly made everything up." The voice, identifying himself as Orion said: "Then I don't know how you knew so much. Maybe I understand, though. I understand those things."

"What things?" Gail asked.

"What I'm trying to say is that Ballantine knows that, ELVIS: WHAT HAPPENED? Is not the truth. But they publish it. You shouldn't let them have ORION. I don't think it's right."

"What isn't true?"

"A lot of it. Especially the drug thing. And the part about Elvis throwing a pool cue at a young lady, stabbing her in the chest. Those boys who wrote it said Elvis did it deliberately. That's not the truth and they know it. Elvis wasn't playing good, got mad and turned and threw the cue. He wasn't aiming. It was an accident. It's not good to have a temper but it was an accident. That's the truth. Those boys told it wrong. It's simply not true."

Sometime later Gail Brewer-Giorgio was attending a concert by Jimmy Orion Ellis, also being allowed backstage, when she told him: "By the way. You don't have to worry about my going with Ballantine. My agent placed it with another publisher." Orion, according to Giorgio stared at her perplexed: "Ballantine? I don't know what you are talking about?"

Another very late phone call was recorded with Gail Brewer-Giorgio. Her son, Christopher, then a teenager answered. "It's for you, Mom."

"Who is it?" came from an annoyed Giorgio, who was resting and reading on a sofa. "Who's calling?" her son asked. She recalled: "There was a long pause, and then the man said: 'Ah, tell her it's Orion.'"

Her son Chris became excited, he had heard enough conversations around their home about the possibility of there being two Orions, and that one of them might possibly be Elvis Presley. Chris exclaimed "Orion!", so that the man, started a conversation with him. As Chris told him about him being hunting squirrels. The caller stated that he didn't like killing animals. "But you do like riding horses?" the mystery caller asked. Chris replied with yes, and they talked five minutes about horses. As the phone was turned over to Gail Brewer-Giorgio, there seemed no particular reason for the call.

But then the subject of identical twins came up. Orion said: "You know. Identical twins come from one identical egg. At the moment of the conception there's just one soul, but then the egg divides and becomes two human beings. I believe, the soul also divides, each part going into each body. If one of those identical bodies dies at birth, I believe the soul of the dying twin goes into the living's twin's body. The living twin will have twice the talent, twice the fame—yet also twice the sorrow, twice the pain."

Gail asked: "Are you Elvis Presley?"

"No. Elvis is gone. This is Orion."

Again, Jimmy Ellis denied this call. People magazine, shortly after, ran an interview with Merle Haggard, who was stating as saying, if Elvis might have faked his death: "It would be the first chance of freedom in his entire life, and it could have been a scheme Colonel Parker dreamed up."

Could it be that some talented impersonators were behind all the mysterious phone calls, and even the Mystery Tape as included in the bestseller "Is Elvis Alive?"

The following commentary by Gregory Sandow appeared in the Los Angeles Herald Examiner on Sunday, 9 October 1988:

"Don't look at me: I don't know if Elvis is alive. But "The Elvis Tape" (included with Gail-Brewer-Giorgio's breathless book Is Elvis Alive?) has to be pretty damn uncanny.

It's billed as Elvis, speaking a few years after—as we're supposed to believe—he faked his death. I guess I thought it would sound too dim to rank even as implausible. But not so. It's clear enough to draw qualified approval from a voiceprint expert, and easily clear enough for me to tell you that ... well, it could be Elvis. Whoever's speaking hesitates just the way Elvis used to; that's what gets me. What's Elvis supposed to be doing? You'll have to hear the tape yourself, but a short answer might be that he's thinking things through. And that's another reason not to toss the tape away. Would anyone faking his death resurrected an Elvis who sounds so unsure of himself?"

Discoveries magazine printed in December 1988 the following comment:

"I recently bought the paperback Is Elvis Alive? by Gail-Brewer-Giorgio which included 'The Elvis Tape'. I wasn't very impressed by Gail's ramblings in her book, but the Elvis tape is an entirely different story. The voice on the tape is the voice of Elvis Presley. End of conversation?

Did Elvis Presley actually die on 16 August 1977? He surely could have, but if he did then die, that would make me wrong on the tape.

If the voice on the tape is not Presley's, then it is an absolutely perfect imitation, but such letter-perfect voice imitations have yet to be performed, so the burden of proof regarding the tape has to lie with those who say the tape is a fake. The voice on the tape is Presley's until somebody comes up with the guy who faked it.

In my opinion, it would be much more difficult to fake the tape than it would be to fake a death. Maybe a person would have to be involved recording to really

78

understand just how difficult faking such a tape would be, but I'm not going into any detail about the tape. I have absolutely no question in mind about whose voice is on the Elvis tape. It is the voice of Elvis Presley."

(Prewitt Rose, of Jamesport, New York)

Gail-Brewer-Giorgio noted in another bestseller she penned, "The Elvis Files":

"The tape with Is Elvis Alive? was voice-authenticated by an expert with a major law enforcement agency in Texas; the Watergate methods, were in fact, used. The spectrographs are available on the video Breakthrough and have been available for perusing by anyone on doubt. The conclusion of the first official report states that 'there is data indicating that the unknown and known speakers are the same with a moderate level of confidence.' These were the results of comparing the Mystery Tape (with Is Elvis Alive?) and known interviews with Elvis Presley. On the video the expert states that the voice on the tape and the known voice of Elvis Presley are 'one and the same'."

Even Priscilla Presley was asked in an interview on US National Television, if it was Elvis' voice on the tape. She replied, that it was indeed Elvis speaking, but old interviews spliced together …

This yet, seems unlikely, by the references the "mystery Elvis" makes on the tape:

Elvis never travelled around the world; the Colonel, his manager, did not allow him to perform outside the United States, during his Army years he was in Germany, but did not go out and only visited Paris briefly in 1958.

During his Army discharge interview, filmed at a press conference in Graceland, Elvis Presley said he never even went out to eat.

Elvis was not known for going around wearing a beard, except for his movie "Charro".

When did Elvis "escape" from his life?

He makes reference to people finding out. But what? What wouldn't they believe?

Not completely in hiding. He was walking around freely, that never happened before 16 August 1977.

The speaker also makes reference on being "disappointed". Why? Who put him through pain, and why? Elvis never officially made a comment on the book "Elvis What Happened?" in a press conference …

No biopics were produced about Elvis Presley, before his death.

"The drug thing" This was not made public until after 1977, or at the very least only days before his death, via the book "Elvis What Happened?".

Why would people be hurt by seeing him?

What secret?

Five people have claimed to be the voice on "The Mystery Tape". However when they were asked to be voice-authenticated by the police, they always backed off.

The most controversial person to have claimed until very recently, even on a LinkedIn profile, which is no longer active, to have been the voice was David Warlock:

His first claim came to be standing up during a February 1989 "Geraldo Show" claiming to be the voice. On the programme—to which Elvis' friend Joe Esposito, his stepmother Dee Presley, Major Bill Smith, a Fort Worth/Texas record producer who claims to be an Elvis friend, also the producer of the gold/platinum hits "Hey Baby" by Bruce Channel and "Hey Paula" by Paul and Paula, author Paul Licker, and Elvis Army buddy George Dividinzi and Gail Brewer-Giorgio were invited. Warlock also made the claim via an magazine interview with Bill Burk, publisher of Elvis World, No. 11, 1989.

The man described himself as being:

1) A psychic entertainer and as a spiritual entertainer.
2) Said he was paid 125 US Dollars for a month's work; later he stated he was paid 125 Dollars a week for four weeks.
3) Said the "clicks" on the tape occurred when he hit the "pause" button on the tape to gather his thoughts.
4) Stated that he went into a psychic trance in order to bring Elvis' voice through.
5) Mentioned of being offered a million dollars to be the voice on the tape.
6) Said he was hired by the Eternally Elvis Fan Club in Florida.
7) The Eternally Elvis Fan club, presided over by June Paolillo has never heard of this man—who did not gave his real name.)
8) He also showed a contract dated 1981, listing two men who supposedly hired him.
9) Said the background noise heard was a fan running.

Against this claims comes another television spcial, in which a pararpsychologist makes quite a few statements, which rule out any psychic connection.

David Warlock could have had with the King:

(And even if, then Elvis Presley's spirit, must have thought he did not die on 16 August 1977, but had faked his death, this would have been possible, if Elvis died around 1981, and his "spirit" talked about the few years he had after faking his death, through the psychic entertainer …)

Brian Corelone, was spotlighted in a 1988 TV Special on the Las Vegas "Billy Goodman TV Show":

Billy Goodman: "I'm Bill Goodman, I welcome you to the story behind the story. Today we're looking into the possibility of Elvis Presley being alive. Some folks in Kalamazoo/Michigan, claim they have been seeing him driving around in a red Ferrari and with us is Brian Corelone, who is the Director of Parapsychology in Las Vegas. Brian, you've met Elvis Presley and you were with him more than once. How about telling when you first met him, and the last time you saw him before his death?"

Brian Corelone: "Well, the first time I met Elvis was at a school dance. I was going to a private school with, I don't remember if it was his godson or nephew or something like that. Anyway, this classmate had said that Elvis might pop in to offer the graduating class his congratulations. And we were all out in the inaudible end of the ballroom waiting for him, and he did show up and when I shook hands with him, I was amazed at the … I mean people have described his personality as being electric and there really was some sort of electricity that felt, like, coming off him. Then the last time I saw him was several years later at the Hilton, and I was as close to him as I am to you and the scarves that he used to throw at the audience were going over my head. And I felt that same charisma or electricity or vibration or whatever you want to call it. I've never felt since then anybody with such unique and dynamic vibrations."

Billy Goodman: "What do your attribute that to?"

Brian Corelone: "Well, of course the first time I met him I had not really been into parapsychology as deeply as I am now. The only thing I can figure is, the man had a great deal of wonderful karma; he had so much within him that was dying to get out. I had once heard somebody say that, if Elvis Presley had really let go of everything that he had within him, there wouldn't have been billboards big enough or lights bright enough. And from what I felt coming off him, I agree."

Billy Goodman: "Repeat that again, people were saying there wouldn't be lights bright enough if he were to give off his total energy."

Brian Corelone: "Right. Very often he had a lot of dynamicness (if that's the word) in. I never felt like he was really letting go, even with all the movement on stage there was something restrained in him."

Billy Goodman: "So there was something different about these vibrations. They were so intense you would never forget them."

Brian Corelone: "They were unmistakeable and unforgettable."

Billy Goodman: "Now, Brian, there came a time when a real ardent Elvis Presley fan asked you to go to Graceland to see for yourself because of your parapsychology background. To see in fact, he was in that grave."

Brian Corelone: "Well, she mainly wanted me to try to communicate with Elvis. Since the announcement of his death, I'd been invited to preside over several dark rooms, which is like a séance. Elvis is one of the few people I've never been able to raise. I was curious about that. She was frustrated about it, because usually she was the one who has to talk to Elvis in the dark rooms. So, we flew to Graceland, went on the tour, nobody knew who we were, just a couple of hick tourists. When we went past the gravesite. I felt absolutely nothing. Now, part of my training in parapsychology was being taken through cemeteries. My teacher at the time was Richard King, and he'd point to a grave and say. "Tell me about the person buried here." He did this with maybe three to five hundred graves. I never really kept tab. One time he said, "Tell me what you feel from this one?" I felt nothing. As it turned out, it was a mock grave that had been used for a movie that had been filmed there, and there was never really anybody buried there. I felt that same nothingness from Elvis' grave."

Billy Goodman: "Let's go back now. The vibrations you felt when he was alive at the Hilton. Would they still have been there with the body dead, as a dead body? I don't know about the vibrations."

Brian Corelone: "The characteristics of the vibrations would have been the same. But the intensity would have been far less."

Billy Goodman: "And they were not there."

Brian Corelone: "Nothing."

Billy Goodman: "Nothing."

Brian Corelone: "I may as well have been standing in front of a hatbox."

Billy Goodman: "So you can unequivocally say, as far as you're concerned., Elvis Presley's body was not in that grave."

Brian Corelone: "Not a body as it was presented in the news: the human form in the glass-lidded coffin. If Elvis is in that grave in my opinion, either the body was later cremated or they must have put in in a lead casing, because lead is the only thing that will cut out any kind of electrical frequency. Human vibrations are a form of electricity."

Billy Goodman: "So you're saying, once again, that unless he was encased in lead, or cremated. He definitely was not in that grave."

Brian Corelone: "I tend to believe that he isn't in that grave."

Billy Goodman: "Felt no vibrations."

Brian Corelone: "Nothing whatsoever."

Billy Goodman: "Did you at any time feel any of his vibrations on the property at Graceland?"

Brian Corelone: "Yes, when we went on the tour of the mansion itself. There are doors that lead to what was known as the family wing. This is a part of the mansion reserved for the family and the caretakers and so on. The public was not admitted there. As we walked past those doors, I suddenly could not move. I was literally paralysed with fear, because I felt the same vibrations I had felt when I shook hands with him, and when I saw him at the Hilton. I felt hose exact same vibrations at same intensity level, coming from the other side of those doors."

Billy Goodman: "So, if I'm hearing you correctly, that means as far as you're concerned he was alive behind these doors. If it's the same intensity, and you only feel the same vibrations when they are alive, and they were the same."

Brian Corelone: "Yes."

Billy Goodman: "Then he was behind those doors as far as you're concerned."

Brian Corelone: "He was alive in some sense. Now, I've heard a lot of people theorise that he was not dead when they found him, that he was in a coma, and that maybe he's on life-support systems, behind those doors. If that's the case, that would explain the intensity of the vibrations. When a person crosses over or dies, whatever you want to call it, the life force is no longer here. Only the consciousness. And without the life force to give it that extra energy, the intensity drops."

Billy Goodman: "I understand that. But you are also saying that no matter what condition the body was in, he was alive."

Brian Corelone: "Yes."

Billy Goodman: "So six years ago, the man could still have been in a coma, could have been anywhere. But the vibrations were there and he was alive."

Brian Corelone: "Yes."

Billy Goodman: "It's really becoming more and more fascinating with this man. You also mention the fact that you could not reach him during the dark room on the other side. Is that correct?"

Brian Corelone: "Right. Right, I have been asked to contact Mae West, W.C. Fields, some of the real old-timers, and they've always come through. But Elvis Presley ... nothing comes through with Elvis Presley."

Billy Goodman: "That's amazing, isn't it. Either, he's not there or he doesn't want to come here."

Brian Corelone: "Right. A spirit has the same thought patterns—if you want to call them that—as a living person. If a lot of living people don't want to be bothered on the telephone, they don't pick it up. If a spirit doesn't want to be bothered, it's not going to respond. I tend to believe that Elvis has not crossed over."

Billy Goodman: "Which simply means he's alive. Let's get right down to it."

Brian Corelone: "In one form or another."

Billy Goodman: "Right. He is laid up in a hospital bed or something of that nature, but alive."

Brian Corelone: "Right, yes."

Billy Goodman: "He could even be driving around in that red Ferrari."

Brian Corelone: "Very possible."

Billy Goodman: "Very possible. Brian Corelone is the Director of the Institute of Parapsychology, trained in this. He has no trouble reaching people on the other side. He cannot reach Elvis Presley on the other side. You did say one thing to me, Brian, and I think we should bring it up, that there's a middle place there too, which you never wanted to get involved with when you felt those vibrations down there at Graceland. You thought he could actually pull you through the door."

Brian Corelone: "Yes. I felt like if I had reached out, he would have been able to grab hold of me."

Billy Goodman: "And you wouldn't be here today."

Brian Corelone: "Well, if he was on the other side—I tended to believe that that was his spirit—he could have sucked me right through the veil."

Billy Goodman: "Ladies and gentlemen, you have heard it. Right here, on the story, behind the story. Elvis Presley could be alive. Brian, thank you very much for coming by."

Brian Corelone: "Thank you."

Billy Goodman: "And for enlightening us. And, boy, one question. Do you want to see him come back?"

Brian Corelone: "I would like to just know he's somewhere, and that he's happy and he's at peace with himself."

Billy Goodman: "Do you think he would come back?"

Brian Corelone: "That's something only he could answer. I don't think so, though."

Billy Goodman: "Let's leave it up to him."

Brian Corelone: "Yeah."

Billy Goodman: "'The King' himself."

So was Elvis Presley sighted as well? He was. One of the most credible sightings comes from the journalist Kelly Burgess, who spoke about it in depth on Billy Goodman's KBEG Radio Show, broadcast in the fall of 1988:

Billy Goodman: "We will be listening to Kelly Burgess. Kelly actually met Elvis Presley in August of this year, and she's going to tell us what happened at that meeting. Welcome back to this 'story behind the story' in the Elvis Presley controversy—whether he's dead or alive. Our next guest is Kelly Burgess. Kelly, you've got your background, Detroit News—tell us something about yourself."

Kelly Burgess: "Well for ten years I was an editorial feature writer and sometime columnist on the staff of the Detroit News."

Billy Goodman: "… and there came a time when you left the Detroit News?"

Kelly Burgess: "Yes, I left the Detroit News—since then I've been writing for national magazines. I have an article in this month's issue of Skin Diver magazine."

Billy Goodman: "I you understand that you actually talked to Elvis. This is great. Tell us about it. How did you ever even think of trying to find him—where did you find him? Let's start from how you got there. Take us on your trip that you told us about today—it's interesting."

Kelly Burgess: "First of all, unfortunately, I was never an Elvis fan. I never had the opportunity to see a concert, never owned a record. When he died, I felt very bad, but it just kind of passed, and I never gave it a second thought until this summer. I don't know if any of you had access to the Michigan newspapers.

There were several sightings of him in Michigan, and that's where I'm from—Troy/Michigan, which is a suburb of Detroit. About the same time, I read Gail Giorgio's book Is Elvis Alive? and I became quite intrigued by the research she did, and what she uncovered. And the more I read about the sightings in Kalamazoo—as a reporter—it was a challenge. One day, around the first week in August, I told my twenty-two-year-old son, 'Let's go to Kalamazoo today.' I went totally expecting to find nothing. I had heard about the lookalike. And when we arrived in Kalamazoo, we went to Burger King and to the YMCA."

Billy Goodman: "Tell everybody what happened at the YMCA. We can't let that go by."

Kelly Burgess: "I went to the YMCA and spoke to the director of the fitness centre and I said, 'Does Elvis Presley work out here?' He said: 'Just a minute, I'll have to check the roster.'"

Billy Goodman: "I think that's great, I really do. Nonchalant as can be …"

Kelly Burgess: "… which he did, and he came back and said, 'No. Elvis Presley does not work out here.' Let me tell you first that there is a lookalike running around in Kalamazoo creating an uproar. Many people have seen him: he hangs around Burger King, goes into the supermarket, could be spotted driving a car. I've even heard he throws parties and invites people an hands out T-shirts. That is not Elvis Presley."

Billy Goodman: "Where did you find Elvis Presley?"

Kelly Burgess: "I went to an hold hotel in Main Street. Now, Kalamazoo is small college town with very antiquated buildings. I went to this hotel, which was built in the 1890s—there's a renovation underway there now—it's being converted from an old hotel into an office complex. Three gentlemen bought the hotel in 1985."

Billy Goodman: "Where did you find Elvis?"

Kelly Burgess: "You want to hear the details? The mystery behind it?"

Billy Goodman: "Well, maybe we could go back afterwards to it. Where did you find Elvis is what I want to know."

Kelly Burgess: "I went into the building and started surveying. There's five stories, a five-story building with an atrium elevator. I started surveying every floor. I had three encounters with security guards. They told me to leave. They said: 'You're not allowed in here.' My next step was to go into some of the offices; there are several tenants doing business in that building. I went into offices asking for Elvis Presley or Jon Burrows. They all looked at me, quite incredible. I mean, here's these business people and I'm asking for Elvis Presley. At one point some of the people said, 'Elvis is not here, but we've seen his illegitimate son, Elvis Presley Jr.,' which turned out to be a joke. The last office I went into was off the main floor and lobby. I spoke to a receptionist and asked her the same question. She said, 'just a moment, I'll get my manager.' So the manager came out and I was speaking to him about Elvis, and he seemed quite interested, and asked my reason for being here. We talked about five minutes: I had my back to the office door. Suddenly, he said, 'There's the man you want to see,' and I turned around, Elvis was standing there; it was almost as if lightning had struck the room!"

Billy Goodman: "You're there—it was Elvis. Tell us about what happened then."

Kelly Burgess: "His presence was overwhelming. Now mind you, I've been a reporter: I've seen and worked on all kinds of stories. This was the first time in my life that I was stunned. I didn't know what to say. He took his finger—like this—and said, 'What are you doing in this building bothering the tenants? I will not have this.' He was very angry. I said, 'I'm with the Detroit News and I'm doing a story on Elvis.'"

"I do not care if you're with the Detroit Star, I will not have this!" Yet in the next moment his mood changed entirely. He was very kind. I could feel that he did not feel threatened by me: I was not aggressive. I started talking to him and he did not say a word for about five minutes. I started outlining some of the facts in Giorgio's book: "Why didn't anyone collect life insurance? And why didn't Vernon accept the flag for the coffin?" He stood there and listened; he didn't say one word. At one point, I turned around and he was standing at a kind of angle. I turned so that I could look directly into his eyes. He had on gold-rimmed glasses, a modified version of what he used to wear; they had a slight tint to them. But I looked in his eyes, and he had the Elvis Presley expression in his eyes, which I think the most people are familiar with—that kind of sparkle—the same shaped eyes, same-colour yes. Again, I was stunned. It was shining through, what comes through all of us that says: "This is me." It's kind of your soul that shines through your eyes. I said, "You have eyes just like Elvis. Are you a relative?" He said: "Nope."

"See, for some reason, and today I still don't know why, I did not let him know that I thought he was Elvis. I still don't know why. I didn't come out and ask him. After he listened to my questions, he just stood there with a very pleasant look on his face, smiling at times. Just before I walked away, he said, "Yeah, but it's against the law to hoax your death." And I left the building, but then I returned. Should I talk about that?"

Billy Goodman: "What did you return for?"

Kelly Burgess: "To take a picture, to—"

Billy Goodman: "Kelly, what does Elvis Presley look like?"

Kelly Burgess: "He's about six feet, maybe 195 pounds, with a small pot-belly. He looked really good. He had a head of very thick white hair, without sideburns; his hair was done up in a kind of boyish haircut. Same mouth, same cheekbones. I mean, it was Elvis. Anyway, I followed him into the construction office and he sat down at this desk. Then he put his head down. He spoke very little in the short time I saw him. I thought he was looking for a pen so he could write my number down. Evidently he didn't find one and I didn't. I ripped out a deposit slip from my check book and handed it to him. He said, "All right, Kelly." And I left. After that, I did get several hang-ups and hold-ons on my answering machine. It was quite an experience. I'll never forget it for the rest of my life."

Billy Goodman: "I wouldn't think you would."

Kelly Burgess: "I mean, his presence was just electrifying."

Billy Goodman: "You, like everyone else, knew it was him—the vibrations and everything that goes with it, that it was Elvis. Kelly, I understand you're writing a book?"

Kelly Burgess: "Yes, I am."

Billy Goodman: "What's it going to be about?"

Kelly Burgess: "It's going to be about Elvis Presley, from 1977 to 1988."

Billy Goodman: "You're going to tell what he's been doing. How about giving some inside information?"

Kelly Burgess: "No. I'm sorry. I can't do that."

Gail Giorgio noted in her 1999 book "Elvis Undercover" about the late Kelly Burgess: "Kelly Burgess was a credible lady. She was not the new kid on the block career wise, but a mature woman with grown children. (When I was invited to appear on Geraldo, Kelly agreed to appear with me; but, like all other credible guests I was promised, Kelly was "uninvited" prior to the show on the grounds that she was "too credible".) In a later telephone call with Kelly, she related that she had uncovered evidence that was frightening and shocking. When I asked her if she had gotten a picture of Elvis that day, she said she'd rather not say.

After that Kelly told me that she was dropping the idea of the book because the evidence she had uncovered was dangerous and that she felt that a non-involved was best. "Does it have anything to do with the mob?" I asked, "Yes", she replied hesitantly, "It does …"

With permission, the "Elvis Poolhouse" Picture

Graceland, 1 January 1978

On 8 January 1986, when Tim Malloy, co-anchor of a news segment on KCOP TV in Los Angeles, introduced the voice of KCOP's reporter Bob Walsh and then showed what is now known as the Poolhouse Picture, the world took notice. In the words of KCOP:

"Mike Joseph took his family to Graceland for a vacation on 1 January 1978, more than for months after the death of Elvis Presley—perhaps we should say "reported death". At the time the grounds of Graceland were the only part of the estate to the public, but Joseph took snapshots and put them away for safekeeping. Four years later while reading about Presley, Joseph took out his mementos of the Graceland visit, and he noticed something unusual in a shot at the bathhouse behind the mansion. It was a shadow in the lower half of the door. Joseph says he had the picture enlarged and the results were nothing short of startling. Someone or something bearing a remarkable resemblance to Elvis Presley was indeed sitting behind the door … The sequence of pictures including shots of Elvis's grave confirms that the pictures were indeed taken after Presley's death. Joseph says he's not trying to convince anyone that Elvis still lives or that the snapshot is an image of some supernatural phenomenon but there is something there. How it got there and what it is will no doubt remain as much a mystery as the entire Presley mystique."

Two years later, in February of 1988, Mike Joseph was interviewed on Breakthrough, on an independent TV telemarketing program show across the US nation. He said:

"One day, after reading a book, I decided to look at my pictures again. I pulled them out and this time I saw something that I hadn't seen in over the years. Of course, I wasn't really studying them. But the sun had just hit on this picture in such a way that it picked up this image sitting in the doorway—a shadow in the doorway. For curiosity's sake, not that I would know who was there, I wanted to see what it was. I took my son's magnifying glass, put it on the picture, and started pulling it away from the picture to get a good visible view of it and I was just shocked. I couldn't believe what I saw. My God! I had Elvis Presley sitting in the doorway, looking at the fans walking past his grave. Why? I asked myself a million times. Why? I don't know. Did he fake his death? Did he have to fake his death? Why couldn't he go off to an island someplace? Lock himself up in Graceland. I mean, I understand he stayed inside the house for months at a time. I remember the night of the vigil. There was something like 80,000 people outside the gates of Graceland. All of a sudden a car with teenagers in it—they were intoxicated—rant into the crowd, hit three women, who died. Maybe he was gonna come back—come back for the ultimate comeback. He was a practical joker. Maybe now he can't come back because of this accident."

When Mr Joseph was asked how we could sure the photographs were not altered, Joseph replied they were "the only negatives I've had" and that the negatives were examined by Kodak: "They were taken in sequence, uncut. By the negatives being original, they can tell. The emulsion number of the film was manufactured in '77. A roll of film has a manufacturing date in the emulsion number. You couldn't pay Kodak to say something like that if it weren't true." (A letter of Kodak exists testifying to this analysis.)

The interviewer Grant then wondered how Mike Joseph knew it was Elvis in the chair and not simply a photograph, to which Mike Joseph testified that there were indeed also pictures of the entrance with the chair being empty. Mike Joseph further explained: "We couldn't go near to the house. This is a security's guard's car. Things were sorta makeshift. It was too early; the mansion wasn't opened as a museum yet, so the house was closed to the public. Uh, this is Elvis's headstone, and right there in the corner is his mother's. So this shows that this was taken after 16 August 1977, and before '79, when his father died, because his father would be right over here, and in '80 his grandmother, Minnie Mae. This is the shot that I took of people walking and the bathhouse in the distance. We zero in here, and this is the same shot with just the chair, no one sitting in the chair. (Elvis) would be seeing us—and the people walking past his headstone."

After the Poolhouse Picture became known to Graceland, the original poolhouse door was replaced with a solid door. No one could see inside.

Chapter Three
The Presley Arrangement

"If you look back on my life, you will see I have not had as much to say about the way I live as most men do. My life was run by my fans. I'm not complaining. I did want it. People have written that I am a bad influence. That hurt me bad at first. I'd think what do they want from this kid from Memphis? I was but myself. I've got to be Elvis. I'm going to live the way I have to live, and if something should ever happen to me, I hope they remember I was not afraid … There might even be somebody who would say, "If Elvis had lived, he would have made a nice old man." (Elvis Presley in Modern Screen, 1966)

1977 lies more than 40 years in the past, new generations have come of age who never knew Elvis. Even older Americans may now have forgotten the events of 16 August 1977, when America and the world learned that the King of Rock and Roll, Elvis Presley died. Let's refreshen memories or introduce new generations to what happened:

15 August 1977—Elvis Presley was preparing for a twelve-day concert tour that was to begin in Portland/Maine, on the following day.

As his daughter Lisa Marie—who by then lived with her mother Priscilla Presley in California—was at Graceland on an extended vacation, on which Elvis spent much of his time that day, and before, with her. Riding golf carts, planning to watch the movie MacArthur that night on the home screen. (As the projector was not functioning that night, the plan was scrapped.)

Sometime during the evening, Elvis made a telephone appointment with a dentist, Dr Lester Hofmann, asking if he would open for an emergency appointment. (He asked to have his teeth cleaned, as well as some other dental work.) Along with his cousin Billy Smith, his trusted friend and on-stage right hand Charlie Hodge, girlfriend Ginger Alden—Elvis wearing his DEA (Drug

Enforcement Agency jogging suit—headed out at 10:30 pm, to attend his last-minute appointment with Dr Hofmann.

16 August 1977:

Elvis was back at Graceland somewhere between 12:30 and 1:30 am. Reportedly energetic, optimistic, good-humoured, and full of plans for the future.

At 4:00am, Elvis called Billy Smith and Billy's wife, Jo, to join him and Ginger on the racquetball court for an hour's play.

At 5:00am, after racquetball, Elvis played piano and sang songs.

At 6:00am, Elvis and Ginger went to his bedroom, where he changed into pyjamas and then, alternately, watched television and read.

At 8:00am, Elvis told Ginger that he was going into the bathroom—which in addition, served as a large, comfortable lounge, in order to continue reading. (It had its own back entrance.)

For the next six hours, according to the original reports, no one saw or talked with Elvis.

At 2:00pm, Ginger Alden discovered Elvis' body in the bathroom/lounge on the floor in front of his chair, where he had been reading. She called downstairs to Al Strada, Elvis friend/employee, who was in the kitchen. Al rushed upstairs, then called downstairs for Joe Esposito, another Elvis friend and employee. Elvis' personal doctor, George Nichopolus was phoned. Noticing that rigor mortis had set in, Joe called Unit Six of the Memphis Fire Department.

At 2:33pm, the Memphis Fire Department unit arrived. Despite the fact that the body was in rigor mortis, paramedics had been called, and gave CPR.

At 2:48pm, the body was taken to Baptist Memorial Hospital.

At 3:00pm family and friends Elvis was pronounced dead. The public was given a death time of 3:30pm.

At 8:00pm Dr Nichopoulos and Dr Jerry Francisco, the Medical Examiner, were interviewed in a press conference at the hospital.

17 August 1977:

At noon that day, the body was returned to Graceland for private family viewing.

From 3:30pm to 6:30pm, the public viewed the body at Graceland.

18 August 1977:

By order of the Governor of Tennessee, Ray Blanton, flags were flown at half-mast for the funeral procession, At midday, the gates of Graceland were opened and white Cadillac hearse drove through them, trailed by sixteen white Cadillac limousines.

It seems that Elvis had started cleaning house shortly before the year 1977. What is not evident is why? He fired Red and Sonny West plus Dave Hebler. All of them had been part of the Memphis Mafia, since a long time. The relation to Red West was going back to their high school days. Elvis also told J.D. Sumner and other members of his entourage that he would not be performing as much in 1977, as he had been, asking them to start looking for other work. Some asked why, he just stood by his statement: "Look for other work."

Dave Hebler, Red and Sonny West did not understand why they were fired, either for being bitter, or to make an income, the wrote the sensational book "Elvis? What happened?" which according to another Elvis biographer Albert Goldman, in his second book on Presley, focusing on his final 24 hours leads him to the conclusion, that this book was the ignition for Elvis planning suicide ...

Elvis' "cleaning house" was very secretive. Yet, his conversations from early to middle 1977 were filled with hints. At one point Elvis told Larry Geller that he wanted to dedicate his life fully to spiritual matters. He said the life he was leading had to end, that it had "gone on far too long". Elvis spoke about seeking a higher purpose of doing more with his life, and that his destiny had not been met. Despite of the conversations with his spiritual mentor Larry Geller, Elvis left other signs that changes were planned:

In many of his spiritual books, Elvis underlined or even wrote in his own hand the following words: "Should I return, you would not recognise me."

Elvis began saying "adios" at the end of his shows.

During his last concert tour just weeks before his death, Elvis turned down to his stepbrother and said: "Know, what Rick? I may not look good for my television special tonight, but I'll look good in my coffin."

On his final concert tour, Elvis, with is eyes away from his audience, looked down and said: "I am and I was."

Beyond saying things which inevitably seem to say goodbye forever, it appeared that Elvis may have left even tantalising messages in his songs:

He insisted that one of the titles recording during his last sessions be: "The Last Farewell".

Elvis launched his version of the song "My Way" towards the end, yet despite knowing the lyrics well, he deliberately stopped and read each word during a final concert—as of to stress the lyrics rather than the singing. His stepbrother Rick Stanley, that the song, although recorded years before by Elvis, was not added to his live shows until 1977.

There is also some clues in his final album "Moody Blue".

Perhaps in the end Elvis Presley intentionally saw the final curtain …

It came as far, that people attending Elvis' viewing of his body, did not believe that it was Elvis Presley's corpse they had seen:

LaCosta, sister of country singer Tanya Tucker stated in a correspondence with the Elvis Fan Club "The Elvis Special"—"We were right up to his casket and stood there, and God. I couldn't believe it. He looked just like a piece of plastic laying there. He didn't look like him at all … he looked more like a dummy than a real person. You know a lot of people think it was a dummy. They don't think he's dead."

Even Larry Geller, who supposedly did Elvis hair for the viewing, stated that Elvis looked like "a piece of clay".

Could it be that it indeed was a dummy, but not because Elvis had faked his death, as so many millions believed after his death? But simply, because he looked terrible after dying? (…)

Others, like Elvis' cousin Gene Smith, spoke about the "beads of sweat" on the body in the coffin. Since dead bodies do not sweat, this raises legitimate questions. Joe Esposito, Elvis Presley's right hand man, also acknowledged it on Larry King's TV Show in conversation with journalist and author Gail Brewer Giorgio, explaining that "it was very hot that day".

Those who believe all the official reports believe that if Elvis really wanted to escape his life, and faked his own death, why the circus-like funeral? Maybe, because his life was in danger, and he was given a new identity with the "Witness Exchange Programme" and had to "proof" to those who possibly threatened him and his family, that he was indeed dead. After all, Elvis Presley said only weeks before 16 August 1977: "I know I look fat now and I'll look terrible for my TV special coming up. But I'll tell you this: I'll look good in my casket."

According to Elvis Presley biographers, there are two birth certificates on Elvis Presley. The first was filled out by the attending physician, who used the traditional biblical double A spelling on Elvis' middle name: Elvis Aaron Presley. However, it was the parents of Elvis, Gladys and Vernon, who dictated that Elvis' middle name be spelled with a single because of a dead twin, Jesse Garon. Thus Elvis would always know by looking at "Aron" that he was a part of "Garon". A second birth certificate with "Aron" appeared, this second version is sold in reprints as souvenir.

This birth certificate has the spelling, the Elvis chose when he signed with his full name: Elvis Aron Presley. Patsy Guy Hammontree, Assistant Professor of English at the University of Tennessee, in her extensive researched work "Elvis Presley: A Bio-Bibliography" states Elvis' middle-name as being spelled "Aron", with his twin brother's name spelled Jesse Garon. The majority of fan publications use Elvis Aron Presley, in particular Elvis Now and The Elvis Special. Sue Wiegert, president of the Blue Hawaiians for Elvis Fan Club, relates in her book "Elvis: For The Good Times" that once, she asked the singer to autograph a book, he told her personally that he spelled his middle name with a single a, admitting also that there were those who mistakenly used the biblical spelling. Also the Tennessee Historical Commission states that Elvis Presley's middle name was Aron.

The Elvis Presley International Memorial Foundation purchased the marker, which was authorised by the Tennessee Historical Society. This marker, presented five years after 16 August 1977, negating the rumour that Elvis might have changed his name legally sometime in the 1970s. In the note of appreciation by Elvis' family, it was also thought that "The family of Elvis Aron Presley ..." Further high school diplomas, Army papers, marriage licence all display him as being named Elvis Aron Presley.

But why is the name misspelled on his tombstone?

According to Elvis Presley's uncle Vester, as stated by Gail Brewer Giorgio, that it was Elvis himself who had instructed his father Vernon to make sure that there would be Elvis Aaron Presley written on his grave stone.

Some thoughts suggest, as also the name of Elvis dead born twin is misspelled, that no one is actually buried in the Memorial Garden of Graceland. Further as common in the South, the bodies buried there are not facing east or west, as suggested in the Holy Bible. Although Elvis' interest in law and order was immense and sincere, he really was all about spirituality. One of his library's books was "The Passover Plot" by Hugh J. Schonfield, in which Jesus escapes death, through hoaxing it. The book is also on display in Graceland, and some die-hard believers that Elvis did not die in 1977, see in it, a clue that Elvis Presley left behind ...

Elvis also read the book "The King" by Morton Cooper. The book is about a forty-four-year-old singer who is "the King". He has decided to leave his way of life and go to work in the President's administration.

The jacket of the book, published before Elvis returned from his movie career to live performances reads as follows: "In the posh Manhattan hotel suite of President Joseph Haywood, Orlando brushed off the fawning hangers-on and left for Madison Square Garden … And as he sang, he said a silent goodbye to it all, because he decided to get off the dizzy merry-go-round of his life, trade it all for a job in President Haywood's administration … It would give him a last chance to do something that would make him proud to look the world in the eye."

In 1985, the novel "Fairytale" was published. This mysterious book is the story of a rock star named Aaron Wade, whose death is questionable. The book has a Joe Esposito type character who with the main protagonist is planning "the death". Finally, there is "The Presley Arrangement" written by Monte Nicholson, a veteran of the Los Angeles Sheriff Department. In his novel, the subject is the possible hoaxing of the death of Elvis based on facts.

In 1981 an album was released under the title of "Do You Know Who I Am" credited to Sivle Nora. For many years, there have been speculations who the mystery singer was, some say Jimmy Ellis others stay with the intended answer to the album's question—Elvis Presley. Ten songs are on the LP, the song "I Love A Rainy Night"—a hit for Eddie Rabbit—was not written until after 1977 … During singing "Loving You" the mystery singer stops and says: "Wait a minute, man, wait a minute—hold it, hold it. Somebody—somebody just told me that, ah, that President Reagan and some other people have been shot. I'd just like to say that I hope they're not hurt badly." President Reagan was not shot until March 1981.

Songs on the LP included were: "Do You Know Who I Am?", "Reconsider Baby", "Are You Lonesome Tonight", "Blue Christmas", "If That Isn't Love", "Hawaiian Wedding Song", "I'm So Lonesome I Could Cry", "That's Allright", "Loving You" and "I Love A Rainy Night".

Some questions on the death of Elvis Presley remain:

Why did Elvis' father refuse to have his son's coffin draped with the American flag traditionally given to all dead Army veterans? Did he know that the coffin did not contain his son's body?

Were all the post 1977 sightings, photos and tape recordings of Elvis mere hoaxes or wishful thinking by the many fans who will not let the King of Rock and Roll die?

Chapter Four
Elvis Presley and Law Enforcement

"He had a million badges and a blue police light in his car. He liked nothing more than putting that light on his car and pulling people over. He'd walk up to the window, show off his official badges and say, 'Son, you were speeding. Just wanna want you to slow down.' The driver would look up, see who was talking to him and remain speechless." (Priscilla Presley)

Was Elvis Presley also a Federal Agent? Because Elvis Presley was a collector of law enforcement badges, the debate whether Elvis' federal badge was honorary or real, continues. Most of those who followed Elvis remember the story of his December 1970 visit with US President Richard Nixon at the White House. Witnessing the historic meeting were Jerry Schilling and Sonny West; two of Elvis' trusted friends and members of his inner circle.

Most Elvis biographers state that the badge was real and that the purpose of Elvis' trip to Washington was to obtain a real, not an honorary badge, as well as to offer his services in drug enforcement. Yet Priscilla Presley, offering only a few pages on Elvis fascination in Law Enforcement in the book "Elvis by the Presley's" plays it down, with the following comment from it:

"Elvis wanted the ultimate badge from the ultimate law enforcer, the President. He reasoned that the badge would give him the freedom to carry around all the prescription drugs and guns that he wanted. His trip to Washington, though, started out as a mystery. He and his dad gotten into an argument about the Colonel. Elvis wanted to fire him and Vernon didn't. Frustrated, Elvis stormed out and disappeared for several days. This wasn't like him. We had no idea where he was. Later we learned he'd wound up in Washington. While on the plane he wrote a letter to the President.

At first they wouldn't let him through. You just don't show up in Washington without a prior appointment and waltz into the President's office. Yet that's

it my way through my communications with people of all ages. First and foremost, I am an entertainer, but all I need is the Federal credentials. I am on this plane with Senator George Murphy and we have been discussing the problems that our country is faced with.

Sir, I am staying at the Washington Hotel, Room 505–506–507. I have two men who work with me by the name of Jerry Schilling and Sonny West. I am registered under the name of Jon Burrows. I will be here for as long as long as it takes to get the credentials of a Federal Agent. I have done an in-depth study of drug abuse and Communist brainwashing techniques and I am right in the middle of the whole thing where I can and will do the most good.

I am Glad to help just so long as it is kept very private. You can have your staff or whomever call me anytime today, tonight, or tomorrow. I was nominated this coming year one of America's Ten Most Outstanding Young Men. That will be in January 18 in my home town of Memphis, Tennessee. I am sending you the short autobiography about myself so you can better understand this approach. I would love to meet you just to say hello if you're not too busy.
Respectfully,
Elvis Presley

P. S. I believe that you, Sir, were one of the Top Ten Outstanding Men of America also.

I have a personal gift for you which I would like to present to you and you can accept it or I will keep it for you until you can take it.

Mr President
    These are all my PVT numbers

Beverly Hills	278-3496
	278-9535
Palm Spring's Pvt #	325-3241
Memphis Pvt. #	397-4427
	398-4882
	398-9722
Col P.S. #	325-4781
Col B.H. #	274-8498
Col. Off M.E.M.	870-0370

Room 505–506
Under the name of Jon Burrows

PRIVATE
AND CONFIDENTIAL
Attn. President Nixon
via Sen. George Murphy
from
Elvis Presley

A Memorandum of the White House dated 21 December 1970 reads as follows:

MEMORANDUM FOR: MR H. R. HALDEMAN

FROM: DWIGHT L. CHAPLIN
SUBJECT: Elvis Presley

Attached you will find a letter to the President from Elvis Presley. As you are aware, Presley showed up here this morning and has requested an appointment with the President. He states that he knows the President is very busy, but he would just like to say hello and present the President with a gift.

As you are well aware, Presley was voted one of the ten outstanding young men for next year and this was based upon his work in the field of drugs. The thrust of Presley's letter is that he wants to become a "Federal agent at large" to work against the drug problem by communicating with people of all ages. He says he is not a member of the establishment and that drug culture types, the hippies elements, the SDS, and the Black Panthers are people with whom he can communicate since he is not part of the establishment.

I suggest that we do the following:

This morning Bud Krough will have Mr Presley in and talk to him about drugs and about what Presley can do. Bud will also check to see if there is some kind of an honorary agent at large or credential of some sort that we can provide for Presley. After Bud has met with Presley, it is recommended that we have Bud bring Presley in during the Open Hour to meet briefly with the President. You know that several people have mentioned over the past few months that Presley is very pro the President. He wants to keep everything private and I think we should honour his request.

I have talked to Bud Krough about this whole matter, and we both think that it would it will take very little of the President's time and it can be extremely beneficial for the President to build some rapport with Presley.

In addition, if the President wants to meet with some bright young people outside of the Government, Presley might be a perfect one to start with.

Here is the Memorandum which was sent to the President:

THE WHITE HOUSE WASHINGTON December 21, 1970

MEMORANDUM FOR: THE PRESIDENT

SUBJECT: Meeting with Elvis Presley
December 21, 1970
12:30 p.m.

1. PURPOSE

   To thank Elvis Presley for his offer to help in trying to stop the drug epidemic in the country, and to ask him to work with us in bringing a more positive attitude to young people throughout the country.
   In his letter to you, Elvis Presley offered to help as much as possible with the growing drug problem. He requested the meeting with you this morning when he presented himself to the guard at the Northwest Gate bearing a letter.

2. PARTICIPANTS

   Elvis Presley
   Bud Krough (staff)

3. TALKING POINTS

   We have asked the entertainment industry—both television and radio— to assist us in our drug fight.

You are aware that the average American family has 4 radio sets; 98% of the young people between 12 and 17 listen to radio. Between the time a child is born and leaves high school, it is estimated that he watches between 15,000 and 20,000 hours of television. That is more time he spends in the classroom.

The problem is critical: As of 14 December 1970, 1022 people died this year in New York alone from just narcotic-related deaths. 208 of these were teenagers.

Two of youth's folk heroes, Jimi Hendrix and Janis Joplin, recently died within a period of two weeks reportedly from drug-related causes. Their deaths are a sharp reminder of how the rock music culture has been linked to the drug sub-culture. If our youth are going to emulate the rock music stars, from now on let those stars affirm their conviction that true and lasting talent is the result of self-motivation and disciplines and not artificial chemical euphoria.

Suggestions for Presley activities:

1. Work with the White House Staff.
2. Cooperate with and encourage the creation of an hour Television Special in which Presley narrates as stars such as himself sing popular songs and interpret them for parents in order to show drug and other anti-establishment themes in rock music.
3. Encourage fellow artists to develop a new rock music theme, "Get High on Life".
4. Record an album with the theme "Get High on Life" at the federal narcotic rehabilitation and research facility at Lexington/Kentucky.
5. Be a consultant to the Advertising Council on how to communicate anti-drug messages to youth.

Another interesting note from Bud Krogh:

"Presley indicated to the President in a very emotional manner that he was 'on your side'. Presley kept repeating that he wanted to be helpful, that he wanted to restore some respect for the flag which was being lost. He mentioned that he was just a poor boy from Tennessee who had gotten a lot from this country, which in some way he wanted to repay ... At the conclusion of the meeting,

Presley again told the President how much he supported him, and then, in a surprising, spontaneous gesture, put his left arm around the President and hugged him."

However, on the second page of the memo Haldeman's response in pen was "You must be kidding", it appears that Haldeman was not as enthusiastic as President Nixon and his assistant. However, Haldeman did sign his initial on the approval line.

Many DEA agents appear to be "drug users" and "pushers" in order to do their undercover work. It is not unusual to find undercover agents who look very young taking on the role of high school or college students in order to get on the "big guys". There is little doubt that Elvis could get to anyone at any time, especially if he gave the appearance of a user. This falls in line with what was even stated in the book "Elvis: What Happened?" when one of the guys former members of Elvis inner circle wondered if Elvis was ever as whacked out as he sometimes appeared … Maybe after all, he was an actor also in that sense?

But could it be, that all the cryptic remarks by Elvis, as well as some of his clues to a "Last Farewell" by him, lead to the fact that the man committed suicide?

In the 1990 June issue of Life magazine, a story on Elvis Presley appeared with the headline "THIRTEEN YEARS AFTER THE DEATH OF ELVIS PRESLEY NEW EVIDENCES POINTS TO AN INESACAPABLE CONCLUSION: SUICIDE."

This story was based on a new book by Albert Goldman, who had previously penned the unflattering biography of Elvis Presley. He and Elvis stepbrother David Stanley had appeared prior on National Television to plug a new Albert Goldman book, which focused on Elvis Presley's final 24 hours.

Would this book, as many Elvis fans had felt with the prior Goldman book, again be a negative portrait of an obese, drug-ridden Elvis, a one-sided account?

The life article which was written by Albert Goldman himself told that he was revising the death of Elvis Presley, admitting that he prior had been wrong that Elvis accidentally took a drug-overdose. He should have read the signs more closely, he said: he now as convinced that Elvis Presley committed suicide. Part of the new conclusion came from David Stanley's statement that Elvis had said goodbye to his stepbrother a few days prior to 16 August 1977. Informing David that he wasn't going to be seen by him anymore. David was now convinced that Elvis knew, in fact, his demise was imminent—that indeed, he was planning it.

David Stanley, his mother Dee, and brothers Rick and Billy in 1979 had written "Elvis, We Love You Tender" (telling their accounts to Martin Torgoff). Besides Elvis' saying goodbye to David, the Stanleys reported in their book that, during Elvis Presley's final tour in June 1977—moments before he was televised—he turned to his stepbrother Rick and said: "Know what, Rick? I may not look good for my television special tonight, but I'll look good in my coffin!" Does David Stanley's conclusion a decade later, come from that statement of Elvis Presley?

Others think that Elvis Presley's deep-religious nature would have been appalled by the idea of suicide. In fact, David Stanley himself wrote at length about his feelings about it in "Elvis, We Love You Tender". He recalled a time when he and Elvis were watching television and the news of Freddie Prinze's suicide was broadcast. David reported in the book, that Elvis turned away from the TV in disgust and said, "That's really the chicken-shit way out!" David Stanley went further to tell he did not believe Elvis would ever hill himself purposedly, startling, moreover that Elvis held a strong religious resistance to suicide. "The Lord's way would never be to kill yourself", Elvis is quoted saying by David. He further told us about Elvis: "Elvis' sense of manhood and dignity would never allow him to take the 'easy' way out." Other events clearly speak against the suicide theory as well, prior to 16 August 1977:

Elvis' nine-year old daughter, Lisa Marie, had been at Graceland on an extended vacation. Now, Elvis if he had planned to do away with himself would certainly not be doing it on one of his precious daughter's visits!

What's more Lisa's bedroom was the only other bedroom upstairs at Graceland, further she had access to her daddy's bedroom. Can one imagine, Elvis Presley, in event of suicide, not taking into consideration that his body would be possibly discovered by his little girl? If suicide was on his mind, he would have made sure before that his daughter would be back with her mother Priscilla in California.

And what about Elvis' father Vernon? The most important people in Elvis' life in 1977 were his daughter and his father. The fact that Vernon Presley had suffered several severe heart attacks was a constant worry to Elvis. Certainly, he would now have committed an obvious suicide and chance his father's finding the body, possibly bringing on Vernon's death? This is not the Elvis his friends, family nor fans knew.

Plus, everyone at the time told that Elvis had been in good humour and spirits, especially with his daughter Lisa Marie being at the mansion. They had spent the two weeks prior, together, with many excursions to Memphis' Libertyland Amusement Park, where they had a great time. "They had a ball," Paul Lichter wrote in his 1989 Elvis book "All My Best". There were movies to see, golf carts to ride …

As for the drug stories themselves: Most who knew Elvis agree that he did not take street drugs but did overindulge in prescribed medication. He was known to have taken sedatives for sleep. At times, he also performed while he was sick, one time with the flu, at other times with temperature. Most of his tours were gruelling and exhaustive. "Last week I was sick for a day", he said during one of his performances. "I had 102 temperature. I had the flu and missed two shows. They said I hadn't been sick but that I was strong out on drugs. I heard from three different sources that I'm dependent on heroin. Never in my life have I been strung out. They don't vie a black belt if you're on drugs. Reports like this hurt my daughter, my family, everyone …"

Displaying a certificate to the audience, Elvis continued his announcement: "This is from the International Narcotics Enforcement Association. This certificate gives me special honours and a lifelong membership. I've been wearing a federal narcotics badge for six years. They don't five you that if you're strung out." But the rumours had begun. Elvis took drugs, everyone seemed to agree. Yet when one examines the big picture, especially since this speech to his audience was given in 1976, during a time of the Operation Fountain Pen FBI operative, when Elvis' involvement might have cost him his life, those same rumours might have been his cloak of protection. After all, who would suspect a drugged entertainer of being a federal agent?

Without question if Elvis Presley had the spirit, patriotism and bravery that if, asked to serve his nation, he would gladly serve.

Through a 1992 letter from the Department of Treasury Bureau of Alcohol, Tobacco and Firearms in Washington, D.C. it is known that Elvis Presley provided cover for an agent from 1974 to 1976. At this time, Operation Fountain Pen moves into the picture. An operation the government was investigating. The case involved racketeers who conned billions of dollars from unsuspecting citizens, Elvis being one of them. A simple fact, Elvis was involved. Which is intriguing. In a larger sense it helps to paint a more complex historical portrait of the King of Rock and Roll and in the end may explain why Elvis might have been forced to fake his own death. These FBI files were not declassified until 1985, almost eight years after the death of Elvis Presley. Over six hundred pages of this file are still classified top security, many of them national security and foreign policy reasons. This leads one to wonder:

1) What was Elvis Presley's involvement in this case?
2) Why the continued secrecy?
3) What was Elvis doing that we are not allowed to know?
4) How would this information affect the security of the United States of America?

This is an enormous amount of government files encountered in the course of the Fountain Pen investigation. These materials included, but are by no means limited to FBI files, trial transcripts, and White House logs—approximately thirty thousand pieces of paper so far uncovered. We shall focus in this presentation of Fountain Pen as they pertain to Elvis Presley's reporting of his death. The secret part of Elvis final years. What was going on between Elvis Presley and the FBI?

Ironically, "Pen" began around 1974 the same year that Elvis Presley began to give cover to an undercover agent who posed as musician in his band. A second irony appears when the Pen files reveal that this FBI investigation continued through 1975, 1976 and 1977. Of most particular note are numerous FBI memos and reports transmitted between the Memphis field office of the Federal Bureau of Investigation and its headquarters in Washington, District of Columbia. Stated in this case ("the Presley case") would be presented to the Memphis grand jury on or before 15 August 1977.

On 16 August 1977, Elvis Presley was gone. Until the moment he died, Elvis Presley was a chief witness against the major criminal organisation that made no bones about its philosophy. A good witness is a dead witness, must have been their slogan. This FBI undercover investigation focused upon an organisation called "the Fraternity"—described by the FBI as being composed of approximately thirty to forty of the world's top racketeers, with some members being connected to the powerful mafia bosses, including the notorious Gambino family. One "fraternity" member was an old partner of New Jersey mafia boss Sam "The Plumber" DeCavalcante.

No question, many of the members of the Fraternity were gangsters, described as "very dangerous men who would stop at nothing to scare their victims from testifying". Beyond its ordinary criminal activities, the Fraternity had victimised countless numbers of people worldwide for sums exceeding three billion dollars. By the time the FBI succeeded in infiltrating the Fraternity in 1976 and 1977, they were on an all-time high, with their criminal activities. Two FBI agents who infiltrated managed to gain the confidence of one of its top men, Philip Karl Kitzer, with whom they travelled extensively.

This gathering of evidence against its members would be more powerful and more prosecutable if the FBI could convince victims to testify. Which was becoming almost impossible, since the same victims knew that to testify meant to be possibly killed. It meant that they, or their loved ones would be in danger. Even under the best of circumstances, these witnesses would probably have to enter the government's witness-protection programme. Could it be that Elvis Presley did have to enter the witness-protection-programme also?

Did the FBI's frustration with finding appropriate witnesses end, when Elvis Presley fell victim to the Fraternity? Very likely, Elvis was not only a gifted entertainer in the favour of the public eye. He was also a full member of the DEA, and honorary as well as full-fledged to many law enforcement agencies ...

In May of 1976, Elvis Presley and his father Vernon Presley became victims of the Fraternity in an amount exceeding one million dollars, due to entering a sophisticated sale-lease agreement with a man named Frederick Peter Pro regarding Elvis' airplane the JetStar. This was due to recommendation of Nigel Winfield, Elvis' personal airplane broker, who had introduced Elvis and his father to Pro. At this time, the Presley's had not reason to be suspicious. Not even Elvis' attorney was suspicious. All were comfortable with the deal and the deal maker. Briefly, this sale-lease agreement came about because Elvis was having financial problems: investments, high payroll costs, expensive gifts, too many assets to maintain, including four airplanes: a Jet Commander, a Dassault Falcon, a Lockhead JetStar, and a Convair 880 (known as the Lisa Marie). Liquidating at least of these airplanes appeared to be a good financial move. Nigel Winfield was contacted.

Winfield was a former Marine flier and Elvis thought him to be the biggest and greatest thing at the time he was recommended by Winfield to deal with Pro, associated with the Fraternity, unbeknownst to Elvis, it seems. D. Beecher Smith, Elvis lawyer was stated: "And during this period, Elvis thought a lot of Windfield and Mr Presley had no reason to distrust someone that Nigel Winfield called his friend, and Mr Winfield introduced Pro to us, and because of Elvis Presley's feeling towards Winfield, he accepted that man and wanted to give him a chance."

After various negotiations between the Presleys and Pro it was decided that the best way for everyone to profit would be for the Presleys to sell the JetStar to Pro on a sale/lease/sublease repurchase plan that was based on the JetStar being upgraded to meet commercial aircraft standards. Pro and another Fraternity member were to borrow a sum of $950,000 which would be used to liquidate the balance of the approximately $612,000 mortgage taken by the Presleys when the aircraft was originally purchased. The remaining $338,000 would be applied to the upgrading that needed to be done, thereby increasing the JetStar's market value to a million dollars. This upgrading, would guarantee that Pro and his people could lease the JetStar out on a commercial basis and everyone would be making money.

Elvis could also lease the plane back from Pro and his associates on an arrangement that would result in a $1000 a month profit. Elvis would have use of the airplane and make a profit, rather than the use of it with a debit. Further, since the plane was considered private property at the time of the upgrading, being still reserved for Elvis' personal use, the JetStar was not then subject of regulations applying to commercial airplanes. Pro realised he could make a substantial profit. Confiding to friends—by trading on the added value of the Presley name—he hoped to turn the JetStar into a shuttle service for major cities like Las Vegas. The lawyer of Elvis Presley D. Beecher Smith explained: "The transaction involved the sale of the JetStar to WWP Leasing Group, WWP was to borough money from the Chemical Bank of New York to cover both the paying off the present indebtedness of the aircraft, which is over $600,000, and also upgrading this aircraft in order to qualify it for Federal Aviation Regulation 121 Maintenance Program.

This upgrading had an estimated cost of $350,000. Upon completion of the upgrading, the plane allegedly would be valued on the open market at approximately $950,000. With WWP purchasing the plane, the contractual agreement was for Elvis Presley to lease the plane back for 84 months at a monthly rental of $16 755. Thereafter, Presley would sublease the plane for 17 755 per month for 84 months to Air Cargo Express. This would result in a $1000 a month profit for Presley, and at the end of the seven-year period Presley had the right to buy back the plane for $1.00. However, the contractual agreement would allow Air Cargo to continue another three years, paying a reduced rental of $10,000 per month."

Robert Caggiano and Raymond Baszner, both members of the Fraternity, were given via their World Aircraft Exchange company the responsibility of supervising the JetStar's upgrade.

Vernon Presley issued two checks, each in the amount of $16 755 to WWP Aircraft Leasing Company in payment for the first and the last month's leasing by Elvis Presley of his own aircraft. In order to do is part, Friedreich Peter Pro drew three checks payable to Elvis Presley, the first two in the amount of $17 755 each, to cover the first and the last of his lease payments, and a third payment in the amount of $40,000 given as a bonus to the Presleys. With an investment of approximately $75,000, Pro took possession of an airplane valued over $600,000 and accompanied by his group, left for Miami on board his new acquisition. No sooner that the aircraft had taken off, Pro telephoned another member of the Fraternity with the following: "Hi Phil. This is Fred. You're not going to believe it. I pulled it off ..."

After Elvis found out about the scam he had fallen into, one can only wonder how he have felt? Elvis Presley the victim of an organised criminal network, might have been the only man both willing and able to help the FBI in one of its most dangerous undercover investigations. Would he help? For many people, that's maybe the most apparent question to ask of a man known to the world primarily as an entertainer. But in this case, one has to remember that Elvis Presley was already a federal agent-at-large with the DEA. In addition, if Elvis and his father Vernon chose to initiate a civil suit against this band of criminals in order to recover their lost million dollars, it could place the FBI's entire undercover operation in jeopardy. Would the victims, rather than pursue their suit through the civil courts, instead choose to aid the government investigation and ultimately testify, in criminal proceedings, for the FBI?

In this instance, the Federal Bureau of Investigation would have had the duty to tell Elvis Presley just how dangerous this men under investigation were estimated to be. Would Elvis Presley, the most revered entertainer on the planet, help the government bring down this dangerous criminal organisation?

Can one imagine the soul searching that must have occurred when Elvis and his father realised how dangerous these men were?

This was not a movie with fake bullets and fake blood; it was not the cartoon hero donning a cape, intent on saving the world from destruction. This was for real. Elvis could say no. But if he did, would he ever look at the man in the mirror again?

And certainly his steps he would have to take would require a courage that might go unwitnessed by history—except for the knowledge of a chosen few people, no one else could or would know the details. After all, if Operation Fountain Pen was so dangerous for the FBI agents that the bureau found it critical to surround them with surveillance, how much more dangerous was it for a victim who might testify, especially if this victim represented a threat to the entire worldwide network of the Fraternity? Elvis Presley had become that threat.

As it happened, from the beginning the plan Pro set did not run smoothly. The Chemical Bank of New York refused the contract presented and thus refused the $950,000 load. Chemical Bank wanted a well-defined contract—that is, an agreement that completely clarified and assigned the responsibilities of each party. The bank drafted a new thirty-page contract, that move would delay completion of the transaction for at least three weeks. Since Pro had counted upon money from this loan to cover the three checks he had issued to the Presleys, the checks were returned as "insufficient funds".

Further, WWP had added a clause to the new contract drafted by Chemical Bank stating that WWP was no longer responsible for the authorisation of upgrading funds. WWP then convinced Vernon Presley to authorise these disbarments, in so Vernon released WWP of all legal responsibilities. For "some reason" Vernon agreed—this seemed at first a grave mistake. Now handling the funds, Vernon ordered Robert Caggiano to bring him the $338 048.33, representing the balance of the $950,000 Chemical bank loan. To Vernon Presley's shock, when Caggiano arrived in Memphis with the check, he also presented the Presleys with five invoices totalling $341 500 which represented the sums owed to the companies that supposedly performed the upgrading work on the JetStar. This upgrading work had never been done!

Gail Giorgio wonders in her book Elvis Undercover if there might have been another scenario altogether:

"An obvious question: Vernon was known to be tight with money. Plus the Presleys were cash short. Why would Vernon 'pretend' to the point of advancing money for work not done? Was this entire situation a setup from day one, and/or was Elvis (along with, perhaps, Vernon) called to action earlier than the declassified FBI files show? Is this why there are still so many classified files? Remember, we're talking about May of 1976 to August of 1977, when it's known that Elvis and his father became connected with Pro and his group. What about the letter from the government clearly stating Elvis had given cover to an agent from 1974 through 1976? Recall also that the FBI began its undercover operation in 1974. Consider this:

1) The FBI needs a 'victim' to testify against the Fraternity.

2) The name Pro appears. As the FBI investigates Pro, the name Nigel Winfield comes into play.

3) Winfield and Pro are connected.

4) Winfield and Presley are connected.

5) Presley is a federal agent-at-large with the DEA.

Upon discovering that Winfield is Presley's airplane broker, is it possible that the FBI began contemplating a setup whereby Presley would become a willing victim of Pro and his group via an innocent introduction by Winfield? The FBI then contacts Elvis privately; Elvis' father Vernon has to be let in on it, as he handles most of the financial transactions having to do with Elvis. Since the operative is in its embryonic stage, the FBI isn't quite sure exactly how far its plans will take them or what role Elvis will play. For starters, the FBI assigns an agent to Presley and, so as not to arouse suspicion, this agent becomes a member of Elvis' band. Possible? (…)"

The government stated in its letter confirming that here was an Undercover agent in Elvis Presley's band the following: "Mr Presley was not actively involved in any of the investigations, his assistance in this regard made it possible for our agent to develop a number of quality investigations" (during the period from 1974 throughout 1976).

Would it be that human nature would have it during these investigative years that Elvis Presley knew what was going on? After all, Elvis Presley was known for his curiosity and he also knew that people would tell him things that they'd never tell others, maybe even government agents. After all, he was Elvis Presley.

Plus there was Elvis love for law enforcement; it is known how he loved to hang out with law enforcers. It would be out of the question to not believe that Elvis had many gabfests with this secret agent in his band; Elvis no doubt admired the man. Elvis was known to be great in keeping secrets, known to love plots and plans. This was the same Elvis Presley who sneaked off to the White House earlier this year. This investigation surely excited Elvis, but may at this point have been not dangerously. The real danger developed after the Presleys began doing business with Pro—and became involved in dealings with the Fraternity.

Let us return to the point where Vernon was presented the invoices for the upgrading not done to the Presley JetStar. In this sequence, we witness Vernon's transactions with Pro and his group, the Fraternity, and follow the path of the Presley money involved. We can see precisely how this same money trail resulted in the Presleys becoming, perhaps willingly, victims of Pro and other members of the Fraternity. After lengthy discussions with Pro's group and his lawyers, Vernon Presley agreed to issue certified checks on the invoices to go to the stipulated corporations. Pro immediately cashed the $17 500 check at Presley's bank and put the money in his briefcase. A second check was made out to Air Cargo Express and Dallas Air Motive.

Unbeknownst to Vernon, Dallas Air Motive had not been in operation since 1968 and did not even exist in July 1976. Pro realised that it would be impossible for him to cash the check without an endorsement from Dallas Air Motive, and suggested that Vernon issue another check bearing Air Cargo Express's name only. The third check was issued to Transworld Industries, Inc., which was owned by Fraternity associate Lawrence Wolfson: the fourth check went to World Aircraft Exchange, owned by Baszner and Caggiano. The last payment was reduced by $78,5000 and was intended to cover the three band checks Pro had given Vernon earlier.

A certified check in the amount of $38,990 was handed to Pro in settlement of Invoice No. 506. Pro and his associates left Memphis with a small treasury in their pockets. Now the only thing left for them to do was to perform the upgrading work for which they already had been paid. When Frederick Pro's second lease payment on the JetStar came due, he gave Vernon another check that bounced—again returned to Vernon marked insufficient funds. Alleging a delay in the transfer of funds that were coming from Jamaica, Pro apologised to Vernon, assuring that the money was about to be put in his (Pro's) bank account.

How could this man Pro—who only a week before was worth approximately $90,000 suddenly having difficulties meeting a $17,500 payment?

A few days later, on 19 July 1976, Vernon received a strange visit: Pro had sent a certain R. Warren to obtain from Vernon his authorisation to replace the WWP Aircraft Leasing Company with AGM Financial Limited. AGM was being incorporated under the laws of the State of Florida at the same time R. Warren, AGM's secretary was knocking at Vernon's door.

Disagreements had arisen between Pro and Hans Achtmann concerning's Pro actions. Achtmann (who presided over WWP) had from the very beginning sensed the nebulous character of Frederick Peter Pro. Especially the agreement between Pro and the Presleys. Achtmann being constantly on Pro's back, had requested that Pro take out a $950,000 personal insurance policy in order to cover the loan by the Chemical Bank—just in case something happened to Pro.

Pro took the initiative of replacing WWP Aircraft as intermediary with AGM Financial Limited. Vernon felt he was unable to authorise the transfer from one comp any to another, directing R. Warren to his attorneys, who categorically refused Pro's request. Despite his inability to meet his first payments on the JetStar, Pro was interested in making a second deal with the Presleys, this one involving the Presley's Dassault Falcon airplane. Little more than a month had passed since the first deal: the Presleys felt that Pro was capable of handling this kind of transaction. For them, it was just a question of time until Pro was able to meet his financial obligations. The same sale/lease/sublease concept as used in the first agreement was retained this time. However, because Pro did not want to deal with WWP anymore, he suggested AGM should be responsible for authorising the disbursement of upgrading money. Vernon began negotiating the terms of the second deal.

On 30 July 1976, Pro, Vernon, Winfield, and AGM held a meeting at D. Beecher Smith's office. The Presley lawyer, who also handled the first deal, took care of the details of the second transaction. The scenario repeated itself, of course: Not having any personal checks with him, Vernon issued two counterchecks. The first was for $52,000, representing the first and last payment to AGM. This was immediately cashed at the Presleys bank. The second check, in the amount of $6000 was given to Nigel Winfield as sales commission. For Pro's part: He gave three checks to Vernon. The first two were in total of $28,915.68—which covered the first and last payment. The third check was in the amount of $40,000—another bonus for the Presleys.

Once again, none of the Pro checks were honoured at the bank. Fortunately for the Presleys, AGM was unable to find the necessary funds to finalise the transaction. Presley was obliged to terminate the agreement for breach of contract by AGM Financial. Meanwhile, AGM received a visit from two men sent by Pro to give back the $52,000 paid to AGM by Vernon Presley. As lease payments came due in August and September on the Presley JetStar, D. Beecher Smith sent a notice to default to Pro, stating that Presley would repossess the aircraft if payments were not made immediately. On 11 October 1976, Pro temporarily resolved the problem by sending a telex to Presley's bank from Seven Oak Finance Limited in England:

"With regard to Elvis Presley—Ai Cargo Express transactions, by the request of Frederick Pro, Seven Oak Finance Ltd had bank confirmation that Air Cargo Express has an account in excess of $500,000 US dollars.

Regards (signed(AC Scott-Brown, Seven Oak Finance Limited"

Frederick Peter Pro had just committed one of his biggest mistakes. The telex would become the primary piece of evidence upon which the U.S. attorney's office in Memphis would rely in order to indict several members of this important criminal network. The telex secured Vernon, but it was nevertheless the last known time the Presleys had contact with Pro. On the pretext of leaving the US to get money so he could cover the numerous rubber checks he had issued, Pro disappeared which severed all his links with his American companies. By this time, Vernon Presley had taken enough. At the end of October, the Presleys repossessed the JetStar and took the aircraft back to Memphis. It was a major catastrophe for the Presleys.

Vernon had spent $262,000 to pay the upgrading invoices for the plane. He had also paid AGM $52,000 at the beginning of the negotiations for the Dassault Falcon—plus of course the $6000 commission he had paid Winfield. Moreover, Pro owed Vernon $115,000 for the insufficient funds checks. From May to October 1976, the Presleys were taken for $435,000 in cash as well as becoming liable for a $950,000 bank loan. In the end, the financial loss was $1 385,000—nearly $1.5 million. A disaster that even an Elvis Presley could not afford.

Why did the Presleys deal with the Fraternity?

The official story is that the Presley lawyers decided, along with other government interventions, to present the case to the FBI. However, by presenting this case to the grand jury for criminal indictment and prosecution, the chance that the Presleys would recover their losses, was next to nothing. By litigating in a civil court, a recoup of the money would have been easier and far less dangerous. In the end the FBI had their witness, they won their case, and Elvis "lost his life" … as he knew it!

What is the role of an Undercover Agent? According to "My Undercover Life in the Mafia" (New York 1989) by Joseph D. Pistone with Richard Woodly: The understanding is, that the role of a federal undercover agent is playing, is the one that he is not the type to be suspected. It makes also a great viewing, in the Johnny Depp starring movie, based on the book—"Donnie Brasco".

It is obvious that the most effective agent is the one least suspected. The one who has a legitimate other job, and as in the case of Elvis Presley, and his role in the DEA, who would get to people others would not. This was precisely the service offered by Elvis Presley to President Nixon in December of 1970. Also, according to Larry Geller's book "If I Can Dream": Elvis' Own Story): In June 1977 during what would become Elvis' final concert tour, Presley showed Geller a book at the Netherland Hilton Hotel in Cincinnati, a small black book issued each year from the US Justice Department listing the names of narcotic agents— a book only agents who are listed are given. Elvis during that conversation with Larry Geller, was very excitedly talking about his love to America and his willingness to help in any way possible.

Some months earlier, Larry was also witness to a telephone call Elvis received from President-Elect Jimmy Carter—a call lasting about ten minutes. Elvis told Larry Geller, that President Carter had asked for a meeting with him at the White House after the Inauguration, with the President planning to appoint Elvis as Special Advisor to him on the youth of America, the music scene, and other projects. "President Carter is planning to create a special post for me.", Elvis said to Larry and to others. "And I promised him I would serve my country and use whatever influence I had, especially with the war on drugs."

From 1970 to 1977, Elvis Presley was connected to two United States presidents, both wanting his services to help with the war on drugs. Also a letter confirming this to the president of The Elvis Special Fan Club, Maria Columbus, from 29 November 1982 from the Department of the Treasury's by Bob Pritchett, that during the years 1974, 1975 and 1976: "Mr Presley provided one of our undercover agents, who was a musician, a job cover."

In this letter it clearly states also that: "President Nixon recognised Mr Presley's contribution and assistance to the Drug Enforcement Agency."

Also in a second letter to Maria Columbus—it states that the "files are Criminal Investigative files."

This means that Elvis Presley was giving cover to an agent, being a DEA agent himself, for over three years to an agent, whose identity still remains secret, On 15 August 1988, Pritchett wrote to an Elvis fan, stating that: "Our Undercover Agent ... does not want his name known to the public."

As there are some 663 FBI pages, one can conclude that Elvis Presley was not just an honorary DEA Agent, but an agent at large. We also know that Elvis Presley was a visiting guest at FBI headquarters, once an appointed DEA agent, further he was connected to the future President of the United States Jimmy Carter, as far back as 1973, when Carter was Governor of Georgia. A well-known photograph shows him with the Governor and Mrs Carter. Governor Carter subsequently proclaimed 8 January 1974 as "Elvis Presley Day in Georgia". Both President Nixon and President Carter held great respect for Elvis Presley, both speaking with him shortly before 16 August 1977. Elvis wanted to speak Carter privately, this wish was forwarded to Carter by an FBI agent.

Two weeks after their conversation, Jimmy Carter had to issue a tribute, for 16 August 1977, the day the world learned that the King of Rock and Roll Elvis Presley was gone:

"Elvis Presley's death deprives our country of a part of itself. He was unique and irreplaceable. More than twenty years ago he burst upon the scene with an impact that was unprecedented and will probably be never equalled. His music and his personality, fusing the styles of white country and black rhythm and blues, permanently changed the face of American popular culture. His following was immense and he was a symbol to people the world over, of the vitality, the rebelliousness, and good humour of this country."

Many journalists noted this tribute, noting also that although it was not unusual for local leaders to comment on a celebrity's death, for the President of the United States to issue a formal statement, was unusual.

Further questions arise: Since Elvis Presley was an agent-at-large of the DEA and was a least involved in providing cover, for three years, for another undercover agent together with is ongoing associations with at least two United States Presidents—both of whom he spoke shortly before 16 August 1977. Would it be possible that Elvis became the target of some drug dealers who were the focus of the 1974–1976 investigations. And if, was Elvis and his family under serious death threats due to his DEA involvement. Could Elvis Presley turn to the US government for protection?

Even if no drug dealers or the Mafia had an interest in Elvis Presley being dead, the pressure of his superstardom, was a threat to his and his loved ones security: Ed Parker, a karate master, who was a confidant and a bodyguard to Elvis Presley recalled in the 1988 issue of the American Karate magazine when in Florida a terrorist group threated Elvis' life in order to make him an example of how they could get to famous people—thus blackmailing them into contributing to their causes. "We will plant a bomb in one of the gifts offered Elvis at a concert", was the threat. Police authorities were summoned and whatever threat there, it was never materialised. Still, living under such constant threats had to take its toll on the entertainer. As long as he was "alive", he and his family could be targets. But dead ...?

Once Elvis was a DEA agent, it appeared he began to surround himself with law enforcement officials such as John O'Grady, who had earlier been in charge of the Narcotics Division of the Los Angeles Police Department. Also around the time, he became committed to law enforcement, he hired Dick Grob, formerly a fighter pilot with the U.S. Air Force and a sergeant with the Palm Springs Police. Therefore the picture of Elvis in the 1970s: an undercover agent acting as a musician in his travelling band an surrounded by two lawmen in top security positions. But Elvis Presley remained in danger. If he wanted higher protection, could he for instance, call in on the FBI? The President of the United States? How are other agents protected? And was Elvis Presley frightened at any time in his life enough, to call in for this super security scheme?

Larry Geller also recalls in his book, that Elvis felt asleep and said something in his sleep. Mumbling his daughter's name, telling her to stay away from a trap. According to J.D. Sumner, friend and backup singer for Elvis, Presley was always concerned that someone might kidnap his daughter. Therefore he did not allow her to fly commercially. If this was the case, why was Lisa Marie still in Graceland on 16 August 1977, when Elvis was due to perform in Portland/Maine? Should she not have been back with Priscilla on the West Coast already?

This questions have been raised before ... Under normal circumstances, Elvis would have had Lisa flown home on August 15th via the Lisa Marie, so that the plane would be available for the upcoming tour. One report states that an

Elvis staff member planned to escort Lisa on a commercial plane back to the West Coast, this in stark contradiction with Elvis concerns.

Did Elvis want his daughter to be with him for another day. Not really, as he had requested not be wakened until later in the afternoon. Was there even a plan to send Lisa home? What was the reason, that Elvis wanted her to stay until the last minute? Mary Jenkins, Elvis personal cook, reports in her book "Elvis, The Way I Knew Him" that she was called around 2.00am in the morning on the house phone, asking that she come upstairs to straighten his bed. When she arrived, the room was quiet and empty. All the televisions were off, this was strange, since Elvis was known to keep a TV on at all times. Thinking he was in the bathroom, she changed the bed, then took his water bottle to Lisa's bedroom in order to fill it in her bathroom. Since no lights were on, Mary turned on the light's switch. She was startled: There was Ginger Alden and Elvis Presley sitting on the side of Lisa's bed in the darkened room, whispering. Mary said it was all so strange … so unlike Elvis.

Where was Lisa Marie? Nine years old, two in the morning … Was something to happen?

Had threats against Elvis and his family escalated? Having been informed by more than one law enforcement official that a break-in had occurred earlier on, that items had been taken from Lisa's bedroom and mailed back to Elvis as proof how close they could get to him and his daughter, it is understandable how terrified Elvis was. Could the reason be that Mary was called upstairs to get her out of the kitchen (from which a back staircase led to Elvis' bedroom)?

Priscilla Presley states the following for 16 August 1977 in her book "Elvis and Me":

1) Hearing the news that Elvis Presley died around noon in Los Angeles.
2) Sending for the plane Lisa Marie, which was in Memphis, boarding at 9.00pm L.A. time (which is 11.00pm Memphis time). Considering flight time, she would have arrived in Memphis around 3.00am.
3) She was sped in a waiting limousine to Graceland.
4) Lisa, according to Priscilla was outside riding around in her golf-kart.
5) There are thousands of fans and the media, but Priscilla leaves her outside?

In her film adaption of the book, Priscilla plays the arrival complete opposite, showing it to be in the broad daylight. It would not have been the afternoon of 16 August 1977, because Elvis Presley's body was not discovered until around two that afternoon and Priscilla was in California, according to her own book.

In February 1989 Gail-Brewer Giorgio who wrote several books on the possibility that Elvis Presley went into witness exchange programme or some other sort of a new identity scheme, with the help of the US Government, guested on the Geraldo Show. With her was also Elvis right-hand man and trustee Joe Esposito. Asked by Gerald Rivera about his (Joe Esposito's) reaction to the news about Elvis' death, Joe Esposito replied: That he was concerned about Lisa and Priscilla being in Graceland. Was this the reason, for the Priscilla's journey to Memphis, on hearing upon the news on Elvis' death, making hardly sense?

Is it because there had to be a reason for the plane Lisa Marie to fly from Memphis to Los Angeles? The reason not to pick her up, but to fly Elvis Presley on board the Lisa Marie? Be flown privately out of the States, or to an island (Hawaii) as the Mystery Tape, transcribed fully in this book, hints us to believe. The Lisa Marie arriving in LA, in plenty of time to refuel. The nit waits for Jerry Schilling (a close friend to both Elvis and Priscilla) to board. Joan Esposito, the wife of Joe, boards also. Priscilla's immediate family boards. The Lisa Marie leaving for Memphis at 9.00pm LA time. A few others were disappointed not being allowed to fly with the Lisa Maire to Memphis, was it only open to a few trusted ones, who knew more? It has substance.

"I've always been a dreamer. I read comic books and I was the hero of the comic book. I saw movies and I was the hero in the movie. So every dream that I ever dreamed has come true a hundred times. These gentlemen over here, you see, you see, these people who care, are dedicated, you realise, is it not possible that they might be building the Kingdom of Heaven? It's not too far stretched from reality.

I'd like to say that I learned very early in life that without a song the day would never end, without a song a man ain't got a friend, without a song the road would never bend, without a song. So I'll keep singing a song." (Elvis Presley's acceptance speech to the Jaycees for being one of the Outstanding Men In America).

If Elvis is alive, he would still hold this dream.

Chapter Five
Elvis and Priscilla

Priscilla Ann Presley, birth name Wagner, changed after adoption to Beaulieu was born on 24 May 1945 in Brooklyn/New York.

She is also renowned as an actress and businesswoman of Elvis Presley Enterprises (EPE), the company that turned Graceland into one of the top attractions for tourists in the USA. Priscilla had a starring role as Jane Spencer in the highly successful comedy movies "The Naked Gun 1–3" alongside Leslie Nielsen. Also played Jenna Wade in the long-running TV series, *Dallas*.

Her maternal grandfather, Albert Henry Iversen, was born in 1899 in Egersund, Norway and later migrated to the US. There he wed Lorraine, who was of Scots-Irish and English decent. Their only daughter, Anna Lillian Iversen, was born in March 1926, her name later changed to Ann, before giving birth to Priscilla at the age of 19.

Priscilla's biological father was US Navy pilot James Wagner, son of Kathryn and Harold Wagner, who married Ann at the age of 23. The couple had been dating for three years. Tragically, James was killed in a plane crash while returning home on leave when Priscilla was just 6 months old. She later discovered that family secret, though clues in old wooden boxes of family keepsakes. Ann advised Priscilla to not let her revelation beknown to her half siblings, lest it "endanger our family closeness."

Ann Wagner met a United Air Force officer named Paul Beaulieu, from Quebec, Canada during 1948: The couple getting married within a year. Paul took over raising Priscilla, who announced his death on January 4th 2018 on her social media accounts. She took also his surname, while heling to care for the growing family over the next few years. While her new father's career took the family from Connecticut to New Mexico, followed by Maine. Priscilla described herself during this times as a "shy, pretty, little girl, unhappily accustomed to moving from base to base every two or three years."

She later confessed how uneasy she felt having to move so often in her childhood and youth. Wondering if she could make friends in the new place, or if she would fit in with the people. After they had settled in Del Valle/Texas, Paul Beaulieu was soon transferred to Wiesbaden in Germany. Priscilla being crushed by this news, fearful of leaving her friends behind, and afraid of finding new ones.

When the Beaulieus arrived in Germany, they stayed at the Hotel Helene, but after three months, decided to move, as of financial reasons. The family settled into a large apartment in a "vintage building, constructed long before World War I." Soon after moving in, they realised it was a brothel, but had little choice, but to remain.

Elvis Presley met Priscilla during his Army career, on 13 September 1959. She attended a party at his home in Bad Nauheim, West Germany. Although only being 14 years of age—she made a huge impression on him. Elvis being described as being like acting "awkward and embarrassed", like a boy next door figure in front of her. Only able to compose him by the end of the evening.

Priscilla recalled it this way: "I wore a blue-and-white sailor dress, and I was petrified. The drive seemed to take forever. I didn't open my mouth. When we finally arrived, the first person I met was Vernon, Elvis's dad. He couldn't have been nicer. He led us to the crowded living room where Brenda Lee was signing 'Sweet Nothin's' on the record player."

"And there he was. He was wearing a red sweater and tan slacks. He was breathtakingly handsome, far more handsome than his pictures revealed. He was friendly and inquisitive and full of fun. He presumed I was a junior or senior in high school. It took me a while to tell him I was in the 9th grade. When I answered his sarcasm with a little sarcasm of my own, he liked it. He thought I was spunky and I guess he thought I was cute. There was an entourage—besides his dad, there was a large group of friends."

"There was a risqué poster of Brigitte Bardot on the wall which I found intimidating and finally there was Elvis himself sitting at the piano and singing 'Rags To Riches'. Before the evening was over he did a great impersonation of Jerry Lee Lewis. Afterwards, he took me into the kitchen and introduced me to Grandma Minnie Mae who was busy frying bacon. H wanted to know about Fabian and Ricky Nelson. He asked, "Who are the kids listening to back home?""

"You," I said. I could see he was nervous about losing his popularity. And I could feel he found it easy to talk to me. "What kind of music do you like listening to?" he asked.

"I love Mario Lanza."

"You're kidding", he said. "How do you know about Mario Lanza?"

"I love his album, The Student Prince."

"That's my favourite." He thought I had the taste of someone older than fourteen. As he downed five huge bacon-and-mustard sandwiches, he spoke more openly. He was lonely. He missed Memphis but, even more, he missed his mother. He was still mourning her death and looking for a connection back to his fans in the States. I found him extremely vulnerable and sweet. He had beautiful manners and an open heart. There was nothing false about him. When Currie said it was time to drive me home, Elvis wanted me to stay longer. I didn't take it as a sexual come/on but merely the request of someone eager for companionship. "I promised her father I'd have her home on time," said Currie. Fog delayed us two hours, and my parents were up waiting.

"He's a perfect gentleman," I assured them.

Priscilla's parents were not too happy about the late return by their daughter. It put any other meetings or future rendezvous under suspicion of never materialising. With Elvis promising to take care in the future personally of having her brought home, led them to agree that Priscilla and Elvis would meet again.

Following Elvis Presley's departure from Germany, Priscilla was inundated with requests for interviews from media outlets around the world. Making headlines as the "Girl he left behind". She also received mail from lonesome GIs, as well as from Elvis fans. Due to gossip magazine rumours that Elvis was having an affair with Nancy Sinatra Priscilla believed that she and Elvis had no future, anymore. That she would never see him again. After his return to the US, she stayed in touch with Elvis by phone, but both did not see each other until the summer of 1962. Priscilla's parents agreed on a visit by her daughter to Los Angeles. Elvis would have to cover the air costs and have her chaperoned at all times. They also insisted that she would write home at all times.

Priscilla flew to LA. On a short notice Elvis informed her that they would be going to Las Vegas. So he had her pre-write a postcard for every day they would be away, being mailed from Los Angeles, by a member of his staff. While on the trip to Las Vegas, Priscilla was first offered amphetamines, which she took, she also had to take sleeping pills to keep up with the lifestyle of Elvis. Following another visit at Christmas, her parents agreed that Priscilla would move to Memphis permanently in March 1963. Elvis arranged for her to attend an all-girls Catholic school, the Immaculate Conception High School in Memphis. While she would live with Elvis' father and his new wife Dee Presley, just a few blocks away from Graceland, in a house on Hermitage Drive 3650, until she would graduate from high school during June 1963. Priscilla stated in her autobiography, "Elvis and Me" (1985) that she "spent entire nights with her Grandma at Graceland and gradually moved her belongings there. She said: 'The move was natural. I was there all the time anyway.'"

She was also keen to go to Hollywood with Elvis, but he kept telling her that he did not want to take her there. That he would rather prefer if she would stay in Memphis.

Priscilla described Elvis in her book, Elvis and Me, as a very passionate man, not overtly sexual towards her. They waited before marriage before having intercourse. Elvis said to her: "I'm not saying we can't do the things. It's just the actual encounter. I want to save it." The couple married on May 1st 1967, at the Aladdin Hotel in Las Vegas. Obviously or not surprisingly the wedding was arranged by Elvis' manager Colonel Tom Parker to maximise publicity. But the guest list was small, with a handful of guests, the ceremony was over in just about eight minutes.

It was followed by a short press conference and a $10,000 breakfast reception, attended by friends, family, and business associates from MGM, RCA, and the William Morris Agency. The wedding led to thrifts within Elvis' close circle the "Memphis Mafia": Red West and his wife had been personally invited by Elvis to Las Vegas, having already been dressed for the occasion, they were told at the last minute—they wouldn't be present. For Red, who had been with Elvis since the start of his rise to fame, with Elvis Presley having been his best man, at his own wedding, it was a big enough insult that he quit his job working for him. His other friends were also disappointed, having their grudge aimed at Colonel Tom Parker, rather than Elvis, blaming the "old man Manager" for their exclusion from Elvis and Priscilla's most important day.

Following the reception, a private jet was boarded by the couple taking them to a short honeymoon in Palm Springs/Florida. On May 4th, they flew back to Memphis, retreating to their private ranch, just over the Mississippi state line—

the Circle G Ranch. Most of the part the couple was left alone, to enjoy each other's company without the intrusion of the Memphis Mafia.

Priscilla: "What seemed like a new life had begun. We spent our honeymoon at the Circle G. I look back at those weeks as remarkable lull in the midst of a storm. I've never seen him so free—free of his entourage, the press, the Colonel, the incessant demands of his career. I was just the two of us at the ranch house. I loved cooking his eggs and frying his bacon. I even loved doing his laundry. We shared a new intimacy. After breakfast, we'd saddle up and ride our horses through the hills. Sometimes he'd rode alone. I remember one day I happened to look out the window. It was twilight. The sky was aglow in misty blue and radiant pink. There was Elvis, walking Rising Sun, his Golden Palomino. I saw them as silhouettes against the darkening sky. Elvis was walking slowly. I could practically hear him breathe. His breath was easy, his body relaxed. At that moment, I was convinced my husband had finally found peace.

Sadly, the peace was not long-lived. Forces he could not avoid—or chose not to avoid—were calling him back. His world would not remain calm. Neither would our marriage, despite the birth of our beautiful daughter. Neither of us could know about the tremendous obstacles ahead. But the future would include more than obstacles. It would include music, absolutely thrilling music, some of the most memorable music Elvis ever created." (From the book Elvis by The Presleys).

Priscilla wrote in Elvis and Me that around the time Elvis was filming "Live a Little, Love a Little" (1968) she was taking private dance lessons, becoming strongly attracted to the instructor, known as Mark. In the book, she confessed, having had a short affair with him, but concluding: "I came out of it realising that I needed much more out of my relationship with Elvis."

Despite's Priscilla affair, the first few years of their marriage seemed a happy time for the couple. After the 1968 preparation for Elvis to return to the stage, with the acclaimed NBC Television Special, him being on the concert stages again, leaving Priscilla alone with Lisa Maria in Memphis—things turned sour.

Elvis was a keen Karate student, including many of it as part of his stage movements in his show, but also seriously studying it. He persuaded Priscilla to take lessons also, as it would help pass the time she spent alone, a hobby and a shared passion would not hurt them, he thought. Priscilla began taking lessons from Mike Stone, a karate instructor whom she had met backstage at one of Elvis' concerts in 1972, soon beginning an affair with him.

She stated in her book: "My relationship with Mike had now developed into an affair. I still loved Elvis deeply, but over the next few months I knew I'd have to make a crucial decision regarding my destiny. Elvis must've perceived my new relentlessness." A couple of months later, Elvis supposedly asked her to his hotel suite, where as she wrote in her book "forcefully made love to me … saying, 'This is how a real man makes love to his woman.'"

Priscilla later regretted her choice of words in describing the incident, saying that it was an overstatement.

"What really hurt was that he was not sensitive to me as a woman and his attempt at reconciliation had come too late." Here Priscilla referred the lack of interest Elvis had in her as a woman, after she gave birth to their first daughter. Priscilla also stated in her book: "He'd mentioned to me before we were married that he'd never been able to make love to a woman who had a child." So it began, that she noted: "I'm beginning to doubt my own sexuality as a woman. My physical and emotional needs were unfulfilled, this was not the gentle, understanding man I grew to love."

Elvis and Priscilla separated on 23 February 1972, filing for legal separation on July 26th the same year. She avoided to make her home address available on public records, not risking hers and their daughter Lisa Marie's safety outside of Graceland. A month after their divorce, Elvis apparently stated: "There's too much pain in me … Stone (must) die." Elvis had such an outburst that even a doctor could not calm him, despite large doses of medication. After another two days of raging, his friend and bodyguard, Red West, was making enquiries about arranging a contract killing of Stone, he definitely was relieved when Elvis said: "Aw hell, let's just leave it for now. Maybe it's a bit heavy." The divorce was finalised on 9 October 1973.

The former couple agreed to share custody of their daughter Lisa Marie Presley, with Priscilla being paid an outright cash payment of $725,000, as well as spousal support, child support, 5% of Elvis Presley's new publishing company's and half the income from the sale of their former Beverly Hills home. They had agreed on a financial less rewarding settlement for Priscilla originally, though Priscilla was encouraged by her lawyers to ask for more. As she wanted to prove that she could make it on her own without Elvis, she had agreed with Elvis on a one-time $100,000 payment, $1000 a month spousal support, and $500 child support. The lawyers argued that a star of the statue of Elvis Presley could afford more to his former wife and to his only daughter … So the new settlement was arranged. Priscilla and Elvis remained close, leaving the courthouse on the day of their divorce, hand in hand.

Following her split from Elvis, Priscilla set up a joint venture with her friend and stylist Olivia Bis during 1973. The pair opened a clothing boutique in Los Angeles called Bis and Beau. Elvis was very supportive, contracting several friends in public relations to help for the launch. In an interview with advertising the launch she was quoted as saying: "After the separation, I had to make up my mind about what I wanted to do, and since I'd worked with Olivia for such a long time on my own clothes, I decided to try it professionally. We both do the designing for the shop, and have people who sew for us." The boutique was successful, with celebrity clients such as Cher, Lana Turner, Barbara Streisand and Natalie Wood shopping regularly there, before it closed in 1976.

After Elvis's death on 16 August 1977, in 1978 Priscilla acted as executor for his only heir, their daughter Lisa Marie Presley. Who was only aged nine. Graceland's cost for one year were $500,000 in upkeep with expenses and taxes due on the property. Lisa Marie's inheritance dwindled down to $1,000,000. Faced with having to sell Graceland, Priscilla went for a new direction. She hired a CEO, Jack Soden, to turn Graceland into a tourist museum attraction. Which opened to the public on 7 June 1982.

Only 4 weeks after opening Graceland's gates the estate had made back all the money it had invested. Priscilla Presley becoming the chairwoman and president of EPE—Elvis Presley Enterprises. Under her guidance the trust growing to be worth over $100 million.

She launched her own range of fragrances during 1988, gullwing it up with a range of linen, plus helping to produce a couple of movies, including Breakfast with Einstein and Finding Graceland. Priscilla was elected to the board of directors at Metro-Goldwyn-Mayer in September 2000. She also was the executive producer of the 14-track album "If I Can Dream"/Elvis Presley with The Royal Symphonic Orchestra during 2015. A follow up was released. Other contemporaries of Elvis such as Roy Orbison, Buddy Holly and Johnny Cash were also honoured with new albums and backing by The Royal Symphonic Orchestra. She stated in 2015: "If Elvis was here, he'd be evolving and taking risks< seemingly like everybody else today."

In that year, yet another Elvis Presley stamp (after one in 1993) was issued by the US Postal Service. It featured a black and white shot by William Speer from 1955.

The 1993 stamp was one of the most popular edition of stamps of the US Postal Service history.

Hal B. Wallis, the Hollywood Producer who had financed many of Elvis Presley's earlier films, had shown an interest in signing Priscilla to a contract. But Elvis had no intent of allowing this. Also was not too happy about her interests in dancing and modelling. She once modelled for a local store, as soon as Elvis heard about that, he asked her to not pursue further.

After her time with Elvis she was offered the role of one of Charlie's Angels, but turned it down, because she didn't think so much of the show. Her debut on TV came with "Those Amazing Animals" during 1980. Her first professional acting happened on a season 2 episode of The Fall Guy, titled "Manhunter" in 1983. After that she was cast in a role in the television movie "Love Is Forever", starring alongside Michael Landon. Although she was treated well by most of the cast and crew, with her acting being recognised positively by her co-stars, she found Michael Landon difficult to work with.

She then was seen as Jenna Wade in Dallas, the third actress to play that role, playing it for the longest, leaving the show during 1988, after five years.

After three "Naked Gun" movies, she made her pantomime debut in Snow White and the Seven Dwarfs at the New Wimbledon Theatre, Wimbledon, London, during Christmas of 2012, starring opposite Warwick Davis. She is also Ambassador of the Dream Foundation since 2003, a Santa Barbara-based wish-granting organisation for terminally ill adults and their families.

Reports that she had left the Church of Scientology in October 2017 were refuted by Priscilla.

She spoke out against the Tennessee Ag-Gag Bill during 2013, citing her and Elvis Presley's love for horses, expressing her concerns that the bill would hinder animal cruelty investigations. While reducing protection of horses and other farm animals.

Her longest relationship was with Marco Garibaldi, with whom she lived for twenty-two years. Their son Navarone was born on 1 March 1987, while she was starring in *Dallas*. Her pregnancy was written in the storyline of the soap. The couple's relationship ended in 2006. She has a square named after her in Egersund, Norway, on the street where her grandfather was born and lived. The opening ceremony took place on 23 August 2008.

Priscilla wed Elvis on 1 May 1967, in Las Vegas/Nevada. She was 21 and he was 32. It followed a seven-year romance. Elvis was earning a $4 million a year as an actor and singer. Their daughter Lisa Marie would be born on 1 February 1968. They separated during August of 1972. Elvis filing for divorce in 1973. As they waited for their divorce to become final: Elvis lived in a large, 5-room penthouse which was worth $500,000, a Holmby Hills estate, he once shared with his wife Priscilla. Her living in a large 5-room penthouse apartment overlooking a small marina on the Pacific Palisades.

When Priscilla was aged 10, her father, Captain Beaulieu, was transferred to Austin/Texas. Four years later the family moved to his new post in Wiesbaden, Germany. Not far from Bad Nauheim, where Elvis Presley was serving in the United States Army 3rd Armoured division. It was in Bad Nauheim, where Elvis, 25, met Priscilla, 14.

The author of the book "Elvis Presley and Priscilla Presley" (ISBN 9781716993664) met Priscilla at the Pacific Palisades apartment, describing it as follows: "The décor was sheer and soft, with billowy organdie curtains and calico sofas, there being a conspicuous lack of anything masculine. There wasn't a photograph or a memento in view to suggest that Priscilla had been the wife of Elvis Presley. The smell of jasmine wafted into the living room as she entered from the kitchen carrying a tea tray, standing 5 ft, 2 ins tall, weighing 110 lbs, being stylishly dressed in a splashy, purple print blouse and pants. More impressive than who she was or what she was wearing was her aristocratic bearing, everything about her suggesting grace and poise. Priscilla was beautiful, perhaps the most beautiful kept secret in Hollywood, as outside the inner circle of Presley's friends, few people knew what his wife really looked like."

Priscilla handled herself with ease and confidence, saying as she poured tea that she was reluctant to talk about her life with Elvis, her desire to protect her own privacy being as strong as her impulse to shelter him, having guarded her life with Presley since she'd first met him. Even before she got to Germany, Priscilla had thought about what it would be like to meet Elvis: "I didn't have great fantasies about meeting him but I do remember that when my father told us he was being sent to Wiesbaden Air Base, I mentioned jokingly that Elvis was stationed nearby and maybe we'd get a chance to meet him. My mother said: "I wouldn't let you walk across the street to see Elvis Presley," which seems funny now, doesn't it?"

Then, a week and a half after I got to Germany, I was eating in a little place where most of the military kids went, when a guy asked if I wanted to meet Elvis Presley. I said, "Fine", thinking it was all a joke. For my so-called date with

Elvis, I didn't dress up: I just wore a little sailor dress, because I still didn't believe it but the next thing I knew I was on my way to his house, which he shared with his father, Vernon Presley. Three or four friends were with their dates, and a couple of girls dropped by. It was a very casual evening—a family atmosphere. Elvis was sitting in a chair when I arrived, before he got up to shake my hand. Then reality hit me, and I thought, "What am I doing here?"

In that interview she also recalled that her parents were waiting up when she arrived back home, stating: "They asked me how it was, and I told them exactly what had happened: that Elvis was very nice and warm and cordial, but I never thought I'd see him again. Then he called."

Priscilla admitted that: "At first, my parents said that I shouldn't date Elvis, that I was too young, which was true but my mother felt that it was a once in a lifetime opportunity and besides, it wasn't harming me. Finally she prevailed upon Dad to allow it but he set up a 12 o'clock curfew. Each date with Elvis was the same. Usually he'd have his father pick me up in a car. Elvis's mother Gladys had died in 1958. In Germany, Vernon was dating a pretty blonde named Devanda 'Dee' Elliott. Sometimes they'd join us and some friends for a movie or something. No, I was never impressed with dating Elvis. Perhaps I thought that it was all a dream, or maybe because Elvis was very down to earth. He made me comfortable. Elvis fit in with everybody, too. Elvis wasn't aggressive with me, he never pushed. He was very gentle."

The interviewer describes Priscilla Presley further: "One of her outstanding qualities was her sensitivity to Presley, never breathing a word to anyone during the whole time she dated him. When asked why, she said, 'Oh, there were so many possible reasons. I felt that he was publicised so much already; it was my own life, my own business, or maybe it was because Elvis is so self-protective. He's his own man, a very understanding compassionate person, and he accepts people fully but as far as his personal's life's concerned, he's very secretive.'"

Priscilla points out: "When Elvis was discharged from the Army, I was still in Wiesbaden. I had no idea that I'd ever see him again. I was dumbfounded when he asked me to spend Christmas in Memphis—and then he asked if I could remain there. Of course, my Mum and Dad said definitely, no but Elvis called then talked to them, so I finished my senior year at the Immaculate Conception High School in Memphis."

In the book "Elvis by The Presley's" Priscilla recalls: "When Elvis and I met in Germany a few months before the end of his army stint, he kept describing

Graceland to me—how much I would love it, and how much his mother would have loved me were she still alive. He pined for his home and he pined for his mother. I was a young girl then—only fourteen—and couldn't begin to understand the importance that Graceland held in Elvis's heart. As years went by, though as I myself lived in Graceland and Graceland became part of my heart, I understood that it was much more than a place. It was Elvis's refugee from the storms of life. It was where he dreamt of raising a family and finding simple peace. Sometimes he found that peace, sometimes he didn't, but he never stopped trying. Graceland symbolised his hopes for a happy life. That's why he always came home. The attic in Graceland seemed to call to me."

"Elvis's paternal grandmother, Minnie Mae, who lived with us in Graceland, claimed she heard noises coming from Glady's ghost. Well, I didn't believe in ghosts and was determined to see exactly what was up there. One day while Elvis was off making a movie in Hollywood, I ventured upstairs. I can't say I was apprehensive. It was a stormy afternoon. Heavy rain. Thunder and lightning."

"I slowly opened the attic door. It creaked like it hadn't been opened in years. Inside, it was pitch dark. I took a couple of steps forward and found the light switch. The yellow bulb lit a long line of clothing racks. These were Glady's clothes. Elvis had saved everything. All her precious belongings were here. I could feel her spirit. I was excited and moved. One by one, I examined her blouses, skirts and dresses. They were simple, not extravagant, and gave me a sense of her character. It might sound strange, but I would bring these articles of clothing to my face and breath in their essence. I knew this was as close as I would get to Elvis's beloved mother. I tried on a couple of coats. It was as though she was embracing me."

"And just as I was lost in a reverie, thinking of how this charismatic woman shaped my husband's charismatic personality, the door flew open. I screamed! Seeing me, the woman who had opened the door screamed even louder! It was Hattie, one of the housekeepers. She was certain she'd seen a ghost. It took us several minutes to get our bearings. When we finally did, we were able to laugh, but the experience of discovering Glady's wardrobe and feeling her presence was something that lives within me to this day."

Priscilla led a Cinderella existence in Memphis, her every dream having become reality. When Elvis was at home, he tried to make up for the time he'd been away, giving her presents. "It was difficult for Elvis to buy for me, and a lot tomes he would just tell me to get what I wanted, which I liked. He gave me all of the cars I've had. We stared out with a little red Corvette, then a Chevrolet, a Tornado, and Eldorado then the Mercedes, a white one, which I drive now." She recalled in the 1970s. When Priscilla was not driving her own car, Elvis chauffeured her in a Lincoln Continental, equipped with a little TV and a bar: "It only served soft drinks, because Elvis didn't drink or smoke. Well, recently I think he's begun to smoke a pipe. We had a day cook, who prepared simple American food. Elvis would rent an entire cinema, invite friends and we'd talk loudly to each other without worrying that the manager would throw us out. Elvis loved good, action-packed movies, some Westerns he loved. A Shot in the Dark with Peter Sellers. No, Elvis never showed his own movies. He just preferred not to see them. Maybe he didn't say a line right or he thought that his hair didn't look good, or that he appeared fat. He just didn't want to see himself. He's very self-critical."

Priscilla visited Elvis in Hollywood occasionally, staying away from the set when he was due to be filming. "I didn't think that he could do his best if I was around. I felt that was his job, his business, so it wasn't my place to be there. Most of the time I stayed in Memphis, occupying my time at the dance studio, or went to dinner with a friend. I was perfectly happy the way it was."

For years, Priscilla and Elvis seemed happy not to marry. But finally got married in a double ring ceremony at the Aladdin Hotel in Las Vegas. Priscilla wore a gown of white organza, trimmed in seed pearls with lace sleeves and a full train. A ¾ length tulle veil was held by a crown of rhinestones. Her wedding-engagement ring was a three carat diamond, surrounded by 20 smaller diamonds. 14 guests attended the wedding: Vernon, Dee, the Beaulieus and selected members of Elvis' entourage.

"As a wedding present, Elvis flew in my mum and dad from his new post at Fort Ord/California. I remember how overwhelmed they were, how happy, too. Of course, they thought it was about time, as we'd been dating for years! Although many people thought our wedding was sudden, Elvis and I had been talking about it in stages. One day he showed me the ring then simply asked me to marry him. Even though he was perfectly content the way we were, at that time it wasn't nice for people to live together."

"After their two-month honeymoon in Palm Springs/California, the newly-weds returned to their $400,000 mansion in the Truesdale Estates. Elvis had just completed the film "Double Trouble" and filming for yet another movie was scheduled. Their hit-and-run lifestyle continued from their relationship into their marriage. Priscilla did not complain, saying: "For Elvis to come home from a trip then leave again was routine. At first I wanted to go along and it was difficult for me to understand why I couldn't. Sure I was disappointed, but I got over it. The times that Elvis couldn't make an anniversary became a way of life. I may've been hurt, but it's an adjustment that you make as a wife. I kept thinking. 'It's going to work itself out—we'll make it somehow! I had to, because if you think I'm always going to be alone, you'll go crazy. You have to live one day at a time, hoping that things aren't always going to be like that.'"

"It was an adjustment, but I kept busy. I began studying karate. I won my green belt and was ready to test for my brown belt when I decided to drop out. I felt karate wasn't very feminine. So I decided to go back to ballet. I'd studied ballet years before with a woman named Maylee Kaplan. I enrolled again in her dance company; I stayed for c. 3 ½ years. I danced and worked out every day and did a couple of recitals with them, Elvis didn't mind, so long I was happy."

A blessing came for them with the birth of their daughter Lisa Marie Presley. Not only did it provide them with a much wanted child, but the baby gave Priscilla a new outlet for her energies: "Elvis and I were ecstatic over the birth of our daughter. If the baby had been a boy, we were going to name him John Barron. I liked the name Barron. It has a very strong feeling to it but when it was a girl we decided on Lisa Marie—for no special reason, only because it's a very feminine name. She definitely has her father's eyes, but she has my features and petiteness. You know, the movie magazines have had me having 5 miscarriages: I've never had a miscarriage."

Priscilla enjoyed being Mrs Elvis Presley: "I felt very flattered when people stared at me in public, at a restaurant or on an opening night. I guess I'd be less than honest if I didn't say I liked the attention. Yet I never invited it by going to posh places where people go to be seen. That wasn't what I wanted. Maybe Elvis had a lot to do with that because he never associated with the movie people. He had always had his own friends from his hometown. I was very happy to see that he was entertaining those people but I was also worried about someone getting hurt or Elvis getting sued and things like that." Priscilla objectively relates to Elvis "because I know what it is. I know exactly why Elvis is up there on that stage, and it goes beyond seeing him as a superstar. He's a human being, and I can sense when he's nervous or if he's not doing the song as well as he did it the time before. I didn't see Elvis as a superstar, I saw him as my husband."

When the Presley's had a $550,000 home in Holmby Hills, Elvis was most of the time on the road, so Priscilla decorated the house herself. Her favourite room became the den, she furnished for Elvis. "I did it the way he wanted it: antiques, very manly. For the fireplace, I searched everywhere for wrought-iron and irons with eagle heads, and I bought antiques from all over Beverly Hills. I got old books and beautiful antique bar stools, and a desk that furnished with a telephone and intercom. Elvis liked the room; he spent a lot of time there. The sofa was done in suede—brown suede. The game room was done all in suede, with pinball machines and a pool table. After all, you've got to do what a man likes. He's got to live in it, and he's not going to be happy with anything feminine, that's for sure. The kitchen was very country and the breakfast nook was pleated and wicker, which didn't bother Elvis." There was still a gap in between raising Lisa Maria and seeing Elvis: "Someone once said in jest that I should see other men, simply as friends, and that it would take my mind off being alone but when you're married, you just don't date other men."

Priscilla could also have had a career of her own as early as being with Elvis: "It's untrue that we argued about it, or about my becoming an actress. The dance studio also had drama classes, so I attended one class. Someone started the rumour that I wanted to be an actress, which actually had never entered my mind. I did get offers to be in motion pictures, and Elvis left that up to me but it could never be, especially with a little daughter. Besides, I could never live that life. I saw how Elvis had to be. I mean, so publicised. I could live my life and wo what I wanted, but it wasn't possible for Elvis to do that, which was a shame."

Always hoping for more time with each other, and to solve their issues in marriage, the couple saw a turning point in 1972:

"In mid-1972, I finally realised that things weren't going to change and that we had completely separate lives."

After filing for divorce on 8 January 1972, after their official separating in August of that year: Elvis still knew that Priscilla was there if he needed her. Priscilla said she was worried about Lisa Marie, shielding her away from publicity: "Lisa Marie is so sensitive that harsh would crush her, but happily, she seems to have adjusted to the separation of her father and myself. She thinks daddy is on a business trip, so it works out and Elvis is no absentee father. When he's on tour, he often calls her, and when he's in town, he sees her a lot. She spent last weekend with him, and I took her to watch him perform in Las Vegas for her birthday."

Priscilla further enrolled Lisa Marie to "a very exclusive academy where they speak French—and she's only 5! I've also been thinking about giving Lisa some religious background, and have been considering the religion of Science ... I don't know much about the church, but I plan to look into it. I want to see for myself if I like it. I want Lisa to have a religious foundation, and I feel, I need it, too. I was raised Catholic, but I don't believe that is the way for me. I think that everybody needs some kind of support though and I'd like to get into something different—a more realistic religion."

In her spare time, next to setting up a boutique, she thought a lot about live, men, and marriage: "When you've lived a kind of sheltered life, you're a little hesitant about being out in the world with other men. It's an adjustment. I went through stages where I didn't want to go out but I'm dating someone now, which is very good, because I have a secure feeling. His name is Mike Stone, and he's Hawaiian-born. He's a black belt karate champion. He's very much of a man to me, and treats me like a woman. I'd never go with a guy who wasn't boss. I mean the man would definitely have to be the more dominant person. His schedule is flexible, so we can do things together. We both enjoy riding, and have horses, which we keep at the sables in Huntington Beach. Mike had his horse here and I brought Domino, a gift from Elvis, up from Memphis."

At this stage in her life, while being in the relationship with Mike Stone, Priscilla ruled out a reconciliation with Elvis, but also to marriage: "I really can't say for the future—I only know about today and how I feel—but I don't have any plans for marriage. I think that there can be a very good relationship between two people that marriage can ruin. In marriage, you can really easily take each other for granted. You begin to feel obligated. I see it happening to my friends/everyone is divorced—and I saw it happen to me. It's a slow gradual change. Whatever it is that marriage does, it changes you. It may be the obligation; it may be the responsibility. People become less sensitive to each other's needs. They do something because they have to, not because they want to. So I'd rather be the girlfriend than the wife."

"For some reason 'wife' is a bad word to me. So much is expected of you. It's a role, and if something doesn't turn out, it's your fault but I don't feel resentful or regretful. It was an experience. Today, I feel I'm a better person than I was 10 years ago, because I know a lot more, I've learned a lot. Life just kind of does things, you know. I can't change, and Elvis had his work and the things he had to do, and he can't change. One day you realise that it's going to be this way forever, so you have to make adjustments and when you know where you stand, you no longer have to please anybody but yourself. Then you can begin to live and have an identity without depending on someone else—no matter who that someone else may be."

Chapter Six
The Elvis Sound

There has been a lot of razzmatazz, speculation and distortion surrounding the name Elvis Presley since his death in 1977. Despite of it being his music, that has kept the legacy alive. In a recording career that spanned twenty-two years, he had made some of the most famous and enduring records of the twentieth-century. Among them "Heartbreak Hotel", "Blue Suede Shoes", "Hound Dog", "Don't Be Cruel", "Love Me Tender", "Suspicious Minds", "Burning Love", "If I Can Dream" … everyone has a special favourite, the records, many of them highly collectable, have sold in countless millions throughout the world. The making of this records is the subject of this chapter of "Elvis Presley". Producers, musicians, backing singers and songwriters, contributed to this unique era of American recording history and in many cases took part in the sessions. An aspect of Elvis Presley, the singer, largely not fully explored. So let's dive in the recorded history of the greatest musical icon, that America has ever given to the world. Elvis Presley, The Recording Sessions 1954–1976!

On a cold morning, late in October 1976, an enormous mobile truck bearing the letters "RCA" on its side drove up the curving driveway of Elvis Presley's southern colonial mansion known as Graceland in Memphis/Tennessee. Driving round the imposing building, partly shielded from eyes of passers by a high stone wall and several clusters of trees, the truck stopped at the building's rear. Over the next few hours a small league of technicians were busy in running miles of cables and batteries of complex recording equipment, speakers and microphones through the doors and windows into the large room facing over the gardens, known as the Den. This activities might have puzzled some passers-by, more so though it was of vital importance to those directly involved.

As Elvis Presley had recently been in increasingly poor health, suffering from respiratory infections and crash-dieting to keep down in his increasing weight, plus showing a general disinclination to go into a recording studio, in between live performances … His producer Felton Jarvis therefore decided to set up a session in Elvis' own home. The same exercise had been carried out earlier in 1976, in February, as the results had been good—maybe even better than expected—Felton Jarvis was hoping to obtain some more recordings for anxious RCA Records, which was eager on releasing more recordings by their top selling Star Elvis Presley. Little did Felton Jarvis, or any of the other technicians and musicians involved in setting up the quarter of a million dollars-worth equipment, realise that what would follow was to be the 41 year-old-singer's very last recording session …

Graceland, a colonnaded building on the crest of a rolling hill in the Whitehaven section of Memphis was purchased by Elvis in 1957 and he had it extensively renovated and enlarged. Apart from giving the King of Rock and Roll privacy, it also enabled him to indulge into his fancy of collecting cars and further provided him space for a sports complex and a swimming pool. The grounds also accommodated his menagerie of animals. In the mansion itself, as well as the various bedrooms, living rooms, the large kitchen, Elvis also had a music room installed which was completed with a grand piano, there was a television room where he also kept his large record collection, and the Den on which he had lavished particular attention when it was added to the building in 1965.

The Den had been created because there had previously been no informal living space on the ground floor win which Elvis could relax. At first, it looked rather like the setting for a jungle movie: both the floor and ceiling were carpeted in green, while its dark-stained wood furniture was covered in intricately carved animals. The furnishings, too, including lampshades, cushions and rugs, were in fake animal fur, and a number of animal paintings, statues, carved masks, and tropical plants completed the room. With little surprise, after Graceland opened its gates to the public, the Den got even more spoken of, as the Jungle Room!

The story of how the Den came to be furnished in this extraordinary style is a typical example of Elvis Presley's impulsiveness. It was his father Vernon who apparently saw the furniture in a Memphis store and cold not help remarking on how weird it looked. Overhearing this, Elvis promptly bought the entire suite and had it delivered to Graceland before the startled elder Presley had time to say another word …

In the Jungle Room, Elvis liked to sit in a huge chair, so big it had to be brought into the room through one of the window, watching television and eating the occasional meal. It was his favourite room—and also the one Felton Jarvis thought Elvis would be at his most relaxed for recording, even though most of the furnishings had to be removed to allow space for the equipment and to set up the various microphones for the musicians and singers. The acoustics were an obvious problem and there was no way of isolating each instrument, but Felton Jarvis did his best. He felt he owed it to Elvis for what working with him had done for him. In 1972, Felton had suffered from a kidney disease which could have proven to be a fatal one. Had Elvis not heard about it and insisted on paying the cost of finding a kidney donor and ensuring the operation.

Elvis recorded at night, that evening as the technicians and musicians waited for him to appear and take up the position that had been set aside for him at the southern end of the room, next to as staircase leading to a sundeck above the Jungle Room: Felton Jarvis kept up everyone's spirits with a string of jokes and reminders they had recorded in February. Assembled in the room were guitarists James Burton and John Wilkinson, augmented by Elvis' long-time-companion Charlie Hodge, bass player Jerry Scheff, the singers Kathy Westmoreland and Sherill Nielsen, plus Elvis favourite group—J.D. Sumner and the Stamps. All of them had special admiration for Elvis and were also anxious in trying to raise his spirits, to allay worries about his father who had suffered a heart attack a few months earlier. The session in February had begun with a new song by one of Elvis Presley's favourite country writers, Larry Gatlin, a slow ballad entitled "Bitter They Are, Harder They Fall". With lyrics about a broken marriage which must have brought back echoes of his own divorce.

The album which would be entitled "Moody Blue" had indeed a blue mood. Songs like "Bitter They Are, Harder They Fall", "Never Again" written by Billy Edd Wheeler and Jerry Chestnut and "Blue Eyes Crying In The Rain" by Leon Rose, were full of despair, maybe also despair in Elvis' life, at the time. Most of the songs continued the vein: Mark James's "Moody Blue" though it was sounding far more optimistic, than the afore mentioned songs, "Hurt" by Jimmie Craine and Al Jacobs (which would be Elvis Presley's next single release), the recent Neil Sedaka hit "Solitaire". "Danny Boy", the Irish ballad, was heavy fare also, variety was brought by "For The Heart" to this, written by Dennis Linde and "I'll Never Fall In Love Again", a hit for Tom Jones, one of the Entertainer friends of Elvis.

There was also the beautiful and haunting ballad "The Last Farewell" by English composer-singer Roger Whittaker, that had provide a high point of the session. There was still plenty of evidence that the great voice of Elvis Presley was very much intact, if not better than ever!

One of the people who helped to preserved that incredible voice was Charlie Hodge, who lived in Graceland in an apartment above the garage. A professional rhythm guitarist who had played and recorded with Roy Rogers and Gene Autry before meeting Elvis in the Army, becoming lifelong friends with him. He recalled that there was hardly a day that passed, when Elvis wouldn't sing: "It was the one thing that would stop him brooding. I usually played guitar and we would duet on all sort of things—"Danny Boy" was one song he was always playing on the piano. We even sang together on some of his records like "I Will Be Home". Elvis liked to have me around taking care of business.

During the six previous years lead guitarist James Burton had been taking care of business as far as Elvis' band was concerned: "I started with Elvis in 1969 when I put this group together for him and out of all those years I never missed a show with him. I remember the day we first met. It was just like we had known each other all our lives. I had always been a fan, but I never expected to get a chance to play with him. He hand-picked each musician for the group with me and I really loved that. We all just did what he wanted, learning the songs he picked from demo records, just putting it all together as we went along. We got accustomed to Elvis feeling the music the way he liked it and working from there."

Rhythm guitarist and backup singer John Wilkinson says about Elvis Presley: "There were times at his house when we would be listening to records and he would start playing and singing. H would sing old, old songs that I just never knew even existed and we'd go on until five in the morning sometimes. When we got to rehearsing, he would often pick up a guitar and beat on the top of it as he was singing. His rhythm was just perfect, you couldn't beat it. He knew what he wanted to hear and never missed a thing. He'd know if something was wrong and he'd stop and say, "That's wrong." No matter what was going on around him he just knew if something wasn't right. If it wasn't for Elvis there's a lot of big name entertainers today who wouldn't be where they are. Some admit it, but a lot of others don't. He influenced so many people, everybody grew up with him. Look he spanned almost thirty years—that's three generations. There are kids today that are using the basics of that old Rock and Roll sound that Elvis evolved for all of us."

Petite, soprano vocalist Kathy Westmoreland, who had started to back Elvis in August of 1970 said about Elvis: "I had worked with a lot of stars before him and I was not really an Elvis fan. I actually thought his songs were nonsense. But that was what he was doing—making people happy with nonsense songs so they could forget everything. No heavy message, we're just here to have a good time and make people happy, was what he'd always say about songs like 'Hound Dog' or 'Blue Suede Shoes'. They were silly but they made people happy. Because we had totally opposite musical tastes I wondered how on earth a Rock and Roll artist could use a soprano. But once I started to work with him I couldn't help but being impressed by his musical ability and also see what a generating force he was. You'd have to be dead not to feel what he was doing. All those musicians from different musical backgrounds just followed the feeling. There was place for everybody and everything. He also taught me the joy of singing. I had learned, technically, how to sing, and I always sang with feeling, but he gave all of us a new spark."

"Go deeper into yourself and let people see that," he would say. "If you're hurt, let them see it in your song. If you're happy, let them feel it. In fact, he was a man of emotional extremes. One minute he'd be happy, the next sad, one minute friendly, then angry. I remember one time when we were all singing and having a good time by ourselves. It was a happy song and he said, 'Thank God for songs like that,' and he started laughing. His smile lit up the whole room. The next instant someone mentioned his mother and his face just changed instantly and you could almost see a little tear in his eye. Elvis taught me the pure joy of sharing music with others. He gave everybody who came into contact with him a positive attitude to life. He lived his faith and loved his music."

The importance of his faith to Elvis was also well-known by J. D. Sumner, leader of the gospel group, The Stamps, who had actually had the longest association with him of any of those gathered in the Den that October evening. J.D. Sumner known as "Father of Gospel Music" and credited as 'the world's lowest bass singer", always remembered meeting a 14 year old Elvis Presley.

"Back in the late 40s and 50s, I was singing bass with the Blackwood Brothers Gospel Quartet and we used to appear a lot in Memphis. I kept noticing this skinny, greasy-haired kid always hanging around. Then he didn't show up for a while and when he reappeared I asked him where he had been. He was real embarrassed about it and said his mother had been sick and there wasn't the money for a ticket to the show. I could tell he just loved gospel music so I said for him to come and see me and I would see that he got in. After that, I used to sneak him in the back door at all our gospel shows. It was a funny thing, he used to sit in the auditorium and listen to me sing and he never did lose that respect for me. He never did believe he was a bigger star than I was. He said many times, 'J.D., I never thought I'd have the privilege to sing with you.'"

After Elvis had become a household name in the music industry and a star, J. D. Sumner and the other members of the quartet often visited Graceland to give impromptu gospel concerts in the music room for Elvis and his family and friends. "Elvis loved gospel music," said J. D., "and he always liked to have a gospel quartet backing him up. He loved the fullness of the sound. When he started out he had the Jordanaires, then the Imperials joined him when he decided to go on the road again. It was in 1970 or 1971 when he called and asked us to sing with him. One of the songs he loved to hear us sing was 'Sweet, Sweet Spirit', and we often sang it for him just moments before he went on stage. He often said to me, 'I need it, I've got to have it.' Many times, we would gather round the piano in his home and sing gospel songs for hours. It was a way for him to relax."

"Elvis was not only a religious man, he was also a very generous man. When the old bus the Stamps and I were using started breaking down all the time he gave us the money to buy a new one. He just wrote out a cheque and told me to fill in the amount. When we got that bus I took it up to Graceland and it had the TCB logo on the side and he really loved that!"

Sherill Nielsen, an Irish tenor singer and former member of the Imperials, who also accompanied Elvis on stage and in in recording sessions during the last decade of his life, also recalled being a recipient of Elvis Presley's generosity. Idly remarked one day that he was worried about his thinning hair and the fact that his teeth needed capping, both features were taken care of by a plastic surgeon and dentist—all paid by Elvis. "He was a generous and sensitive man." Nielsen recalled and continued: "Of course he was moody at times and could be very unpredictable, but all these stories about guns and pills, well, all I can say is I never saw him take anything stronger than a sleeping pill, and although he did love guns and had a huge collection of them, I never saw him fire one or anything like that."

Sherill Nielsen also vividly recalled Elvis Presley's last recording sessions: "The funny thing is, they say a singer really doesn't hit his peak until he's between forty and fifty. Well, just before he died, Elvis was singing better than he ever had. He had more range and more expression. He may have showed up a little in his movements on stage, but I think that comes with maturity. But as a singer, he was just reaching his peak."

Four songs suitable for release were cut on the final recording session for Elvis Presley: "It's Easy For You", a slow ballad by two young English composers, Time Rice and Andrew Lloyd Webber, who would soon become among the most famous musical show writers. Elvis also tried his hands on the Jim Reeves country number "He'll Have To Go", a hit from 1960. Another dated ballad was "Pledging My Love" a huge hit for former Rhythm and Blues Star Johnny Ace in the 1950s. The last song from the session was "Way Down". It would be his final single, and a posthumous Nr. 1 hit-Felton Jarvis' last memories of Elvis Presley were not, however, of the final session, but of visiting the singer in Graceland to present him with the final mix of the upcoming album "Moody Blue":

"I arrived near sundown, and Elvis was lounging on the front porch in his pyjamas. He seemed very happy, in a real good mood, and didn't seem like he had a care or worry in the world. We played the album and then Elvis got to talking. He seemed to like to talk about the past and how he had got started with Sun in the Fifties and all the things that happened down the line. He surprised me, though, when he told me his biggest ambition was to tour Europe and Japan. He said as we sat there on the porch, 'That's one thing I got to do and I don't want to wait until I'm too old and have to over there with a walking stick.' But it was one of those kind of things where he'd always add, 'We'll do it tomorrow, because today I'm too busy.' And, of course, tomorrow never came ..."

Although the actual date is the subject of some controversy, it seems likely that it was Saturday, 18 July 1953, when Elvis Presley made his first recording at the Memphis Recording Service Studios—slogan "We Record Anything—Anywhere—Anytime" at 706, Union Avenue in Memphis/Tennessee. In the unassuming, single-storey brick building, the young truck driver cut a 78rpm disc which legend has long maintained was intended to be a birthday present for his mother Gladys. This same legend also claimed for many years that the rare disc had long since been worn out and irretrievably be lost. But "My Happiness" was released on the early 1990s RCA compilation "The Great Performances".

And as a matter of fact, neither of these stories is true. Gladys Presley's birthday had actually come and gone several months earlier and the record itself remained safely in the possession of one of Elvis Presley's former classmates until the late 1980s. On hearing the recording today, Elvis who already had ambitions to be a singer, wanted to hear what his voice sounded like on disc, at the same time intending to get a recording contract.

The owner of the Memphis Recording Studios, 31 year old Sam Phillips, a former amateur musician and radio engineer, was out of office on that Saturday afternoon when Elvis came in with is guitar and the four dollars he had saved from his wages to record two songs. Sitting at the reception desk was blonde-36-year-old Marion Keisker, a local radio personality with her own interview show "Meet Kitty Kelly", who also doubled at weekends as the office manager. (Or assist everything as she liked to call it herself.) It was Marion's job to supervise the making of personal records—everything from weddings, funerals and bar mitzvahs to walk-in singers. A side line which Sam Phillips had introduced to help subsidise the more precarious business of producing commercial discs by local artists.

In a rare interview, shortly before her death in 1989, Marion Keisker recalled meeting Elvis Presley the first time:

"When Elvis first came in, I wondered if he wanted a handout. We got a lot of drifters along Union Avenue and his hair was long and shaggy and his clothes were all worn. He was obviously impatient and ill at ease and just mumbled that he wanted to sing. I asked him what sort of things he sang. "I can sing anything," he replied. I asked him if he sang popular music or Country and Western and he just nodded, "Sure". I asked him who he sounded like and he said, "I don't sound like nobody." He was about halfway through his first song when I realised he was someone who Sam ought to hear.

"Sam had been saying for some time that if he could find a white boy who could sing like a black man he would make a million dollars. And Elvis had this amazing voice that could swing from high tenor to resounding bass, mixing all sorts of styles together. Unfortunately, I only had tis old piece of paper to hand, and by the time I had fitted it into the machine and turned it on I had missed most of the first song, 'My Happiness'. But I did get the whole of the second one, 'That's When Your Heartaches Begin'. They were both popular songs by the Ink Spots, of course, but I'd never heard them sung that way."

Sam Phillips, Elvis Presley and Marion Keisker outside of SUN Records:

Sam Phillips: "The greatest thing in the world to me is the human voice and hearing these different kinds of singers made me want to record them. I knew that I would never be a great musician, but I felt I had the ability to get the best out of potentially great musicians and so I set up my little recording studio in Memphis. I was especially interested in the black musicians and I think Elvis first became aware of me through Little Junior Parker, Ike Turner and the other black artists on my label. He was only 18 when he first came to my studio, but already he knew so many songs by all sorts of artists such as Hank Snow, Dean Martin and the Blackwood Brothers Quartet. Now most people think that Elvis wanted to make his first record as a birthday present for his mother. But I believe he wanted to sing something so that I would hear him and perhaps get him to make a record. He didn't want to compromise his independence, so he thought that if he paid me it was a way to get in."

Sam Phillips in an interview coinciding with Elvis Presley's death said also: "There was no question in my mind—my business was to hear talent, no matter what stage of polish it was in. Of course, none of us knew he was going to be that big, but the minute I heard the guy sing he had a unique voice. Now there are very few things I'm gonna say are unique, that there's nothing like them. A bit later I called a guitarist I knew named Scotty Moore and told him to get hold of Bill Black who played bass. I said, "I've got a young man and he's different." I told them to go and work with Elvis and added, "He's really nervous and timid and extremely polite. It took us quite a while. We worked on and off with Elvis for about five to six months. I knew there were a lot of things we could have cut, but they weren't different if you get my meaning. It was up to me to see the uniqueness of his talent and to go, hopefully, in the right direction with it."

The first time Elvis Presley went into Sam Phillips' studio at the owner's invitation rather than by courtesy of his own hard-earned cash was in early May of 1954. Sam had received a demo disc from Nashville of a new title named "Without You". Marion Keisker thought of Elvis in trying and interpreting the ballad, which was to be sung with the accompaniment of a single guitar. But Elvis could not achieve the sound that Sam Phillips was looking for. The decided to try another song—"Rag Mop" written by Johnny Lee Willis, and also ran through some popular songs of the catalogue of artists Elvis admired such as Dean Martin, Billy Eckstein, Hank Snow and Hank Williams. Though nothing became of it, Sam Phillips was now convinced that it was just a matter of time in finding the right song for the aspiring young singer.

Scotty Moore, lead guitar, vividly remembered what happened when he, Elvis Presley (vocal and rhythm guitar) and Bill Black (bass) went for a session to 706 Union Avenue on 4 July 1956: "Sam had called Elvis and asked him if he would mind coming into the studio as he would like to put his voice on tape and see how it came back. Which of course, he readily agreed to. Bill and I only went in to provide some kind of meagre accompaniment so he wouldn't be standing alone in the studio. The first song I think we put down was 'I Love You Because'. We also went through several different songs, but the problem was for him to sing something we knew because both Bill and I played by ear. And Elvis played by ear and sang by ear."

"Anyway, we went through some more songs and were when taking a break, having a coffee or a coke, when Elvis suddenly started clowning around. He just picked up his guitar and started fooling and singing 'That's Allright, Mama'. That was all he was singing, 'That's Allright, Mama', and dancing and cutting up in general. Bill picked up his bass an started slapping and clowning, too, and then I joined in with just a rhythm vamp. Sam was in the control room with the door open at the time. Suddenly, he came out and said, 'What ya'll doin'?'—that sounds pretty good through the door, so see if you can do it again the same way. We'll put it on tape and see what it sounds like."

"Well, we kind of looked at each other and said, 'What, were we doin'?' Well, we backtracked and tried to do it again, and I think we did it twice—once for Sam to get a balance and then we put it on tape. And that was it."

Sam Phillips also recalled this moment of history, generally acknowledged as the birth of Rockabilly music:

"As soon as they started playing, I knew that was what I was looking for. I had been around artists long enough to know when something was 'in the groove'. This was it: I had found the white boy who could sing like a black man."

"That's Allright" the song Elvis had begun to sing purely by chance, had been a success in 1947 for black Rhythm and Blues composer and singer, Arthur "Big Boy" Crudup and it had helped make his reputation for the Chess label. Elvis was an admirer of Big Boy's songs, and a story told in Memphis maintains that the young singer actually had met Crudup on Alabama Street in Memphis in 1953, when the bluesman's car broke down. Elvis, so the story goes, helped Crudup to change a flat tyre and it was only when the musician was to drive away and was thanking young Elvis, that he told him who he was.

"An open-mouthed Elvis is said to have stuttered out how much he enjoyed Arthur Crudup's songs and that one day, he too, hoped to be a singer. Elvis Presley never confirmed nor denied this story, it is certainly true however that Elvis recorded three of Arthur "Big Boy" Crudup's songs and later helped to finance the older man's recordings for the Fine Records Label. (The other songs Elvis cut by Crudup were "My Baby Left Me" and "So, Glad You're Mine", both cut at a single session in New York in 1956.)

Spurred on by Sam Phillips' approval for their version of "That's Allright", Elvis, Scotty and Bill played on into the night cutting several other numbers which were to prove crucial in the young singer's future career. These included a fast paced rockabilly version of Bill Monroe's bluegrass favourite "Blue Moon Of Kentucky", a rendition of the Rodgers and Hart classic "Blue Moon", as well as "I Love You Because" by Leon Payne which the Sun Studio archives indicate was actually the first song to be successfully waxed at the session. It took four takes. The first released version used takes two and four spliced together, and it was not until 1974, that the unabridged take one, complete with spoken middle section, was released on the LP "A Legendary Performer Vol. 1".

"That's Allright" was received in many parts of the south indifferently, selling well in Memphis, Nashville and New Orleans. It encouraged Sam Phillips to set up another session with Elvis, Scotty and Bill on September 13th 1954. This time the trio waxed an echoing cover version of Roy Brown's/Wynonie Harris' "Good Rockin' Tonight". Roy Brown, an R&B composer like Arthur Crudup, was another one of Elvis' favourites, there is definitely no doubt that Elvis had already seen him perform at least twice in Memphis. Once when Elvis was still at high school, and later in a local night club. On both occasions, Roy Brown sang "Good Rockin' Tonight", a 1947 hit for him, and later for Wynonie Harris. The session also produced "I Don't Care If The Sun Don't Shine", as the B-side for "Good Rockin' Tonight".

Rhythm and Blues Star Roy Brown

Around Christmas 1954, the three musicians found time to go back into the recording studio, on an almost constant touring schedule. On December 16th 1954, Elvis registered another milestone in his recording career when he stopped midway through "Milkcow Blues Boogie" and exhorted the two other musicians into a faster version with the line "That don't move, now let's get real gone, for a change ..." They also cut San Kesler and Bill Taylor's "You're Right, I'm Left, She's Gone". After this productive session, a return to the Sun Studio on 24th January 1955 managed to produce the song "I'll Never Let You Go", a Jimmy Wakely number.

A session, which produced the likes of quality as "That's Allright" and "Blue Moon Of Kentucky" had been happened to be on 5 February 1955, in which "Baby Let's Play House" and "Mystery Train" were produced. Bill Black, with then 28 years, the oldest of the trio, particularly remembered this 5th session for its good humour. Later, after Bill Black had parted company from Elvis Presley, and was fronting his own group, The Bill Black Combo (who had a hit with an instrumental version with "Don't Be Cruel" in 1960), was to say: "There's been a lot of talk about the Elvis Presley sound. Well, it wasn't something we set out to create—it just happened. The fact we had fun playing and singing together was the beginning; and once we knew we had something, we built on it."

"We got a lot of laughs in the studio on some of those records like 'Baby, Let's Play House' and crazy things happened to us on the road, too. In the studio you could never be sure what Elvis would do next, what trick he would pull. He just broke us up sometimes with his pranks, and there were times when Sam Phillips would get mad because tape was expensive stuff to be wasting in those days. Elvis needed to relax before he could record and as far as I know it was a habit he never got out of."

One final Sun session came to be on 6 July 1955 and introduced a drummer for the first time on an Elvis Presley recording—Johnny Bernero. Perhaps after the enjoyment of cutting "I'm Left, You're Right, She's Gone", Elvis was in the mood for tongue-twisting lyrics, he went to record "I Forgot To Remember To Forget", another Stan Kesler tune, co-written by Rockabilly singer legend Charlie Feathers, this time Elvis gave it a gentler Country and Western feel. "Tomorrow Night" had been an earlier hit for Lonnie Johnson in 1948, and was revived by LaVern Baker in 1954, this SUN recorded song, did not see the light, until 1965 when released by RCA Records.

The label enhanced it with a new backing by Nashville's A-Team Chet Atkins and Grady Martin on guitars, Buddy Harman on drums, Henry Strzelecki on bass, Charlie McCoy on harmonica and backup vocals provided by the Anita Kerr Singers. Also the Sun version of "When It Rains, It Really Pours" remained in the vaults for years, the same for Elvis 1957 version, of the song, cut in Hollywood. Which was eventually first released in 1965 on the long play "Elvis

For Everyone". There is still mystery surrounding the Sun days of Elvis Presley, and as Sam Phillips did not keep track of sessions and recording dates as detailed as major labels, some of the sessions and the songs produced in it, remain questionable. But Sun Records did play a significant role in launching the career of Elvis Presley, the future after Sun would bring international acclaim for his discs and superstardom for the man himself!

Elvis Presley's switch from the small, regional Sun Records label to the multinational recording giant RCA Records was engineered and planned by his ambitious new manager, Colonel Tom Parker, and Steve Sholes, RCA's man in the south. Sholes, an A&R man in Nashville for several years, had been following the same trail as Sam Phillips, searching for a new sound. Steve Sholes explained later: "I will never forget the first time I heard Elvis Presley sing. One of the RCA field reps sent me a copy of his first Sun record, 'That's Allright'. I had been looking for something, I didn't know what—it was a sound or a beat—and I'd been looking for it a long time. When I played that record I knew I'd found it. I called Sun records straight away but I was told that Elvis had just signed a seven-year contract."

For the time being, Steve was in disappointment but not for a moment did he lose track of what was happening in the career of Elvis Presley. Single-minded determination was very much part of the character of this man who had risen in the RCA hierarchy from messenger boy to near the top. He himself was also a talented saxophonist and clarinet player. He too had the feel, that there would be a successful fusion between black and white music, just as some of the musicians and singers, who had searched for it, and took years until they accomplished it, successfully, for instance Bill Haley.

When Colonel Tom Parker was looking for a major label for his new protegee in 1955, Steve Sholes did not hesitate, and RCA bought all of Elvis Sun recordings and his contract from Sam Phillips, for the then unheard sum of $40,000 for a newcomer. Steve Sholes explained: "The deal, which brought Elvis to us cost $40,000 which was a lot of money in those days. I knew it could be the making of RCA—or the breaking of me! The deal also included ten master waxings from Sun which had already been issued and six more that were suitable for release. I wanted to make sure no one could muscle in on our sales by issuing previously recorded material from the can. In fact, two-thirds of Presley's first RCA album were those Sun masters. My policy really paid off."

Having signed Elvis, Steve Sholes wet up his new artist's first recording session on 10 January 1956, in RCA's studio at 1525 McGavock Street in Nashville. He knew, beforehand, that there would be problems with the studio's very basic sound system: "The building was a two-storey place we rented from the Methodist Publishing Company. The sound-proofing wasn't too good on the top floor where we recorded, and there was a stairwell leading to the rear of the building which was used as an echo chamber. But the problems of the building were nothing compared to those of recording Elvis! The thing was he would hold his guitar close to his mouth and play it so loud we couldn't pick up his voice on the mike. There was no such thing as tracking in those days, so we had to keep moving the mike around and gave him a felt pick to keep the sound of the guitar down."

"He also couldn't keep still when he sang and that didn't help either! Elvis took as much interest in everything as we did, and sometimes when I thought a take was OK he would still say he thought he could do it better and want to try again. When you meet an artist like that, you just know he is going to succeed."

It was also at RCA that Elvis Presley would meet legendary guitarist and producer Chet Atkins, who remembered their collaboration as follows:

"I was in this bar in Nashville where a lot of the guys in the music business used to hang out." A writer named Vic McAlpine said to me, "I want you to hear this record," and played me "Blue Moon Of Kentucky". After he had played it, I said, "Who in the heck is that?" Vic said, "Do you think he is black or white?" And I said that he sounded black at times and at others like bluegrass. I asked what his name was. Vic told me it was Elvis Presley and I said, "That's the worst name I ever heard!" Well, I soon found out all about Elvis and I heard that when he was on tour you couldn't get him off the stage with a fire hose—the girls just loved him. I surely never expected to be producing his records, though. He came in silk pants with blue stripes and was really polite. He called me "Mr Atkins" and "Yes, sir" and "No, sir" until it became excessive. He was a shy sort of person, and I am too, so we never talked very much. We worked in the studio together a lot but never had any real conversations to speak of.

"Elvis played a pretty good guitar and he could also play the piano. He played an old Gibson guitar, but I don't think he did more than just hold it and strum it on those early sessions. I think he could have been a really good guitarist and piano player if he had worked at it. I played rhythm guitar on those first hits like

'Heartbreak Hotel', 'I Got A Woman' and 'I Want You, I Need You, I Love You'.

'He always moved around a lot when he was recording and during one of those early sessions he ripped his pants. One of his people went out and bought him new ones, throwing the old ones in the corner.' Later, a girl who worked in the building asked me what she should do with the pants. I said she could have them, but to take good care of them as Elvis was going to be famous. She wasn't really sure, but she kept the pants and six months later she turned up on the TV show 'I Have A Secret' with Elvis' pants."

Chet Atkins

The story of how Elvis Presley catapulted to fame lies in the song "Heartbreak Hotel". It would become a world-wide hit. Accompanying Elvis in the studio apart from Scotty Moore and Bill Black were the drummer D. J. Fontana from the Louisiana Hayride show, who had become the regular drummer for Elvis, Floyd Cramer on piano, and three singers known as The Jordanaires: Gordon Stoker and the brothers Ben and Brock Speer. The first song cut for RCA wasn't "Heartbreak Hotel" though, but a cover of the Ray Charles hit "I Got A Woman". You either love or don't give a coin for "Heartbreak Hotel" being played in a jukebox, Sam Phillips didn't like it, same for Colonel Tom Parker, others describe it as breathless, dramatic, sexy and instantly as an memorable song.

Mae Axton had penned it. Mae, the mother of folk singer-composer Hoyt Axton would write over 200 songs, but this one song, "Heartbreak Hotel", which has sold around 18 million copies worldwide, remains her best known. Back in 1954 she was also working as a journalist who worked occasionally with Colonel Tom Parker helping to promote his shows. She saw Elvis perform in December of that year in Jacksonville and afterwards conducted one of Elvis' radio interviews.

At that time, in her mind, the idea of writing a song for Elvis was already born. "Heartbreak Hotel came about by pure chance" she said nearly 40 years later and concluded: "I was working in my office one night when a friend named Tommy Durden with whom I'd written a few songs came in. He had a newspaper in his hand and showed me this photograph of smartly-dressed, handsome-looking gentleman beneath a headline that read, 'Can You Identify This Man?'

The story said he had torn up all means of identification and, after writing on a little slip of paper the words, 'I walk a lonely street', had killed himself. The story stunned me, it seemed such a waste of life. I looked at Tommy and said, 'Everyone, regardless of their position in life, rich or poor, good or bad, has someone who cares, and when they see this picture they will be heartbroken. So here as to be a Heartbreak Hotel at the end of a lonely street.' Tommy just looked at me and said, 'Hey, that's a great idea for a song!' Twenty minutes later, we had it down on tape."

Although originally written as a ballad, Mae Axton saw it as an up-tempo song, and she had it dutifully recorded by Glenn Reeves, who was capable of imitating Elvis, and had it sent to him as a demo via Colonel Tom Parker. Though Glenn Reeves said it was the "silliest title I've ever heard", Elvis liked it and insisted on waxing it on his very first RCA recording session!

When released, "Heartbreak Hotel" credited Axton, Durden and Presley as composers—a fact that has puzzled many fans. Mae later explained the reason: "In fact, Elvis didn't write a word of it. He got his name on the record because of something he said when he was on tour in Florida. He was looking at the sights and he said to me. "Mae, if I ever make enough money, I'd love to bring my mommy and daddy here." I said to Elvis, "If "Heartbreak Hotel" becomes your first big hit on RCA then I'll give you a third of it, and that way you'll have enough money to bring your folks to Florida." And that's why Elvis is credited on the song."

After cutting the song by Mae Exton, Elvis turned onto a classic—"Money Honey", which had been a big hit for Clyde McPhatter three years earlier. His satisfaction with "Heartbreak Hotel" can almost be sensed in this driving, Rock and Roll performance backed by another great accompaniment on the piano by Floyd Cramer. Cramer's bravado accompaniment is most evident on the sessions' ballad "I Was The One" with superb backing vocals by The Jordanaires to Elvis' rangy singing. The first session for RCA extended for a total of nine hours, through the night of 10 to 11 January 1955.

It left Elvis Presley exhausted but exultant. Although he might have not known at all, when he left, but his place in music history was already assured. It was to be only three weeks before Elvis recorded again: This time in RCA's much better equipped studios in New York, at East 24th Street in the heart of Manhattan. Elvis was in the city to appear on five TV stage shows for the CBS network. On the nights of January 30th to 31st, and on February 3rd he laid down wight songs in four three-hour sessions. Scotty, Bill and DJ Fontana were again in support, although local session man Shorty Long replaced Floyd Cramer on the piano.

Elvis was far away from home, and never felt home or at ease in New York, there were close ties in the first three numbers he cut. Two more Arthur Crudup songs, namely "My Baby Left Me" and "So Glad You're Mine", as well as his rendition of "Blue Suede Shoes". It had been a Top 10 Country, Pop and R&B hit for its author the King of Rockabilly Carl Perkins. Perkins, and his band, consisting of his brothers were en route to the Perry Como Show to plug their careers even further. Though were involved in a car accident, leaving them in hospital for a long time, unable to do anything musically. Elvis recorded "Blue Suede Shoes" to guarantee a royalty check for its composer, former fellow SUN Records artists Carl Perkins.

Though "Blue Suede Shoes" in some circles became more associated with Presley than Perkins. Carl Perkins, however, earned his own place in musical history. A guitarist, singer and composer born in Jackson/Tennessee, he was vastly influential in inaugurating a new style of guitar playing, and of course popularised the Rockabilly style during the 1950s, and during its Rockabilly Revival of the 1970s and 1980s enormously. He also produced a string of popular tunes, several of which were also recorded by Rick Nelson and groups such as the Beatles. It is, though, for the pounding defiance of "Blue Suede Shoes", one of the first songs to stress the importance of teenage fashions, that he will be always remembered. During a visit to the United Kingdom in 1980, he talked about the creation of this classic Rockabilly/Rock and Roll song:

"In the early fifties, I did a lot of little country shows with Johnny Cash who also recorded for Sun. One time Johnny told me how when he was in the US Air Force servicemen would line up for pay or food in their brightly polished footwear. If anyone got a bit close, they'd say, 'Hey, don't step on my boots!' A bit after this, I was playing at a dance in Jackson when I overheard this young guy tell his girl not to step on his new suede shoes. It all sort of came together then. I actually got up at 3 am with the lyrics in my head, went downstairs and scribbled them out on a brown paper bag there was no writing paper around. 'Blue Suede Shoes' is actually a real country song."

"There never was a man who appreciated a pair of shoes like an ole country boy, and them city boys don't drink liquor or fruit jar. That's country. It was a country song and it had a beat."

Although Elvis Presley achieved the greater fame with "Blue Suede Shoes" than Carl Perkins. Carl Perkins had never expressed a word of bitterness, contrary to what audiences were shown in the musical "The Million Dollar Quartet". Following Elvis Presley's death he also wrote and recorded the tribute song "Elvis, We Love You, The Whole World Misses You" as well as recording with the Class of 55 consisting of Carl Perkins himself, Jerry Lee Lewis, Johnny Cash and Roy Orbison the title "We Remember The King".

Carl Perkins and Elvis Presley

In a tribute to Elvis, Carl Perkins said: "Elvis and I went back a long way, we were poor boys together. We shared the same label and we toured together in '55. All we really did was take country music and colour it up—that was our style of Rock and Roll. Elvis was a phenomenal guy and nobody swung a guitar like him—he used it as if it was an extension of his body. I well remember that occasion in December 1956 when Elvis dropped by the Sun studios and did some numbers in an impromptu jam session with me and Johnny Cash and Jerry Lee Lewis. An engineer taped some of the session and it's since been issued on an album called The Million Dollar Quartet."

The other songs which Elvis cut at his session in New York in January 1955, included a version of Little Richard's "Tutti Frutti" very much in Elvis' own style, a reprise of Lloyd Price's "Lawdy Miss Clawdy" and Big Joe Turner's "Shake, Rattle and Roll", which had turned out to be the first golden disc for Bill Haley and His Comets. A second session was scheduled for April 11th '55 in Nashville, the fact remains only a single record was produced there—"I Want You, I Need You, I Love You". The plane taking Elvis to Nashville nearly crashed, and this is the reason why Elvis wasn't in the best shape for this session. Elvis was full of confidence again, when he returned to New York in July of 55 to record Jerry Leiber and Mike Stoller's "Hound Dog" and Otis Blackwell's "Don't Be Cruel".

These three songwriters were all to prove highly influential in the career of Elvis Presley. According to Bill Black, Elvis decided to try his vocal chords on "Hound Dog" after hearing the song during his the time of his first doomed Las Vegas appearances: "He heard it at the Sands where Freddie Bell and the Bellboys were playing it. He learned the lyrics from them, and then one night just came on stage and told us he was going to sing it. We just had to grab hold—it was every man for himself!"

The song originally written in 1952 for Texas blues singer Wille Mae "Big Mama" Thornton, climbing rapidly to number one in the Rhythm and Blues charts. It was the first big hit for the songwriting partnership of Leiber and Stoller. The lyrics "You ain't never caught a rabbit … you ain't no friend of mine" were added by Freddie Bell and The Bellboys, who also appeared with Bill Haley in the 1956 movie "Rock Around The Clock" thereafter. Elvis Presley turned "Hound Dog" into a shout of defiance on behalf of the younger generation, and when he performed it on television it was shows only from his waist upwards to spare older viewers the sight of his gyrating hips. On the Steve Allen Show however, he had to sing it to a Bassett dog, in a tuxedo.

Anyway he put all his energy into the song in the recording studio and was only satisfied after thirty-one takes. Otis Blackwell contributed to one of the biggest hits of Elvis Presley—"Don't Be Cruel" and remembered: "It was Christmas Eve and I was standing at 49th and Broadway in New York. It was pouring with rain and sleet and very cold. I didn't have a hat on my head and there were holes in my shoes. A friend of mine who was an arranger took me over to a publishing company by the name of Shalimar Music. I played seven songs for them and they took all seven, advancing me $25 for each song. So I bought me a pair of rubbers, an umbrella and a hat and went home with a little Christmas money. One of those songs they bought was "Don't Be Cruel". About three weeks later I was called in by the publishing company and told that a fellow by the name of Elvis Presley was going to record my song. He wasn't big then, but they had a feeling that he was going to be. Wow, were they ever right!"

Though Otis Blackwell never met Elvis, his musical relationship with him lasted well into the Sixties, and the regularity which Elvis cut Otis' songs demonstrated their mutual admiration for one and another. Now it was time for Elvis to prepare himself for the next big step in his career—Hollywood and the movies.

Elvis' meteoric rise to stardom was given an immense boost when Colonel Tom Parker launched his movie career. His first film, a Civil War drama to be called "The Reno Brothers", was scheduled to begin shooting in Hollywood in late August 1956. As soon as 20th Century Fox, who were to make the picture, sensed the nationwide hysteria that would surely meet the young singer's debut on cinema screens in the country, it was decided to inject four songs into the script and re-title the movie from one of them—"Love Me Tender".

There was gossip in Hollywood that Elvis Presley was no actor, while in music circles it was felt that he and his Nashville musicians were not capable of making satisfying movie music. Elvis however surprised with an astonishing mature performance for a young man with no formal training as an actor. As for the music, 20th Century Fox did not take any chances, and for the session to be held on August 2nd at their studio in Beverly Hills, Elvis for once and for the first time was not surrounded by familiar faces since staring his career for Sun Records. The veteran Hollywood music maker Ken Darby was assigned to the project by the producer David Weisbart. Who was no stranger to the James Dean Fan Elvis Presley, as Weisbart was famous for making another teenage star most popular picture "Rebel Without A Cause".

Darby on the other hand was most talented, a composer and singer as well as conductor and arranger, leading a number of successful vocal groups during the Forties and Fifties, among them the King's Men and the Ken Darby Singers. The Ken Darby Trio was assigned with himself for the movie. Ken was not to be tempted to write rock music for the periodical movie, but opted for country music which not only fitted the film's theme but also provided it's star with a chance to demonstrate how well he handled moody ballads. If the movie lacked in terms of drama and quality, the music by contrast revealed another dimension to the talents of Elvis Presley.

"Love Me Tender" was the first track to be laid down by Elvis. It was based on the old Civil War ballad "Aura Lee". The other songs were "Poor Boy", "We're Gonna Move" and "Let Me". Although Ken Darby wrote all for tunes credits went to Elvis Presley and Vera Motson on all songs except "Love Me Tender". The lady was the wife of Ken Darby.

From 1 September to 3 September 1956, a three-day session was to commence. It included "Old Shep", a sad story of a boy and his dog, plus some more up-to-date songs such as three by the other King of Rock and Roll Little Richard—"Long Tall Sally", "Ready Teddy" and "Rip It Up". On the last song, Little Richard was outsold by the version of Bill Haley. The session began with several gentle numbers such as "How Do You Think I Feel?" by country singer Webb Pierce who back in August of 1954 headlined a show in Memphis, with Elvis as his support act. At that time, Elvis "Good Rockin' Tonight" had completely eclipsed the performance of Pierce, which caused the ladder to growl "Sonofabitch" at the young singer as he left the stage to roaring applause.

Not so much of a surprise that another new song by Otis Blackwell was included in the session—the staccato Rock and Roll song "Paralysed" with powerful support on the drums by D.J. Fontana. Chet Atkins contributed his composition "How's The World Treating You?", written with well-known Nashville songsmith Boudleaux Bryant, and "Love Me" another song by Jerry Leiber and Mike Stoller, in which the emotional intensity of Elvis was beautifully underscored by The Jordanaires. First released on an Extended Play, the song became so popular that it remains the only song by Elvis Presley never released on a single, making it all the way up to Number One.

With "Hound Dog" and "Love Me" Leiber and Stoller's contribution to the career of Elvis Presley were cemented, though the collaboration did not end then. Although both Jerry and Mike had been born in 1933 on the East Coat of America, Leiber in April in Baltimore and Stoller in March on Long Island, both were to fulfil their musical ambitions on the other side of the continent when, independently, their families move to Las Angeles. Jerry in 1945 and hist partner-to-be four years later, in 1949. Jerry first found work in a local record store, scribbling tunes in a notebook during his spare time, while Mike Stoller considered a classical pianist until Jazz and Blues fired his interest towards another direction. Both men were introduced to each other by a mutual friend, a drummer for whom Jerry had been trying to write some material, the pair soon found out that they both had a fascination for mainly black artists.

In their teens, they penned their first song together: "That's What The Good Book Says", which was recorded by Bobby Nunn and The Robins. Further collaborations with black artists mainly vocalists was to lead to smash hit records for vocal groups and R&B singers such as Johnny Otis, Clyde McPhatter and Ben E. King., The Coasters, The Drifters and The Dixie Cups. It was the involvement of Elvis Presley however, which made them international recognisable names. Jerry Leiber recalled the somewhat tortuous history of the song "Hound Dog", before Elvis laid his hands on it: "We wrote it for 'Big Mama' Thornton and then when it sold half a million copies she claimed to have written the song herself.

The same time, Johnny Otis who had been producing her records also said he had been the writer. So we had to go to a court to win back control which we had got by the time Elvis recorded 'Hound Dog' in 1956. Sure, 'Big Mama' changed the original a bit—like Elvis did, too—but the song was still ours. As soon as 'Hound Dog' was a hit for Elvis, his people came after us for some more numbers. But we just didn't have anything on the stocks then, wo we pulled out this ballad 'Love Me' which Willy and Ruth had recorded in 1954. To us it seemed like the worst song we ever wrote, but Elvis turned it into something else. He really liked the song and he went on singing it at concerts for the rest of his life. If Mike and I had our misgivings about 'Love Me', we certainly weren't going to turn down the royalties from Elvis! After that, we worked on the musical scores of a number of his movies, and he also did cover versions of our earlier numbers which had been recorded by groups like The Coasters and The Drifters. Elvis just loved those R&B groups."

That session, apart from the informal jamming with fellow Rock and Roll/Rockabilly Stars Carl Perkins, Jerry Lee Lewis and Johnny Cash, at Sun, soon the be known as The Million Dollar Quartet Session, in December, was the final recording output for Elvis Presley in the year of 1956.

He returned to official recording in Hollywood on 12 January 1957, laying down the third great hit from the pen of Otis Blackwell—"All Shook Up", as well as cutting his first gospel music recording. The session opened with a quiet rendition of "I Believe" which had been a big hit for Frankie Laine in the early 1950s, followed by the country ballad "Tell me Why" which was not to be released for eight years. Then there were the up-tempo rockers "Got A Lot Of Livin' To Do" and "Mean Women Blues", both soon to be covered by Jerry Lee Lewis. For "All Shook Up" Elvis banging the back of his guitar like an extra drum. Then Elvis closed with sacred music, which fascinated him, since his childhood days—"Peace In The Valley". "Take My Hand Precious Lord" closed the session, with intense backing by The Jordanaires. Released on the groundbreaking EP "Peace In The Valley" two months later.

Another session at Radio Recorders on 19 January 1957 would become memorable for Elvis' singing of the hymn "It Is No Secret", before he switched to his own version of the Fats Domino recording "Blueberry Hill", at that time becoming an international hit for Domino. The emotive piano of Dudley Brooks gave both songs a distinctive sound. With hardly time to breath, Elvis Presley began on work on his second film "Loving You", a poor-boy-makes-good story not unlike his own. Three sessions were aligned for the soundtrack, including the title track, written by Jerry Leiber and Mike Stoller. They also contributed, next to this ballad, the rocker "Hot Dog".

The first track Elvis cut at these sessions was the novelty song "Teddy Bear", a song that became forever associated with him. Lyrics had been written by Kal Mann and Bernie Low, a Philadelphia songwriting duo, who had read about Elvis' ability to win teddy bears in amusement parks. Released as a single with "Loving You" on the flip-side, it stole the chart thunder and also resulted in Elvis being deluged with thousands of teddy bears from adoring fans.

In contrast to the innocence of this song, Elvis recorded the very same evening the song "One Night", a raunchy number written by Dave Bartholomew and Pearl King, which had been given its full title "One Night Of Sin" when recorded by Rhythm and Blues Artist Smiley Lewis, in 1956. Although the lyrics, which were either about an orgy or about a visit in a brothel, were adapted for Elvis Presley's younger market, the sexual undertones in lyrics and deliverance, were still there. The song came close to some of the raw emotions of "Heartbreak Hotel".

Elvis' last session for "Loving You" held of February 23rd to 24th, included a great rendition of the Cole Porter song "True Love", which had been a hit for Bing Crosby and Grace Kelly in the film "High Society". Elvis also recorded "I Need You So", the first of a trio of songs he was to record by the blues singer and composer Ivory Joe Hunter, whose work Elvis had admired for years and who was later to stay with him in Memphis.

The song "Jailhouse Rock" is as instantly recognisable for Elvis fans as "Don't Be Cruel", "Heartbreak Hotel" or "Hound Dog". It is certainly part of some of the finest and early hours of Rock and Roll music alongside Bill Haley's "Rock Around The Clock", Gene Vincent's "Be Bop A Lula", Eddie Cochran's "Summertime Blues", Buddy Holly's "That'll Be The Day" or Jerry Lee Lewis' "Great Balls Of Fire".

Another song from the Leiber and Stoller partnership, it was once again written by order, this time for Elvis' third film "Jailhouse Rock", which went into production in April of 1957. It was cut with several other numbers for the film, including no less than three more by Jerry Leiber and Mike Stoller, at a session on 2 May 1957 at Radio Recorders. The song, the movie and the clip of Elvis performing "Jailhouse Rock" in the film remains indelibly in the minds of fans. Mike Stoller explained their participation in what was undeniably a milestone achievement:

"We didn't get to meet Elvis for the first time until the summer of 1957 when Jailhouse Rock was actually being filmed. Before that MGM had called us up and asked us to go to New York to write some songs for the movie. Well, it was nice to go back to where we had been as kids, and for the first couple of days we just looked around and had a good time. But after a week they started asking where the songs were. Finally, Jean Aberbach, who was Elvis' agent, cornered us in our hotel and said he wasn't going to let us out until we came up with something. It was amazing."

"We just grabbed the script, looked where they wanted to slot the songs, and they seemed to jump right into the paper. In one afternoon we wrote 'Jailhouse Rock', 'Baby I Don't Care' and 'Treat Me Nice'. A couple of days later we came up with 'I Want To Be Free' which both Jerry and I really liked and on which Elvis did a fantastic job."

The involvement of the two didn't end there. Both later flew back to Hollywood and attended the recording session. Jerry sitting in the control room and Mike in the studio. Mike later appeared in the movie itself as the pianist in Elvis' little band. Also featured were Scotty Moore, Bill Black and D.J. Fontana. "Although they gave me a part and they knew I could play the piano, it's not me you hear on the soundtrack, it's Dudley Brooks."

Mike Stoller sets the record straight and concludes: "But it was a great experience and afterwards Elvis asked us to write some more material for him. He particularly asked for a love song, and over one weekend we wrote 'Don't.' He was just really nice and appreciative about it. 'Thank you,' he said, 'that's really pretty—just what I wanted.' What both of us wanted, though, was the chance to produce some of his records, but it never came up. Of all the artists we have produced he had perhaps the greatest vocal range. Oh, sure, we made some sound-alike demos for him so he could hear what the songs would be like, and some of the backing tracks we made may even have been used on his actual records, but we still never got to be his producers." D.J. Fontana, Elvis' drummer also has a special memory of recording the song "Jailhouse Rock": "One day they told us they had this scene of Elvis breaking rocks and they needed some kind of sound to go along with the picture. Well, Scotty and I kicked it around trying to figure out what to do. Eventually we came up with that thing that played it to them, they said, 'That's great—leave it just that way!'"

Two more songs composed by Aaron Schroeder, one of the other songwriters to compose numerous songs for Elvis, rounded off the May session: "Young And Beautiful" and "Don't Leave Me Now". Both songs were cut in different versions for the soundtrack and the movie. If there was one song from the session which seemed to hold potent for the future it was surely "I Want To Be Free", for already Elvis Presley was becoming a prisoner of his fame and would soon be just as surely trapped in a series of movies which would dominate his life and career for almost a decade.

Colonel Tom Parker's policy of broadening Elvis Presley's appeal continued on 5 September 1957, when Elvis returned to Radio Recorders to cut his first festive LP, "Elvis's Christmas Album". Once again, Elvis was to demonstrate his versatility, with standards such as "Silent Night" and "White Christmas". Jerry Leiber and Mike Stoller provided three new songs for this session: "Treat Me Nice" which was also featured in the movie "Jailhouse Rock" (also released as flip-side to the film's title track), "Santa Claus Is Back In Town", the powerful ballad "Don't", to go to the top of the Billboard charts.

Jerry Leiber later said about Elvis and "Don't": "It was really one of the most beautiful interpretations that Elvis did on any of our songs. The mix and the performance and the arrangement were particular good." Elvis himself was very pleased with "Santa Claus Is Back In Town". Jerry Leiber: "We were told about the Christmas album only a few days before they were due to record. We hadn't finished the song when they called us over to Radio Recorders, but we managed to get it in shape just before Elvis started his final session around four in the afternoon. We rushed into the control room with the sheets of music and there was Colonel Parker. He took his big cigar out of his mouth, looked at the song, and then said, 'What took you so long, boys?' We heard later that Elvis said this was his favourite Christmas song."

Elvis, who had a very religious upbringing, tackled "Silent Night" and "O Little Town Of Bethlehem" beautifully.

Another number from the session with a strongly spiritual feel to it was "My Wish Came True", written by Jivory Joe Hunter, with The Jordanaires giving a backing vocal accompaniment not uncommon in sacred music. It was a song with an added meaning for Elvis, for he had long admired the composer's work and had recently spent some hours with him perfecting his technique as spiritual singer. Ivory Joe Hunter had been raised in Beaumont/Texas by a father who was a guitarist and a spiritual-singing mother. Forming his own band in which he played the piano, he also began composing and wrote numbers for various artists, including Nat King Cole, Eddie Fisher and the McGuire Sisters, earning him the nick-name "Mr Versatility" in the music business.

While visiting the United Kingdom in 1958 he also recollected on his meeting with Elvis in 1957: "I was visiting Memphis for a recording session and was invited to meet Elvis at his home by a mutual friend. Frankly, to begin with I was not sure about the idea because I'd heard he was colour prejudiced, but once we met it didn't seem like that to me. In fact, he showed me the greatest courtesy and it seemed he had known my music for years. Well, we talked for a bit and then graduated to the piano. I got the impression Elvis was happiest when he was playing, it made him feel more at ease—especially if it was the kind of music that suited his mood. We spent hours and hours at that piano, taking it in turns to play, and singing spirituals and blues numbers. Elvis is very spiritual minded and as far as his spiritual knowledge goes, he has a negro background. I believe he can sing spiritual numbers with more feeling than any other white singer of his calibre. On the second day, I spent with him, I met Elvis' mother and she told me that when he was younger he used to collect my records. That flattered me very much, and later I was glad of having the chance of writing some songs for him."

"My Wish Came True" was not to be released until July 1959, as B-side to the Rock and Roll song "A Big Hunk O'Love". The same year Elvis cut Ivory Joe Hunter's "Ain't That Loving You Baby", which remained in the vaults until 1964, when being released on as single with "Ask Me".

The session was rounded off with more Christmas songs, namely "Blue Christmas", "Santa Bring My Baby Back To Me", "Here Comes Santa Claus" and "I'll Be Home For Christmas".

But the new year held a completely new challenge: Elvis Presley had received his Army callup papers and military service would present him either filming or recording. (His Army stint was to last from March 1958 to March 1960.) Plans to complete his fourth movie—"King Creole", and record enough material to be released while he was away in the Army, were quickly put into operation. On January 15th 1958 with Scotty Moore, Bill Black, DJ Fontana and The Jordanaires Elvis went to Radio Recorders to cut songs for the movie King Creole. Again Leiber and Stoller came up with three numbers, the classic "King Creole", the moody and menacing "Trouble" and the school song "Steadfast, Loyal and True".

Both men would also attend the recording session, Jerry Leiber involved into the engineering, while Mike Stoller played the piano. It was a session that the Jordanaires would long remember, because the witnessed one of the few and rare outbursts of anger by Elvis. The members of the quartet Gordon Stoker and Neal Matthews from Tennessee, Hoyt Hawkins from Kentucky and Ray Walker from Mississippi, were then becoming increasingly seen as Elvis' permanent backing group, although the quartet itself, with different members, had been in existence since 1958 when they had started singing spirituals and barber shop songs.

In 1956, the Jordanaires broke into the recording industry in Nashville with a new type of vocal harmonising which made them very popular as backup singers for recording stars such as Jim Reeves, Marty Robbins, Patti Page, Tennessee Ernie Ford, Elvis Presley and later Ricky Nelson. The group had first met Elvis back in 1955, when they appeared together in Memphis on a bill starring Eddy Arnold. He had told them that if ever he got a recording contract that would lead him to Nashville, he would want them to back him—a promise that none of them paid much attention to.

Elvis had been as good as his word, and at a concert in Detroit the four men suddenly realised they were involved with someone truly extraordinary, as Gordon Stoker explains: "It was as if someone had suddenly turned loose millions of bees. The crowd literally began to swarm: they filled the aisle, climbed on the stage, grabbed the music, stands and all, there was nothing that could stop them. With Elvis in front we rushed down the stairs and into the a waiting car surrounded by policemen. Our buttons had been torn off, our coat pockets ripped, our pocket handkerchiefs taken. We were pushed into the car, the doors slammed and locked and off we went."

"We were completely exhausted and, to be honest, downright scared. And we didn't feel any better when Elvis said, 'Man, we were lucky that time! In a crowd like that I usually always lose a coat and a shirt!' About the recording sessions Gordon Stoker remembers the following: 'Recording sessions with Elvis were always a delight, he'd always come into the studio with a big smile on his face, shake hands with everyone there, no matter who they were. He'd tell jokes and kid around, put his arm around your shoulder and pick at you about something—the shirt you had on, the way you wore your hair, anything. He just wanted to warm up to the session and get everyone else in the same mood."

"Other entertainers usually wouldn't speak to you when they came in to record. But Elvis was fun to be with. Then he'd usually sit down at the piano and start singing spirituals and we'd join in. He might sing for an hour or two before we cut the first side. In all the years I travelled and worked with him, I never heard the man raise his voice at anybody—except one time. That was when we were at the sound studio recording the tracks for King Creole. We sang spirituals until the noon break and all these officials and technicians were standing around, just dying. During the break, they came over to us and told us they were terribly upset, that the session was costing them a fortune, and for us not to sing spirituals with Elvis when he came back from lunch."

"When Elvis came back and sat down at the piano, we didn't go over and join him as we always had before. He finally looked around at us and said, 'Hey, fellas, what's the trouble?' So we went over and told him that the studio had told us not to sing with him around the piano after lunch. He really got mad. He said, 'Look, if I want to bring you guys to Hollywood and sing spirituals all day long, that's what we'll do.' Then he walked out of the studio. The next day he came back and finished the sound track—but it taught the studio a lesson. Elvis always did finish his job during the time the studio had budgeted for it. But he liked to mess around until he could get in the right mood to do what he had to do. Then he did it and he did it right. After that, nobody bothered Elvis."

Apart from Jerry Leiber and Mike Stoller, a number of other songs for King Creole were written by composers who would provide material for Elvis' later films: Men such as Claude Demetrius who penned "Hard Headed Woman", as well as "Dixieland Rock", Sid Tepper and Roy C. Bennett contributed "New Orleans", Sid Wayne co-authored "Lover Doll" with Abner Silver and the prolific Fred Wise-Ben Beisman team who wrote the ballads "Don't Ask Me Why" and "As Long As I Have You". The sessions on 15 and 16 January 1958 completed the soundtrack for King Creole, with a second session needed for a revised version of "King Creole". The song was to exchange the original title track "Danny", which was inspired by "A Stone For Danny Fisher" the novel on which the screenplay was based. It was revived by Conway Twitty as "Lonely Blue Boy" and covered in the UK by Marty Wilde.

The Army dominated the life of Elvis Presley for the next two years. But on 10 June 1958, when Elvis was given a two-week furlough after basic training, a recording session was scheduled for GI Presley. Elvis was also able to slip into a screening of King Creole. The Nashville overnight session produced three outstanding numbers: "A Big Hunk O' Love", "I Got Stung" and "I Need Your Love Tonight". The session also introduced some new musicians to the line-up of Elvis recording musicians: Hank Garland and Chet Atkins on guitar, Bob Moore on bass, Floyd Cramer on piano, Buddy Harman on bongos, The Jordanaires as usual on backing vocals and D.J. Fontana as ever on drums.

A sadder and more mature Elvis was discharged from the Army on 5 March 1960, for his much-loved mother had died in the interim, creating a void in his life which he never completely filled. The world of pop and rock music had changed and in one of his first statements to the press, he acknowledged this: "There isn't too much wild stuff, the artists have started adding strings and receiving better arrangements. And the sound is now of much better quality than when I first started to record."

For Elvis Presley's first recording session, after his Army stint RCA chose their new Studio B on the outskirts of Nashville, at 17th Avenue South, a studio far better equipped than the old building on McGavock, which would allow Elvis to record in stereo for the first time. As there was tremendous interest among fans about when and where Elvis would cut his first discs, RCA, aided and abetted by Colonel Tom Parker, decided to use a little deception. Booking the session for 8 pm on Sunday, 20 March 1960, the company gave the impression that the artist using the studios was the popular Country and Western singer Jim Reeves, who agreed to go along with the ruse.

Another disguise was to name the singer Sivle Yelserp, but this was so obvious, Elvis Presley's name in reverse, that while Elvis was recording, news broadcasters announced that he was recording in Nashville. As one hundred hamburgers and cups of sweet milk were ordered by Crystal Hamburger in Nashville, it was clear that Elvis was in town. "When one of the guys said that RCA was paying for them we knew that a hundred hamburgers plus the record label equalled Elvis in town!" said an employee of the Hamburger place. Another reporter said that the two policeman who stood guard on the studio had only a small handful of fans to contend with, although one intruder did get as far as the reception room in the building. "Ironically, he was not a typical fan, but a personal member of Elvis' own profession whose courage had been temporarily enlarged and who tried to join Elvis in song," added the report.

The session lasted twelve hours and reunited Elvis with virtually the same line-up that had played on his last RCA recording date, plus the return of Scotty Moore in place of Chet Atkins, who was now RCA's A&R man in Nashville and supervised the recording. A fitting reward for his tremendous work on behalf of RCA Records. Bob Moore was on bass, and had replaced Bill Black, he concluded on the session: "It wasn't like your normal session. There's usually a lotta urgency about most Nashville sessions because running overtime costs the companies extra money and they don't like that. But with Elvis it was the case of long and leisurely, expense no object."

When he first came into the studio he must have played around on the drums for ten minutes and more. And when he stopped singing and did something else, everybody just let it happen. Nobody said anything. But he's a nice guy to work with, a gentleman. He never tries to tell you how to play or what to do. He tends to his singing and lets you tend to your playing. I heard someone ask him at the end of the session how it had gone and he said, "After two years it was sort of strange at first, but after singing for a couple of hours it all came natural again."

Elvis returned to his roots, now with a great Rock and Roll feeling in his more mature voice, with "Make Me Know It" composed by Otis Blackwell. This was followed by the song "Soldier Boy", then "Stuck On You", which turned out to be his next single, within a couple of days. This was backed on the b-side with "Fame And Fortune". "Stuck On You" had advance orders of over a million copies from fans before a note had even been sung. Not surprisingly it hit the number one spot in the charts before the end of April. Even its success, though, was to be overshadowed when Elvis went back to Nashville Music City USA on April 3rd 1960. The material selected for this session ranged from Peggy Lee's "Fever" to a new Leiber and Stoller song—"Dirty, Dirty Feeling" and the Bunny Paul, Drifters, Johnnie Ray hit "Such A Night".

Also, the immortal classic "Are You Lonesome Tonight?" was recorded It would become Number one for six weeks when released as a single in 1960, selling in excess of five million copies. "It's Now Or Never" would also take the record buying public by storm. The song, by Aaron Schroeder and Wally Gold, was actually an adaption of the Italian song "O Sole Mio", made famous by Entrico Caruso, and after the session Elvis himself explained how he had come to record it: "O Sole Mio" has always been one of my favourite songs. I liked the Tony Martin version "There's No Tomorrow" and I often played the record by Ian Pierce, the opera singer. I used to sing it myself and maybe add some piano. That's the way I did it with "It's Now Or Never". It wasn't Rock and Roll, but it did have a beat and I think it has turned out pretty good."

British fans very nearly did not have a chance to agree or disagree with Elvis Presley, for it appeared that there might be a copyright restriction preventing the release. When it was released it hit number one in the United Kingdom, breaking records with its sales. If the copyright issue would not have been resolved, a release in the UK would have been delayed for seven years. The record turned out to be a worldwide seller, with nine million copies being sold and, as one critic later wrote, would "lock Elvis furthermore into the tradition of the popular romantic ballad".

The movie "GI Blues", which Elvis made on his return to civilian life, was to herald a decade which his activities would be confined almost totally to making films, with the occasional recording sessions thrown in. The former Rock and Roll King who had changed contemporary music was now being groomed into an All-Round Entertainer, whose work could be enjoyed by people of all ages. Whether it was a path that Elvis himself chose to travel on, or if he accepted it on recommendation of his manager Parker, will probably be never known. GI Blues drew heavily on Elvis' own experiences in the US Army in Germany, and it took him two sessions at the RCA Studios and Radio Recorders, to lay down the soundtrack on 27–28 April and 6 May 1960.

The title track, complete with the Jordanaires, was as effective as the train number, "Frankfurt Special". Another Army song "Didja Ever" was cut before Elvis slowed down for the ballad "Doin' The Best I Can", written by the famous songwriting duo Doc Pomus and Mort Shuman, in Rock and Roll History equalling an importance with Jerry Leiber and Mike Stoller. The duo, had been prove to be most effective, for the Elvis competitor Fabian Forte. A problem of copyright again arose with "Tonight Is So Right For Love" which the composers Sid Wayne and Abner Silver had based on "Barcarolle" by Jacques Offenbach.

It was later rearranged to "Tales From The Vienna Woods" by Austrian composer Johann Strauss, which was not under the same copyright restrictions. "Wooden Heart" was based on "Muss Ich Denn Zum Staedtele Hinaus", adapted by Fred Wise and Bert Kaempfert. A tremendous success for Elvis in Britain and Germany. "Pocketful Of Rainbows", which Fred Wise also contributed with his partner Ben Weisman, was of interest as the first song in which a female co-star provided a few lines of accompaniment, in this case Julie Prowse. And a pattern other actresses would follow for Elvis Presley soundtracks.

By this time, in the career of Elvis Presley, an interesting system had been established to provide him with the material he would record. Two music publishing companies had been set up in his name: Elvis Presley Music and Gladys Music (named after his late mother), material would be submitted in them and in so to Elvis himself via the giant Hill and Range organisation based in New York. The man in charge of overseeing the submissions was Freddie Beinstock who had been added to Elvis' entourage shortly after the singer had joined RCA and thereafter acted as the link between Hill and Range, Elvis' companies, and Elvis the artist. It was Beinstock, in fact, who was responsible for bringing together the team of writers, almost two dozen strong, including Otis Blackwell, Doc Pomus, Mort Shuman, Sid Tepper and Roy Bennett, who for the next decade would supply virtually all Elvis' material, mostly to order.

The preferred method of submitting new songs to Elvis was by way of demonstration recordings by artists with a voice similar to his own. The centre for the production of these discs was a recording studio, Associated Recording, near the Brill Building in New York where Hill and Range had their headquarters. Once material was selected from a huge pile, recording sessions with the soundalikes would be set up using four studio session men. One of the first producers of these demo discs, or dubs, as they were called, was Phil Spector, later to become famous for producing the Ronettes, the Righteous Brothers, Ike and Tina Turner and the Beatles. Singers used were Brian Hyland, P.J. Proby and David Hill, among others. P.J. Proby would later portray Elvis Presley in the musical "Elvis".

P.J. Proby recalls recording the demos for Elvis as follows: "I left Houston when I was 17 because there was no show business there and went to Hollywood. I worked in B movies of the hot-rod era and then, because I had always wanted to sing, got into making demos for Elvis movies. I'd record all the numbers sounding just like Elvis, so when he got through acting he could come and learn the songs straight off my demos. He liked to hear the way things would sound when they were recorded. Many times he would follow the demo disc to the note, and if he liked a lick or a riff he wanted it on his own version. Phil Spector once told me that Elvis sometimes even used the demonstration track and just sang over it."

The next stage in the system took place in the studio when Elvis arrived for a session. DJ Fontana, for many years Elvis Presley's drummer provided an insider's view of what went on: "In the early days we actually recorded in mono because that's all there was. Then they came up with two-track, three-track and four-track and it made things a little easier. In the early days, Elvis didn't like to overdub in the first place. He didn't want to go back and redo his vocals. He always wanted to be in with the band, live. The procedure went through in the studio was always the same. There would be a stack of demos, maybe 25 to 50 songs. And he'd play a demo and throw out those he didn't like. He would kinda sling them on the floor! After hearing the first eight bars or so of something he liked, he'd say "We'll hold this one."

"Then if he decided he would record something we'd play it over and over again. We'd learn the tunes like he would, right there on the spot. He had a memory that was ungodly. He'd learn his part real quick, although it took us a little while longer. He always knew exactly what he wanted in the studio, right back when we did "Heartbreak Hotel". He knew the sound he wanted. He'd tell us, "Now, boys, don't play anything fancy. I want every band in every club across the country to be able to play these songs. I want everybody to hear these songs." The one time I saw him upset was with some songs they wanted him to sing in the movies—especially the later movies. You think some of the ones recorded were bad—you ought to hear some of the ones he wouldn't record. He'd shake his head and say, "Fellows, I don't think I can do this. Can't you rewrite it?"

Another soundtrack session was followed with the first gospel LP for release at Christmas. Elvis mastery of this kind of religious material was evident from the first cut of the classic "His Hand In Mine", which had been one of his favourite tunes from childhood. Impressive versions of "Joshua Fit The Battle" and "Swing Low Sweet Chariot" were followed by his own beautifully simple rendition of "Crying In The Chapel", which had been a hit for several earlier artists such as Sonny Till and The Orioles and Adam Wade. It was an even bigger hit for Elvis Presley, when released on a single with "I Believe In The Man In The Sky" as a single. Before Elvis could enjoy Christmas himself, there was another date in Hollywood to cut the tracks for his next movie, Wild In The Country, which was held on November 7th to 8th.

The title song, a gentle ballad, contrasted nicely with the up-tempo "I Slipped, I Stumbled, I Fell" which was made even more effective in the movie where Elvis sang it while driving a truck and revved the engine to accentuate the beat. On the set of the movie he also did a duet with co-star Hope Lange on "Husky Husky Day". In March 1961, Elvis Presley recorded the album "Something For Everybody". Afterwards he talked to journalist Jon Whitcomb about the way he picked his songs and recording them: "I know right away which songs are right for me. When I'm picking songs to record I listen to everything that comes into my music company. Of course, it's screened first by someone who knows what I like. Folk songs and classics are usually out—the rights are too difficult. Dozens of people pop up and claim they were the writers. After I recorded "Hound Dog" a bunch of people turned up, among them a man who said he had written a song called "Bear Cat" and, he claimed, it had exactly the same tune. When he tried to make trouble a Memphis newspaper said "Bear Cat Sues Hound Dog."

"For my recording sessions, I work with ear musicians and not sheet musicians. They're great. You just hum or whistle or sing a tune for them once and then they go to work. Inside a minute or two the place can be jumping. I take my time to do the right thing. I can't properly explain it, but it all begins with listening and more listening. It all narrows down gradually. When I'm down to the songs I think I'll want I'm ready to go. I can cut fifteen songs on a session. Me and the boys sometimes get together late at night and it's late morning when we call it a day."

The March session was also a memorable one for pianist Floyd Cramer, for it was to repay a debt to another composer-pianist, Don Robertson, the writer of two of the songs laid down: "There's Always Me" and "Starting Today". Floyd Cramer: "In the early Fifties I used to go to Nashville from time to time for recording sessions. And it was Chet Atkins at RCA who advised me to settle there. After that, I was hardly ever out of work. Chet also encouraged me to develop a distinctive style of piano playing, and because I'd always liked Don Robertson's honky-tonk style I sort of copied him. I found out when we were recording those songs of his in Nashville that Elvis liked his music, too."

Saxophone player Boots Randolph, who also played on this session, added his own comments: "Elvis is a very easy person to get on with. He knows what he wants but everyone contributes something to the sessions. Elvis has got a terrific personality. He can walk into a crowded room and generate electricity— you know he's there even if you haven't seen him. But he is a very shy and nervy person." But Elvis did not sign of nerves on such excellent tracks as "Sentimental Me", "Gently", "I Feel So Bad" and "It's A Sin". The long play was truly "Something For Everybody".

Later in March, Elvis Presley laid down the soundtrack for one of his exotic movies—"Blue Hawaii", once more at Radio Recorders in Hollywood. His backing ensemble was considerably enlarged to help the create the sound of Hawaiian music and included drummer Hal Blaine, a specialist in Hawaiian instruments, Fred Taveras and Alvino Rey on ukuleles, and another vocal group, the Surfers, to augment the Jordanaires. Elvis enjoyed adding new elements to his work, saying after the sessions held between March 21st and March 23th: "I happen to like Hawaiian music and the beat and we sure got lots of Hawaiian music in the picture.

Some of them are standards which have been rearranged, like "Aloha-oe". For "No More", Don Robertson was responsible, while "Can't Help Falling In Love", was based on the classic "Plaisir D'Amour", rated among the greatest love songs ever recorded by Elvis, by critics and fans alike. Ben Weisman was the songwriter behind four of the other songs, which were cut in an attempt to mix rock with Hawaiian music, the best received "Rock-A-Hula-Baby". Charles Curran directed Elvis once more, they had already collaborated on "Loving You", "King Creole" and "GI Blues", where some scenes were also directed by Curran.

He gave an impression of the singer to the press: "It's my job to study the script and work in the songs to the situations so that they merge without slowing down the storyline. First we record all the songs in the recording studio and then on set we play back the tapes as we film the visual part of the picture. This often means that I must make Elvis, who need not actually sing but just move his lips in tome to his recording, look as if he's singing. It have to coax him along like a cheer leader. I usually just stand beside the camera and tell Elvis to mimic me. Sometimes I'll have the members of his group, Scotty, Bill and D.J., with me to play off screen. When there's a lull in shooting, they often start off a jam session with Elvis to keep him relaxed and happy. In fact, they earn money just as much as by being in the films. We did most of the exteriors at Oahu, the island next to Hawaii, which has far fewer tourists and where Elvis found he could walk around in public without being mobbed and asked for his autograph. I think the best song in Blue Hawaii is "Hawaiian Wedding Song" which is like the national anthem of the islands, and Elvis sang it superbly with a backing of 100 Hawaiians and the Hawaiian group, the Surfers. I can tell you the scene brought tears to my eyes! I also remember the scene where Elvis has his inevitable brawl and winds up in jail, where he sings "Beach Boy Blues", an amusing song in which he refers to his pineapple-growing family and his predicament. The words were, "I'm a kissin' cousin to ripe pineapple and I'm in the can".

"Elvis really enjoys putting over songs with funny lyrics. After the shooting, the crew on the picture were entertained to what would be the most expensive lounge-room attraction in the world: Elvis and Patti Page (who was with me having a holiday) singing together long into the night. Elvis would strum his guitar as accompaniment on the terrace of the Cocopalms Hotel with the lagoon bathed in moonlight. They went through dozen of numbers 0 it was amazing how many they knew. And if Patti knew one Elvis didn't, or vice versa, they'd want to learn it."

Elvis' return to Nashville in June produced more memorable tracks, five in number: Three by the songwriting duo of Doc Pomus and Mort Shuman, another Don Robertson composition—"I'm Yours", and "That's Someone You Never Forget" which is credited to Elvis and his long-time friend Bobby "Red" West. Elvis and Red had been friends since meeting at Humes High School in Memphis, and when Elvis Presley became famous, he employed Red West as his bodyguard. West later became a singer and writer, while remaining a member of the "Memphis Mafia". Their relationship was a stormy one and after Elvis fired Red, along with his cousin Sonny West, and another bodyguard, Dave Hebler, the trio wrote a controversial and scandalous book about the use of drugs by Presley. Entitled "Elvis: What's Happened?" it was published just 15 days before Elvis died.

These events were in the meantime, more than a decade away, when "That's Someone You Never Forget" was waxed by Elvis. A haunting and beautiful song, it was apparently written with Elvis' mother Gladys, in mind. Elvis put a lot of emotion in it, when it was recorded on a June evening in Studio B. Doc Pomus and Mortu Shuman already had contributed "A Mess Of Blues" and "Surrender" to the Elvis Presley catalogue. Shortly before his death, in March 1991, Doc Pomus, born in 1923, talked about Elvis, his partner Mort, and their music: "I started out singing around some of the joints in Brooklyn where I was born. Me and Otis Blackwell would sing for a few beers and a little change. We were both trying to get started as songwriters. Everything changed for me the day I first heard Elvis. I was in a local bar and this new sound came out of the jukebox. It was Elvis singing 'Mystery Train'. The sound captivated me as it was like nothing I had ever heard before."

"A few weeks later I saw Elvis on the Dorsey show on TV and I became an instant fan. I said to myself: 'Man, would I like to write a song that this guy could record.' Later I got a job writing material for Aberbach (music publishers in New York) which is where I met Mort. I played him 'Mystery Train' on the juke and he was grabbed by the sound. But we wrote a lot of songs for other artists before Elvis recorded one of ours. Strange thing was, it all came about in London. We were there taking care of some business when we met Lamar Fike, a friend of Elvis, who was on his way to Germany to see him. He asked us if we had any songs we would like him to take to Elvis. One of the songs we just had written was 'A Mess Of Blues', so we gave Lamar a demo of the song, We never expected to hear from him again."

But contrary to their belief, a partnership was soon established, and an association began which lasted well into the Sixties, with Elvis singing some of the pair's songs in concert right up to his death. With Elvis' love for the Inks Spots in mind, the pair wrote for him the ballad "Doin' The Best I Can". On the strength of "It's Now Or Never" they wrote him "Surrender". Other popular Elvis songs, the pair wrote for him, were "Kiss Me Quick", "Little Sister" and "His Latest Flame". Elvis Presley could sing anything—rock, country, rhythm and blues, ballads and gospel.

Doc Pomus: "So no matter what we came up with he could do it. I'm telling you as a songwriter, he was the best singer for my money that ever sang popular songs. He even made so many mediocre songs sound great. There are many great singers, great stylists, but they're all like branches of a tree, and he was the tree. Another thing that impressed me was every time I wrote a song for Elvis, after recording it he would tell me something about it that I even didn't notice. He understood music and songs in such a way that when he finished it, it was your song … but with a plus." Ironically Doc Pomus and Mort Shuman never met the singer Elvis Presley personally.

Before 1961 was over, Elvis had recorded the soundtrack for this next two films—"Follow That Dream" and "Kid Galahad". Highlights were "Follow That Dream", "What A Wonderful Life" and "King Of The Whole Wide World". A session in Nashville followed, on the evening of October 15th, when five tracks were cut, RCA hoped for some hits of this session, as well. Don Robertson contributed "Anything That's Part Of You" and "I Met Her Today", then there was "Good Luck Charm" soon to be a Nr.1 hit, a composition by Aaron Schroeder and Wally Gold.

In March 1962, Elvis spent another two days in Studio B cutting tracks for the new album Pot Luck and a single: "Easy Question" by Otis Blackwell, "Just Tell Her Jim Said Hello" and "She's Not You" by Jerry Leiber and Mike Stoller, "Gonna Get Back Somehow", "Nigh Rider" and "Suspicion" by Doc Pomus and Mort Shuman, plus one by Doc Pomus and Alan Jeffries—"I Feel That I've Known You Forever". Pomus and Shuman contributed other great songs to the Fifties and Sixties, such as "Save The Last Dance For Me" by The Drifters, "A Teenager In Love" by Dion and The Belmonts, "Sweets For My Sweets" for The

Drifters … Though their paths separated when Mort Shuman moved to Europe, finally settling in London during the Beatles era, they remained friends and, by coincidence died within less than eight months of each other.

For the movie "Girls, Girls, Girls" Elvis revolved a Leiber and Stoller track, which had been an earlier hit for The Coasters, then there was the movie's song "Return To Sender" which had been written for him by Otis Blackwell, and was released on a single in October 1962. Otis Blackwell's "One Broken Heart For Sale" was also selected as a single, from another Elvis movie—"It Happened At The World's Fair". Though the song had merit, and was of high production quality, it failed to make the Top 10. 1963 rolled in, Elvis continued much in the same groove, seemingly unconcerned by the Brit Invasion. Three soundtrack albums were released that year.

In January and February 1963, Elvis worked on the film "Fun In Acapulco". "Bossa Nova Baby" was originally a hit for The Clovers, and Elvis effectively tied the dance with Rock and Roll. He also showed great versatility with his version of "Guadalajara". Elvis further cut "Please Don't Drag That Spring Around", an up-tempo Otis Blackwell number, followed by "Devil In Disguise", composed by Bill Grant, Bernie Baum and Florence Kayne. Both songs were released as a single. Also cut was "Long Lonesome Highway" which became the title track for the Elvis movie "Tickle Me".

In July, Elvis Presley recorded the songs for his upcoming movie "Viva Las Vegas" which had him co-starring with Ann-Margret. The session saw the introduction of several new musicians, such as Glen Campbell, then an accomplished studio man who would later become a very successful solo artist and friend of Elvis; further Billy Strange, an outstanding guitarist who would be featured on a lot of Elvis' later discs and would also pen some songs for him. The beautiful Ann-Margret, sang two duets with Elvis, the humorous "The Lady Loves Me" and "You're The Boss" which was revived many years later by Brian Setzer and Gwen Stefani on the Grammy award winning album "The Dirty Boogie" credited to The Brian Setzer Orchestra.

Ann-Margret also hummed to Elvis version of "Santa Lucia" which he sang partly in Italian. The title track "Viva Las Vegas" was penned once more by Doc Pomus and Mort Shuman, the ladder remembering the composing with affection: "I had been doing a lot of travelling about that time and among the places I'd visited were Latin America and some of the Pacific islands. I liked the rhythm I heard there and started playing around with them. I wanted to go away from just rock and blues. 'Viva Las Vegas' sort of mixed the samba and rock and I thought it worked pretty well."

The fans agreed, and the song is remembered as one of the most remarkable Elvis Presley records, a hymn to Sin City. Audiences also enjoyed the other Pomus and Shuman contribution to the movie, the ballad "I Need Somebody To Lean On", as well as a couple of very different classics which were included on the soundtrack. The first was a belting version of Ray Charles "What'd I Say", a song which also saw a brief return to the charts for Jerry Lee Lewis in the early 1960s. As fell as "Today, Tomorrow and Forever", based no Franz Liszt's "Liebestraum". Next up was recording for the movie "Kissin' Cousins", two quite different versions were cut of the title track in Nashville in October. The first version, by Fred Wise and Randy Starr, had an element of the blues in it as well as some great and outstanding drumming by D.J. Fontana and Buddy Harman. The second version, used as the title song of the film, is faster, and has lyrics by Bill Grant, Bernie Baum and Florence Kaye.

In 1964, Elvis recorded the Chuk Berry rocker "Memphis/Tennessee" and Joe Byers' ballad "It Hurts Me". The rest of the year, was taken up with two more movies, "Roustabout" and "Girl Happy", both made naturally in Hollywood, with the soundtracks produced there also.

Outstanding songs were "Poison Ivy League" and the old Leiber and Stoller song "Little Egypt". The ladder song, the story of a seductive belly dancer, had earlier been recorded by The Coasters, but because of its lyrics had been banned by many American radio stations. On a trivia note for movie buffs, just before Elvis sings the number "Poison Ivy League", a young girl destined to become one of the screen's most famous sex symbols makes her film debut with a solitary line of dialogue. Her name was Raquel Welch. Doc Pomus was responsible for the title track "Girl Happy", co-written by Norman Meade. "Do The Clam" was pointed out by many music writers as a plain silly song, though it did well in England. In 1965, Elvis recorded film soundtracks only. This was extraordinary, in view of the fact that the year marked the tenth anniversary of his association with RCA Records. There had been plans for an Elvis Anniversary album, which was never realised.

As it was RCA, RCA put out an album consisting solely of previously unreleased songs from earlier sessions, entitled "Elvis For Everyone". A highlight of 1965 in the musical career of Elvis Presley was certainly the release of "Crying In The Chapel", which had been cut five years earlier. It appeared, appropriately, at Easter and made the Top Ten in America as well as in several other countries. Elvis might have overdubbed his voice on quite a number of the tunes for his 1965 movies, "Harum Scarum", "Frankie And Johnny" and "Paradise Hawaiian Style". Charlie McCoy, Kenneth Buttrey and Victor Feldman, some of the session men involved, do not recall seeing much of Elvis for the sessions.

"Hey Little Girl", another Joe Byers rocker, stands away above the other tunes in the movie vehicle "Harum Scarum", a fine cha-cha sounding "Kismet" was also recorded for it. Elvis sang with his co-star Doona Douglas, in two of the songs for "Frankie and Johnny": "Look Out Broadway" and "Petunia, The Gardener's Daughter", it was also in this movie that he lay his hand on "When The Saints Go Marching In". A decade earlier a smash hit for Bill Haley and His Comets as "The Saints Rock and Roll". 1965 and 1966 saw Elvis Presley busy recording the soundtracks to his movies "Paradise Hawaiian Style", "Spinout", "Double Trouble" and "Easy Come, Easy Go". A turning point recording wise came in May 1966, when after three years of recording soundtracks, Elvis went back to his roots in Nashville. The session there was to be consisting of old spirituals and modern hits.

Among them, the recent Bob Dylan success "Tomorrow Is A Long Time". The session was masterminded by Felton Jarvis, who would not only help to revitalise Elvis, but would gut his great talent in new directions. Felton Jarvis had previously recorded Vince Everett, an Elvis soundalike, when Everett's recordings had been re-released during the Rockabilly Revival years, some dubbed them as the 1960s material Elvis should have cut back then.

On top of that, he had masterminded hits for Fats Domino and Tommy Roe, including Roe's Buddy Holly sounding signature hit "Sheila". Felton remembered: "I think one of the reasons we go on so well right from the start was because we both shared the same crazy sense of humour. You remember Elvis kept that pet chimp? Well, I had my own pet, too—a fifteen feet boa constrictor! I kept it in a burlap sack on the floor of my office. I just loved to watch people's eyes when the sack started to move around. The first time Elvis saw it he just hollered with laughter and said it was the craziest thing he'd ever seen!"

The band for the session featured Scotty Moore, D.J. Fontana, Floyd Cramer and the Jordanaires, young trumpeter Ray Stevens (who would become a recording star in his own right), organist David Briggs, guitarist Chip Young, steel guitarist Peter Dranke, the vocal group The Imperials (Jake Hess, Gary McSpadden, Armond Morales and Sherill Nielsen). The first song cut, was the gospel "Run On" which Elvis arranged himself. The mood continued with "How Great Thou' Art". Elvis also cut new versions of two other hit singles, namely "Love Letters" (Ketty Lester scored with it in 1962) and the Leiber and Stoller penned The Drifters hit "Fools Fall In Love" (1957). In all the session extended four nights and produced no less than 18 new songs. When the album featuring the gospels was released in 1967, under the title "How Great Thou' Art" it deservedly earned Elvis a Grammy award.

The sessions ended on May 28th, just two weeks later on June 10th Elvis was back in the studio. He recorded "If Every Day Was Like Christmas" written by Red Weste, and a Christmas tree was planted in the studio, to get Elvis in the right mood for the recording. An almost identical line up of musicians worked under the shade of that tree.

Two moody ballads were also recorded "I'll Remember You" and "Indescribably Blue".

Felton Jarvis certainly did a lot to revitalise Elvis Presley's recording career, but he always was modest about it: "All I ever did was follow what he wanted. He picked the songs, did the arranging and told everybody what he wanted them to do. He hardly ever had written arrangements. They were mostly head arrangements. You see, he was very loyal to his friends and had been using the same musicians for years. Because they were his friends, when he arrived to record they would all stand around talking for a while before getting down to business. Some of the people might not have seen Elvis for months, so they would have little-get-togethers in a corner before the session started. The music just sort of evolved as the session progressed."

"Elvis always had to record according how he felt at the moment. He wanted to feel a particular song at a particular moment in time. If, say, RCA wanted a gospel album then Elvis would ask for a week of studio time and sing whatever came into his mind at any given moment—blues, rock, pop, gospel. Then by the end of the week there would be enough gospel songs for the album. Some nights, though, nothing would get put on tape at all because Elvis was having too much fun just horsing around with the musicians. When he did begin learning a song, he learned it fast, and he carried everyone along with him. He'd always speak to every guy on the session, the musicians, the engineers, whoever, and shake their hands and say, 'Hello—it's good to see you again.'"

In September 1967, after completing the soundtracks to "Double Trouble", "Easy Come, Easy Go" and "Speedway" Elvis was back in Music City/USA. A brilliant guitarist and composer was with him in the studio, Jerry Reed. He had written as song for Elvis called "Guitar Man". Jerry Reed remembered: "Elvis and I had never met, when I got this message that he wanted me to play guitar on the session. So I turned up with three days of beard. I was making enough money for him not to scare me none. And I treated him like I'd known him for years. I talked to him like I'd talk to anybody and he just sat me down and said, "Let's pick." I tell you he was just an ole Mississippi boy. We got along just great. And you know something? That boy was so good-looking it was a crime. I drew real close to him and said: "You know something, boy, you're such a good-looking-guy it dam well hurts."

"It kinda threw him. I just walked in there and I didn't vie him a chance to scare me none." Next to a satisfying version of "Guitar Man" which soon would chart for Elvis, he also cut a rocking "Big Boss Man". He recorded songs prior recorded by other artists such as Jerry Lee Lewis, Bill Haley and Stevie Wonder ("High Heel Sneakers"), "You Don't Know Me" (Ray Charles) and "You'll Never Walk Alone" (Gerry and The Pacemakers).

1968 saw him return to the pinnacle of modern music. Following another session in Nashville in January, which continued in the same vein as its predecessor, he cut the soundtrack for the movie "Live A Little, Love A Little" and then went into the rehearsals of the Christmas TV spectacular which has since gone down in pop music legend as the "Return Of The King Of Rock". Jerry Reed was again among the musicians in Nashville in January and once more brought a new number for Elvis, "U.S. Male". Elvis cut a very cool sounding version of the Chuck Berr hit "Too Much Monkey Business". Mac Davis and Billy Strange's composition "A Little Less Conversation", released as a single, was a great first taste of Elvis with Mac Davis composition.

Featured prominently in his movie "Live A Little, Love A Little". The making of the hour-long NBC TV Special, is featured as its own chapter in this book, so we like in this chapter, quote it's producer Steve Binder on it, to capture the quintessence of it: "I felt very strongly that the Special would be Elvis' moment of truth. If he did just another movie-type show he would wipe out his career and be remembered only as a phenomenon of the Fifties. But if he could do a special and prove he was still number one, he would have the whole rejuvenation thing going for him. I got Elvis involved right from the start, making his own decisions and just listening to the Colonel. Parker wanted to do a traditional Christmas show with holly and snow and a couple of dozen Christmas songs like Andy Williams or Perry Como. But I desperately wanted Elvis to say something and let the world see what kind of man he really was."

"I didn't want him to just finish on a song like "Silent Night" and say goodnight like everyone does. I wanted something that would blow everyone's mind. I talked about this to my choral director, Earl Brown, and he went home and rang me the next morning. "I've got it," he said. "What Brown had was the song 'If I Can Dream', a plea for peace and understanding in the world, which Elvis Presley delivered with the passion of a man who agreed with every word."

Elvis completed two movies in 1968 also: The tough western drama, "Charro", for which he only had to sing the title track under the musical direction of Hugo Montenegro (famous for his theme tunes for the Clint Eastwood Westerns); and "The Trouble With Girls", where he performed "Clean Up Your Own Backyard" written for him by mac Davis and Billy Strange. In 1969, Elvis was ready for even more changes in his life: He returned to live concert performances for the first time in almost a decade. Choosing Las Vegas as the chosen place. It was almost as if he wanted to go back where it all had begun to ensure the complete the revival of his talent. For recording that was to be the Memphis located American Sound Studios, run by Chips Moman. He would record 34 songs there, many of them numbered among the greatest of the latter part of his career. Situated at 827 Danny Thomas Boulevard, the studios were a converted dairy in one of the poorest parts of the city of Memphis. As unimpressive as the Sun Studios at 706 Union Avenue from the outside.

Chips Moman, the owner of the American Sound Studios, had by that time produced over one hundred chart records with his brilliant six-man session team, artists as diverse as Wilson Pickett, Neil Diamond, Dionne Warwick and Dusty Springfield.

Elvis did, in fact, know most of the musicians, though he had never played with them before. Reggie Young, a guitarist, Bobbie Emmons who played the organ and had worked with Bill Black, Gene Chrisman, the drummer had been in Jerry Lee Lewis' band. Almost all the musicians had worked in Sam Phillips studios too, so even that Elvis was without the old faithfuls Scotty and D.J., who, would never record with him again, he was being backed up by some experienced down-home talent in all the departments of record making. Chips Moman: "Those guys all admired Elvis and were pleased to have a chance to work with him. We went right through the night that first time and the sun was coming up when Elvis went home. Just before he told me, "It felt good, man, those musicians are good. I just want to prove I can do it again, record some good hits. Number one records." Four hit singles resulted from the sessions: "Don't Cry Daddy", "In The Ghetto", Suspicious Minds" and "In The Ghetto". (Recorded between 13th and 23rd of February) with "Kentucky Rain" following a month later.

In March 1969, just before "In The Ghetto" became an international hit, Elvis Presley started to work on what was to be his last feature film, "Change Of Habit". The story of a young doctor, practising in the slums, who falls in love with a nun. Off-screen Elvis was reverting to being a live performer, also changing the material he was due to record. From now on, his songs would be predominantly ballads. Due to, what his experiences had been working with Chips Moman in his American Sound Studios, Elvis would also revert to the practice of overdubbing.

As if to motivate himself for his return live performance, Elvis laid down some exemplary tracks for Change Of Habit in the Decca Recording Studios in Los Angeles. It was in the 2000 seater showroom in the International Hotel in Las Vegas that, on the evening of July 31st, Elvis reappeared before the public for the first time in nine years. The event was much heralded in the media, eagerly awaited by fans and proved to be the return for "The King". No doubt, from the ecstatic reception that the audience and the press had given Elvis, live performances were to be his future and also destiny. Felton Jarvis taped Elvis new energy and motivation to be out singing for the public again on the acclaimed album "On Stage", pictured below.

Featuring the Beatles numbers "Yesterday" and "Hey Jude", he stormed through "Mystery Train", sang his current number one "In The Ghetto". AS well as bringing his own versions of modern standards such as The Bee Gees' "Words", Chuck Berry's "Johnny B. Goode", Ray Charles' "I Can't Stop Loving You" and Del Shannon's "Runaway".

Fine recordings with the TCB Band would follow, such as "See See Rider" originally done by Ma Reiney, the 1969 Creedence Clearwater Revival hit "Proud Mary", Tony Joe White's "Polk Salad Annie" or the delightful "Let It Be Me", "Release Me" and "The Wonder Of You".

In June 1970, Elvis agreed to do another studio session for RCA, but since his last recordings in Memphis two factors had changed. Chips Moman's studios had moved of the State and Felton Jarvis had left RCA at the beginning of the year. Jarvis, however agreed to supervise all Elvis' concert and studio recordings, and he set the venue in the familiar surroundings of Studio B in Nashville. A group of local session men were hired to work with James Burton: During five nights 30 songs were laid down. A whole set of excellent recordings emerged from the sessions, including Elvis' reading of "Bridge Over Troubled Water", "The Fool", "There Goes My Everything" and "You Don't Have To Say You Love Me" became 1970s classics in the Elvis Presley catalogue.

In August Elvis was live again at the International and his performances were filmed for the MGM documentary movie, "That's The Way It Is", masterminded by the leading Hollywood producer Dennis Saners. The film remains to this day a permanent reminder of Elvis Presley's unrivalled talent as a performer.

Being briefly in Nashville the following month, Elvis recorded the Jerry Lee Lewis classic "Whole Lotta Shakin' Goin' On" and "Rags To Riches" which would chart for him.

The year 1971 was also very productive for Elvis in the studio, with three sessions resulting in 40 songs. Producing such fine sides as "Amazing Grace", "For The First Time I Ever Saw Your Face", "Help Me Make It Through The Night", "Don't Think Twice It's Alright." Sixteen months had passed since Elvis had last been in a record studio, when on 21 July 1973, he began work on some new songs. A new venue had been chosen, this time, he had told Felton Jarvis that he did not want to travel outside of Memphis. The Stax Studios on McLemore Avenue were in some aspects rather like Chips Moman's American Sound Studios.

Situated in a poor, black neighbourhood, they were rather unimpressive from the outside but well equipped and highly functional. The owners, Jim Stewardt and Al Bell, had also built a reputation for producing hit records. Some with Otis Redding, others with Booket T And The MGs. Elvis was, of course, aware of the studio, and as it involved only a car ride from Graceland he agreed to work there. Elvis laid down "Three Corn Patches", "I've Got A Thing About You Baby" and "For Ol' Times Sake". "Raised On Rock" written by Mark James, the composer of "Suspicious Minds" was also cut, but later failed to chart.

The album was titled "Raised On Rock" and reached the shops while Elvis was in Palm Springs, and there RCA again tried to pursue Elvis to cut some songs. In the house in Palm Springs, Elvis laid down "Are You Sincere", "Sweet Angeline" and "I Miss You". Other songs produced were "Mr Songman" and

"My Boy", this ballad becoming a hit single later. "If You Talk In Your Sleep" written by Red West proved to be a great song in the interpretation of Elvis also.

In 1974 the live album "Elvis As Recorded Live On Stage In Memphis" was released, Elvis seemed to be reluctant of going into recording studios. But as with "Aloha From Hawaii", he still had the energy to release live albums and give great concerts.

Chapter Seven
Where Were You When Elvis Presley Died?

Good question, right? Actually, when the author of these lines was not born yet. I came to see the world on 13 May 1978; Elvis had passed on 16 August 1977. But I was an Elvis fan at the age of three. How's that, you wonder? Well, when Elvis died, a lot of folks went to buy his records. More on this, and the legendary RCA Meeting which was held during his final hours, later. My parents also picked up some Elvis releases on Vinyl. The budget Camden RCA releases with songs from his movies, some non-movie hits, some not even ever released on a single. Now treasured in my music collection. So most probably I heard Elvis already in the womb. Plus, I remember seeing some of Elvis Presley's light-hearted movies on television.

His movie years are some of the most criticised—though as there was no MTV yet, some of them were actually good Video Clips. Only much longer than a music video since the late 1980s. Interestingly when MTV started, they had so few clips of artists that they played the Stray Cats up and down, and helped the rocking' scene which was just at the crossing point of Teddy Boys to Rockabilly's in Britain—finding a new identity … Most of the early Stray Cats songs hit at one time or the other. There's even more to it, the producer of Brian Setzer (lead guitar), Slim Jim Phantom (drums) and Lee Rocker (bass) was none less than singer/guitarist Dave Edmunds.

He had produced the music for the movies "That'll Be The Day" and "Stardust" both based on John Lennon's early life, but still fictional. The main character portrayed by David Essex finally forms a band named Stray Cats … Even Beatle Ringo Starr had a role as Teddy Boy in the movie. So, the soundtrack-maker of the fictional Stray Cats now produced three New York school chums under the same name, as the band for which he provided the soundtrack—Stray Cats!

The film showed Ringo Starr back to the roots, a Ted as he was before German photographer Astrid Kirchheer invented the Beatles haircut, when Ringo returned to the days when the quiff was King.

"That'll Be The Day"—a sequel named "Stardust" followed, but is as much forgotten as the sequel to "American Graffiti".

Elvis Presley—where were you when he died?(An excerpt from the German language book by Schirmer/Mosel) published to Elvis Aaron Presley's 40th anniversary of having passed. An uncredited writer presents the foreword:

"Many singers became popular during the first decade of Rock and Roll, but only one of them reached everlasting life, except: Elvis Presley (January 8th 1935–16 August 1977). His appearances were clean dynamite: exalted, revolutionary and sexy—before he was disciplined by the US Army and Hollywood's Marketing Machine changed this raw diamond to an industrial product.

During his early years, somewhere between 1954 and 1960, Elvis still had the unbounded power and the proletary charm of the southern boy. With that he was the man of the hour, the one who enriched America's prude Entertainment industry with sexuality and new sexual phantasies. The one who with a single hip-swivelling the secret wishes of a million of Teenagers. Far away from the prescribed order of the Nixon-Era to please. In these early years, he became one of the major leaders for youth rebellion. That at the end, he was not capable of living with fame and fortune, live up to being an icon and an idol, does not disturb his fans—for them he was and will always remain Elvis Presley.

The introduction words of this book come from the pen of the legendary music critic Lester Bangs (1949–1982), whose brilliant essays, for scene magazines like Rolling Stone, Cream and Village Voice—to the most original and most influential ones for pop-criticism belong. In so, these magazines were the most influential trade papers for popular music. Under the title "Where were you when Elvis died?" he brings up once more an unforgettable moment of world-spanning grief and generates the most suitable tribute about work and effect of the "King of Rock and Roll".

(Uncredited writer)

Elvis had written already a letter on the plane taking him to Washington, where he would check in a hotel as Jon Burrows. Elvis Presley offered his services to America again, after two years of Military service. He received what he had asked for a BNDD badge. (Anti-Drug Agent). For many a paradox …

(On the morning of 21 December 1970, Elvis Presley personally delivered a letter to the northwest gate of the White House. Written on American Airlines stationery, the five-page letter requested a meeting with President Nixon. Presley intended to present the President with a gift of a World War II-era pistol and obtain for himself the credentials of a federal agent in the war on drugs). Page 1 of the letter Elvis wrote to President Richard Nixon.

The Teddy Boy subculture came from England (where it developed in London in the early 1950s and swept the island, thereafter). The fashion was long jackets (Drapes), tight trousers (drainpipes), crepe-soled shoes known as Creepers, slim ties (Slim Jim), and a waistcoat. Topped off with a Tony Curtis hairstyle—a quiff, with a DA at the back.

America had two more important factors to give to the Teddy Boy movement. Fashion and music.

Let's talk about the origins:

Zoot Suit Riot

The Zoot-suit a predecessor suit of the Edwardian suit was noted at the end of the 1930s in the United States of America. It was the clothing of the Hepcats, the Jitterbug dancers. At the very beginning, people with a shady image wore it. This led to its bad image. Then the Latin-American working class kids adopted the style. Mostly on the West Coast: San Diego and Los Angeles—the "Pachucos". The boys and girls wore a zoot-suit and a Ducktail hairstyle (Argentine style)—this to stand out from the non-Hispanic ethic origins. For a period, the Zoot suit was banned by law. Reason for this were the "Zoot Suit Riots", in the year 1943, in Los Angeles. Sailors and Pachucos, got into a brawl, due to racial tensions.

Spivs

Contrary to America the Zoot Suit never spread in such a way. A small group of working-class teenagers adopted a similar suit. These people were referred as "Spivs" and made "business" with rationed goods. The Spiv was a small fish, but had connections to the criminal elements of the UK. Through wearing a Zoot Suit showed his occupancy. In the US, the Zoot Suit was for Caucasian-whites as well as for Afro-Americans a way to dress. With the birth of the teenage-era, Zoot Suits and Jitterbug, had begun.

In 1948, the British Tailor Magazine "Tailor and Cutter" showed how to make an American broad-shouldered jacket. In Summer 1948, this "Bold Look" was a feature of the magazine. In August 1948, the Edwardian Style appeared in London. Some sources say that it was worn by the first Jamaican immigrants came with the former battle ship "Empire Windrush" in Tilbury. The Tailor and Cutter sent it's photographers, which showed what the "well-dressed Jamaican men of today wears, today": Zoot suits. There was an entire photo series with Zoot Suiters from Jamaica, on the streets of London.

In August 1951 the Journal "Custom Tailors and Designers Association of America" reported that the "Edwardian Look" was now approaching the wardrobes, of the well-dressed American. Soon factories started production of the Edwardian Dress. In Manchester male models were thrown on the catwalk by Elem Clothes Ltd, sponsored by "Sir". For the fashion industry, these new trends seemed to be a blessing.

Cosh Boys

In 1952, the first newspaper stories on Cosh Boys appeared. Cosh Boys seemed to hang around in any dark alley. The ignition for these fears, was the murder case Craig-Bentley: At a burglary in a storage house in Croydon (London): Policeman Miles lost his life. He was mortally wounded by a bullet believed to be shot by sixteen-year-old Christopher Craig, who committed the burglary with the 16-year-old sub-normal Derek Bentley. Both youngsters wore wide hats, long overcoats, long jackets and crepe-soled shoes. Craig also impersonated an accent he believed to be the one of an American tough guy. But under pressure, he chose to speak the same accent as Bentley—South London. Craig's gangster fantasy went as far, that he carried a gun since he was twelve years young. The Daily Mail of November 3rd 1952 concluded in its headline "Chicago Shoot-Out in London".

Edwardians

The Edwardian look was first adapted by the Royal Guards. It's roots came from the Edwardian Dandy, but also from the older, crime-driven elements of South London. The Edwardian style was worn by upper and middle class, only for a brief time though. The Edwardian style held all through the 1950s, but the meaning for wearing Edwardian clothes, changed dramatically. As long as worn by the higher social classes, it seemed to be a satisfying innovation. But as soon as working-class youngsters adapted the Edwardian look, the meaning changed. Edwardian suits disappeared in Mayfair, first the look of a business man, now the uniform of the "Dancehall Creepers". Before the war, working class and most middle-class kids had shared everything with their parents. They had danced to the same music, sat through the same films, worn the same clothes. (Nik Cohn) John Taylor of Style Weekly added: "They tried to dress like their fathers, they wore tweeds and smoked pipes. It was like lamb dressed as mutton and, even if they tried to be different, all they could get was a sixpenny pie from Woolworth's." Nik Cohn, in "Ball the Wall, In the Age of Rock":

Austerity was a result, and even that after the war, things stayed tight. But by the early fifties, austerity was ending and it was possible to experiment. Teenagers made up to 20 GBP a week, and so the teens started to look for things to spend it on.

Teddy Boys

King Edward VII (reign 1901–1910) was the King, for the Edwardian Style—the Daily Express on 23rd September 1953 shortened Edward to Ted, and the Ted was born:

"IN TERMS OF ENGLISH TEENAGERS TEDDY BOYS WERE THE START of everything: rock 'n' roll and coffee bars, clothes and bikes and language, jukeboxes and coffee with froth on it—the whole concept of a private teen life style, separate from the adult world." (Nik Cohn)

Cohn, concluded on the beginnings of the subculture: "In the beginning, this wasn't easy. Since the adolescent market had always been minimal, there was no businessman aiming for teenage customers. There were no teen clubs and no teen music, no teen foods, or clothes. Nothing that didn't apply equally to adults. By the middle fifties, the gap would be filled. Catching on fast, businessmen began to bombard the market with gimmicks and a whole new industry was launched. But when the Teds first started, around 1952, they had none of this. They existed in a vacuum, and from there they spread southwards, to Streatham and Battersea and Purley, and westwards, to Shepherds Bush and Fulham, and then down to the seaside towns, and up into the Midlands until, by 1956, they had taken root all over Britain."

The suits the Teddy Boys wore (mostly tailored) were not exactly what one would call value-for-money for the working-class teenagers. 50 GBP were something which was easily asked for. But the Teds couldn't care less, they didn't give too much of a damn about Zeitgeist morals, politics, philosophy or similar subjects—the most important thing was the style, and they followed it.

Teddy Girls

The photographer Don McCullin remembers, his involvement with a gang of Teds. He lived in Tottenham and hung out with them, but never got fully involved. His recollection, was recounted by Nik Cohn in his piece on Teds with: "I was making 3 pounds a week on the railways, how could I keep up? The Tottenham Royal was the biggest Centre in North London and, the moment you walked in, all the birds would put a price on you. Your jacket, your shoes, even your tie clip—before you'd noticed them, they'd have you costed down to your socks. There was always a greasy comb around. That was a major instrument of attraction. Before you'd asked a girl to dance, you'd stand in front of her and comb your hair, staring at there, with sort of hooded eyes."

"Most of the time, we used to hung around the amusement arcade in Seven Sisters Road and play pin-ball, for a cigarette a replay. Right across the road, there was Greys Dance Hall, where the policeman was stabbed. Bert Assirati, the wrestler, used to be on the door and if he caught you with a razor or bicycle chain, he'd fling you on the street. But there were fights just the same, and knifings and slashings—that's where it all really happened."

The Teddy Girls of which McCullin spoke about were not the typical Petticoat wearing period Teenager as seen in American movies, of that era. The Teddy Girls wore no simple ponytails, they had a shorter haircut, wore caps, trousers, a feminine styled drape jacket, and most of the time carried an umbrella.

Rock Around The Clock

The vacuum, subculture intensity could not last forever. First Ted's had danced to dancehall music by British led Orchestra's. They even had their own dance "The Creep", recorded by The Ted Heath Orchestra. But since Bill Haley's 1953 release of "Crazy Man Crazy" on the London label, the change of musical taste had begun. Lita Roza covered it, and by 1955 when "Rock Around The Clock" as theme song to the Glenn Ford starring youth drama about juvenile delinquency entitled "The Blackboard Jungle" hit cinema's in Britain. Rock and Roll became their music, to this very day.

Ted's slashed cinema seats at the Bill Haley starring films "Rock Around The Clock" and "Don't Knock The Rock" (1956) released by Columbia Pictures.

Tore up the seats, to dance in the aisles. From a minority, it had turned into a more or less mass-appealing lifestyle for young kids. But it did not last forever, National Service was still, young Teds were drafted. The teen-idyll ended. Soldiers also were not allowed to wear Teds' style when leaving the barracks. But the end for the new style came by the newly-converted. Creepers were substituted by winkle-pickers, long-drape jackets were abandoned for the shorter Italian-style jackets. The original Teds, settled down after National Service, other die-hards became the first motorcycled Rockers or Ton Up Boys. And a few, who had sworn in a lifetime, were soon outnumbers by other teen-lifestyles.

In the lean years, middle-aged men, acted like a sect, like a secret society. Organised, like the North Finchley Rock and Roll Preservation Society, they met in back rooms of pubs and appeared once more in their fineries, the velvet drapes and spangled waistcoats and tights, and their hair, or what was left of it, still thick with grease, and sideburns which would make a 'General Sideburn' the alleged names giver for it, proud. Sitting in corners speaking of Eddie Cochran, of James Dean and Mamie Van Doren, remembering a bygone age, when men were men and died as they lived, and women all had big breasts. That was fifteen years after The Teds heyday, seeming distant, stiletto heels, beehives, red ruby lips, Vince Taylor, anyone remembers Sabrina?

Rock 'n' Roll Revival

In 1968 "Rock Around The Clock" by Bill Haley and His Comets was listed again in the UK, US and German Pop-Charts among others. Even the old Columbia pictures had starred in were re-screened. Some new bands such as The Wild Angels (UK), The Houseshakers (UK), The Rock 'n' Roll Gang (FR), Shakin' Stevens and The Sunsets (UK), Crazy Cavan and The Rhythm Rockers … This return to the Roots Rock and Roll was soon to go down in history as "The Rock and Roll Revival".

In the 1970s, a new generation of Teddy Boys was looking for its own identity. Hairspray substituted grease; drapes were at times in the brightest colours one could imagine. The Rockabilly sounds of regional stars who followed the trail of Elvis Presley, who by the way, was someone who followed Bill Haley, and was a lifelong member of his fan club: Soon discovered the Burnette Brothers Johnny and Dorsey with their wild Rockabilly sounds cut for Capitol Records—"The Rock and Roll Trio" augmented live by Paul Burleson, in the studio by Grady Martin, Charlie Feathers, Hank Mizell. (His "Jungle

Rock" is seen as the birth cry of the Reborn Edwardian Generation, and hit the UK charts in 1976.)

Warren Smith, Billy Lee Riley, Charlie Rich, Hayden Thompson, Janis Martin, Wanda Jackson, Carl Mann and many others—soon enjoyed a second career on the British Isles, bigger and more appreciated by their audiences as in their home states south of the Mason-Dixon-Line. Continental Europe was soon to follow. Rockin' Ronny Weiser's "Rollin' Rock" Label soon spread for a Rockabilly resurgence in California. And soon his Original 50s Rockabilly Stars, who recorded now for his label—Mac Curtis, Johnny Carroll, Ray Campi, Jackie Lee Cochran were on demand, once more. Rockin' Ronny Weiser was also the one, who recorded Gene Vincent for a final time.

Rockabilly Rebels vs Teddy Boys

The renewed interest in Rockabilly spread the Teds Gospel further. New bands such as Crazy Cavan and The Rhythm Rockers, The Flying Saucers, The Riot Rockers exported their new-unique sound, today labelled by the New Rockabilly Scene as "Revival" or "Teddy Boy Rock and Roll" and "British Rockabilly" to new shores. It was a more melodic sound, played with electric bass, simply as "Double Basses" and good players of it, were hard to come by in the mid-1970s. The Revival Sounds, played an important role in keeping the longest running 20th and 21st Century Subculture going. New former Teds, soon went for American Vintage clothing, and abandoned the Edwardian rooted Ted's style.

Teddy Boy Band Matchbox dedicated them the song "Rockabilly Rebel" composed by their lead-guitarist Steve Bloomfield, sung by the former lead-singer of The Houseshakers, and new Matchbox singer Graham Fenton. The song became an international smash. There was a bit off a tension between Teddy Boys and Rockabillies, but nothing as big as the Teds vs. Punks riots …

Punks vs Teds

The Teds felt threatened that their image as "The Wildest Cats In Town" was overshadowed by the Punk movement. Some Teds claimed that the Punks stated they would "wipe Teds out", but their hair-colour will be red soon, blood-red" … In London's Kings Road Teds would soon fight with Punks. Don E. Sibley and Dixie Phoenix recorded "Punk Bashing Boogie". The Melody Maker and The Sun Newspaper oiled the fraction with their articles. Originally Vivienne

Westwood's "Let It Rock" Shop was a Teddy Boy boutique, and later she changed it and sold to Punks. So, this could be also one of the reasons for the fights, as well as the re-arrangements of some of Rock and Roll Classics by Punk Bands such as The Sex Pistols and The Clash …

The 1980s Teds Style

The 1980s were a lean time for youth movements in the UK. Un-employment and a general lower interest in the Rockabilly Revival caused by bands such as the Stray Cats, The Polecats and The Jets were critically lesser acclaimed after 1984 … Bands lost chart-momentum and were not booked as often, as before.

Tennessee Rockin'

The Tennessee Rock and Roll Club in North London, led to a renewed interest in the media, thanks to its host Ritchie Gee, who still holds two annual Rock and Roll Weekenders in Pakefield—"The Wildest Cats In Town Rock and Roll Weekender" Summer and Christmas Parties. The death of Sunglasses Ron Staples, named King of The Teddy Boys, was a great loss on a personality level for the Teds. As for a decade he was the spokesperson for the subculture. Evening Standard and TV News reported on the death of Mr Staples, who had died of cancer.

16 August 1977 Teddy Boys gather at Christ Church Cockfosters, London, for a memorial service for American rock singer Elvis Presley. Hundreds of fans were locked out of the service forcing a second one to be hastily arrange.

Let's go back now to see how the world reacted to the death of the King of Rock and Roll, at the untimely age of 42 years old. Why are there since his death Elvis' sightings, so far as we are in this book, it can only be, that the Baby Boomer Generation—lost its dreams with Elvis. That the Baby Boomers were falling at the first sightings into some mode of "Middle Age Craziness" not wanting to accept that the youth of America had left the building, when Elvis Presley did. A similar conspiracy theory exists for James Dean. 1.) He was physically so hurt, when his Porsche Spyder hit the car of Donald Turnipseed (who gave wrong hand signs):

Lester Bangs asking:
Where were you when Elvis died?

As I was not born yet, I rely on information on other people for this part of our Elvis Documentary. Let's see what Lester Bangs had to say, but at first let's see what it was all about that made Lester Bangs such a sought-after Rock-Historian, being in the league of the late Nick Tosches:

Leslie Conway "Lester" Bangs was born on 13 December 1948 in Escondido, California. Whereas his mother was practicing the faith of a Jehovah's witness, his father was an alcoholic. His father supported the family with money he made as truck driver. He died in a fire, when Lester Bangs was only nine years old. His mother raised him in El Cajon in San Diego County, California. He attended the El Cajon Valley High School. He developed a love for writing, jazz music, science fiction and comic books, that getting him through his childhood.

Very briefly, he studied at San Diego State College in 1968. After he was a drop out, he managed to have his first album review in the Rolling Stone Magazine—a year later. He continued to review long plays for Rolling Stone until 1973. Jan Wenner, the editor/publisher fired him finally, for the reason that Lester Bangs reviews seemed to the editor most disrespectful to the artists. Six years later in 1979 he was re-hired for the Rolling Stone. At that time, he began to write album reviews for the Detroit/Michigan based rock-magazine Creem. Lester started writing album reviews for the publication Creem. Having his first work published in an edition in Detroit Creem in 1970.

Lester Bangs later moved to Detroit. There he was promoted to be not only a member of staff but also a head writer for Creem. He influenced the music scene through that mag, until quitting being head writer for Creem in 1976. At this time, still in his Creem days, he became an expert for the burgeoning punk rock music movement of the 1970s and he was able to carve a niche for him as one of the most colourful, distinctive and opinionated rock music critics of his generation. Outside of the Rolling Stone and Creem he also wrote for Fusion, Playboy, Penthouse, New Musical Express and Phonograph Record Magazine.

After departing the Creem team—he moved to New York City and wrote album reviews for the Village Voice. He also recorded a few singles himself, and wrote a book on the band Blondie. He died aged only thirty-three on April 30th, 1982 from an accidental drug overdose, he duly got credit for being one of the great gonzo rock music critics. His love and passion for music is still with us, in his writing.

Where were you when Elvis died? What did you do at that time, and for what doing did you give his death reason? That's what we will talk about here, when remembering this important happening. Like Pearl Harbour or the murder on Kennedy, only individual memories remain. Maybe that must be that way, as Elvis left us alone, as alone as he was himself towards the end. He truly wasn't a man of the people anymore. If you get my drift. If you don't get it, I will allow myself to be more defining. I will take myself away from Elvis and will turn towards the question, why our idols always cement our loneliness.

Not respecting the audience is one of the deadliest sins of any artist. Those who sin that way, will be the one talked about badly, by those who he kicked with his own feet. If he lives forever like Andy "white face" Warhol or fashionably dies early in life like Lenny Bruce, Jimi Hendrix, Janis Joplin, Charlie Parker or Billie Holiday. There end did differ to the end of Elvis for two things: (whereas their drug addicted-careers had much in common): They all died as outsiders of society, and none of them had his audience seen in the way as a God-given present. That makes it harder to see a tragic person in Elvis. To me he seems like the Pentagon, a gigantic out shielded institution. Nobody knows about what it is for or what it stands for and does.

Without the exception that it's power is legendary. Clearly, we all preferred Elvis over the Pentagon, but by now you will have realised, that this is a flat way out comparison. Towards the end Elvis' disrespect to his fans—was obvious—in the creation of "new" albums with already released songs plus one new song on it. That all of us fools would buy them. In our own way of disrespect, which we had in our inner selves for this man. He was god-like like Carlos Castaneda, until the army tamed him and created a dumb square, or rather showed his squareness, which was there already at the beginning. And as sub-normal we waited through two decades that he would show himself as the wild one again. Possibly that he knew that in his own heart, plus the fact that this would never ever occur again. He knew it better himself.

His reason of heart was openly not the reason of our own heart. He himself was a poor dumb Southern boy with an overprotective father-like manager, who kept him away from the outta world. His manager kept him away from everything that could change the fact the he was a nappy-boy, which was responsible to support his family. (…) At last the rock-critics who still felt appreciation towards him, celebrated him for everything he did.

Elvis was a pervert; only a real pervert could release something like "Having Fun With Elvis On Stage", a 1974 stage-album on which only pause filling stage gibberish thaws, which was so redundant, that even Willi Burroughs and Gert Stein shameless in the form of red faces been cemented, should they have listened to it. Elvis was marketing the boredom, while Andy Warhol was still making shoe-adverts, but he sinned again, not realising that his fans were not pervert—they loved him without any prejudice; no matter with what doing he would sing or act for them. They supported him like as if it was a duty to do that.

That's why I feel pity for these poor idiots, more for them, than for Elvis. For whom would we stay a night in the rain, is no one left. The great tragedy is that a whole generation does not give up on their youth, they can't say farewell to their (former) youth. Even though when she already feels her menopausal belly reacting differently and her hair over the horizon starts to miss. Including Elvis and all the other things she believed in her life. Will she still be touched or thinking about the last 20 years of his life?

All their hair is missing over the horizon—including Elvis and all the others things, on which these generation believed in. Will somebody five years from now on, still care what he had done the past 20 years of his life. Certainly Elvis' death is a more sidewinded, ironic moll accord, for those who are living in the general future-lyre. Maybe his death can be symbolised as the 1970s had nothing but warmed-up and brutal demystification; These days three of Elvis' former bodyguards sat together with a grease-finch of the New York Post and are responsible for vomiting a book, from which all the negativities spread against us, if reading it.

Elvis was our last holy cow, which was slaughtered in public; anyone knows that Keith Richards like his Heroine, but if Elvis appears stoned onstage, nobody whispered about amphetamines … In a way it was good or bad at the same time. Good because Elvis did not allow his fellow human beings to assume that he was cool, as of wandering around like a psychopharmatic-book. Bad because that certain Nixon virtue of holding information behind, sold in the USA for some years as the right way, was broken. You could see in Elvis rightfully not only a phenomenon which appeared like thunder and striking in the 1950s and helped to break out of the cage of the soul in the 1960s.

Primarily an exact cultural content of what the Nixon era stood for. Not that his star shined brighter or higher at that time, but his preference for a secluded life, allowed him to neutralise his fans without being made responsible for it.

Clearly stated: It would not be a bad thing for all of us to think if we should not wave him with the middle finger. ...

I learned about Elvis' death while I was sitting with a befriended music journalist borderlinking on his fire ladder over the 21. Street in Chelsea sat. Chelsea is a pleasant district; if you put aside that the where my friend lives, a crazy woman day and night keeps him awake with telling him off in tirades, he decided to stay there. He admires the communities multi-cultureless. There are many wools wearing old communists besides human beings of all races and colours. People who like to be thrown into ethnic groups.

As we have had heard of Elvis' death, we knew that we had to celebrate a night on his death. So, I walked to the next shop, and bought a stack of beer cans. As I stepped out of the house, I passed a few Latinos, who hung out at the entrance door of my friend's house. "Did you hear? Elvis is dead." I told them. They looked me down with a disgust against my person "And so?" was their reply. Maybe I would have gotten a reaction from them, if I told them Donna Summer had passed.

I remember walking through the street with a T-Shirt which proclaimed "Disco is for dumbs", which caused a lot of negative reactions. Which only proved that Elvis was not for everyone the reigning King of Rock and Roll and that Rock and Roll was not the music, many people could relate to it. In the meantime, every correct social person looks for his/her own niche in which she/her can freak out: Whereas the 1960s were very narcissistic, the 1970s were ruled by the Solipsism us and that was nowhere else as obvious as in the world of popular or "Pop"-music. Maybe Elvis was the greatest soloist of them all.

At the store, I asked for two six-packs and told the man behind the counter the news. He seemed to be 50 years old, starting to get grey, had a fat belly, but still life in his eyes and he said: "Damn, what a shame. Now we can only hope that the Beatles will reunite ... Fifty years old. I mean, with that seen through my eyes the absolute fall of human kind would have been reached, and despite of that the Stones should disband now to keep us from further embarrassment. He laughed, told me the way to a butcher down the road. There arrived I asked the sales-man the same question as the man before. He also was around fifty and he said: "You know what? I don't care, if that pig is dead. '73 in Vegas I and my wife went to one of his shows, we paid 14 dollars per nose, he appeared and sang for about twenty minutes. Then he fell. He got up again and sang a few more titles, then he fell again. So, he says "What does it matter, I can also sing it while sitting." He asked the band what songs they should do, but before he got a reply he complained about the lights. "They are too bright. They blind me. Turn 'em off, or I won't hit a single note anymore." They did it.

"So, me and my wife sit in complete darkness and listen to that boy, how he sings songs, which we knew and loved, and if it would have been only his goddamned songs, but he messed them all up. That shitguy. I do not want to say that I am happy that he is dead now, but I know one thing. When I went to see Elvis Presley back then, I had myself soaped in."

The only time that I got to see Elvis was when they soaped me in, but in a very different way. That was in fall 1971, and it happened at the editorial meeting of the magazine Creem, for which I worked then, two tickets for an Elvis show appeared. It was decided, that two employees who had never had the opportunity and privilege to have seen live, would get the tickets. That's how Art Director Charlie Auringer and I landed in the first row of the biggest hall in Detroit. Charlie made the statement: "Do you know how much money we could earn, if we would sell these two damn tickets?" I did not know, but the worth of both tickets, their true worth was clear to me the moment Elvis had entered the stage.

I have never seen a singer, with the exception of him, who stimulated me sexually; it was not a real sexual arousal, more an erection of the heart; when I looked at him, I felt missing, greed, respect and identification-need. It went into excitement. Even Mick Jagger, whom I have seen in 1964 and twice in 1965, could not compete with it, not at all. There Elvis stood, with this There Elvis stood, in a ridiculous costumed white suit, he looked like a threatening stronghold from the times of King Arthur!

He was overweight, and his belt buckle was as big as the head, only that the head of it was not made out of pure gold, and anyone below Elvis would have looked like a caricature of Neil Diamond. But it definitely suited Elvis! What would not have suited him? Never, how lousy his records had turned, never matter, how much he allowed himself to be satisfied with mediocracies, always something seemed to point at something, it still shined and stroke from the days when … well I didn't live them, that's why I won't allow myself a comment on these days. Only saying: Elvis Presley was the man, that enriched the American Entertainment Business (with it the country itself, because mentioning America and Entertainment-Art in one line is almost tautology.

It was said that he was the first white who sounded like a black, which factually was wrong, but culturally it has it's correctness. More meaning comes

197

to it, when Elvis started to do hip-swivelling, and Ed Sullivan denied to show that on Television, the whole nation a hefty breakdown in sexual frustration experienced. Followed by long-lasting dissatisfaction, which reached its highest toll in the beginning of a psychedelic-militant folklore culture: That was the 1960s. Now don't mention Lenny Bruce, man—Lenny Bruce openly spoke offensively and chose freely to become a martyr.

Besides of that Lenny Bruce was hip, too goddamned hip, if you ask me, that broke his neck. While Elvis never was hip. Elvis was a goddamn truck-driver, who adored his mother and who would never have said in her presence shit or fuck. But nevertheless, Elvis hit the nose of America with the fact, that he had hips, which categorised asking remained unfulfilled. Lenny Bruce showed us how far you could go in a repressive society and how much it allowed one to do so. While Elvis put hits like "How Much Is That Doggie in The Window" away and substituted them with "Let's fuck". Under this storm, we still stagger.

In our times, there is sexual chaos, but from these streaming real understanding and harmony could become reality. However, Elvis opened almost singlehanded all of the channels. That night in Detroit, an evening which I never will forget, he only needed to move a bit with a shoulder muscle, not even do things with his arms, that the girls who were hit with his stream, screamed and lost their consciousness or cried. Sinatra, Jagger, the Beatles—you won't find anyone else on your mind either, whoever created such a mass-hysteria. And that after one and a half decade made shit records, decades in which Elvis never tried to overwork himself.

Should love really go out of fashion—forever, I'm not a believer, then to all of our trimmed non-interest about our fellow human beings a further dislike to our objects of desire will become reality. I found, it was Iggy Stooge, you found it was Joni Mitchell whoever brought you out of your painful and seldomly ecstatic life being, on a definitive strictly instrumental point musically to describe. That's how we all will become individuals, because now it seems all enjoy solipsism us. It is a king, which power even numbers Elvis out. But I can guarantee one thing: Never again, we will have such a similar opinion like on an icon like Elvis. So, I won't make myself the work to farewell his body. I rather say farewell to you. *(Lester Bangs)*

Rock and Roll Fan Bernadette Coombs remembers where she was the day Elvis died as follows: "Between two of those days, I was at home, with my family as I first heard of the devastating news in the evening on our daily TV evening prime time news, on August 16th of the year. We were getting ready to travel on our Summer vacation, and during the next day in the morning, just before we left home for our vacation, we heard the sad news again on the radio, BBC World News which used to air daily at 8:00 or 9:00 in the morning. Otto, that was one of the most heart-breaking times of my whole life. To me, it was the most tragic death since the violent death of President John F. Kennedy in 1963. Both me and my mother, who was also a loyal fan of Rock and Roll and other Rock genres, she was just as devastated as I was. That is my story."

Dennis Plateothores who would make a career in the hotel business was in his early teens, when he learned that Elvis had died: "I was 14 years old already a fan and I remember it like yesterday! It was a hot day and I was working at my dad s stationary store and hearing whispers on the street as I would take breaks outside—Elvis is Dead!—I literally went in a state of numbness, turning the radio on confirmed my horror and fears-I cried all the way home!"

Glenda Metivier from Ontario, Canada reacted the following: "I was in my kitchen with the radio playing, when the news came on about Elvis passing, I sat down at my kitchen table and could not believe what I had just heard … I was in shock."

Carol Petitt: "I was working in the garden and heard it on the radio we had outside. It broke my heart."

Marcia Allsbrook Royal: "I was cooking dinner for my family. A friend, who was a huge Elvis fan (who took me to see him in concert in 1976), called and told me among many tears that Elvis was gone. I turned on the TV and there it was. I cried for many days—still cry to this day!"

Trudi Boyle: "I was lifting a patient from her bed to a commode, I heard it on the morning News (in Australia) … I nearly dropped her, I had to sit down and calm myself … I couldn't believe what I was hearing, this couldn't be right, not Elvis! Devastated, I sat home that night by myself watching everything on TV and crying all night … and I'm still not over it!"

John Symes: "4:30 am on way to work; I was 17."

Ian Mc George: "I was at home. My family told me to come and watch the TV news. Still remember it very clearly. The newsreader on UK TV (Reginald Bosanquet) said, "I for one, hope it's not true.""

Redden Transporters: "I was 16 years old when he passed away and I couldn't believe it; at first I thought it was a bad dream. I enjoyed his movies and songs."

Bertha Shrivjer-Pol: "I was 31 years old and that day, I didn't speak, I was silent, my daughter she was six years old, she remembered that day very well because her mother's behaviour was very strange!"

Anthony DiStasi: "I was to see Elvis at his next concert at the Coliseum in Long Island NY. In his honour, I still hold the tickets today on the wall in my office. Long live the King!"

Lori Tiller: "I was home listening to the radio when it came over the air, I was shocked and I cried."

Edward Moller: "On my way to a softball game."

Pat Rice: "I was with the family at the championship soap box derby race in Ohio my youngest son had won the race in Charlotte and was racing for the national championship. The news came over the TV. I left my room and went to my friends' room and we stood there and held each other and cried."

Sabrina Lavocah: "I was at home just got back from London after visiting my uncles grave who was a big Elvis fan, and had passed away 2 weeks before, watched the news and was so shocked and saddened by it, the next morning went to the news agents really early and bought different newspapers."

Nadine Davis: "I was at work my husband picked me up told me Elvis had died I just started crying didn't stop for 2 days I love Elvis and always will."

Robbie McCurdy: "I was working at my father's furniture store in the warehouse my two brothers came in and said they had bad news that Elvis had died. I was a big, big fan had all his records I even had a band that I played with and I did all Elvis music but all my friends called me to tell how sorry they were about it."

Fran Beach: "I was babysitting it on the radio. I was devastated! I have been a fan since I heard Elvis sing on the Ed Sullivan show. It broke my heart and I cried for a week. I would have given anything to go to Graceland for his funeral. He was and still is my greatest singer of all times and I will hold him in my heart forever."

Cindy Sharp Dobson: "I was 10 years old; I was playing outside and ran in the house for a drink. I ran past the television just as the News Anchor said Elvis had died. I bolted to the kitchen to get my Mom, who was fixing dinner, we both ran back to watch and just cried and cried. My sister came in to the house looking for me and found us both just bawling ... scared the daylights out of her. I will never forget it."

Shirley Garrett: "I am so glad I got to talk to Elvis shake his hand I will never forget him and I got scarce."

Pallavi Ghosh: "All my buddies who were in the US were missing me and wondering how to reach this tragic news to me. I couldn't find our before the 18th of August, as those days communication was a challenge. I couldn't believe he had just gone. A part of India still doesn't."

Judy Young: "I got in my car and when I turned on the radio, I then found out that Elvis had died. I was devastated and so was everyone … It was a big deal on the news (probably as big as the Corona Virus). They played his music and talked about him for days."

Cissie Low Long: "School shopping in Cinti. Ohio."

Theresa Bretta Schletter: "I was watching The Gong Show. When a friend came over and told me! I couldn't believe it, a world without Elvis. I was 15 at the time."

Cindy Todd: "I was feeding Tommy to. It took my breath."

Jillene Cook: "I started housework heard on radio my mouth fell open couldn't believe turned on radio to check then thought it's the day the MUSIC DIED!"

Judy Tullis: "I was half way between Nashville and Memphis, on my way to Graceland. I was driving so I couldn't get to upset. I was more determined to get here. It was my first-time visiting Graceland."

Sandra Morgan Lee: "I was working at the dress shop when our old boss who had moved to Memphis to run a dress shop there, called and told us at the shop, I was devastated, I had been a fan since 12 years old, then my old boss sent me all the clippings from the Memphis paper."

Alan Raymond: "Mum woke me up just before I had to get up for work was in shock all day at work, I remember just playing Elvis songs for a week."

Ted Carpenter: "I was at Swinnerton Army training camp when the news came on the radio. A sad day."

Help Me Make It Through the Night

Memphis/Tennessee: The Memphians are suffering from a heat wave, it is a Monday, 15 August 1977—every morning the temperature rises after a subtropical wet night to 40 degrees. The windows of the houses, typically for the US all equipped with air-conditioners, are wet with condensation. The air is not really of any breathing quality. The streets look like at the raceways of Formula

One broadcasts of the time. The sun glows like a heating plate on an oven of the time.

Graceland is a Southern Mansion, more conventional than other mansions, but the white columns clarify the house and its inhabitants as Southern. We are in the heart of Dixie, in Whitehaven. Today a predominately African-American community in Memphis/Tennessee. Originally founded as a neighbourhood for upper-class families. Today, its inhabitants are 50,000 people.

Some of the other founding family names a Francis White, who settled early and became a major property owner. He was also very influential in having the rail line run through what was at first called White's Station. Later it was renamed to Whitehaven. This Mississippi and Tennessee Railroad enterprise was chartered in 1853, the first trains were seen in 18856. IN 1871, so quite a while after, the first "White Haven Post Office" was opened. Roads and railway connected the cotton farms of the Mississippi Delta to the markets of Memphis. Strong commercial links were established. The family's Raines, Hale, McCorkle and Harbin moved to the area in the 1880s and opened a store close to where Whitehaven High School is situated today on Elvis Presley Boulevard. The store of Hale's was a landmark for many decades.

WREC Radio began operating in Whitehaven in 1926—two years later, as early as 1928 Hoyt B. Wooten an inhabitant from Whitehaven was given one of the first six television licenses in the US. His original home is the c centrepiece of a private development called Lion's Gate. Carrington Jones and Lacy Mosby were responsible for the baby boomer residential and commercial development Whitehaven experienced. It was like today moving outside the city to a more pleasant environment, similar to cities of today in Europe like London, Vienna or Brussels. With that, the old transformed plantation tracts were now the neighbourhoods of the 1940s and 1950s.

In 1950, Whitehaven had a population of 1 311. Ten years later, in 1960, when Elvis returned there to his home Graceland the population had grown to 13,894. Officially, Whitehaven was annexed to the city of Memphis on 1 January 1970, the integration into Memphis had begun by the late 1960s. Today it is proclaimed as the capital of South Memphis. Ba. Nock to Monday, 15 August 1977—it's still very quiet at Graceland. Nobody is at work in the building. No Party, no games. The highlight is a nine years old Lisa Marie Presley, Elvis' daughter who drives in her blue-custom made golf car around the lanes of the building. Upstairs in the former bedroom of her parents her dad Elvis lies in the

2,74 x 2,74 extra-large double bed. He is already ten hours to bed. It's 4:00pm, the usual time for Elvis to get up from bed.

The room due to air-conditioning is at 20 centigrade, outside rain and lightning pushed down the hot day to 25 centigrade. In the bedroom is an extra climate machine on the windows, it's the one which guarantees for 24h perfect sleeping temperature for the man who is seen by the world as The King. Elvis makes his living in the heat of the stage, lightning, stage shows, camera flashes are not easy to bear for the 42-year-old. So, he prefers coolness when he can allow it to himself. He doesn't like lighted and heated rooms, some say he even despairs.

The big windows which were part of the architecture Graceland with the thought to show striking views to the green lawns, in a sunny light, are always darkened. The windows glass is with the same material darkened: Imitated leather, with black buttons. The only light tender lightning light bulbs, which are built in a gold green, black dots Naugahyde-blanket filled.

In this pillowed mussel, which is comparable with the backseat of a limousine, Elvis rests for days, sometimes also in unconsciousness. In forgetting he seeks his freedom from all the worries, which give him a hard life. He explains it often with a standard line, that he is quoted by often: "It's better to be unconsciousness than to feel depressed terrible."

The key to forgetting are prescribed-medications. Elvis relies on them for many years, he takes high doses. He seems to be unhealable of ever getting rid of these psychopharmacologies. It seems to be impossible that he will ever be clean again from medication. As one of his doctors denied him to let him sleep for three days in a row, Elvis got up on the cocktail table, took two 45 guns out and shot on the ceiling of the suite of the Hilton Hotel. "Then I buy a goddamned pharmacy!" he screamed, and did just that.

Every night when he goes to bed, he takes a high number of pills, which could narcoticize a horse. The reason is that he is sleepless, that's what the claim of his is. To get rid of this symptoms Elvis' personal medic Dr George Nichopolus, who would also treat Elvis former rival for the title King of Rock and Roll Jerry Lee Lewis, would subscribe a bizarre mixture of prescriptible drugs, which became the most important routine on the King's household. Elvis usually goes at 4:00am to bed, all his life he was a Noctambuler, a human being who preferably and most of the time lives at night. At this time, he dresses in a blue, green or yellow nylon-pyjamas (if he didn't wear it already during the day). He weighs 1125 kilos and most of the weight is centred around his belly.

Albert Goldman who wrote two books on Elvis, giving him among Elvis Fans the saying, the he won't ever enter Rock and Roll Heaven, described Elvis as looking like his own mother Glady's who according to Goldman was an alcoholic, whereas he sees a drug addict in Elvis. Both is not quite right, Elvis was not a street drug user, he relied on the pharma-industry. Plus, in the 1950s it was not common to have a drink against a negative or for a positive experience. I recently made a, why if I re-recognise faces, and I don't see in Elvis his 46 years old mother who was very sick, died premature. Probably she was the same over-protective mother Hank Williams had …

As soon as Elvis feels comfortable in his bed, he asks one of his helpers to give him the first doses, his sleeping pills, he yearns, to be sleeping soon. The helper, mostly a well-built muscled man, gets a small brown paper bag, with eleven sleeping pills and three one-way injections are. Filled with Demerol. These drug packets are prescribed to him by Dr Nichopolus, handing it to Senior-nurse Letitia "Tish" Henley. She works during the day at Dr George Nichopolus Doctor's surgery. In the evening, she can be found on the grounds of Graceland, she and her husband Tommy live in a caravan. Tommy also has his job on the grounds of Graceland. Trish job it is to check the consumption of prescribed medication of Elvis.

Now the helper gives light-coloured pills and capsules to Elvis—Elvis calls them his "little jewels". Elvis takes them directly in his hand, and drinks fast, and full of routine with spring water down. When Elvis has taken all of his pills, he rolls out of bed and puts on his pyjamas-top. The helper looks for Elvis Acne suffering back for a right position to give him the Demerol-injection. Elvis prefers it under the shoulders, close to his spine. Because then there are no marks left on his back, his hips, his bum or his thighs. This regularly injection have left his skin leather like. Sometimes the needle gets damaged. The tablets are mostly calming for the central nerve system. Mostly the Barbiturates, Amytal, Barbital, Nembutal and Seconal. All make the user dependent, but are neutralised in calming, after the user has developed an immunity against them.

Notes, as published by Albert Goldman, translated from the German language of his book on Elvis last 24 hours:

Generally, the beginning of Elvis' drug addiction was blaming a Sergeant of the US-Army in Germany, who gave his soldiers tablets, that they would not fall asleep when pulling guard at night. This story should show Elvis in the light as a human being, who was without the ability to blame his person, while serving the Army, became addicted to prescribed medication. In truth Elvis had taken drugs years before serving for Uncle Sam—Uppers. In question is—how that occurred? Colin Escott, the author of an upcoming Elvis Biography about the record label SUN Records, quoted in the music magazine GOLDMINE, in an Interview with a man named Jimmy Denson, that Elvis was still a teenager when both (Denson and Presley) were close.

Escott asked Denson, how from the shy, soft and rarely speaking, passive "Baby Elvis" the wild Hillbilly Cat became. Jimmy Denson's reply was "Drugs". He needed them, to get out of himself. Dewey Phillips (the first Disc jockey, who ever played a recording an Elvis Presley recording on the radio, and is renown as someone who popped pills) gave it to Elvis—Amphetamine's and Benzedrine. That set his energy's free. On the other side, it's not the day someone tries drugs out, it's rather the day when the addiction sets in.

For Elvis this did not happen until 1972, when he was feeling the pain of his break-up with Priscilla. From this time on, he became a hopeless drug addict and continued to experiment with other drugs, especially barbiturates and narcotics. A few years after Elvis had passed on, in January 1980, Dr Nichopolus was asked to a appear at an hearing. The commission came to the conclusion that there were at least 10 patients which were overprescribed by legal drugs, by the Doctor. They removed him his legal allowance for operating as a Doctor for three months.

For the next three years, he was under watch. In May 1980, a law-suit came in front of a judge, the jury of the county Shelby blamed him for two cases in which he hopelessly overprescribed. The court ruling happened in October. After five weeks, Nichopolus was cleared in all cases. His lawyer was James F. Neal, the state attorney in the Watergate case. It took five weeks until Nichopolus was cleared. Viewers of the judgement meant that it was James F. Neal who got him cleared, and blamed also partially the mistakes of the local authorities. Neal had built his defence on the "good Samaritan".

As of that, Dr George Nichopolus risked his doctorship for the treating of one hopeless case not with knowing that this could or would break his neck for his profession. He saw the danger for his professional reputation, as he saw it *as his duty as a medic, to protect his patients he took that risk full knowingly. To keep his patients away from Doctors who had no fear of prescribing from illegal sources to this patient. The further tactic of the defence was that he indeed prescribed Elvis Presley 19,000 cans during the 31 ½ life-months of Mr Presley with thinking that these drugs were paid fully by Elvis Aron Presley but consumed by him alone.*

Some people might come to the conclusion that this alone makes him guilty, while others would claim that these were partial facts at least. Proof was also that Nichopolus also gave prescriptions to Marty Lacker, who in eleven months got 1,745 Placidyl, approximately 5 tons of tablets. Despite of that the complete number of drug-cans, were 5 1110 for a year. Would you count the drugs to that, which Elvis took to stay alive and functioning, and badly relied on at home and on concert tour, the 19,000 cans of prescribed drugs seem to be accurate?

This makes Elvis increasing the doses, which is very dangerous, as the body is used to it too quickly and the increased dosage seems always too low. In any handbook of prescribed medication, there is a diagram, on which both lines—the used being to it—the increasement. When both lines meet—the patient dies. The little package of Placidyl and Quaalude, which are chemistry wise different to barbiturates, but have a similar affect—are as dangerous as the barbiturates. Adding Valium, Americas most drug abused medication, to calm, plus Valmid for restlessness and sleeplessness. Demerol eases pain, while it is used instead of morphism, but makes one as addicted as the last mentioned. Elvis' pain is of psychological nature.

More of these drugs together, has to be made with great care. To take all of it ruins your health. It means risking one's life every time resting his health on a pillow. Elvis did this for years. He seems to be the only case of that nature. Dr med. Norbert Weissman the leading director of the bio-science laboratories in Van Nuys, California, who checked Elvis death body for chemical substances. Was stated as saying he never found a body with so many drugs as Elvis'. The immense amount and the various drugs cannot be taken under consideration for medical reasons. They show one of Elvis' traits: the man who has an unbound and unsatisfiable appetite. He was compared with the young Dionysus, who drives his crazy fans into a frenzy. In reality he is closer to the kid Gargantua, that giant baby and it's immense appetite for eat and drink, which is only equal to gain satisfaction with other beings, like onaniating …

I am so lonely I could die—it's so easy to die and so hard to lead a life.

Heartbreak Hotel turns into suicide glam

Elvis has luck: He is still alive. Again and again he survives overdoses after overdoses. The adding of crises such as these and the consistent increasement of taking drugs like these, seem to ensure that he will live not for much longer. Dying suddenly, but not unexpectedly. He seems to develop a yearning to die. Often, he says: "It's easy to die, but hard to live." He's also scared most of his employees as if he acted as he was planning suicide.

In his family, suicide was well known. Two cousins of Elvis, Junior and Bobby Smith, took their own life. Bobby Smith took an overdoses of the poison Arsen. When he rehearsed onstage for his upcoming CBS TV Special, he told his guys, "I might not look good currently, but I will look better in my coffin." January his grandfather passed, at the funeral, while passing the coffin he made the statement: "It might not last long from now, until I am ready for that." He talks often about the Hawaiian Medicine Man and Magicians and Healers, who know exactly when they will pass on. David Stanley the son of Dee Presley, the second wife of Elvis father Vernon, which he married after Gladys had passed stated: "He talked himself into death. It circulated all around dying. Until he did."

Even positive experiences were recounted after they occurred in a negative way by Elvis. He had met his former wife Priscilla at their house in the Canyon in Beverly Hills. They had a good time together; trustfulness and positive vibes were noted. But on the way back Elvis turned melancholic and said: "Lisa will be taken good care of." David Stanley asked: "What you are talking about? You will see her again real soon."

"That will show." Elvis replied. Maybe it was an alarming sign, a cry for help, that he was considering suicide but did not have the guts to do it, and asked his surroundings for help, getting him away from it, trying to overcome this crisis, that he was in, at the relatively young age of 42 years. Not young for a Rockstar, but definitely too young to die. Everyone who knew him, who was close, was worried, but there was not much that they could do for him.

Like a little Caesar, the almighty rules in his own small very private kingdom and makes all around him to appreciates of what he is doing. The others work so hard, that they haven't much time of thinking of much else. Joe Esposito, who served with Elvis in Germany in the Army, stated that at the end they did not know much what was going on around in the world. No news, no papers, it was all their little kingdom being with their boss and friend Elvis Presley. No one has the authority to speak against Elvis, or keep him from doing something he wants to do.

A few years ago, Colonel Tom Parker, his manager was an almost equal partner who influenced a lot of the important decisions in Elvis life. But they were never buddies. Over the years the relation even cooled and they treated each other sometimes as enemies. Elvis said he would fire Parker for various reasons, mostly because he never toured Europe because Parker prevented him from doing so. Shortly before Elvis died, Parker tried to sell his 50% interest in his business interests in Elvis Presley. Love and money make Elvis not different. He remains morbid.

The closest relationship he ever had with a woman after Priscilla was with Linda Thompson, a former Miss Tennessee. Linda was the ideal woman for Elvis, until she betrayed him for his piano player David Briggs. Priscilla left him with his Karate-instructor Mike Stone. No wonder Elvis was in a deep crisis, he had felt a kinship to both woman and as he was a very spiritual person, since meeting "New Age" hair stylist Larry Geller, with whom he had planned to write his auto-biography, he was in a very special way religious and/or spiritual. Linda Thompson had the ability to engage in all of Elvis moods, was he passionate, so was she, she got him all worked up for the "Aloha from Hawaii" TV Special, in 1973. His career peaks.

In one moment, she was sexy, then the beautiful lady of the South, in the next she helped him to overcome things in not a motherly, but very adult female way. She was neither weak nor dumb. She saw what the drugs did to Elvis, and she was partly successful in getting him off or to decrease the doses he took. On tours, Elvis got often rude and finally she knocked at the door of Elvis piano player and had intercourse with him. He was not special, just lucky to be awake, while Elvis either read in one of his books of Larry or was simply asleep.

Elvis had a special relationship with his father. I would not necessarily point out that it was a hateful one. Rather that Elvis fathered his own dad. Maybe he took that role after Gladys died. Also, Gladys was more of the ruler of the then young family. Elvis always wanted to tell his father what to do, be it in love life, or professionally. Elvis and his dad used the same body language, so they were very similar. Maybe too similar which led to tension. For a while the Memphis Mafia, Elvis bodyguards copied Elvis way as well. His walk, his expressions, until they saw it with Vernon. Wondering if Vernon was copying his son, but then realising that it was Elvis who had a lot of his father.

Elvis always followed the advice of his mother, but not so with Vernon, his dad. Albert Goldman describes Vernon Presley as a weakling and simulant, who never cared much about work or responsibility. Educated guess neither Goldman nor me knew Vernon or were behind the gates of Graceland, when father and son were alone. So, this statement cannot be a simple fact. True that Vernon was in jail for writing out a cheque that wasn't covered in Tupelo/Mississippi—Elvis' birthplace. 4 months in jail must have had an aspect in Vernon's further life.

He also bootlegged alcohol—and it was for that—that the family moved from Tupelo to Memphis. As a young man Elvis often was full of anger about his father, but towards the end of his life, Vernon was severely heart sick. His doctor asked him not to walk further than 15 meters, without taking a break from going that small distance. It took Elvis some time to accept that his Daddy married after Gladys, a younger lady who would be Dee Presley.

By 1977 Dee had left Vernon, and he looked for love with the nurse Sandy Miller. Sandy was a nice and caring person, perfect for the older care-needing Vernon Presley. But Elvis wanted Vernon to return to Dee. He told her son David Stanley: "Tell Dee, I pay her 10,000 Dollars, if she comes back and discusses with me her return to Daddy." But Goldman's conclusion in his second book on Elvis is correct, Vernon was the black sheep, and Elvis overtook the role of being the father of his own father.

The man who should be worried the most about Elvis Presley's health would be his doctor: Dr George Nichopoulos, indeed he tries to keep Elvis away from other sources, that can provide overdosed medication. Sometimes Dr Nick, as he is called by Elvis and entourage also gives his patient placebos. At every fall out with Dr Nick, Elvis has another medic who is eager to prescribe him whatever he wants. Medicine is help, but like everything in the world it is based on economics. There would be dozens of medics who would take the opportunity with both arms to be Elvis Presley's personal Doctor.

How about Elvis himself? His only forthcoming, next to the scriptures he reads, all provided by Larry Geller his spiritual guidance and hairstylist, are drugs.

When Elvis' drug condition worsened, Larry Geller was no longer part of the Memphis Elvis Presley Crew, as Geller emphasised with Elvis' wish to actually separate from Priscilla Presley and marry his 1964 co-star from "Viva Las

Vegas", Ann Margret, he was kicked out by the Colonel, with many warnings indirectly before.

A day before the wedding of Elvis Aron Presley and Priscilla Beaulieu set for 1 May 1967 in Las Vegas, Nevada—Elvis once more overprescribed his medications. I doubt it was a suicidal action, as the Elvis at this time was too much of a seeker for why we are here, and where we should go, and what it is that we should achieve for our undying soul or spiritual wellbeing. But I find it reasonable, that he tried to get admit into a hospital, and so jeopardise the wedding—and somehow win Ann-Margret back. Larry Geller who also wrote two books on Elvis, found Ann Margret as a Female Elvis, possibly if you'd translate it into Geller's and Presley's personal language—as his twin soul, incarnated to find him and marry him ... To state it down-to-earth, they were made for each other, and maybe, but just maybe she could have done for him what June Carter did for Johnny Cash—get him off the uppers and downers ...

Elvis had proposed to Priscilla shortly before Christmas 1966, some source claiming that she had threatened to "take her story to the press" ... This source also claims that her father would have threatened him to have Elvis charged under the Mann act; "taking a minor across state lines for sexual purposes". Plus Colonel Parker insisting on the moral clause in Elvis Presley's RCA records recording contract.

Priscilla recalled the proposal in the book "Elvis by the Presleys" as follows: "Elvis was a non-conformist. In many ways, though, he was an old-fashioned gentleman who loved tradition. Christmas always put Elvis in a good mood, but this year he seemed especially happy. I could hear it in voice when he knocked on my dressing room door and said we needed to talk. Before I let him in, I jokingly demanded that he stated our secret password. "Fire eyes", he said. Fire eyes was the name I gave him when he lost his temper and his eyes lit up like flames. Other times, his eyes were soft and gentle. His eyes, the windows of his soul, reflected his changing passions.

When he opened the door and walked towards me, I could see his eyes were fiery, but it was a fire of joy. He dropped to his knees and handed me a small box. Inside was a magnificent diamond engagement ring.

My heart's desire had been realised. What could I say but yes? We'd lived together for five years. In those years I had learned to love him on a deeper level. I knew his problems. I saw them first-hand. I worried about the pills he took, I worried about his mood swings, I realised his soul was uneasy, that he was searching for spiritual answers that had eluded him. But none of that had stopped our love. The love grew, I very much wanted to be his wife." Priscilla's father, Captain Paul Beaulieu said: "Elvis honoured the commitment he made to me when Priscilla left Germany for Memphis. I respected him for that. And still do."

As most psychological issues lie in one's childhood—it should be also so with Elvis Presley:

Elvis counted himself all of his life, maybe unconsciously among the poor. He was spoiled as a kid, but due to the poor financial stand of his family, plus the fact that the lived in a shack near the Afro-American community, at that time in the South as what people called him and his family—"white trash". As pupil without much favour by fellow students because of his bizarre clothes from Lansky's in Beale Street, he dreamed of making it as a singer—maybe even so as a Gospel singer. Gospels remained his favourite music during his entire life.

He was very similar to Johnny Cash; both auditioned at SUN, trying to present themselves as Gospel singers, but as Philips saw no money in it, they both became worldly singers, but always with the possibility by their labels to release Gospel recordings, perform it on TV, or on concert stage. Both thought to be special in the way of their faith—and all their life they worried about their souls and the souls of their next-neighbours. "Love thy neighbour as thyself" (Jesus Christ). Both fell for the same woman—June Carter Cash—yes also Elvis was interested in here, she kept his love letters her entire life, and left them behind for the world thereafter.

Elvis' first two years in the music industry were immensely successful, scandalous, rebellious, filled with the right amount of rockability, but soon he was sent to Germany by the Army after training in Fort Hood, Texas. In the two years serving his country as GI, he was very worried that other young singers would put him in second row, the same Elvis intended to do with Bill Haley who was crowned to be The King of Rock and Roll after a string of hits like "Rock The Joint", "Crazy Man Crazy", "Live It Up", "Fractured", "Shake, Rattle and Roll", "Dim Dim The Lights" and most of all for "Rock Around The Clock" The source for Elvis actually being possessed with becoming the next King of Rock and Roll is his best man George Klein, for Elvis' wedding with Priscilla, who wrote it in his book on Elvis Presley!

Maybe even more worrying to him might have been the fact that it was actually Colonel Tom Parker who supposedly advised Uncle Sam that Elvis Presley should serve. As he was 1a Level at the test for health and abilities, he had to serve straight away. Colonel Tom Parker's intention was to get Elvis out of the scandals he was in. He shocked the nation, while Jerry Lee Lewis "corrupted the American youth" (Lewis later stating this at a live show more than a decade later) with "Whole Lotta Shakin' Goin On". His mother Glady's Love Presley was shocked and became depressed, especially when she heard that he would have to serve in Germany. Remember the war was still pretty fresh in people's mind, World War 1 even part of the story in the Elia Kazan directed "East of Eden" starring James Dean—and there the Germans were the bad guys once more ... Though the hate was shown towards them, when they got abused on the street, for being of German decency.

While he was serving, his mother got hepatitis and died shortly after, this changed the young Rock and Roll Kid forever ...

Would he consider suicide to see his mother, was all the Gospels aimed that he sang, often still for hours after shows, with his back-up singers a prayer to be with God, and leave his earthly being?

A Mansion on the Hill to Die In?

Elvis Presley's home for twenty years of his life. The address was 3764 Elvis Presley Boulevard, Memphis/Tennessee, 38116 (Telephone: EX 7-4427. Located in the suburb of Whitehaven (annexed by Memphis in 1969), Graceland had been used as a church by the Graceland Christian Church. Its 13 ¾ acres of land was purchased by Elvis in March 1957 from Ruth Brown Moore for USD 102,500 (40,000 Dollars in cash, 55,000 Dollars for the Presley's house on Audubon Drive, and a 37,000 note carried by Equitable Life at 4 percent interest), beating out the Memphis YMCA's bid of just 35,000 Dollars. Graceland was established as a farm during the American Civil War (1861–1865) by publisher S. E. Toof of the Memphis Daily Appeal, on land that originally covered 500 acres in Whitehaven. Toof named his estate Graceland after his daughter, Grace Toof. The present estate house was constructed in the late 1930s by Dr Thomas and Ruth Moore. Ruth was the niece of Grace Toof. The couple's daughter—Ruth Marie was a professional musician who sold Graceland to another professional musician/singer—Elvis Presley.

The two-story mansion was constructed of tan Tennessee limestone and originally contained twenty-three rooms, including five bedrooms. Elvis painted the mansion blue and gold, which glowed at night. The front room featured a white marble fireplace and Louis XIV furniture, Elvis added several rooms, including a trophy room. This room was forty-foot long and built over the back patio. It began as a playroom where Priscilla had given him a small set for Christmas in 1965. Now it displays Elvis' sixty-three gold singles, twenty-six platinum albums, and thirty-three gold albums. When Elvis died, there were sixteen TV sets at the mansion. On the grounds, Elvis built a barn and a racquetball court. Alabama fieldstone built the wall that was constructed in 1957 to surround Graceland.

He also built a 200,000 Dollars private recording studio at Graceland. A portable mobile recording studio was brought to Graceland by RCA on two occasions in 1976—2–8 February and 29–31 October. Some of the songs recorded at Graceland include "Way Down", "Pledging My Love", "Moody Blue" and "Solitaire". After 16 August 1977 Graceland was valued at 500,000 Dollars but it's annual upkeep was running reportedly 500,000 Dollars with a 12,000 yearly utility bill. Rather than selling the estate, Priscilla acting for Lisa Marie, decided to open it for the public, charging 5 Dollars a visitor. On the Graceland tours visitors can see the living room, music room, dining room, music room, TV room, pool room, jungle den, and the automobile collection in the Elvis Presley Automobile Museum.

Over the years, Graceland has had an average of about 2500 visitors a day. In 1986, singer Paul Simon recorded the album Graceland, in which he sings. In 1988, the songs about Graceland as a symbol of redemption. This long play won the Grammy's award for the year 1987. In 1988, the song "Graceland" won a Grammy award for Record of the year. The album won the Grammy for album of the year before.

According to Lucy de Barbin in her book "Are You Lonesome Tonight"— Elvis was inspired to buy Graceland because it was located on Bellevue Road, Bellevue being Lucy's middle name.

When Elvis was discharged from the Army in 1960, he focused on continuing his movie career in Hollywood. He felt lonely and was sensitive and lonely. That's how it came that he built his "Memphis Mafia", paid friends who isolated him from the to him foreign Hollywood and boosted his self-esteem. He was ready to fulfil his dream of being a movie-star, an actor he never really became, thanks to Colonel Tom Parker—his film career went downhill at the end of the 1960s. His beach movie like films would become little recognition by the film industry of Hollywood. Worse was that the soundtrack albums were the songwriting work of third-class songwriters, who were ready to give 1/3 of ¼ royalty payment to Elvis.

For years, he had hits, but nothing in the league of his former quality hits. At this time, Elvis met Larry Geller, and learned about the spiritual world. He thought that he became not for no-reason a megastar. That he had his purpose in life. This led to choose his futuristic stage-wear in the 1970s. At the end of the 1960s, the radical change of the music industry reached Hollywood. Especially when producer Hal Wallis was stated as saying that the Elvis movies were made, to produce proper work with the money the generated. But in 1968 it came to a return to original Rock and Roll especially in Europe, where Bill Haley and The Comets would lead a Rock and Roll Revival, this had reached in 1969 the US with the Richard Nader Rock and Roll Revival Shows which had every big 1950s and early 1960s Rock and Roll Star appear either at Madison Square Garden or go on package tours—Bill Haley, Chuck Berry, Jerry Lee Lewis, Bo Diddley, Fabian, Jimmy Clanton, Dion, Chubby Checker, Little Richard only Elvis was left out.

He only revisited his early work in the 1968 NBC TV Special, a live show in 9 years—today known as 1968 Comeback Special which Elvis didn't like, as he never saw himself career-wise down. He and Sam Phillips also despised the name Rockabilly which they felt as bringing a Rock and Roll singer down to be a rockin' Hillbilly. Today the Rockabilly industry still has its own niche in the music field, whereas almost no money is generated for many who contribute to it. According to Ronny Weiser who had formed the Rollin' Rock Music Magazine and Rollin' Rock Records after he did the final recordings with Gene Vincent and rediscovered regional "Elvises" like Mac Curtis, Jackie Lee Cochran, Johnny Carroll, Ray Campi—regional Rockabilly singers of the 1950s who would make a bigger career during the Rockabilly Revival Years of the 1970s and 1980s—the term Rockabilly was reintroduced to differ the music's styles from the progressive sounds of groups like the Rolling Stone and others who appeared at Woodstock—with the exception of the "student project" The Sha-Na-Na who would appear at Woodstock!

Anyway, Elvis and the Colonel were financially on the lane down, Elvis spent his money on cars, expensive toys, and gifts to his friends and fans, whereas the Colonel lost his money at the Roulette tables of Las Vegas. The movie-star who made three films a year for a million dollars per movie, was in financial trouble.

Rock and Roll had changed there was the Rock and Roll of the long-haired groups for the teenagers, from which most original Rock and Roll Stars held back. They concentrated on nostalgic warming up of their old hits, with some exceptions when recording. Elvis also chose the audience of his youth, the over 30 years. His music had evolved in a new style suitable for the posh stages of Las Vegas!

When Elvis re-appeared on stage and bid Hollywood farewell for good, his career had an uplift. But generally you could differ Elvis career in four parts— The Rockabilly years at SUN, the Rock and Roll pre-Army days of RCA, the GI Blues All American Boy, and the light-hearted movie making Star of the 1960s who in that way did not lose momentum or at least presence like all the other first generation Rockers, and even teen idols like Ricky Nelson, Fabian, Frankie Avalon, Bobby Rydell, Jimmy Clanton and co. Others like Carl Perkins who had jumped from SUN to Columbia with Johnny Cash, could not reproduce his "Blue Suede Shoes" days became an alcoholic, and part of the Johnny Cash Stage Show, whereas Chuck Berry after an arrest of bringing a minor of the state-line, still generated hits and was a hero to the Beat Groups. Jerry Lee Lewis did his part in Rock and Roll Extravaganzas with Bill Haley, Bo Diddley, Little Richard and Chuck Berry—The London Rock and Roll Show in 1972 also featuring notably British Rock and Roll Stars like Screaming Lord Sutch, Heinz or The Houseshakers.

The ladders being Rock and Roll Revivalists as mentioned when the story of the Teds subculture was briefly told in this book. But generally re-inventing himself as a Country Star. Whereas former label mate Johnny Cash did appear at Folsom Prison and San Quentin sympathising seemingly with the Jailbirds and showing mistreating of humans and other issues becoming the protest and later Outlaw Country singer "The Man in Black". Elvis did participate in all of this, but not sharing billing with his former rivals or competitors of the 1950s—and he did it the Elvis way. So different that he, also thanks to good posthumous management could not be forgotten.

But over the years, the continuous touring became as tiring as the provincial SUN Records days, the army, the Hollywood years … Throughout the 1970s Elvis started his tours with the stage program from Las Vegas. He gave hundreds of concerts in stadiums and arenas of provincial towns. He sold out everywhere, but as an artist he risked of having his career taking a dip. He started to mechanically recreate show after show, he went the easier way of entertaining with the same repertoire and the same jokes. Almost as if he self-persiflaged Elvis. In 1977, he finds little motivation of going on tour. He seeks freedom from these repeated public appearances.

In the summer of 1977, he cleared his personal relations, as if he was waiting for judgement day. A few weeks before 16 August 1977 he asked his oldest step-brother Billy Stanley for a meeting. Years ago, when Priscilla left Elvis with or for Mike Stanley his Karate teacher, Elvis sought revenge; the only thing that came to his mind or that evolved out of the situation was that he seduced Billy Stanley's wife Angie after a motorcycle ride together at his Circle G Farm in Mississippi. This ruined Stanley's marriage and both stayed away from Graceland. Under tears he asks his stepbrother for forgiveness, and it was granted to him.

"Ricky, man, I really like you. I will always be with you." The late Elvis biographer Albert Goldman would point this into the direction that Elvis was preparing for his suicide, Larry Geller his spiritual guide would say that Elvis was furthering his journey back into spirituality, Gail Brewer Giorgio—who wrote four books on the possibility that Elvis is indeed still alive, and why not as this is written during the Corona crisis, Jerry Lee Lewis is still the Last Man Standing and his personal doctor for years was Dr George Nichopoulos, both were born in the same year in 1935—and if we follow John Parker who wrote "Elvis—Murdered by the mob"—"We are closer than ever to the truth about Elvis's death ..." as the back cover of this paperback explains. What do I think? Well, I'm still on my journey, with you dear reader, let's find out what happened ...

Let's dive into it a little bit on the Old School European Side—Austrians love to read their horoscopes, and sometimes some dailies found out what their journalists were astrologically, and wrote little horoscopes for them, to see how the working climate would change ...

Let's see it from the point Horoscopes and Wisdom of the ages:

First a horoscope by Count John Manolescu, who born in Rumania, worked during the second world war was in Service for the English Secret Service: It was published by the magazine Tattler, and two years later used for the book Elvis Presley Report by Henno Lohmeyer (Bastei Lübbe—see Bibliography as for all other sources for this publication.)

"Born on 8 January 1935, at 12.20 am, in Tupelo/Mississippi, Elvis Aron Presley is a Sagittarius with Aries in the ascendant."

The Taurus-Sagittarius Planets can in connection with the "false Stars" destructible. But Elvis has an equalling factor: His moon is Saturn, what minors the negative side of his pre-disposition, mildly, at least what affects surroundings.

Saturn means work and success with the public. But as far as his private life is affected, he is not in such an advantage. With Uranus in the first house Elvis is unconventional, rebellious and difficult with coping with other people, especially those who are close to him. His ascendant can make him aggressive and going into defensive, also going into arguments. But Uranus gives him also a big portion of optimism, emery and sexual potency. He is in the middle of new beginnings, privately and professionally. With Jupiter in his stars he will take off in a positive way. But as soon as the Jupiter constellation will be over 1977 and later, he might face crisis. A crisis which is far more serious, than any he faced before.

Presley will have success in business life in the near future, will produce new recordings and make live-appearances. This can distract him for a while from his private situation. Elvis' moon is in the Gemini sign. This is the reason why he has such a rhythmic and musical talent. This constellation is also responsible for his admiration and worship responsible. Which he currently enjoys, and which encourage him in an interaction.

Advice from his manager and friends will be ignored by him. Presley can stay 27 days of a month in lethargy, unable to cope with daily life, but he only needs two days to make that even. In a period when the moon changes from sign to sign. He has three planets—two positive and one negative—in his sixth house, the house of work and health. There is Neptune with its irritating, conflict-bringing a contradicting influence. But Mars and Jupiter guarantee him times when he can work periodically endlessly. Independent from the predicted.

Always, when Jupiter and Mars are crossing, he will work independently to bad prospects. It was this Gemini-combination, his rehearsal-eagerness, his craft in recognise a chance, and use it to his advantage, which made him a Superstar, nevertheless coming from a poor background. But this Gemini constellation also brings health issues. He literally can work himself to death. Mars and Neptune also cause an in-balance of feelings he experiences.

Elvis has a strong bond to his family, which is obvious from the Moon-Gemini-stand. The missing of one parent and the resulting loss of a deep emotional binding, causes him to be attracted to different women. Bad Venus aspects affect Libra, his house of marriage, and cause difficulties. Sun and Mercury in Sagittarius, his tenth house, the house for popularity and success, show his luck, to meet the right people at the right time.

But Saturn in the eleventh house, the house for friends and family shows towards his egocentric, keeping people away from himself, and the ability to be emotionless in doing this, possibly. This man is scared, when he recognises that he has feelings. He positions himself outsider-ish whenever feelings overcome him, there is danger of psychological disorders, caused by his inner torrness. He really needs the help of people who knows how to handle this. Some signs in Sagittarius show that he does not hand himself in to professional help. He will leave all the sooner or later, he resembles the personality of Voltaire. 1976 will be a good, successful year for Elvis, a new beginning. As long as his optimism, his passion for luck, in that way, the sooner or later he is a damned.

In 1971, Antonia Lamb's horoscope was published in the Elvis Presley Biography by Jerry Hopkins. Jerry's phrase—"Four things America gave to the world: Mickey Mouse, Baseball, Coca Cola and Elvis Presley!" was often cited.

General overview:

Antonia Lamb's horoscope: "The whole picture is schizoid. He is the special blend of one who has no feelings and a sentimental, at the same time. He has the ability to have extreme in. When he does something, he goes for it fully. If he refuses something, you are better advised not to try to make him do it, better wait until he decides it for himself. An idealist, who is always on the watch, for not getting hurt. He is very often in a total defence mode. He has his own ways of being driven—you could call it rare egoism, but there is also lack of personality in his seeking, naivety or the impossibility of his to imagine to go another way. He is the embodiment of the nature law.

There are many conflicts. He is very suspicious on the other hand very gullible. His imagination of the world is idealistic, and his honesty, is based on this conception of the world, he has. He belongs to those human beings, who are always a little angry, that human beings are not as they should be. His worldview is small, stiff, biased, head-based. He can change his views, but not for pleasing others. I imagine his life to be that one of a lovely dictator. He is unbridled, has the ability of wildly losing his temper. He is tortured due to the fact that he thinks he is mistreated, that's why he gets so angry.

He is drawn to employ someone fast, at the same time to give notice for leaving! That's his expression of how he handles his employees. The expression of being erratic with other human beings. He has the ability to give, to present one with wonderful gifts, it's easier to him to give away presents instead of giving out anything of himself.

He is driven in his intentions to ensure that the people who he cares for have no hardships. He can be lovely, but his interest for things is only short-timed.

He belongs to the humans who easily suffer from "paranoia". He lets himself be used at the same time he fears the fact of being used. This explains his mood-swings. He is shy, way too shy, that he enjoys his own shyness. He always needs to have people around him, this gives him a feeling of safety. He is so eager for recognition that he even accepts it from people he himself does not respect. He needs compliments for his self-assurance, at the same time he reacts short-tempered towards criticism, contrary to the fact that the is a self-critic-perfectionist! He really cares about his appearance. His taste is rare, more loud than shy, but at last still conventional. He is against unfairism, but he only cares about the world close to him; he is uncaring; he is not the great philanthropist, which he aims to be. He does many things, only as they fit his image. He doesn't care about politics, but if something is against his worldview, he acts like a revolutionary. He lets himself be eaten by frustrations. He has a long breath, overcomes despair, bites himself through. His belongings change, often bought spontaneously, they lose importance and momentum rapidly for him. He doesn't care much for money.

Feelings/Sexuality

His mental aging is long and only began in the past few years. It takes long, before he is ready to love or gives place to attraction, but if it once has happened, its real long-term feelings, which he does not change or adapt soon. Against his many on the surface beings, these feelings are real, lasting, very traditional and very solid.

As a child he had some traumatic, violent experiences, which scared him, as of that it is not easy for him, to be spontaneous tenderly. Violence also rules his relation to love and pain. This makes him almost a sado-masochist. He honestly is attracted to and adores women, but is also fascinated by the 'sinful' female. He does not mature women, but prefers young appealing ladies, who are capable of motherhood, at least image wise. He has a strong sex-drive, but a lot of this drive is taken by his work. Sex to him is a physical necessity.

Family:

He is passionate about his family. Home and family have their importance to him—and the mother as ruling factor. We can estimate that he is often melancholic—it seems that his mother made him reachable for this feeling, in her life span. She was an alcoholic, this is an open secret, the way of a melodrama.

He possibly did not marry for such a long time, as he did not see himself worthy to his partner. (Naturally, he did not marry partly for a long time, as Priscilla Beulieu, later to be Mrs Elvis Presley, was only 14 when they met, and he did not want to make a fatal move like Jerry Lee Lewis, who married a 13 year old southern girl, when she was 13, he 23, in 1958. Causing a scandal that ruined not only his career.) His feelings as a father are impaired, which could mean, that he cannot have other children, already has his troubles with one child, or that he has a secret child; something is definitely wrong. There is also a secret, that has something to do with incest. He loves children who are out of the toddler age—when they are in the age to make no problems, but already understand many things, are too young to take issues which are rather scary. He would adopt children, or take care of children which are not his own.

Character

His character and feelings lie together closely. He relies almost entirely on his instincts. He can see facts, but reacts instinctively. Intuition rules him more than intellect. I believe that he has the ability for clairvoyance. This ability he is capable of using for seconds, and so he has the ability to direct human beings. He knows what will happen. His notion is true, if he does not engage his feelings in it. But his ability for clairvoyance also works, when he does not seek about it.

Health

He has enormous physical powers of nervous nature, which he takes from the interaction with other humans. That's why he always needs a partner; he can take from their powers. He is imperishable, can walk through great efforts. But it is nervousness or glands, which Doctors fail to see, and he has not the great ability in digesting. He should not eat too heavy and refrain from smoking. He is interested in diets, and can be fanatic about them. Alcohol is poison to him, his love for uppers/amphetamines, is a danger to liver and kidneys.

President Richard M. Nixon meeting Elvis Presley and two of his associates, Jerry Schilling and Sonny West, 21 December 1970

Elvis Presley in his "Washington Outfit"

A radiant Elvis Presley at the beginning of his Hollywood career

Elvis Presley in the 1970s

Elvis Presley with The Jordanaires

The gravesite of Elvis Aaron Presley in Graceland's Meditation Garden

Elvis Presley in the movie, *Jailhouse Rock*

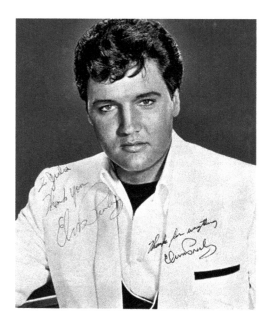

Signed 1960s photograph of Elvis Presley

1954 Publicity Shoot

President Richard Nixon with Elvis Presley

Youthful Elvis Presley

One hour of Elvis - live!

**OTC means you can see Elvis
in 'Aloha from Hawaii' 9-30 Sunday night
on Channel 9. Sydney & Melbourne.
Live via satellite.**

It's a world wide telecast from the Holiday Inn, Hawaii.
It's an entertainment first. It's Elvis Presley at his best.
And it's brought to you "live via satellite" by OTC.
Whenever you see those words on your television
screen it means OTC is at work bringing you a
"first"—in news, international events, or world
class entertainment.

OTC helps you see it happen.
Australia's International Communications Enterprise.

Elvis on stage in Hawaii in 1973

From "Aloha in Hawaii" 1973

On stage in Honolulu in 1973

ELVIS PRESLEY
Exclusively on RCA

RCA Records and Tapes

The birthplace of Elvis Presley in Tupelo/Mississippi

In the movie, "Jailhouse Rock"

Elvis and the President at the White House

Chapter Eight
Elvis in the Movies

"They sent me to Hollywood to make movies; it was all new to me. I was 21, 22 years old and they yelled action and I didn't know what to do. I said Memphis they said that's all we can get out of him." (Elvis Presley)

Elvis' cousin Patsy recalled the first films: "My cousin made love me tender loving you jailhouse rock and kingrail well done in a hurry right after his first hit records and before he went into the army Colin Parker wanted everyone to see Elvis could be more than a musical Idol he could be a big movie star Colonel Parker was right he got Elvis into Hollywood very early that was the 50s when Elvis got out of the army the same thing happened for most of the 60s more and more movies from around 1961 from 1968."

"Elvis was starring in something like free movies a year that meant back and forth from LA to Graceland to allay making movie take a break make a movie take a break in the beginning Elvis was afraid of flying so he or a friend drove a customer's crayon from California to Tennessee and back sometimes I think he was happy to get out of Graceland because he got a little restless but I know he was always happy to get out of Hollywood where he never felt he belonged."

Elvis would conclude "that's how it works you get a record and you get on television and they take you to Hollywood to make a picture but I wasn't ready for that town and they weren't ready for me I did 4 pictures so I got real good and used to do the movie stop it man I'm sitting in the back of a Cadillac with sunglasses on and my feet propped up saying I'm a movie star I'm some *****　hey hey you know eating hamburgers and drinking Pepsis and totally nuts I was living it up man but then I got drafted shafted and everything else so when I was all gone it was like it never happened like a dream but I was in a rut in Hollywood right in the middle of Hollywood Blvd there's a big rut."

Priscilla Presley recalled in the book "Elvis by the Presley's": "I moved into Elvis's life full time during the 60s when he got caught up in his artistic dilemma I saw it first-hand I only Kelly he was a movie buff he watched films all the time Elvis was a serious student of cinema he loved movies like to create escape and the Birdman of Alcatraz old classics like watering hates Florence olive year Mr Skeffington with Bette Davis and Les miserable with Frederic March he had wonderful taste in film and realised he could do whatever he wanted he didn't like love meat end and called it a rush shop but he liked King Creole which was basically intended for James Dean."

Colonel Tom Parker strictly insisted on the fact, that there would be no new Elvis recordings, while Elvis was serving the U.S. Army. When Elvis returned from Germany, the people at RCA had eager appetite in recording Elvis Presley for new material. They accepted almost everything Parker would ask for. Also, in Hollywood TV did strict business. He had a few hard-pill-swallowing agreements with Producer Hal B. Wallis. At the end, both had what they wanted. Wallis a film, Parker 175,000 dollars and an interest in the movie. Twentieth-Century Fox opted in for two new films with Elvis. The three movies of 1960 alone made for Elvis a half million dollars.

MGM showed interest also in signing Elvis for some movies. Hardly time to recreate in Graceland. After the obligatory Press conference in his uniform and in Sergeant stripes Elvis called his friend Anita Wood, met his old pals and visited the former room of his mother, which was left unchanged, as if she was still living there, upon his request. Then he had to come to Nashville into the studio—RCA was impatient. Despite guitarist Scotty Moore, drummer DJ Fontana, the backing group The Jordanaires, Nashville musicians such as pianist Floyd Cramer and guitarist Hank Garland, were on hand, to round off the sessions to be held. Elvis recorded his new-single "Stuck On You" b/w "Fame and Fortune" duly, as well as the title "A Mess of Blues". Before the actual recordings, RCA had labels printed—advertised as "Elvis' 1st New Recordings For His 500,000,000 Fans All Over The World" 1, 4 Million pre-orders went in.

The first stage appearance was a TV Special with Frank Sinatra, who interestingly distanced himself from Rock and Roll in 1956, called artists of that genre "Cretinous goons" and more …, now welcomed Elvis as if he was his son-in-law, and one that he appreciated.

It seemed that either money, Elvis loyal Fans, or a complete change in musical tastes, or the fact that Elvis had served in the Army, changed his attitude on Rock and Roll. Another Colonel Tom Parker managed Rock and Roll protegee—Tommy Sands married his daughter Nancy Sinatra. When both divorced, Tommy Sands career took such a dip, that it was rumoured forever, that it was Sinatra, who sabotaged Sands career. After the Sinatra Show Elvis finished his album "Elvis is Back", which included a version of Peggy Lee's "Fever", "The Girl Of My Best Friend" (turned into an hit by Elvis soundalike Ral Donner) and The Drifters/Johnnie Ray/Bunny Paul hitting "Such A Night". A bluesy "Reconsider Baby" is also part of the album. It was Elvis charisma reaching into that album's music, that he was able to transfer to the screens as an actor, successfully marketed by Hollywood, as early as 1956.

The final product, the LP 'Elvis is Back' included "Fever", "Girl Next Door Went A Walking", "Soldier Boy", "Make Me Know It", "I Will Be Home Again", "Reconsider Baby", "It Feels So Right", "Like A Baby", "The Girl Of My Best Friend", "Thrill Of Your Love", "Such A Night" and "Dirty, Dirty Feeling".

His Comeback on screen, was to be "G.I. Blues. Everything was planned so smoothly, that the machinery around was oiled so well, that if, even maybe without Elvis this could have been done. Asking, how much was Elvis himself involved into that decisions? Elvis had high hopes for the film, according to Priscilla Presley, but wrote her that he was afraid too much music was crammed into it—"Tonight Is So Right For Love", "What's She Really Like", "Frankfurt Special", "Wooden Heart", "G. I. Blues", "Pocketful Of Rainbows", "Shoppin' Around", "Big Boots", "Didja' Ever", "Blue Suede Shoes", "Doin' The Best I Can" and "Tonight's Allright For Love". 12 songs, the length of an LP, so was he teasing "Cilla" as he wrote to her in Germany, about that? The result of the movie was the album "G. I. Blues and vice versa":

In his spare time Elvis chased the girls—he met the 16 year old Hollywood actress Sandy Ferra, had Bonnie Finkley fly into Memphis, she resembled a lot to Priscilla Presley, in optics, flirted with Julie Prowse who starred with him in "G. I. Blues", but was engaged with Frank Sinatra and kept the blankets of the Girl he left behind in Germany—Priscilla warm—with calling and writing. He visited parties held by Sammy Davis Jr. and Bobby Darin, and celebrated his own at the Beverly Wiltshire Hotel.

Rock and Roll seemed, at least in the studio to have lost its momentum for Elvis. Until a week before, shooting his follow up film to G. I. Blues. Elvis, always longed for to record more of his formative years' music—in so—Gospel.

With Chet Atkins and The Jordanaires he recorded in a single night—the Gospel album "His Hand In Mine". 12 songs like "Crying In The Chapel", "He Knows Just What I Need" and "His Hand In Mine". Inspired by his role model Jake Hess (The Statesmen), he fulfilled his dream plus crated a wonderful statement of Gospel music! The album consisted of the following titles:

His Hand In Mine
I'm Gonna Walk Dem Golden Stairs
In My Father's House (Are Many Mansions)
Milky White Way
Known Only To Him
I Believe In The Man In The Sky
Joshua Fit The Battle
Jesus Knows What I Need
Swing Down Sweet Chariot

Elvis was known for his generosity by friends and family. In November of 1960 he announced his first concert, since the Army, would be in February at the Ellis Auditorium in Memphis/Tennessee. A benefit appearance for aid of the Elvis Youth Centre in Tupelo/Mississippi, his birthplace, and 25 local charitable organisations of Memphis. In December 1960, Colonel Tom Parker announced that 50,000 Dollar for the U.S.S. Arizona memorial were missing, that Elvis would make a benefit show for the tragedy of Pearl Harbour, in Hawaii. After both shows, Elvis stayed away from giving concerts, for full 8 years.

More than 62,000 Dollars were raised, and Elvis was in his old good spirits! All movies that would follow, 25 in number, were created under their mission statement given first to screenwriter Allan Weiss: "I was supposed to create a believable and clean plot for 12 songs and a number of girls." On set Elvis was always on time, professionality, respectful towards other actors and film crew; behind that public persona of a professional he was suffering from mood swings and showed the signs of a lonely child. Now that his friends had become his employees, the issue turned worse.

According to some sources, he pulled the hair of actress Christina Crawford in his living room, another time it was said he supposedly threw a billiard cue after a girl who made remarks that the Beatles were stealing his job. Some of his staff reported that he was paranoid and always needed to be the centre of attention, at the same time. The movies became similar, one after the other, the nights longer. It was time for a change, it was time for Priscilla!

In June 1962, Priscilla Beaulieu arrived by plane from Germany in Memphis. For two weeks, she and Elvis were inseparable, Sightseeing, attending concerts, shopping … When she returned to her parents in June, they were shocked by her makeup and her Elvis-like hairstyle. But Priscilla knew—Elvis was her future!

For Christmas 1962, Priscilla flew in with her father Captain Beaulieu, visited Los Angeles, where Elvis was filming the movie "Fun in Acapulco". There the relation was sealed. Priscilla moved to Memphis and began to lead a double life. A.) As a catholic High-school student. B.) As Elvis Presley's best kept-secret.

In May of 1963, Priscilla graduated from High School. After that Elvis and her stayed three weeks in his bedroom, ordered food, watched old movies, had fun with pillow-throwing. Sexually they were passionate and manifolded. But Elvis did not let it go to actual intercourse. "Baby, don't let us do it, let me decide, when the time for that has come. To me that is a sacred thing."

The world and the sunshine waiting on the outside was far away. Kept away by curtains and Alu foil, with which Elvis always dimmed his bed room. But time and Hollywood were not waiting for much longer. In July Elvis was due to star and act in "Viva Las Vegas". When meeting Ann-Margret, almost a female counterpart of Elvis, red haired, Elvis just had to fall in love …

Elvis and Ann-Margret fell for each other, had a romance. This ended with the decision of Elvis to ask Colonel Tom Parker to manage Ann-Margret also. The next day, it was all over the news, that both were engaged. Priscilla naturally was enraged; Elvis had no other chance then to make nails with head. He chose Priscilla. It was Larry Geller who noted in his book on Elvis—"I Was The One", that Ann-Margret could have been what June Carter would be for Johnny Cash. Getting him, like Cash, off prescribed medication. A missed opportunity, possibly. Margret would herself have been not happy, very likely, to be represented by Parker, as she was the one, to tell Elvis that his talent was wasted on second rate songs, for publishing and royalties right. She was also the one to introduce him to the changes in music—Bob Dylan was one of her favourites. Elvis acknowledged that Dylan sang as if he had a sock in his mouth, but would record his composition "Don't Think Twice—It's Alright".

After seeing the film "Viva Las Vegas" it was producer Hal Wallis who wrote to the Colonel, that Elvis looked chubby, that his hair was corny—in a letter of complaint. Nothing negative came of Wallis regarding soundtrack and/or screenplay. Elvis statements were of the quality, that he felt deceived by both Parker and Wallis. But he was 29, in the 90 percent tax bracket. A lot of people, of his entourage relied on his financial income. Parker's tactic was to change the director, as "Viva Las Vegas" was over-production costs, lasting longer to shoot than expected.

Parker chose Sam Katzman who was responsible for celluloid adventure such as "Batman and Robin" (Columbia 1949) starring Robert Lowery and John Duncan, as well as the Bill Haley full-length-motion pictures "Rock Around The Clock" and "Don't Knock The Rock" (Columbia 1956) for Elvis next film, as producer. The circus themed movie—Roustabout. In March 1965 Elvis began his journey with his hair stylist, spiritual advisor and friend Larry Geller. It was on April 30th 1964 that Larry Geller worked for his employer Sebring, cutting the hair of singer Johnny Rivers, when the phone rang. The caller had identified himself as Alan Fortas and belonged to Elvis' inner circle.

Sal Orifice, Elvis' hairstylist, he explained, had resigned and had recommended Larry Geller as his successor for Elvis. "Elvis asks, if you could visit him this afternoon, at four in Bel Air, to take care of his hair." That was Fortas' request on behalf of Elvis Presley. Geller who explains in his book "I Was The One" further that he already knew the important people in Hollywood, and was surprised of himself, that he felt something like nervousness in meeting Elvis. He had felt the bond of fans, the charisma of Elvis had taken him again. Geller had seen Elvis live in the mid-fifties. Geller had the feeling since shaking hands with Presley, back in the 50s, that they had this special bond.

Elvis was still the King for Larry, but he was also aware that times had changed. The love for Rock and Roll was still there, and in so certainly also for Elvis Presley. But the thunder had gone. Beginning with 1960 most of his films were middle-of the road—fair pictures—but not special anymore. Not surprisingly this had occurred, the path of showbusiness. Elvis made it to Hollywood's a league something not accomplished by his fellow Rockabillies such as Carl Perkins, Jerry Lee Lewis, Roy Orbison, Warren Smith nor Johnny Cash.

Larry Geller also stated in his book "I Was The One" (written with Joel P. Spector and P. Romanowski):

"He would always have stayed The King for me, even if he would have disappeared from the limelight altogether in 1958." Larry Geller also describes the life of Elvis Presley, before he would join the Presley Entourage:

Elvis made three films in black and white:

-) Love Me Tender
-) Jailhouse Rock
-) King Creole

Elvis Presley films grossed a reported $150 million at the box office.

Colonel Tom Parker, as most Elvis fans know, was listed at the technical advisor in most Elvis films. These are nine films in which he was not listed in the credits as the technical advisor.

1. Wild in the Country
2. Viva Las Vegas
3. Frankie and Johnny
4. Stay Away, Joe
5. Speedway
6. Live a Little, Love a Little
7. Charro!
8. The Trouble with Girls
9. Change of Habit

A number of performers made their screen debuts in an Elvis Presley film. Here is the list (movie by movie):

1. Dolores Hart (Loving You)
2. Scotty Moore (Loving You)
3. Bill Black (Loving You)
4. D. J. Fontana (Loving You)
5. Vernon Presley (Loving You)
6. Gladys Presley (Loving You)
7. The Jordanaires (Loving You)
8. Jennifer Holden (Jailhouse Rock)
9. Leticia Roman (G. I. Blues)

10. Sigrid Maier (G. I. Blues)
11. Priscilla Tauron (G. I. Blues)
12. Kerry Charles and Terry Earl Ray (G. I. Blues)
13. David Paul and Donald James Rankin (G. I. Blues)
14. Christina Crawford (Wild in the Country)
15. Flora K. Hayes (Blue Hawaii)
16. Gavin and Robin Koon (Follow That Dream)
17. Orlando de la Fuente (Kid Galahad)
18. Ed Sander (Kid Galahad)
19. Laurel Goodwin (Girls, Girls, Girls)
20. Vicky Tiu (It Happened at the World's Fair)
21. Raquel Welch (Roustabout)
22. Annette Day (Double Trouble)
23. Susan Trustman (Stay Away Joe)
24. Patti Jean Keith (Speedway)
25. Ross Hagen (Speedway)
26. Ursula Menzel (Love a Little, Live a Little)
27. Lynn Kellog (Charro)
28. Marilyn Mason (The Trouble with Girls)
29. Nicole Jaffe (The Trouble with Girls)
30. Anissa Jones (The Trouble with Girls)
31. Pepe Brown (The Trouble with Girls)
32. Jane Elliot (Change of Habit)

Conversely, a dozen performers made their last screen performances in an Elvis film:

1. Judy Tyler (Jailhouse Rock)
2. Ludwig Stossel (G. I. Blues)
3. Jason Rothards Sr. (Wild in the Country)
4. Philip Reed (Harum Scarum)
5. Carl Betz (Spinout)
6. Una Merkel (Spinout)
7. Frederic Worlock (Spinout)
8. Frank McHugh (Easy Come, Easy Go)
9. Hal Peary (Clambake)

10. Richard Carlson (Change of Habit)
11. Ruth McDevitt (Change of Habit)
12. Elvis Presley (Change of Habit) (Last acting appearance)

THE ELVIS PRESLEY MOVIES:

1. LOVE ME TENDER (1956) with Debra Paget, Richard Eagan, Robert Middleton, William Campbell and Neville Brand

Directed by Robert D. Webb

Twentieth-Century Fox, A David Weisbart production. Running time: 89 minutes, Elvis Presley's first feature film as Vince Reno.

Elvis first film—Love Me Tender is set in the period, shortly after the American civil war. Elvis character is married to Kathy (Debra Paget), formerly the girl of his older brother Vince (Richard Egan)—everyone believes to be dead—until he turns up again. On his trail the law, for having robbed a train, with his buddies. By the time Elvis had made the film, he was already a national star, having released seven gold singles in 1956 alone. So the title of the movie was changed from "The Reno Brothers" to Love Me Tender. Elvis is still unfolding his acting skills in this movie, but the film itself is a treasure, maybe just for that—as well as for its aesthetics, not forgetting seeing the Boy King of Rock and Roll on the screen for the first time. It was reported that Glady's Love Presley, Elvis' mum had difficulties seeing the end of Love Me Tender, in which Elvis gets shot and mortally wounded, dying in the arms of his brother …

1. LOVING YOU (1957) with Lisbeth Scott, Wendell Corey, Dolores Hart, James Gleason and Ralph Dumke

Directed by Hal Kenter

Paramount, A Hal B. Wallis production. Running time: 101 minutes, Elvis' second film.

Elvis radiant, in great from and in blazing colour. Just 22, with his sandy-blonde hair dyed into blue black, Elvis stuns one as uniting the coolness of some of the method actors, notably Marlon Brando and certainly another one of his role models when it came to acting, James Dean. What a great stage outfit he is wearing, many people know him singing "Teddy Bear" from the movie's footage, even if they did not watch Loving You itself. His musical numbers are close to his early live performances, a lot of hip-swivelling, shaking, bumping, grinding and just goofing around. At the end, Elvis sings "Got A Lot Of Living To Do", he stops in front of a large woman in a blue dress sitting in the aisle. It's his mother Gladys, devastated by her death in 1958, it is said that Elvis never watched Loving You again …

2. JAILHOUSE ROCK (1957) with Judy Tyler, Dean Jones, Jennifer Holden, Mickey Shaughnessy

MGM. An Avon Production. Running time: 96 minutes. Elvis Presley's third film.

Directed by Richard Thorpe

Marshall Crenshaw noted on this production in his book on Rock and Roll related movies "Hollywood Rock", on Jailhouse Rock—"In which Elvis teaches us how to dress."

An early Elvis movie, when young Mr Presley was still a fresh face in Hollywood. MGM had not quite worked out the kinks in his film persona—yet. Difficult for the watchers of the later Elvis movies to imagine, here we do not find a nice guy in Elvis role. More of the persona Jerry Lee Lewis displayed or the image JLL had created for himself …

Elvis is neither an innocent, he portrays a convict, serving a stretch of one-to-10 in the state pen for manslaughter. He shares the cell with the older Country and Western singer (played by Mickey Shaughnessy), who takes him under the wings and a TV show live from the prison is held. Elvis gets more fan letters than everyone else participating in this special show. But is given the letters, after serving, he tries to perform in a bar, once released. But has no success. There he meets a talent scout, as portrayed by young actress Judy Tyler. A must watch is the choreography Elvis had worked out for "Jailhouse Rock", the first-on-scree haircut before the one by Uncle Sam. The scene in which Elvis grabs Judy Tyler, his love interest in the film, kisses her. She pushes him back with the line "How, do you think such cheap tactics would work on me?" following. To which Elvis replies: "That ain't cheap tactics, honey—that's the beast in me." Judy Tyler passed shortly after the film's competition in a car accident. Another film vehicle Elvis refused to watch, as of her death.

3. KING CREOLE (1958) with Carolyn Jones, Dolores Hart, Dean Jagger, Liliane Montevecchi and Walter Matteau

Paramount 1958. A Hal B. Wallis production. Running time: 116 minutes. Elvis' fourth film.

Directed by Michael Curtiz

An almost evil Elvis we can watch in Michael Curtiz vehicle for Elvis. The Austrian director is also remembered for having Humphrey Bogart given the ultimate film, one must watch before to die—in "Casablanca". Elvis plays Danny Fisher, who has problems with his wimpy father, similar as James Dean in his role as Jim Stark in "Rebel Without A Cause". Whereas Dean finds a father-like-man in the Police officer, Elvis looks for a father-ersatz in the crooked owner of the Club Creole, portrayed by Walter Matteau. Elvis is split between two women, the good and the bad girl, yet lures the good girl in sleeping with him, though his emotions are at that time stronger for the baddy lady. Elvis to her: "God didn't give you those charms for what you're using them for." The bad girl: "That's funny, and I read the instructions so carefully."

4. G. I. BLUES (1960) with Juliet Prowse

Paramount, 1960. A Hal B. Wallis production. Running time: 104 minutes. Elvis Presley's fifth film.

Directed by Norman Taurog

Elvis got out of the army in 1960. Paramount did not waste any time—Buddy Holly, Ritchie Valens and The Big Bopper were dead, Chuck Berry was in jail, Little Richard had forsaken Rock and Roll for Seventh-Day Adventism, Jerry Lee Lewis' career had been undone by his marriage to his thirteen year old cousin second-grade. Bill Haley was preparing to flee over the Texas border to Mexico, as of tax debts. The first generation of Rock and Roll Stars was slowly substituted by teen-idols by the likes of Fabian, Frankie Avalon, Bobby Vee, Bobby Rydell or Frankie Sardo. Elvis plays Tulsa McClean in GI Blues, his dream and ambition is to open a nightclub, once out of the army, back in Oklahoma. Tulsa needs money. He bets that he can seduce nightclub star Lily (Juliet Prowse). She finds out, a lot of hurdles are to overcome, finally they work out as a couple. A cool scene for trivialists Elvis gets disturbed playing live, when somebody pushes "Blue Suede Shoes" in the jukebox …

5. FLAMING STAR (1960) with Barbara Eden, Dolores Del Rio, Steve Forrest and John McIntire

Twentieth Century-Fox, 1960. A David Weisbart production. Running time: 101 minutes. Elvis' sixth film.

Directed by Don Sieger

Flaming Star is not only a return to a dramatic role, after the lighter hearted, more musical approach in "G.I. Blues", but also Elvis Presley's contribution in a movie to the race debate, as well as to the wrong the white settlers done for centuries to the Native Americans. It's difficult to see G. I. Blues and Flaming Star in one man's filmography, what is even more astonishing is, that both films were made in the same year. "Flaming Star" reduced Elvis the singer to Elvis the actor. Elvis on the other hand reduced the actor to be the character he played: Pacer, a young man, born to a white father and a native mother, or a half breed … A tension between the white settlers and the local tribe mounts, Pacer and his family are torn apart. Similar to John Ford's 1956 classic The Searchers, Flaming Star addresses issues of race and racism. Better dialogue, a more believable script to Pacers almost supernatural powers of sight and sound, could have make the film more believable. Nevertheless, Elvis the man who brought together blues and country, as a doomed half-breed is an statement in 1961, itself. "I will return, then, when the sun has killed the stars in the sky."

6. WILD IN THE COUNTRY (1961) with Hope Lange, Roland Winters, John Archer, Angela Lansbury and Nancy Walters

Twentieth Century-Fox, 1961. A Company of Artists Inc., production. Running time: 114 minutes. Elvis' seventh film. Directed by Philip Dunne.

One of the Elvis movies which should have been close to the King's heart. Not only is the character he portrays a seeker of faith like Elvis. At times yet wild and untamed, just like Elvis. Someone who cites from the Bible, at the same time sins, is a tempted men. In this movie, it is at first two girls who try to steal Glenn Tyler's heart—but at the end he finds solace in the arms of his therapist, played by Hope Lange. A tragic film, yet going for the positive end, as two alternative endings had been shot. Yet, the more favourable by the people's choice at pre-screenings was chosen. Elvis discovers his talents as a writer, and heads off to college … Elvis quoting Jesus on the cross, at the request of a Reverend "Father, father why have you forsaken me?" in Aramaic as well as in English, brings tears to some eyes, especially those who knew about his faith quest, his seeker's role in life.

7. BLUE HAWAII (1961) with Joan Blackman, Roland Winters, John Archer, Angela Lansbury and Nancy Walters

Paramount 1961. A Hal B. Wallis production. Running time: 101 minutes. Elvis' eighth film.

Directed by Norman Taurog

The eight of the Elvis Presley movies did very well on the box-office, it was usually shown as a double-feature with Ricardo Montalban's Spanish-Italian film Desert Warrior. The first of the Elvis Hawaiian Trilogy: Blue Hawaii, Paradise Hawaiian Style and Girls! Girls! Girls!

"Of the three, this one's probably the most difficult to watch, often losing the viewer as it ventures deep into that familiar surreal world of the generic Elvis musical." Marshall Crenshaw attests in his book "Hollywood Rock—A Guide to Rock and Roll in the Movies" (Plexus).

Chad Gates (Elvis Presley) has returned to Hawaii from serving in the Italian army. He has the struggle most young men have, to find themselves. Most of the time, he finds a lot of girls, plus sticky situations involving them. Angela Lansbury's role is the one of his mother. He avoids her as much as he can, as her intention is to get him the job within his father's fruit company. Stepping into dad's shoes is not Chad's dream. Elvis gets pretty sexist in this movie, but on the other side, he gets any jerk off the lady's back, defending their honour.

Towards the end of the film, he opens a travel service by the name of "Gates of Hawaii". Scenes that make up for some great viewing: Elvis singing "Can't Help Falling In Love" beautifully, backed by an Austrian Jukebox; Elvis spanking a girl over his knee. Dialogue that stands out: Mrs Pentice—"Do you think you can satisfy a school teacher and four teenage girls?" Elvis' reply: "Well, uh, I'll sure try, ma'am. I'll do all I can."

8. FOLLOW THAT DREAM (1962) with Anne Helm, Joanna Moore, Jack Kruschen, Arthur O'Connell and Simon Oakland

United Artists, 1962. A Mirisch Company production. Running time: 110 minutes. Elvis' ninth film.

Directed by Phil Karlson

Based on the 1959 novel "Pioneer Go Home", this story of hillbilly's attempt to settle down in Florida, raised concerns by its author Richard Powell, that Elvis would try it play funny, as soon as he found out that the plot, was that one of a comedy. But Elvis Presley as the boy from the backwoods, delivered his scenes pitch-perfect, straight and with superb timing. He was directed straight throughout the film. As author Eric Braun stated: "Presley's portrayal of guileless innocent has never been bettered." Reviews pointed out that Elvis was able to show his versatility, without the wiggle factor: "A charming vehicle as well as a nice story based on the American theory that good, simple folk will always triumph over city slickers ... the script is witty, the direction clever and Elvis's part brilliantly conceived."

In the plot we meet Elvis Presley as the naïve but upstanding Toby Kwimper, singing a spirited "What A Wonderful Life". The unconventional family, the Kwimpers, are on the road, journeying along the Florida coast. Pop (Arthur O'Connell), in a role to be reprised in "Kissin' Cousins", a sweet-former baby sitter Holly (Anne Helm), unofficially adopted twins, and last but not least a young orphan girl named Ariadne. While the Kwimpers run out of gas, they decide to spend a night on the beach. During the next day, they are discovered by an official, who learns that they virtually rely on the government for money: Toby is a discharged Army veteran, his father in receipt of tax relief. Pop declares that they intend to settle down on the unclaimed land. The official H. Arthur King, portrayed by Alan Hewitt and a child-welfare-manager Alisha Claypoole (Joanna Moore), to gangsters Garmine and Nick (Jack Kruschen and Simon Oakland), all try to get rid of the Kwimpers, one way or the other.

Toby, meanwhile, fishing, catches a giant tarpon. As a passer-by offers him 20 $ for the catch, he forms the idea in his mind, to start a fishing business. But to fund it, they need a bank loan, offering their luxury john (restroom) as security for a loan of $2000. Bank president Mr Endicott (Herbert Rudley) sees his customers sincerity, and grants them a character loan instead. Alisha, now monitoring the clan's "moral fitness" tries to seduce Toby in the woods. He is tempted to a kiss, but resists anything more by reciting his multiplication tables. Seeing the flirting pair, Holly feels left out, and pushes Alisha into the river. Alisha responds to that with taking the twins and Ariadne into social care. A day in court follows, where the Kwimpers plead to be fit as guardians. While the mobsters try to turn the land into another Las Vegas, with a mobile casino, in turn Toby is made into a Sheriff. This is responded by the mobsters in planting a bomb to take him out, but luckily neither this attempt to drive him and the others out succeeds.

The cast, the acting, the plot are all good Elvis singing the aforementioned "What A Wonderful Life" a very uplifting song, as well as the welcome Rock and Roll song "I'm Not The Marrying Kind" and not to forget the evergreen "Angel" at the happy ending, in a romantic scene to Holly.

9. KID GALAHAD (1962) with Gig Young, Lola Albright, Joan Blackman, Charles Bronson and Ned Glass

Directed by Phil Karlson

United Artists, 1962. A Marisch Company production. Running Time: 95 minutes: Elvis' tenth film.

Praised as a movie in which Elvis "gave on of his very best performances"

"Kid Galahad" was a remake of the 1937 silver screen classic by the same name for Warner Brothers, then directed by Austrian director Michael Curtiz, who had worked with Elvis Presley on the movie "King Creole" based on "Rebel Without A Cause" starring James Dean.

The original "King Creole" had starred Humphrey Bogart, Bette Davis and Edward G. Robinson. Contrary to the 1937 black and white movie, this remake filmed in colour, featured music numbers. Naturally. Also the United Artists reprisal was not as dark as it's forerunner. Though featuring considerable action in the ring. According to Walter Gulick, who assumed the boxing handle of Kid Galahad, Elvis did very well, ex-pro boxer Mushy Callahan was the coach for Elvis Presley for the fight scenes, and praised Elvis ability.

The movie was shot in late 1961 in Idyllwild/California and Hollywood with top-notch acting talent. Charles Bronson, a few years away from leading-man status played Elvis coach, but they two did not get on very well. Gig Young, a lovely Lola Albright (remembered fondly by many as Peter Gunn's nightclub singer lover interest) was also in the cast. Like in "Blue Hawaii" Joan Blackman portrayed Elvis' girlfriend. Memphis Mafia tough men Red and Sonny West had unbilled parts in the movie, reportedly not shy for swinging punches in private life.

Six songs were recorded for the soundtrack on 26 and 27 October 1961 at Radio Recorders in Hollywood. Musicians included Scotty Moore and Hilmer "Tiny" Timbrell on guitars, Dudley Brooks on piano, Boots Randolph on saxophone, Bob Moore on bass, plus D.J. Fontana and Buddy Harman sharing drum duties. Vocal harmonies handled by The Jordanaires. One of the movie's best songs "King Of The Whole Wide World" came from the songwriters Ruth Batchelor and Bob Roberts. Another great song was the Bert Weisman composed "I Got Lucky". The remaining songs not to be underestimated were "This Is Living", "Riding The Rainbow", "Home Is Where The Heart Is" and "A Whistling Tune". Placed by Variety as one of the 1962 top-grossing movies "Kid Galahad" proved that with the right cinematic material, Elvis Presley could do no wrong in the movie world.

10. GIRLS, GIRLS, GIRLS (1962) with Stella Stevens, Laurel Goodwin, Jeremy Slate, Guy Lee and Benson Fong

Directed by Norman Taurog

Paramount, 1962. A Hal B. Wallis production. Running time: 106 minutes. Elvis' eleventh film.

Colonel Tom Parker proved right that with material closer to "Blue Hawaii" there was a lot of money to be made. Not that "Girls, Girls, Girls" did as good as "Blue Hawaii", it proved that the formula of colourful locations, likeable, laughing characters and an uncomplicated story in the era of the Beach movies, was a winning formula. But it was also the only Elvis movie to be nominated for a Golden Globe Award for Best Musical. Given the film's title and the footage over the opening credits one could mistake the movie for raunchy fun. But the character portrayed by Elvis is rather interested in catching fish than girls. Elvis plays straight and honest through "Girls, Girls, Girls" only appearing to enjoy himself when singing.

Norman Taurog, the director who had signed responsible as such in "G.I. Blues" and "Blue Hawaii", helped, especially as the pair Taurog and Presley got along well. Norman Taurog was experienced, having directed is first movie for

Vitagraph in 1919. The Hawaiian fisherman Ross Carpenter, portrayed by Elvis Presley, works on a boat he built with is how-deceased father, owned by a friendly Greek man and his wife. They must move to Arizona, for a climate change, as of health reasons and plan to sell the boat, to cover their expenses. Ross is devastated, there are some dramatic twists and turns, but also enough music material to ensure that the movie was not nominated for a Golden Globe for Best Musical without reason.

The character Elvis plays has a relationship with a nightclub singer played by Stella Stevens. An alternative love interest comes up with Laurel, played by Laurel Goodwin. She plays with a cheeky innocence that suits Elvis' character Ross Carpenter well. The interactions between the two actors Elvis Presley and Laurel Goodwin are among the best moments of "Girls, Girls, Girls". The success of "Girls, Girls, Girls" cemented Elvis Presley's future in Hollywood.

11. IT HAPPENED AT THE WORLD'S FAIR (1963) with Yvonne Craig, Joan O'Brian, Vicky Tv and Gary Lockwood

Directed by Norman Taurog

MGM, 1963. A Ted Richmond production. Running time: 105 minutes. Elvis' twelfth film.

In this film, Elvis' child co-star Vicky Tiu performs a wonderful double act and brings out some of the most memorable moments of the film. Next to Elvis Presley sitting in a mesmerising scene, where he sits unspeaking for the duration of the moving ballad "They Remind Me Too Much Of You" in a monorail at the Century 21 Exposition of Seattle/Washington, held from April through October 1962. The location had been recommended to MGM by the governor of Washington, even though that the film came out six months after the exhibition closed, ticket sales on the box-office were high.

In this film, filled with light-hearted as well as melodramatic content, Elvis Presley could prove what a fine actor he was. Co-stars included the later Batgirl Yvonne Craig, Joan O'Brien, Gary Lockwood and the afore-mentioned Vicky Tiu. The plot for the film, as penned by Si Rose and Seaman Jacobs finds Elvis Presley portraying Mike Edwards, a crop-duster pilot whose plane would be impounded due to gambling debts of his friend and co-pilot Danny (played by Garlo Lockwood, who had appeared previously with Elvis in "Wild in the Country").

Needing funds, the two young men hitch-hike to the world's fair in Seattle, where Danny attempts to set up a deal with the shady mobster-like old friend he has in mind since losing the money. In the mean-time, Elvis as Mike tries to defrost the heart of the nurse Diane (Joan O'Brien).

Elvis' wardrobe, on a trivia note, for the movie cost $15,000. It suits him, originally the sister of Vicky Tiu was cast for the film, but she had an engagement to play piano for President John F. Kennedy's birthday party, after having appeared with Elvis in "Girls, Girls, Girls". The songs of "It Happened At The World's Fair" are mostly easy-listening, with one up-tempo showing Elvis former glory as Rock and Roll King "One Broken Heart For Sale" which scored for him in the UK on Position 12, and the US on Number 11 on a single, released prior to the film.

The critics weren't too kind to the movie, but although a lightweight compared to other Elvis movies, it remains a film that the whole family from children to grandparents can enjoy. Kurt Russell was also cast in the film, to get attention of the his love interest, a nurse, Elvis asked the boy played by the later action star Russell to deliberately kick him on the knee. Which he did, twice, once unasked. Kurt Russell would play Elvis Presley in the first of the Elvis biopics "Elvis" in 1979, which won him an Emmy.

12. FUN IN ACAPULCO (1963) with Ursula Andress, Els Vardenas and Paul Lukas.

Directed by Richard Thorpe

Paramount, 1963. A Hal B. Wallis production. Elvis' thirteenth film.

Elvis had high hopes for the movie "Fun In Acapulco", not only would it reunite it him with the director of "Jailhouse Rock" Richard Thorpe, but also introduce him to two leading ladies of interest, more than their mere beauty: Ursula Andress who was the first Bond Girl, and also a love interest of his acting role-model James Dean, as well as the Mexican actress Elsa Cardenas. (She appeared in James Dean's final film "Giant"). He also hoped that the film would be shot on location in Mexico, but due to safety concerns expressed by Colonel Tom Parker, shooting remained to be within California. "Fun In Acapulco" would be his final movie, before the British Invasion of Merseyside rock groups such as The Beatles. Critics already noted, that the Elvis Presley films became more and more formulaic.

The character of Elvis, Mike Windgren, was trying to find work after being canned as a boat hand. Being hired as lifeguard and club singer, also struggling to overcome a trauma had experienced in his early career as trapeze artist. Elvis who worked well with Richard Thorpe was very convincing once more, though some say that the off-screen magic he had with his female co-stars wasn't transferred to the big screen. Maybe in part also that Director Thorpe was known as a one-take director.

13. KISSIN COUSINS (1964) with Arthur O'Connell, Glenda Farrell, Jack Albertson, Pam Austin, Cynthia Pepper and Yvonne Craig

Directed by Gene Nelson

MGM 1964. A Four Leaf production. Running time: 96 minutes. Elvis' fourteenth film.

The trailer of "Kissin' Cousins" promised "feuding, fighting and fallin' in the water … love of hungry mountain girls … the two greatest lovers in the Smokey Mountains. Elvis Presley and Elvis Presley". So two Elvises, a tight budget for Elvis 15th film, "Viva Las Vegas" was shot before, ran over production-costs and would be released after "Kissin Cousins" produced by Sam Katzman. Who basically crafted the first Rock and Roll musical starring Bill Haley—"Rock Around The Clock" (Columbia Pictures, 1956) which established the market for Presley films like "Jailhouse Rock".

With Sam Katzman looking over director Gene Nelson's shoulder, the budget restrictions were quite obvious: artificial looking studio sets that resembled a stage musical at times. Nevertheless, it proved also to nominate writers Gene Nelson and Gerald Drayson Adams to be nominated for the Writers Guild of America Award for Best Written Musical, only to be beaten by the Julie Andrews and Dick Van Dyke classic evergreen movie "Mary Poppins". The presence of two Elvis Presley's guaranteed not only more love interests, with once more Yvonne Craig, as well as Pamela Austin who competed for blonde Josh, Cynthia Pepper who falls for the dark haired Private First Class Midge Reilly. But also a horde of females named the "wild girls of Tennessee" who enthusiastically welcome and intrude the mission of the US Soldiers, trying to settle a treaty with those who live in the woods—the girl gang is called The Kittyhawks.

The soundtrack was recorded in Nashville, the setting would also invite Country music, but it is more of a soulful pop-minded album that came out of the film. Highlights include "Smokey Mountain Boy", "Catchin' On Fast" and the hit "Kissin' Cousins". Critics were not enthused by this Elvis movie outing, the New York Times noted: "Presley's movie status takes a nosedive in his latest Kissin' Cousins. Sam Katzman's production is tired, strained and familiar stuff."

Variety reported: "A pretty dreary effort—Presley needs—and merits—more substantial material than this if his career is to continue to flourish as in the past." "Nevertheless, the film feels good-paced, is uplifting and shows Sam Katzman's enthusiasm in producing fast and reliable another box-office hit for The King Elvis."

With that in mind, it is no surprise that Katzman, Nelson and Adams were retained for Elvis Presley's 1965 movie "Harum Scarum".

14. VIVA LAS VEGAS (1964) with Ann-Margret, Nicky Blair and Cesare Danova

Directed by George Sidney

MGM 1964. Jack Cummings-George Sidney production. Running time: 86 minutes. Elvis' fifteenth film.

The distinguished film historian David Thomson in his "Dictionary Of Film" describes Ann-Margret in "Viva Las Vegas" as "one of the best and most provocative partners Elvis ever had". True, she was an all-round actress, singer and dancer, and RCA had built her up, like Janis Martin before, as a Female Elvis. Plus the chemistry of the pair Elvis Presley and Elvis Presley was remarkable. Not only leading to gossip on set, but also in magazines of the same nature. Ann Margret later said that the felling she and Elvis had for each other, was mutual, and felt from their very first meeting. Reporters on the set noted: "Whenever the dialogue brings Ann-Margret and Presley together, their roles suddenly become more than play-acting. An electricity from the two charges the crew with alertness."

The storyline had Elvis portray race driver Lucky Jackson who wants to compete in the Las Vegas Grand Prix, his car needing a new engine and so, to raise the money, he lands himself a job as hotel waiter. His rival, hot only on the racetrack but also for Rusty, the hotel's swimming instructor played by Ann Margret is Count Mancini, as played by Cesare Danova.

Alongside of working next to Ann-Margret Elvis enjoyed also that character actor William Demarest portrayed his father. He had appeared in the first ever Hollywood talkie—"The Jazz Singer" alongside the legendary Al Jolson in 1927. Possibly the greatest all-round entertainer of the 20th century, Elvis spent a great deal of time asking about Al Jolson, to find out that William Demarest couldn't stand Jolson.

Superbly choreographed dance-scenes all made under guidance of Ann-Margret's personal dance instructor David Winters also make this film stand out. Meanwhile director George Sidney was a veteran of the music movies or musicals, with work in his vita including "Anchors Aweigh" (1945) with Frank Sinatra and Gene Kelly, "Annie Get Your Gun" (1950) with Betty Hutton and Howard Keel and "Pal Joey" (1957) starring Rita Hayworth and Frank Sinatra. His last film would be "Half A Sixpence" starring one of Britain's first answers to US Rock and Roll artists such as Bill Haley and Elvis Presley—Tommy Steele, in 1967.

"Viva Las Vegas" stands out as one of the best Elvis Presley musicals, with a superb and timeless title song, the duet "You're The Boss" with Ann Margret, in the late 1990s reprised by Brian Setzer and Gwen Stefani.

The film made $9 million on the box office, but the Colonel seemed to bit furious about its production costs, possibly also worried about Priscilla and Elvis relation, with all the gossip papers reporting on a stormy affair the pair supposedly had … So the pair never worked on screen together, again.

15. ROUSTABOUT (1964) (with Joan Freeman, Leif Erickson, Pat Buttram, Sue Ann Langdon and Barbara Stanwyck

Directed by John Rich

Paramount, 1964. A Hal B. Wallis production. Running time: 101 minutes, Elvis sixteenth film.

The idea for Roustabout came of Colonel Tom Parker's early beginnings at the carnivals. As technical advisor he probably seems to be accountable for the authentic, realistic, yet so sympathetic setting and people of the carnival. Not least to mention movie legend Barbara Stanwyck as carnival owner Maggie Morgan, who put in a good portion of sympathy for the carnival people to the cinema audience.

A big plus for the movie is also that Elvis once again, after some absence, can play more of a bad boy here again. In the first scene he chases, leather-clad on his motorcycle carnival worker Cathy (Joan Freeman). But her father Joe (Leif Erikson) sends him on a truck to the bushes. Crushing through a fence. Maggie Morgan who is also in the truck, takes care, that the boy gets a chance to have his bike and guitar repaired, with working at her carnival. It does not take long, that after doing some regular carnival jobs, he becomes the teenage appealing sensation—but Charlie Rodgers (the character Elvis portrays) gets a better offer from rival carnival owner Harry Carver (Paul Buttram)—a role with maybe than just more than a hint of Colonel Tom Parker in it.

Reportedly, Elvis was in awe of Barbara Stanwyck, so there is some cinematic magic between them. He also insisted on doing his own fight stunts, suffering a bad cut above his eye as a result. A band aid which he wears in subsequent scenes, had to be written into the script, to avoid a delay in shooting while he healed. Strong support comes from Leif Erikson as a fiery, tough hard-drinking man haunted by the death of a customer. To which he was responsible partly, though it having been an accident. Richard Kiel, of later two Roger Moore starring James Bond movies as Jaws is also one of the supporting actors. Screenwriters Anthony Lawrence and Allan Weiss were nominated for the Writers Guild of America Award for Best Written American Musical, a script and in so full with sharp lines. Songs include "Roustabout", "Little Egypt", "Wheels On My Heels", "Hard Knocks" generally one of the greats among Elvis Presley's soundtrack albums.

"Wheels On My Heels" only a little over a minute long, appears like a music video in the movie, when he rides along a country road, singing the tune. Critics were lukewarm, seeing yet another Elvis formulaic film. The New York Times wrote that "Roustabout has little in the way of dramatic substance", noting that Elvis was "perfectly cast" plus "surprisingly convincing".

16. GIRL HAPPY (1965) with Shelley Fabares, Gary Crosby, Nita Talbot, Joby Baker, Mary Ann Mobley, Harold J. Stone and Chris Noel

Directed by Boris Sagal

MGM 1965. A Enterpre production. Running time: 96 minutes. Elvis' seventeenth film

Elvis plays Rock and Roll singer Rusy Wells whose band y is to eagerly embark to sunny Fort Lauderdale/Florida. But the tough guy managing the club they are gigging in in Chicago (portrayed by Harold J. Stone) informs them that their gig is not at the end. Big Frank (Stone) has a problem, his daughter Valerie (Shelley Fabares) is about to head down to Ford Lauderdale for Spring Break herself. So Daddy's worried about her retaining her virtue. With mobster Big Frank sending them to Fort Lauderdale to keep more than one eye on his daughter. Romantic entanglements evolve and Rusty and Valerie hook up.

Joe Pasternak, the musical's producer, had some experience with Beach movies having produced 1960s "Where The Boys Are" for MGM starring Connie Francis, one of the genre's forerunners. Beach movies were still en vogue in 1964, even though the impact of the British Invasion, Motown and Garage Rock was not to be overheard on the charts. So why not combine the two, Elvis movie and Beach movie, that being the innovative idea behind "Girl Happy".

But the budget was low, and so Elvis even didn't travel down to Florida. The movie being filmed at the MGM Studios in Culver City/California over the course of the last week of June and all of July 1964. Most of the plot was set around the swimming pool and inside the club where Rusty performed, so some movie goers might have noticed that this was not a grand scale production. The title song, was provided by songwriters Doc Pomus and Jerry Ragovoy. The latter doing business under the alias Norman Meade. The RCA Victor soundtrack album was cut at Hollywood's Radio Recorders from June 10th until June 12th 1964 with Scotty Moore (lead guitar) and DJ Fontana (drums). The Jordanaires, several members of Nashville's A-team and LA guitarist Tommy Tedesco in attendance. One of the greatest hits to come out of the movie was "Puppet On A String" which made No. 14 for Elvis in the Billboard Charts. "Do The Clam" was very well received in the UK, while "The Meanest Girl In Town" was also cut by Bill Haley for a return single to Decca Records. Not to forget "I've Got To Find My Baby".

The album to the film made the US Top 10, while the movie itself generated more than three million Dollars on the box office.

17. TICKLE ME (1965) with Jocelyn Lane

Directed by Norman Taurog

Allied Artists, 1965. A Ben Schwalb production. Running time: 90 minutes. Elvis' eighteenth film.

In 1965, Elvis Presley needed some quick money to pay a tax bill. Colonel Tom Parker knew the answer. A movie for the struggling B-movie studio Allied Artists:

A one-off deal was struck. Allied Artists funnelled $600,000 in Elvis' direction, plus $150,000 expenses and his usual 50 percent of the profits. That left $400,000 to make the cheapest move to that date, Elvis Presley starred in, only overrunning the budget with $6000. It was shot on location at the Paramount Studios in California. Thanks to the witty direction of the established "Elvis-director" Norman Taurog and a script by the authors of "The Three Stooges" Elwood Ullmann and Edward Bernds the result was one of the funniest Elvis Presley comedies. Elvis plays Lonnie Beale, a singing rodeo rider who takes a job helping out with horses at a beauty ranch, a big health spa named Yogurt Gulch. The clientele are actresses and models, so this alone ensures a bikini, leotard and towel filled surrounding for Elvis to sing some of his hit songs.

As the budget was so small, no separate soundtrack album was produced, but Elvis Presley relied on prior recordings such as: "Long Lonely Highway", "It Feels So Right", "(Such) An Easy Question", "Dirty Dirty Feeling", "Put The Blame On Me", "I'm Yours", "Night Rider", "I Feel That I've Known You Forever", and "Slowly But Surely".

The non-producing of a soundtrack album was not such a bad case, especially for such an hastily produced film, for which a soundtrack might have been a little bit rushed. All of the songs chosen were good: For instance the Rock and Roll ballad "(Such) An Easy Question", penned by Otis Blackwell and Winfield Scott, which became a hit wen released as single to back off the film. Highlights included the bluesy rocker "It Feels So Right", charismatically performed in a lively restaurant setting with Elvis wearing a striking black western jacket with a white piping over a scarlet shirt, there was another lively rocker with "Dirty, Dirty Feeling" sung in the stables—with the last word spoken by a horse (!). The ballad "I Feel That I've Known You Forever" was comically staged with Elvis as Lonnie Beale wandering around the outside of the house of his miffed lover repeatedly closing the curtains and blinds in his face.

About the plot: Rodeo rider Lonnie Beale (Elvis Presley) is needed by spa owner Vera Radford (Julie Adams, of The Creature From The Black Lagoon) to which he holds the line: "I've heard of this happening to secretaries.", Lonnie quipping when she tries to seduce him. His real love interest, meanwhile, is spa guest Pam Merritt (Jocelyn Lane), who is hunting a treasure, hid by her grandfather, in a nearby ghost town. This leading to a fantasy sequence where they imagine to be in a deserted saloon bar, full with cowboys and card sharks.

Elvis becomes the western-suited Panhandle Kid for one of the movie's funniest scenes. First, he throws his Stetson from the door, landing it on the barkeeper's head. Then he orders his "usual", a glass of milk, and tells the server to "leave the bottle". Later, the movie evolves into a live action version of Scooby Doo, with Pat, Lonnie and his sidekick Stanley (Jack Mullaney) comically menaced by ghosts and wolfmen which are unmasked as crooks trying to scare them away, to claim the box with the treasures for themselves.

At the time that "Tickle Me" as released, the critics might have given up on Elvis Presley appearing in a cinematic classic. The New York Times described it as "The silliest, feeblest and fullest vehicle for the Memphis Wonder in a long time. Both Elvis and Allied Artists should know better." While the Los Angeles Times understood it better: "lousy colour, cheap sets, hunks of stock footage, painted scenery and unconvincing process work. But who's to quibble when the movie is so much fun!"

The movie's success saved Allied Artists from bankruptcy, doubled its investment on the box-office, and rewarded it's star Elvis Presley with a Golden Laurel Award for Best Male Actor in a Musical.

18. HARUM SCARUM (1965) with Fran Jeffries, Michael Ansara, Jay Novello, Mary Ann Mobbley and Philip Reed

Directed by Gene Nelson

MGM, 1965. A For Leaf Production. Running time: 95 minutes. Elvis nineteenth film.

One of the characteristics of most of the Elvis movies is that, apart if the movie is in the league of "King Creole" or "Girls, Girls, Girls" Presley took his acting always serious, and is always worthwhile watching. Maybe this is not so obvious in "Harum Scarum". The film is described by many critics as plain silly. Elvis plays Johnny Tyrone, a singer/actor who is also an expert in martial arts. He is on a publicity tour to promote his latest film "Sands Of The Desert" when he is kidnapped an brought to a deserted place cut off from the rest of the world, for centuries. His kidnappers would like him to use his martial arts to kill a desert king. He tries to escape having to fulfil this deed by joining a troupe of touring musicians.

The possibilities for Elvis were there … The idea of playing in a costume drama interested him. The storyline was based on the silent movie The Sheik (1921), which had starred Rudolph Valentino, one of Elvis Presley's idols. Elvis was sheer fascinated by the Valentino mystique, and the way he used his eyes to project emotion. Some of Elvis' costumes for "Harum Scarum" were modelled on Rudolph Valentino's. Plus the film was shot on the original set of Cecil B. De Mille's biblical epic movie The King of Kings (1927). The movie also reunited Elvis with director Gene Nelson who had filmed with him "Kissin' Cousins".

Elvis admired Nelson who had experience as an actor and dancer himself. Disillusion set in early, especially after Elvis saw the material presented to him, for the soundtrack. Sadly also the set, no matter, what history it had, looked cheap. Priscilla Presley wrote in her autobiography "Elvis and Me" how quickly Elvis' spirits sank: "His morale plummeted. Harum Scarum's plot was a joke, the character he played a fool, and the songs he sang disasters. The film turned out to be another disappointment, and an embarrassing one at that."

Elvis also told his leading lady Mary Ann Mobley, as she recalled in an later interview and had appeared with him in Girl Happy: "This isn't going to make movie history, is it?" Having completed shooting, Elvis handed out gifts—Star of David watches. Director Gene Nelson got an autographed picture with the inscription: "Someday, we'll get it right." Even the Colonel thought of Harum Scarum as turkey. When seeing the finished film, he suggested than an narrator, a talking camel should be added, so that the audiences would think that the film's stupidity was intended. On the box office, *Harum Scarum* made $2 million. The soundtrack reaching the Top 10 for 11 weeks.

19. FRANKIE AND JOHNNY (1966) with Donna Douglas, Harry Morgan, Sue Ann Langdon and Nancy Kovack

Directed by Frederick de Cordova

United Artists, 1966. An Edward Small production. Running time 87 minutes. Elvis' twentieth film.

This cinematic feature on "Frankie and Johnny" based on American folklore, is a vibrant musical-comedy which cast Elvis Presley as a riverboat singer with a gambling problem.

Based on the real-life incident in St Louis in 1899, when an angry young lady named Frankie shot her teenaged lover Albert after he won a cakewalk contest with dance partner Nelly Bly (he died of his wound, but Frankie got off on self-defence). A song memorialised the shooting Albert's name soon shifting to Johnny in the tale. Bluesman John Hurt, guitar wizard Les Paul, Country icon Johnny Cash, Jerry Lee Lewis, Gene Vincent and of course Elvis Presley would cut their own versions of the song. Elvis, as soon as it was decided that he would make a perfect Johnny, for the movie. He portrays a suave singer and riverboat gambler in a movie loosely following the original tale. This 1966 Technicolor feature, directed by Fred de Cordoas, who also directed TV's The George Burns and Gracie Allen Show and The Jack Benny Programme, as well as a string of films such as 1951's "Bedtime for Bonzo" with Ronald Reagan starring opposite a Chimpanzee. The movie wasn't standard Elvis fare, as it was strictly a period piece, with colourful costumes and not an electric guitar in sight, therefore more old-fashioned features.

Donna Douglas, from the Beverly Hills Hillbillies, a top rated US TV sitcom, was cast to play Frankie. Nancy Kovack made a tempting rival Nelly Bly. Veteran character actor Harry Morgan was cast as Hoagy Carichal, also being presented as the author in this memorable movie tale, in the film. Franke and Johnnie happen to be stage performers in a performance, that climaxes in Frankie shooting her Johnny, on stage. There isn't really any Rock and Roll songs in the movie, but plenty of up-tempo production numbers. Johnny sings the lowdown blues on "Hard Luck". There is the tender ballad "Beginners Luck". Further we find "What Every Woman Lives For" and "Please Don't Stop Loving Me" penned by Doc Pomus and Mort Shuman. Elvis also belts out "Down By The Riverside", "When The Saints Go Marching In" and "Come Along". (The ladder written by David Hess, who had the original song of the Elvis hit "All Shook Up" out, a few months before Elvis.)

Other songs included are "Petunia", "The Gardener's Daughter" and "Look Out, Broadway" with the fast paced "Shout It Out" bringing some rockin' change into the set. The film made a little less than $3 Million at the box office, with the soundtrack album cracking the Top Twenty, the only single from it "Frankie and Johnny" and "Please Don't Stop Loving Me" missed the Top 20 in the US, with

"Frankie and Johnny" doing better in the UK, than stateside. The film shows how Elvis Presley might have looked like in a 1940s Technicolor musical.

20. PARADISE HAWAIAN STYLE (1966)

Suzanna Leigh, Donna Butterworth and James
Shigeta

Directed by Michael Morre

Paramount 1966. A Hal B. Wallis Production. Running time: 91 minutes. Elvis twenty-first film.

In what could have been Blue Hawaii part 2, Elvis Presley plays playboy airline pilot Rick Richards, who is canned for saucy behaviour with a stewardess. He returns to Hawaii in search for work. With his old buddy Danny Kohana (James Shigeta), he sets up a helicopter service. Banking on Danny's amount of former girlfriends they recommend their service to tourists. Danny then hires Judy Hudson (Suzanna Leigh) as his Girl Friday. He puts a ring on her finger, telling her to pretend she is married, to put off the attentions of Rick (Elvis). Desperate for customers, Elvis and his associates decide to transport some dogs to the Kuai Hilton dog show.

Elvis sings to four puppies "A Dog's Life" written by Ben Weisman. In trying to land, the canine caper nearly causes an accident. Rick runs Belden (John Doucette) a bigwig of the FAA (Federal Aviation Authority), off the road and into a ditch. Belden pushes for Rick's licence to be revoked. Despite being grounded, he violates the temporary order to set off on a search and rescue mission with Judy to rescue Danny, stranded on a beach with daughter Jan (Donna Butterworth) and nursing a broken leg. At a Polynesian festival attended by special guest Belden, Rick persuades him to think again, and after considering Rick's recent heroics, Belden relents, and Danrick Airways is soon airborne once more. Judy announces she is free. The finale is a flamboyant, full cast set piece, to a "Drums Of The Island" reprise.

Unlike the movie's predecessor "Blue Hawaii" not all songs here are strong. Nine-year-old Donna Butterworth sings "Bill Bailey, Won't You Come Home?", Elvis sings "Queen Wahine's Papaya", "This Is My Heaven", while the dreamy "Sand Castles" didn't make it in the film's final edit. The soundtrack only selling 225,000 copies, while "Paradise Hawaiian Style" itself mad $2.5 million on the box office in five months. Proving once more that the public loved Elvis not as much in dramatic roles as in lightweight musical comedies. The film has some good moments, a glossy travelogue, the locations are lovely, there are authentic dance sequences which were choreographed by Jack Regas from the Polynesian Cultural Centre.

Marianna Hill who played Lani Kaimna, stated how Elvis must have felt about his twenty-first motion picture: "Underneath it all, there seems to be a lot of resentment, defensiveness and hostility." True, Elvis Presley by now was thirty years of age, most likely fed up with the same old movie format, also growing unsure of his place musically in hit parades mostly dominated by British acts. "All Elvis breaks loose in the Swinging, Swaying Luau-ing South Seas!" nevertheless was the movie's most promising tag line, being a long way from Blue Hawaii, only four years later.

21. SPINOUT (CALIFORNIA HOLIDAY) (1966) with Deborah Walley

Directed by Norman Taurog

MGM, 1966. A Joe Pasternak production. Running time: 90 minutes. Elvis' twenty-second film.

Three girls, a rock band and a race car towed by a stylish 1929 model J Duesenberg—in Spinout Elvis had it all, only lacking the serious role he still hoped for.

By the mid-1960s, Elvis was very desperate to elevate the quality of his acting career that he told his friends he'd be willing to take a support role in a big film just to get an opportunity in showing his craft. It had worked for Frank Sinatra in 1953, with fourth billing in "From Here To Eternity"—would it work for Elvis Presley? After Barbara Streisand offered him co-starring in "A Star Is Born", which he most likely had to turn down as of advice of Colonel Tom Parker, that dream was over too …

"Spinout" with racing cars in a way not dissimilar to "Viva Las Vegas", yet minus Ann Margret, but with Norman Taurog to come on board to direct his sixth film with Elvis Presley, is one of the better ones, yet still in the usual Elvis fare of the 1960s. Elvis plays Mike McCoy, who mixes racing cars with being the lead vocalist of a travellin' band. The band had even a beat look about it. But Elvis merely fronting a band is a little surreal, he'd always been out of front his movies as a solo star, just as he was as a musical performer, no matter how accomplished his musicians were, he was always the main attraction. Such, however, was the musical landscape after Beatlemania, that it was written into the screenplay. Mike is a free and easy sort of guy, who would happily enjoy a single life, moving from gig to gig, towing his sports car behind a 1929 model J Duesenberg, But three women chase him. There is Cynthia, played by Shelley Fabares, who had already acted alongside Elvis in "Girl Happy", and who would do so again in "Clambake". Cynthia is the daughter of a millionaire played by Carl Betz. The appeal for audiences was that they had played father and daughter before, in the long running American sitcom The Donna Reed Show. Which only had recently ended, before Spinout hit production. The second girl in line is Diana, played by Diana McBain, who researches a book called "The Perfect American Male". She thinks Mike might fit the description.

Also the female drummer of his band, Les played by Deborah Walley fancies our hero. Privately Elvis, who was studying spiritual matters at this time, introduced her to some of new age's teachings, she at least gave him credit for it. Spinout fared respectably at the box office, also offering some strong music with the Bo Diddley styled "Never Say Yes", written by Doc Pomus and Mortu Shuman, the ballad "Am I Ready" and the blues-shuffle "I'll Be Back". Though of course not all critics liked it, there was a felling it had been the best effort by Elvis Presley in some time.

22. EASY COME, EASY GO (1967) with Elsa Lancaster, Dodie Marshall, Pat Priest, Pat Harrington, Ship Ward and Frank Mettugh

Directed by John Rich

Paramount, 1967. A Hal B. Wallis production. Running time: 95 minutes. Elvis' twenty-third film.

Having been a soldier in "G.I. Blues", an airman in "Kissin' Cousins", Elvis joined the Navy as frogman in the seaborne adventure "Easy Come, Easy Go". On his last day in the service, his character Ted Jackson is defusing an undersea mine when he chances upon a sunken ship complete with treasure chest. On his return to life as civilian, he teams up with his beatnik buddy Judd (Pat Harrington Jr.) to try to recover what he believes to be a fortune in Spanish gold. Determined to beat him is rich, bikini-clad yacht owner Diana (Pat Priest) and her boyfriend Gil (Skip Ward).

The movie opens in breezy fashion with a sharp-uniformed Elvis Presley serenading his crewmates with the jazzy title song, it looks like an attempt to recreate the magic of "G.I. Blues". But for some it stops here, though Variety gave the film one of its most favourable write ups, when noting: "Good balance of script and songs, plus generally amusing performances by a competent, well-directed cat, add up to diverting entertainment." The New York Times however called it "a tired little clinker that must have been shot during lunch hour", while the Los Angeles times said: "aptly summed up in its title> easy to take, easy to forget." It was Elvis last film for movie producer Hal Wallis and Paramount, it seems somewhat that all were just there to fulfil contract engagements for a last time. Elvis did not feel comfortable on the open sea, and for once was not keen on doing his own stunts.

Presley's love interest in the movie is yoga-loving Jo (Dodie Marshall) and a lot of the film's humour is aimed at the hippie community. Some funny moments for instance are, when a girl holds a placard with "We Protest", to which Presley asks, "What are you protesting?" and gets the reply: "If you don't know, then I'm certainly not going to tell you!"

Elvis knots himself in yoga class, with the accompanying song "Yoga Is As Yoga Does", probably the oddest song he ever sung, and far away from the real Elvis, who practices it, privately. While the filmmakers clearly enjoyed poking fun at the counterculture, it might have not done Elvis a favour. Certainly there were not many songs in the soundtrack to convert new Elvis fans. A pity also that Elvis disliked the song "She's A Machine" which because of that, did not end up in the movie, but on the album "Elvis Singing Flaming Star And Others". Recorded in two days, the soundtrack released on an Extended Play sold just 30,000 units, though making Nr. 1 in the UK.

23. DOUBLE TROUBLE (1967) with Annette Day, John Williams and Yvonne Romain

Directed by Arthur H. Nadel
MGM, 1967. A B.C.W. production. Running time: 90 minutes. Elvis' twenty-fourth film.

Elvis Presley never toured Europe, but his character in "Double Trouble"—the nightclub singer Guy Lambert—did. Even if Elvis never left the studio back lot in Hollywood. In the year, 1967, that the Beatles released their "Sgt Pepper's Lonely Hearts Club Band" (a day after the soundtrack to "Double Trouble" by Elvis Presley) swinging London was the centre of the musical world. It made sense to set part of Elvis' newest film there, with the rest in Bruggs and Antwerp. Added was a comic plot about kidnappers and jewel thieves, in the heyday of the Pink Panthers films, adding a trio of Volkswagen Beetles, a year before Herbie made his debut for Disney, this movie was bang on trend.

Mark Brandel's story finds Guy trying to avoid romantic entanglement with an over amorous but slightly underage British heiress—at least for the four days before she turns 18. At the same time, he has to keep her out of the clutches of various crooks who are either trying to kidnap her, retrieve a cache of diamonds planted in her suitcase, or kill the pair in a series of accidents. "I could get shot for this" mutters Elvis as Guy Lambert, a second later, an assassin's bullet almost parts his hair, as he walks the girl out of a hotel. Elvis co-star Annette Day, was spotted by chance by producer Judd Bernard, as she was working in her partner's antique shop in London's Portobello Road. Despite "Double Trouble" being her first and only film, the 18 year old was faultless in every scene and looks genuinely in love with her leading man Elvis.

Some of the 1960s days of British English were also written into the script. To some comic effect. When making tea, she asks "Do you have any biccies?" (meaning biscuits). "Not that I know I know of." Elvis replies defensively. In another scene he says: "I've got to straighten this thing out once and for all."

"Super Duper!" Jill's eyes widen with Carry-on-film suggestiveness. Elvis Presley's performance of "Old MacDonald Had A Farm" is often cited as the lowest of his recording career. Taken out of context, it would really seem as an odd choice for a singer who once shook the world with "Jailhouse Rock". But the scene in which he sings it to Day while they ride in the back of a truck is perfectly entertaining, mainly due to the reactions of the winsome Day.

There is a playful chemistry between both lead actors, which is pure delight. Elvis appreciated Annette Day's acting debut to reward her with the present of a white Ford Mustang convertible. There was no off-screen romance between the two. Maybe because she was in real life only eighteen also, in the film he has the text phrase to say: "Seventeen will get me twenty." The soundtrack was recorded at the MGM soundstage, Elvis turns into fine performances of the Broadway styled "I Love Only One Girl" and a more typical Elvis rocker "Long Legged Girl (With The Short Dress On"). At the box-office the film only took 1.6$, maybe also because it was only released weeks after "Easy Come, Easy Go". It was Elvis' lowest grossing movie to date. Critics however praised the movie's colourful production values, which still look good today. The Los Angeles Times: "The cast never left Culver City, but you would never know it, so cleverly have quaint Belgian streets and other European settings been reproduced on the back lot."

24. CLAMBAKE (1967) with Shelley Fabares, Will Hutchens, Bill Bixby, Gary Merith and James Gregory

Directed by Arthur H. Nadel

United Artists 1967. A Levy-Grandeur-Laven production. Running time: 97 minutes. Elvis' twenty-fifth film.

1967 saw the final Elvis Presley movie being shot for United Artists. Elvis is cast as Scott Hayward, heir to an oil fortune, who is a talented singer on the side, naturally. Scott yearns to know if he's as irresistible to the ladies without all the money burning a hole in his bank account. He trades places with water-skiing instructor Tom Wilson (Will Hutchins, star of the TV Western "Sugarfoot") at a Florida Hotel. The chicks still love him—including Shelley Fabares who is back for a second duty as Elvis Presley's primary love interest. Bill Bixby, co-star of the popular TV Sitcom "My favourite Martian", later of TV's Hulk fame, as Dr Bruce Banner and also host of the two volume special "The Elvis Files" dealing with the question if Elvis did fake his death, and did indeed not die on 16 August 1977—is Elvis rival in this movie.

Director Arthur H. Nadle had a resume heavy on TV Westerns such as "The Riflemen", "The Big Valley", "The Virginian" and "Daniel Boone". His CV on feature films was light. There were only seven musical interludes in Clambake. Elvis belts the rockin' and rollin' theme "Clambake" written by Ben Weisman and Sid Wayne. There is more of a crooner with "Who Needs Money" written by Randy Starr, who also contributed the dramatic ballad "The Girl I Never Loved". Another crooning tune was "A House That Has Everything", sounding more like in an older fashioned Hollywood musical. Elvis also sings Cindy Walker and Eddy Arnold's Country and Western classic "You Don't Know Me." In 1956, a massive Top 10 C&W seller for Eddy Arnold, plus a massive pop hit for Ray Charles in 1962. Sadly Elvis Presley's remake didn't crack the US Top 40 in late 1967. There are bit parts played by Rock and Roll TV producer of such gems on British television as "Six Five Special" and "Oh Boy!" as well as the US TV Show "Shindig"—Jack Good. Plus DJ Sam Riddle, host of the US Show "Hollywood A Go-Go". As there was only seven songs in Clambake, RCA beefed up the soundtrack album with five titles not in the film. Jimmy Reed's 1961 blues hit "Big Boss Man" wonderfully sung by Elvis for instance. The five numbers were of much better fare, than the movie's songs some say. On the box office, other Presley movies had done a lot better, the soundtrack also making a meagre No. 40 on the Billboard album charts. "The wheels were starting to come off the Presley franchise" Vintage Rock Magazine noted in its special edition on Elvis Presley's movie years.

25. STAY AWAY, JOE (1968) with Quentin

Dean, Burgess Meredith, Joan Blondell, Katy
Jurado and Thomas Gomez

Directed by Peter Tewksbury

MGM, 1968. A Douglas Lawrence production. Running time: 102 minutes. Elvis' twenty-sixth film

"Stay Away Joe" opens with stunning aerial footage of the Arizona mountains, over which Elvis sings "Stay Away", a western-styled rewrite of "Greensleeves" in a most affecting ballad voice. Some viewers might have expected a Western with this opening sequence, but were dished out a broad slapstick comedy from the beginning to the end. Elvis portrays Joe, a brawling, bull-riding, Navajo Indian. Having one eye on every passing lady. His other eye is on getting rich quick: His latest scheme a prize bull more interested in sleeping than impregnating the family's cows. "I might have to show him how to do it." Muses Joe, to which his Grandpa (Thomas Gomez(responds "Can I watch?" …

Throughout the entire movie, Joe is chased by gun-toting gas station owner Glenda (Joan Blondell) who is intent on forcing him to a shotgun wedding. His crazy family in the meantime, are preparing their ramshackle home for their daughter's rich boyfriend's and his high society mother's visit. Unfortunately, what set out to be an undemanding drive-in popcorn cruncher drew immediate criticism for its use of white actors as Native Americans. As Variety put it, at that time: "The basic story—contemporary American Indians who are portrayed as laughable incompetents—is out of touch with latter day appreciation of some basic dignity in all human beings. At best … a dim artistic accomplishment; at worst, it caters out to outdated prejudice."

"Stay Away, Joe" is performed with a Bo Diddley beat by Elvis, in his denim jacket and jeans, you can see the inspiration for the look Shakin' Stevens adopted some twelve years later. There is also the musical number "Dominic" in which Elvis urges his reluctant bull to take an interest in the heifers. In the movie, Elvis sings the song chasing a couple of girls performing a striptease as they go. Elvis had Felton Jarvis made promises that he would never release "Dominic" on a record. As there was no soundtrack with "Stay Away, Joe" the song wasn't officially released in 1994 on the compilation album of the movies "Kissin' Cousins"/"Clambake"/"Stay Away Joe", long after Felton Jarvis' death. "Stay Away" was issued as B-side to "US Male" and reached No. 67 on the Hot 100 in its own right. The Hollywood Reporter also argued that the Native American caricatures would rightly offend many, while "The Film Daily" was a little kinder, noting: "What matters is that the picture evokes a mood of mirth and happy, frenzy that is catching."

26. SPEEDWAY (MGM 1968) with Nancy Sinatra

Directed by Norman Taurog

MGM, 1968. A Douglas Laurence production. Running time: 94 minutes. Elvis' twenty-seventh film.

"We didn't sign Elvis to be another Jimmy Dean, we signed him to be Elvis Presley," Hal Wallis once said of Elvis' Paramount contract. It was clear from the films he made for the MGM studio in the 1960s that he was viewed the same way there. "Speedway" was once again directed by Norman Taurog. It was another movie in a breezy line, great to look at, funny in a non-sidesplitting sort of way. There were good dance routines and pleasant songs. Fans of the 1950s Elvis hip-swivelling Rock and Roll outcast must have seen that Elvis was now sanitised for middle of the road movies, which nevertheless made enough money.

So, there was little hope of change, as much as Elvis himself longed for change. By the late 1960s, set against social changes of the times, the wholesome nature of the musicals Elvis starred in, somehow lacked the Zeitgeist. The films were also no longer as profitable as they once had been. "Speedway" can be seen as a lively final stand of the Elvis formula movie. As in Viva Las Vegas, Elvis was once again cast as racing driver, reflecting an era when films about racing were popular fare.

Standout examples include thrilling big screen spectaculars like "Grand Prix" (1966), with James Garner and Yves Montand leading an international cast, and "The Great Race" (1965), starring Jack Lemmon and Tony Curtis, and "Monte Carlo Or Bust" (1969) with Tony Curtis again, both of which focused on veteran cars. "Red Line 7000" starred James Caan as stock-car driver, and teen idol Frankie Avalon had appeared in a youth-slanted effort, "Fireball 500" (1966). "Speedway", possibly drawing inspiration form the James Caan film, had Elvis play stock-car racer Steve Grayson, and carried a lot of live race footage from the Charlotte Motor Speedway track in Concord/North Carolina. Several leading stock car drivers of the day made credited guest appearances. Bill Bixby, showed a good feel for comedy, and played the manager whose squandering of his charge's racing earnings on gambling, possibly loosely based on real-life manager Colonel Tom Parker's gambling habits, put the Internal Revenue Service on his tail for non-payment of taxes.

Nancy Sinatra was cast as an IRS agent who works on the case, and who thereby also provided the love interest of our leading man Elvis Presley. At the time "Speedway" was filmed Nancy Sinatra was on a career-high with smash hits like "These Boots Are Made For Walkin'" and her duet with her father Frank Sinatra "Somethin' Stupid", plus singing the theme song to Frank Sinatra's detective thriller "Tony Rome". Not to forget also singing the James Bond theme song "You Only Live Twice", which had Sean Connery starring as James Bond, before George Lazenby took over. She was well cast, and it is a bit of a shame, that she could not show off her vocal chords or more of her dancing. "Speedway" finished being in the Top 40 grossing movies of 1968.

Though the Los Angeles Times noted: "a script that ran out of gas before Elvis was born." While the New York Times that some fine talents were underused in the flick: "one of the most talented, important and durable performers of our time" had been made into failure to have been made of use. Luckily, a big change for Elvis Presley was just around the corner.

27. LIVE A LITTLE, LOVE A LITTLE (1968) with Michele Carey, Don Porter, Rudy Vallee, Dick Sargant and Eddie Hodges

Directed by Norman Taurog

MGM, 1968. A Douglas Laurence production. Running time: 90 minutes. Elvis' twenty-eight film

Based on Dan Greenburg's 1965 novel "Kiss My Firm, But Pliant Lips"

"Live A Little, Love A Little" is one of the better late 1960s movie efforts starring Elvis Presley. It's an unusual light music screwball comedy with slight adult overtones. Benefitting from gorgeous California exteriors. There is also a lot of chemistry between Elvis and his co-star Michele Carey, which pays off well in the final product. The character of manic Pixie Dream girl Bernice is best described as problematic with signs of multiple personality.

She cheerily tells Greg, the character played by Elvis: "I have different moods for different names."

Carey is very funny, but is also playing a woman with serious issues: She stalks a man she randomly meets on a beach and then sets her enormous Great Dane, Albert, on him when he ho-hums after kissing her.

Greg on the other hand, is an unusual role for Elvis, who is quite suiting it. There is a bit of action and rough stuff, but the film opens with him doughnutting his dune buggy around the beach. He also looks very much at home in the fashion shoot sequences featuring a variety of models. Clearly a riff on familiar scenes from Michelangelo Antonioni's movie "Blow-Up" on swinging London. There is also an utterly bizarre dream sequence when Albert turns into a man in an unconvincing dog costume and starts talking to Greg. This leads into a musical set-piece accompanying the melodramatic song "Edge Of Reality". This dream sequence features the man in the dog suit and some dancers against a modish hot pink cyclorama.

Elvis seems to quite enjoy it, and throws in some of his best old school hip shaking. It turns out that Bernie has drugged Greg, leaving him unconscious for days and resulting in him needing to work two jobs for two different companies to pay the rent. This is a frankly pretty dark thing which happens to the leading character, but Norman Taurog on his final Elvis Presley movie, gets comic mileage from Greg's frantic running between different shoots in the same building. This same slapstick comic riff was reprised in the 1980s for the yuppie office comedy "The Secret Of My Success" starring Michael J. Fox.

At the end, true love wins, and after Bernice dramatically runs off, the film ends with the pair kissing in the surf on the beach where they met. These days "Live A Little, Love A Little" is best known for inclusion of the latter-day hit

"A Little Less Conversation". Mac Davis and Billy Strange's song soundtrack a rather groovy 1960s LA pool party. There Greg picks up model Ellen (Celeste Yarnall) and whisks her away in his convertible in real time. It is a beautifully choreographed scene by Norman Taurog, both funky and funny, Elvis looking the business in his midnight blue suit and white roll neck. "A Little Less Conversation" would of course have a comeback in 2001, when DJ and producer David Holmes included a shorter, more frenetic alternative take of the tune on his soundtrack to Steven Soderbergh's star-studded remake of the 60s Rat Pack movie Ocean's Eleven.

In another turn, in 2002 the Dutch DJ Junie XL remixed it for a Nike campaign for the 2002 FIFA World Cup. The first ever remix of an Elvis song, it did considerably well, topping the UK charts, becoming pretty much an Elvis standard for the Millennium youngsters generation.

28. CHARRO! (1969) With Mary Tyler Moore and Jane Elliott

Directed by Charles Marquis Warren

National General Pictures, 1969. A Harry Caplan production. Running time: 98 minutes. Elvis' twenty-ninth movie.

"There's half-decent revenge western lying under the surface of Charro!" Vintage Rock noted in its special edition on Elvis Presley movies. Contributing to it that it was only half-decent might be, according to Martin Ruddock of Vintage Rock, the director Charles Marquis Warren who was prior responsible to Wild West TV Shows such as "Rawhide", "Gunsmoke" and "The Virginian". It was originally offered to Clint Eastwood, fair to say Charles Marquis Warren was no Sergio Leone, and Clint Eastwood who had spent six years as second lead on "Rawhide" under Warren's guiding supervision.

Eastwood who had just made his name in Leone's "Dollars Trilogy" of westerns, did not seem to be bewildered of renewing his professional life with working with Warren again. Nevertheless, ever the pro, Elvis gritted his teeth on and got on with the role of reformed outlaw Jess Wade. It wasn't his first rodeo, he could handle horse-riding and stunts, and his charisma and stage presence goes a long way. He only seemed a little surprised when in fight scenes some punch was thrown his way. The beard in Charro was also something new in an Elvis Presley movie, and for once there was only a theme song sung by Elvis Presley over the credits, but no songs in the middle. This movie certainly had a darker flair than previous Elvis Westerns, and also flirted at least a little with the Spaghetti Westerns.

Of course, getting such an adult picture past the manager of Elvis Colonel Tom Parker, was a tough job. The opening saloon sequence was originally planned to feature a trio of naked bordello workers, but Warren replaced it with a standard bar room shoot-out between Elvis' character Jess Wade and the outlaw gang. Some nudity almost made it in the picture, when a nude scene was shot with co-star Ina Balin, but the Colonel worried the movie to be X-rated and had it removed. Gang leader Vince Hackett (Victor French) and his trigger-happy younger brother Billy Roy (Solomon Sturges) are both very interesting, and Vince being basically stuck with his liability of a younger brother leads to a rather interesting movie plot.

The gang also captures Wad and brands his neck with a red hot poker to mark him as a wounded in the heist they are framing him for. This could have been one of the movie's most memorable scene, if it would have been allowed to be more graphic and far more convincing. The climax features a tense night time shoot out, Vince is left distraught after Billy Roy is crushed to death by the stolen cannon. After a brief chat with Jess, he surrenders, two minutes later Elvis rides off, his dignity intact with this move, and "Charro!" ends.

29. THE TROUBLE WITH GIRLS (1969) with Marilyn Mason, Nicole Jaffe, Sheree North and Vincent Price

Directed by Peter Tewksbury

MGM, 1969. A Lester Welch production. Running time: 97 film. Elvis' twenty-ninth.

Elvis Presley was back to exhibit his skills as a serious actor in "The Trouble With Girls", a 1969 MGM feature that turned out to be his next-to-last movie. There was room for songs, but these weren't the primary focus in the move. No RCA Victor soundtrack LP was released and only one of the film's tunes saw light of the day as a single. Elvis was cast as Walter Hale, the manager of a barnstorming Chautauqua troupe. Traveling Chautauqua groups who roamed the US hinterlands presenting educational lectures about a variety of topics during the early decades of the 20th century, usually under tents, were quite successful for some time. This was a more mature Elvis movie, than the G-rated sex symbol that happily sang and acted around beaches and bandstands in one movie after the other, during an entire decade. Now he smoked long thin cigars, and sported stylish sideburns that were wider and longer when he first took the musical and movie world by storm in the mid-1950s.

Drama surrounds Walter's troupe after it sets up shop in a small Iowa town. A murder is committed, and the main character as played by Elvis is revealing the actual killer, after a gambler is falsely arrested for a crime he didn't commit. MGM apparently thought it was time to change the formula of Elvis movies, after dwindling box office sales and a lack of movie songs placings in the charts. The screenplay had been kicking around for a decade before Peter Tewksbury would direct it with Elvis Presley as its star. (Glenn Ford and Dick Van Dyke had been previously attached to it.)

Marilyn Mason, Sheree North and Nicole Jaffe were the primary female cast in the movie. Veteran horror actors Vincent Price and John Carradine where plugged into character roles, while former baseball star Duke Snider and ill-fated child star Anissa Jones also appeared in roles. Billy Strange, a veteran Los Angeles session guitarist and arranger, was in charge of the movie's score. He had begun his recording career for Capitol Records in the early 1950s, first with Country, later with Rockabilly music. In the 1960s becoming a rock instrumentalist. He worked with Nancy Sinatra during her hit-making run and co-wrote "A Little Less Conversation" with a young Mac Davis for Elvis in 1968.

The songs for "The Trouble With Girls" were cut on 23 October 1968 at United Artists Recorders in Hollywood. Strange and Davis wrote "Clean Up Your Own Backyard", which managed to climb up to No. 25 on the US Pop Charts and No. 21 in the UK. Ben Weisman and Buddy Kaye penned the ballad "Almost" which was later released on the RCA budget label Camden on the LP "Let's Be Friends" in 1970. There is a cool duet named "Signs Of The Zodiac" and Elvis truly enjoys himself on the gospel "Swing Down, Sweet Chariot". Although "The Trouble With Girls" didn't turn Elvis fortunes around, it was a far more serious asset to his movie career, than most of the 1960s Presley film fare.

30. CHANGE OF HABIT (1969) with Mary Tyler Moore and Jane Elliott

Directed by William Morris

Universal, 1969. A Universal and NBC production. Running time: 93 minutes. Elvis's thirtieth-first film.

"Changes are a-comin', for these are the changing days" Elvis sings for the opening credits on what would be his final acting movie in his entire career—"Change Of Habit". Thanks to the previous year's TV Special (which was made alongside Change Of Habit as part of a package deal with NBC) he was once again on top of his art. He was back near the top of the charts with "In The Ghetto" and about to hit No. 1 with "Suspicious Minds". Elvis Presley's career was about to enter a new phase on the Las Vegas stage, and he did finish his acting career on a high!

His 31st feature is one of his strongest and very different to most of his musical movies throughout his career. One of the things that makes it so interesting is that even though he had star billing, he doesn't play the main character. "Change Of Habit" was conceived as a vehicle for Mary Tyler Moore and although she was eclipsed by Elvis Presley on the billboards, she remains the movie's focus a Sister Michelle, one of three nuns set out in plain clothes to work as nurses in an inner city clinic run by Elvis as Dr John Carpenter. When they first arrive, Carpenter mistakes the women for patients with unwanted pregnancies and asks "Was it the same guy?"

Despite some sharp humour, "Change Of Habit" takes a gritty view of life in a Puerto Rican ghetto community. At a socially charged time in America's history, the film deals with racism, racial tensions, drugs, poverty. Loan sharking and attempted rape. It was the only second movie to explore autism, the first being Run Wild, Run Free, released the same year. There is also a sequence, a testament of the times, when Dr Carpenter uses the then new and controversial—in the movie barbaric looking—Rage Reduction Therapy on an autistic child. The director William A. Graham worked with Elvis on method acting and improvisation, for Elvis as a big James Dean and Marlon Brando fan, not so new, but certainly much aimed for experience. Graham was also responsible for a different haircut that that gives the then 34-year-old Elvis a more mature look.

Does Elvis get the girl in this movie? The movie ends with Sister Michelle having to decide whether to accept his marriage proposal or return to the convent. The audience never actually gets to see what she decides, so it is mostly up to the viewers imagination. It is a grown up film and a very watchable one. A movie that teases us and possibly also Elvis at the time, that there would be more fine acting roles to come. But ultimately, with the wrap of this movie, his acting days lay behind him!

31. THAT'S THE WAY IT IS (1970) (Elvis Live Performances at the International Hotel, Las Vegas)

Directed by Denis Sanders

MGM, 1970. A Herbert F. Soklow production. Running time: 97 minutes.

Elvis Presley's first non-dramatic role since making his screen debut in "Love Me Tender" in 1956 was "That's The Way It Is". It utilised techniques of two previously critically acclaimed documentaries. Experimental elements of Jean Luc Godard's Rolling Stones feature "Sympathy For The Devil" aka "One Plus One" were dispensed. The reportage style scenes of Elvis rehearsing and larking around with his musicians and inner circle humanised the singer. He was now no longer an untouchable celluloid hero, but a working musician and one of the lads. A split-screen technique seen previously in the Woodstock documentary would bring Elvis up to date.

Eight Panavision cameras were used to ensure that no nuance of the performance, from either Elvis or his musicians, would be missed. Cinematographer Lucien Ballard came with a heavyweight CV including the Western masterpiece The Wild Bunch and used a similar short, sharp cutting style to ensure the excitement and momentum of the footage would be not lost in the final edit. Director Denis Sanders had won two Oscars for his 1954 short film "A Time Out Of War". The original concept for Elvis Presley's latest product was to be a countrywide closed-circuit television presentation. But Parker turned the $1.1 million deal down, and the epic concert film released as a theatrical feature for cinemas. Where it did very well indeed!

32. ELVIS ON TOUR (1972)

Directed by: Pierre Aldridge and Robert Abel.

MGM, 1972. A Cinema Associates production. Running time: 93 minutes.

This 1972 US concert film starring Elvis Presley, capturing him during his fifteen city spring tour earlier that year, was directed by Robert Able and Pierre Aldridge and released by Metro-Goldwyn-Mayer in cinema's. After the success of "That's The Way It Is" Colonel Tom Parker arranged a deal for another documentary film with the MGM studio by early 1972. MGM hired Abel and Aldridge who previously documented Joe Cocker's 1970 tour of the United States. The crew filmed four of Elvis' shows that were later intertwined, assisted by Martin Scorsese, featuring the use of split-screens. The film was released on 1 November 1972, opening to mixed reviews, it became a box office smash, winning the 30th Golden Globe awards for Best Documentary Film.

Elvis twice played characters with the surname Carpenter. In Girls! Girls! Girls! He portrayed Ross Carpenter. Doctor John Carpenter was the name of his character in Change of Habit.

In December 1977, Rob-Rich Films acquired theatrical rights to Girls! Girls! Girls!, G. I. Blues, Fun in Acapulco, Paradise, Hawaiian Style, Paradise Hawaiian Style, Roustabout, Blue Hawaii and King Creole. Owner Sidney Ginsberg packaged the films as an Elvis movie Festival to be shown one film for a day a week long. Ginsberg's Festival opened at the Beacon Theatre in New York City on 26 December 1977. Then moved to Memphis/Tennessee, Dallas/Texas and Oklahoma City/Oklahoma.

Chapter Nine
The Million Dollar Quartet—Elvis Presley, Carl Perkins, Johnny Cash and Jerry Lee Lewis

Sam Phillips was at the controls for a Carl Perkins session during the early afternoon of 4 December 1956. This session would turn out to be the only time that on and off SUN Recording Stars Elvis Presley, Johnny Cash, Jerry Lee Lewis and Carl Perkins, who played an inestimable role in shaping popular music, be united at a recording studio. It was Sun's forefront studio in downtown Memphis/Tennessee.

At that time, Elvis Presley was the most celebrated and most controversial of them all. One out of every two records that RCA, who purchased Elvis from Sun Records, pressed was an Elvis Presley record. Carl Perkins was trying hard to recapture the success he had with "Blue Suede Shoes" in the early months of 1956, crossing the Top Ten in the Pop, Country and R&B Charts. Johnny Cash had enjoyed his first hits with "I Walk The Line" and "Cry, Cry, Cry". Jerry Lee Lewis was desperate to join the hit-makers and sure of himself, that he would outshine them soon.

Ladies and Gentleman—The Million Dollar Quartet:

Elvis Aron Presley (born 8 January 1935 in Tupelo/Mississippi, died 16 August 1977 in Memphis/Tennessee)

> *I learned very early in life that: "Without a song, the day would never end; without a friend, a man ain't got a friend; without a song, the road would never bend—without a song. So I keep singing a song."*
> *(ELVIS PRESLEY)*

American Journalist Jerry Hopkins wrote about Elvis: *Four things America gave to the world, Coca Cola, Baseball, Mickey Mouse and Elvis Presley.*

Time put question marks on many faces, when it comes to Elvis. True, hit compilations, remixes, and classically arranged compilations of some of his recordings—still make the charts. But neither contemporary Rock Journalists, nor the writers of the releases to Elvis, seem to separate the man of his image and myth. Elvis himself stated in his later years: *An image is one thing, a human being another thing.*

Elvis made Rockabilly history with his waxings for Sam Phillip's SUN Records labels. It wasn't until the Rockabilly Revival years of the late 1970s, sweeping Great Britain that his record label RCA seemed to notice the historical value of the songs they had purchased from SUN Records, when buying Elvis contract for 35,000 USD from Sam Phillips. As the first SUN Compilation wasn't released until music journalist Roy Carr asked in an article published at the NME—New Musical Express: *What I still can't comprehend is why, after all these years, RCA haven't collated all the "official" released SUN tracks onto one volume and released it with all relevant details as a collector's edition. After all, these are perhaps the most important rock records ever made.* (NME, June 1974). Someone in that year took notion, because in 1975—the first official LP collection of Elvis' Sun material appeared on RCA, with excellent sleeve notes, by none other than Roy Carr.

Sun Records was a tiny studio at 706 Union Avenue in Memphis/Tennessee. The Sun Record Company began its operations on 27 March 1952. Originally bearing the name Memphis Recording Service—being also responsible for the Nr. 1 R&B hit by Jackie Brenston and His Delta Cats with Ike Turner on piano— "Rocket 88"—leasing it to Chess Records.

Sam Phillips had dreamed his vision of his own record company for a long time and getting the company off the ground wasn't an easy task. For revenue, he recorded anything, that was also the motto of the Memphis Recording Service—and so Sam cut audio of weddings, choirs, and even funerals. He also offered people to make an acetate of a song of their choice for a small fee. Enter Elvis Presley …

"We Record Anything, Anywhere, Anytime" was the slogan of the Memphis Recording Service until it hit off the ground—laying the foundation for the careers of Elvis Presley, Carl Perkins, Jerry Lee Lewis, Johnny Cash and Roy Orbison to name Sam Phillips' most famous Rockabilly discoveries.

Elvis was an only child, his twin brother Jesse Garon dying at birth. His mother Glady's being an over-protective mother and his father Vernon, sold moonshine whiskey and it is said Vernon Presley would have avoided hard work if he could. Moving from Tupelo/Mississippi to Memphis/Tennessee, the Presley's lived in a social housing project. Elvis absorbed music from the streets, the radio, and a Pentecostal church, having already appeared at a talent contest at a fair in his former hometown Tupelo. Elvis started to hang out in Memphis Beale Street, learning from black R&B Shouters not only how to move, sing, but also how to dress. He would become one of the few white teenagers to shop at Lansky's in Beale Street—sporting a Tony Curtis pompadour and sharp clothes, usually associated with the Afro-American musicians and singers.

In the summer of 1953 and again in early 1954, Elvis Presley paid to make a custom ten-inch acetate, a single copy record with two sides, crooning pop songs to hear how he sounded, further to impress Sam Phillips' hoping maybe for a contract, and to have a belated birthday gift to his mum, as the myth tells us ...

When asked by Phillips' secretary Marion Keisker how he sounded before one of the acetate's sessions—he said: *I don't sound like nobody.*

The first professional session for Elvis Presley started on 5 July 1954, and continued the next day. Which was, as irony would have it, Bill Haley's 29th birthday. Then about to commence with his reign as the world's first King of Rock and Roll. According to George Klein's book "My best friend Elvis"—it was Elvis' ambition to make it to the top, and knock Bill Haley off the throne ...

Sam Phillips had assembled Elvis Presley (vocal and rhythm guitar) with two local musicians which were far more experienced than Presley himself, namely Scotty Moore (lead guitar) and Bill Black (double bass). The first song they tried to arrange and wax was "I Love You Because", but Sam was far from being satisfied. Presley then started to fool around with "That's Allright", an old blues by Arthur "Big Boy" Crudup from 1947. When the two musicians joined in, Phillips saw something in it, encouraging them and they taped it. For the flip-side, they came up with an equally fascinating song—a take on Bill Monroe's Bluegrass hit "Blue Moon Of Kentucky". A single was released crediting the artists as "Elvis Presley, Scotty and Bill". At live shows, the outfit would be called Elvis Presley and The Blue Moon Boys.

The instrumentation was used on five Elvis, Scotty and Bill "SUN Singles". 19 Songs were cut by Elvis for SUN, many Rockabilly enthusiasts like to discuss how many of them were genuine Rockabilly? So if you want to have a long conversation with a Rockabilly fan, that could be the start of your conversation …

To point out is—the SUN singles "That's Allright" b/w "Blue Moon Of Kentucky" (SUN 209) and "Good Rockin' Tonight" b/w "I Don't Care If The Sun Don't Shine" (SUN 210) are some of the best Elvis Presley outputs ever. Needless to say, almost anyone should agree that they are indeed Classic Rockabilly songs.

Sam Phillips today glorified as somewhat the "SUN KING OF ROCK and ROLL" was truly visionary as author Peter Guralnick noted in the book "Sam Phillips—The Man Who Invented Rock and Roll" (2015): *Sam Phillips had been thinking more and more that the key lay in the connection between the races, in what they had in common far more than what kept them apart. There were always going to be (in Phillips' words) 'some bastard white people, he knew, but far more to the point was the spiritual connection that he had always known to exist between black and white, the cultural heritage that they all had shared. 'Not to copy each other but to just—hey, this is all we've got and we've going to give it to you. This is our Broadway play. This is our Tin Pan Alley. This is what it is. We hope you like it'.*

To Marion Keisker, Sam's assistant, he had begun to talk increasingly about finding someone—and it had to be a white man, because the wall that he had run into with his recordings practically proved that in the present racial climate it couldn't be someone black—who might be able to bridge the gap. 'Over and over I heard Sam say, 'If I could find a white man who had the Negro sound and the Negro feel, I could make a billion dollars!' And he would always laugh, Marion said, as if to underscore that money was never the point—it was the vision.' (...)

This boy had everything. He had the looks, the moves, the manager, and the talent. And he didn't look like Mr Ed like a lot of the rest of us did. In the way he looked, the way he talked, the way he acted—he really was different.
(Mr Blue Suede Shoes—Carl Perkins)

At the beginning of Elvis' career, there wasn't really a word for the music, similar to Bill Haley, it was hard for the press to find a terminology for the young man's style. Naming him *The Hillbilly Cat*, describing him and his music as: *hillbilly singer; a young rural rhythm talent; a white man ... singing Negro rhythms with a rural flavour;* and *a young man (with a) boppish approach to*

278

hillbilly music. Billboard Magazine coined out of this attributes the term "Rockabilly" in the mid-1950s …

Not long after the early success of Elvis, other Rockabilly and Country and Western singers showed up on the doorstep of SUN Studio, hoping that Phillips could work out a formula on them as well, which would launch them into stars. Phillips would record Johnny Cash, Jerry Lee Lewis, Carl Perkins, Roy Orbison, Charlie Feathers, Billy Lee Riley, Warren Smith, Carl Mann, Johnny Powers, Rayburn Anthony, and so many more …

Bill Williams Sun Records publicist recalled: *I think every one of them must have come in on the midnight train from nowhere. I mean, they came from outta space!*

No wonder that the Rockabilly explosion was compared to the one of Punk two decades later …

Other highlights of Elvis Presley's SUN Material, than the afore mentioned are his reading of Junior Parker's "Mystery Train" and his haunting version "Blue Moon". The ladder used with much effect in the Jim Jarmusch movie "Mystery Train". European Fans for many years were divided in being either Bill Haley or Elvis Presley Fans, both artists being the most well-known Rock and Roll Stars who had launched their careers in the 1950s. I asked Haley's lead guitarist from 1974 until 1976 who, he thought to be more important in the evolution of Rock and Roll.

This is the answer of Bill Turner: *Man, that's the hardest question you've asked me so far! Let me just say, that Bill Haley was the 'trunk of the tree', Elvis was one of the main branches—I tell that to everybody, because that's how I view Mr Haley: he was the guy who truly started it! (...)* Bill Turner also told me in an in-depth interview that he met Sam Phillips in an elevator: The year was 1987 when Bill Haley was finally inducted as part of the "Second Class" into the Rock and Roll Hall of Fame, when he met together with Bill's youngest son, none less than Sam Phillips—in the elevator. Sam stated: (to Pedro Haley, then a teenager: *I was just getting my record label off the ground when your daddy had 'Shake, Rattle and Roll' in all the jukeboxes!)*

After RCA had purchased Elvis Presley from SUN Records they and his new manager Colonel Tom Parker made Elvis into a product: The market was flooded with Presley in 1956: eleven singles, eight EP's, one double EP, two albums, a movie, and tons of Presley stamped products like "Elvis lipstick", "Elvis T-

Shirts", "Elvis Guitars" … But saturation was far from being reached for the fans.

In 1958, Elvis Presley served two years as GI with Uncle Sam, having his basis training in Texas, then being shipped off to Germany. Some believe that this saved his career, and took him out of the fir of the anti-rock press and anti-rock movements—making him acceptable to the general public. He returned in 1960 with a TV Special, hosted by Frank Sinatra, being more mainstream than he ever was. Actually being the first time a pop singer for the general public, than the Rock and Roll Rebel persona he had gained in movies such as "Love Me Tender" (1956), "Loving You" (1957), "Jailhouse Rock" (1957) and "King Creole" (1958).

John Lennon famously claimed that Elvis died after the Army … Indeed that is definitely untrue. He continued to be a major force for two more decades—the 1960s and the 1970s. Recording still great hit-singles and albums, with some weaker Soundtrack recordings. Reaching the pinnacle of his career in 1972 with the first ever Satellite-televised TV Special by a single artist—the "Aloha From Hawaii TV Special".

Elvis died on 16 August 1977, worn out, probably tired, but still eager to go on. Hoping his last tour, to commence on the day he would die, 16 August 1977 it *"would be the his best tour ever"*. His health failed him, but the 42 years he lived on Earth, make him more interestingly ever, be it in the Rockabilly, Rock and Roll, Country or Gospel field. Elvis Presley will still be the King, for many decades on, and hopefully a new Generation will catch on with his artistic achievements and talent, as happened with Johnny Cash after his "American Recordings" and the biopic "Walk The Line". Elvis Presley, the man, the music, the actor—the performer still lives in the hearts of millions.

Carl Perkins (born 9 April 1932 in Tiptonville/Tennessee, died 19 January 1998 in Jackson/Tennessee):

If it helped getting your music off the ground. I'm glad you done it.

For some, Carl Perkins is the ultimate loser of the first Rockabilly and Rock and Roll Revolution, never achieving numerous hits like other contemporaries. To others he is simply the "King of Rockabilly"!

Nevertheless, to commercially judging critics he is the big looser, as Carl Perkins, never was able to make big bucks out of his God-given talent. With "Blue Suede Shoes" he wrote one of the most important classics of Rockabilly and Rock and Roll. He was a thunderous and very gifted guitarist. Even some say that his looks and stage persona, as well as his original style, in between Country and Western and Rhythm and Blues would have made him capable of putting Elvis back to second row. But the sharecropper son didn't recover from a tragedy, which lead to the death of a bandmember, who was also his brother—Clayton Perkins.

On the way to the Perry Como Show, the Chrysler chauffeuring the Perkins brothers crashed. Putting all in hospital for several months, not being able to promote "Blue Suede Shoes" and it's follow ups enough. Elvis Presley wanted to help, and recorded his version of it. Though Perkins made the Top 10 of the R&B, Country and even Pop-Charts with his first "shoe-song" (others would follow)—the song became linked to Elvis, more than to Carl Perkins …

Perkins was born in Tiptonville/Tennessee as son of the only white sharecropper family in the area. So he learned about the black community Spirituals and also the Blues. The 'Perkins Brothers" would soon appear at local dances, and in many of the areas Honky Tonks. Sam Phillips who had kept Carl as a Country singer on his label, gave him a shot as Rock and Roll singer, after Elvis had departed for SUN Records. With "Blue Suede Shoes" becoming such a tremendous crossover hit, the RCA Records executives even became unsure if they had purchased the right talent from Sam Phillips. Until of course, "Heartbreak Hotel" became the first Elvis Presley Nr.1 Hit.

Songs like "Boppin' The Blues" and "Your True Love" which had everything to become hits, died a slow death on the charts in the years 1956 and 1957. The years of Presley-Mania brought the career of Carl Perkins to an abrupt halt. *"One of the real Rock and Roll Stars"* (Rolling Stone Magazine) became dependant on the bottle, staying an Alcoholic until the late 1960s when he and Johnny Cash swore off booze and pills.

After hopping with Cash from SUN to the major label Columbia, Perkins was still capable of recording great Rock and Roll and Rockabilly with songs like "Pointed Toe Shoes", "Where The Rio De Rosa Flows", "Levi Jacket" and "Pop, Let Me Have The Car"—but not one of this releases came close enough sales-wise to his immortal "Blue Suede Shoes". While touring the British Isles in 1964, he befriended the Beatles, who recorded "Blue Suede Shoes", "Matchbox", "Honey Don't" and "Everybody's Trying To Be My Baby" giving a royalty fee of 50,000 USD to Perkins, and a boost to his self-esteem.

In the 1960s, he continued to record Country Rock albums, and also had joined the Johnny Cash Show as featured guitarist and guest artist. He stayed with Cash until 1975. In 1970, a tremendous album was made with Country Rock Troup "NRBQ" entitled "Boppin' The Blues". In 1978, a Comeback followed with the album "Ole Blue Suede's Back" and an extended tour of Great Britain. The LP sold 100,000 copies in the UK, then home to a strong continent of Teddy Boys, and a new breed of subculture—The Rockabilly Rebels. In 1981, he worked with Paul McCartney on the album "Tug Of War", and in 1982 Carl Perkins, Jerry Lee Lewis and Johnny Cash were released on the 'Live' album "Survivors". New Wave converted Rockabillys such as The Stray Cats paid their dues to Carl Perkins.

In 1986, the TV Special "Blue Suede Shoes—An Evening with Carl Perkins" was produced in London, with respects paid not only by the audience, but also the all-star band accompanying him, including Stray Cats Lee Rocker, Slim Jim Phantom, Blues-Legend Eric Clapton, former Beatles George Harrison and Ringo Starr, Dave Edmunds, Roseanne Cash and introductory words spoken by contemporaries Roy Orbison, Jerry Lee Lewis and Johnny Cash.

Perkins returned to SUN Records with Roy Orbison, Johnny Cash and Jerry Lee Lewis for the Chips Moman produced album "Class Of 55".

He toured almost right to the end, dying in January 1998 after throat cancer and strokes he suffered.

I've seen Carl Perkins in concert twice, he was a modest, but so gifted, charismatic talent, a Gentleman onstage and offstage. A Legend of our times. I'm grateful to have spent two evenings in my formative years, being entertained and being stroked by the charisma of a man like Carl Perkins.

Johnny Cash (born 26 February 1932 in Dyess, Arkansas, died, 12 September 2003 in Hendersonville/Tennessee):

The things that have always been important: to be a good man, to try to live my life the way God would have me, to turn it over to Him that His will might be worked in my life, to do my work without looking back, to give it all I've got, and to take pride in my work as an honest performer.

During his tenure at SUN Records, Johnny Cash recorded Country, Popular Teen Gems, Gospel and to some minds reaching into Rockabilly. While other think that his limitations in vocal range disqualify him from the last mentioned musical genre.

Today Johnny Cash personifies the younger aged part of the Rockabilly scene more than anyone else, including Elvis Presley. T-Shirts, wallets, bags, hoodies, shirts and much more name Johnny Cash a Rockabilly or Rock and Roll artist. He's ever popular in the rockin scene—to my mind—a large part of this lies in the tremendous movie "I Walk The Line" starring Joaquin Phoenix as Cash and Reese Witherspoon as June Carter Cash, more than his American Recordings, which are far, far away from his early sounds, which was according to Bob Dylan much more optimistic and humorous.

Despite discovering Elvis Presley Sam Phillips also saw beneath Johnny Cash's surface, he probably saw the honest power in Cash voice, and the potential in a band very limited in musicianship. Both attributes made Cash far more accessible to the 1950s Rock and Roll crowd, than any other Country and Western singer who tried his hands on Rockabilly.

Johnny Cash and his guitarist Luther Perkins, to an extent also bass player Marshall Grant to be known as Johnny Cash and The Tennessee Two originally auditioned at SUN as a Gospel trio. But Phillip's didn't see any possibility in marking them into that direction. Phillips asked Cash to return with more suitable material. Some of the prime SUN cuts by Cash were "Hey Porter", from his first single, which he had written years before while serving with the Air Force in Bavaria, Germany. "Folsom Prison Blues" was rejected by Sam Phillips as B-side, and "Cry! Cry! Cry!" was chosen. The first single made the Top of the local Memphis charts, and even cracked into the National Charts. A far less modest start, than Elvis first single. To Elvis credit, like Bill Haley, he had paved the way for other artists with a unique sound, even more so Elvis paved the way, and laid the inspiration for all the SUN Recording artists in the Rock and Roll field, following him—including Johnny Cash, Carl Perkins and Jerry Lee Lewis.

The basic and stark recordings of Cash and the Tennessee Two, were of an honesty, hardly heard before the advent of the new Rock and Roll and Rockabilly stars. A minimal production seemed the perfect element to nail the essence of Johnny Cash as a young man. Maybe Rick Rubin, nailed him down as an old man, but it was Sam Phillips who was there first, and introduced the world to Johnny Cash, as he did with Presley, Perkins and Lewis the other three of what would become known as the Million Dollar Quartet.

Cash would enjoy a Country hit with "Folsom Prison Blues" b/w "So Doggone Lonesome". The follow up "I Walk The Line" which he had written with his first wife Vivian Cash in mind, was his first taste at Pop Charts success. (No 2 Country and Western Charts, No. 17 Pop Charts in 1956).

Cash probably was the first one to make Social Critic Rockabilly or Rock and Roll if you will with "Get The Rhythm" and made a wonderful moody Country song out of "Home Of The Blues". The ladder he penned around the name of a Memphis Records store—"Home Of The Blues". The first one to give Johnny Cash a fuller sound, and in so making him appeal more to the Pop or Teen market was Producer "Cowboy" Jack Clement, who is responsible for Cash's hit "Ballad Of A Teenage Queen". Although Cash went on to heights music wise far from his beginnings at SUN Records, he never returned to so natural to his fundaments as a man, than on SUN Records. Though he had promised after the basic most promising album "American Recordings" produced by Rick Rubin, that his next album would be a "return to his SUN sound"—he broke that promise when having himself being backed by Tom Petty and The Heartbreakers, throwing away that chance as with the falsely titled 1980s album "Rockabilly Blues" … Cash's contribution to Rockabilly lies mostly in his recordings made at SUN Records.

To some puritans, even these do not qualify him as being a Rockabilly singer … To close this chapter, when I've seen Johnny Cash and June Carter Cash live in 1995, they had all that had made Cash what he was in the past, and would be in the future.

"Whole Lotta Shakin' Goin' On"

Jerry Lee Lewis (born 29 September 1935 in Ferriday/Louisiana):

I am what I am, I've always said what I wanted to say, done what I wanted to do and been what I wanted to be, I've never tried to hide anything. Everything I've done has been out in the open. If people don't like that then that's their problem. I've been picked on, abused, sued, jailed, ridiculed, persecuted and prosecuted but I never let it bother me.

My first real Rock and Roll concert happened to be one by Jerry Lee Lewis shortly before myself reaching teenhood. It was marvellous, though until then I only knew a few of his classic Rock and Roll hits such as "Great Balls Of Fire" and "Whole Lotta Shakin' Goin On". I have seen the man now seven times live since, and even was able to welcome him to Vienna, when his plane landed there at the airport. Thanks to a more than one-decade long dedicated Jerry Lee Lewis fan, named Graham Knight.

Jerry Lee Lewis shook my hand, and said "Good to see you, son". It was even greater seeing him soon in Graz, Austria—playing a smaller venue—The Orpheum to a very appreciative crowd. I was also able to stay at the same hotel than the Killer. But sadly, his management didn't allow an interview that opening night of a 2011 tour. But it was great fun, spending the evening with his talented sister Linda Gail Lewis who had opened the night's concert, his niece Ann Marie Dolan and members of his band, most prominently Kenny Lovelace who has been with him as featured guitarist and violinist since the late 1960s.

When Jerry Lee Lewis showed up at Sun Records in November 1956, he was an unknown, having had some experience, but far more important a great self-confidence which never seemed to leave him. He was rightly timed. The tiny SUN label was still hot from having launched the careers of Elvis Presley, Carl Perkins and Johnny Cash. It was far more successful than the major labels, who signed Rockabillys. But never would materialise sizeable hits for young cats such as Johnny Carroll (Decca), Joey Castle (RCA), Johnny and Dorsey Burnette aka The Rock and Roll Trio (Capitol) and others. Competitors like Meteor Records, also from Memphis were not really a commercial competition to SUN Records, though releasing some fine gems of the Rockabilly genre also.

Over seven stormy years Jerry Lee Lewis spent at SUN Records, launching a world career from a local Memphis attraction, and back to a popularity or rather a career so unhelped by Managers, Radio and Television personalities, after a huge scandalised British Tour in 1958. During which the British Foreign Office ordered Jerry Lee Lewis and his wife Myra, including their entourage to leave the country.

Interestingly Rock and Roll Wildman Jerry Lee Lewis is a far more sophisticated artist, than his early image, cartoonised almost in a biopic starring Dennis Quaid entitled "Great Balls Of Fire" from 1989, as many interviews and two autobiographies should make clear.

He is a seasoned performer who feels home in Rockabilly/Rock and Roll, Country, Gospel, Boogie-Woogie or whatever you would call it—to him and to his fans it's Jerry Lee Lewis music. Born in 1935, like his major competitor and rival Elvis Presley—Jerry Lee grew up on his family's struggling cotton farm, where he was immediately attracted to music and religion. This duality between worldly Rock and Roll and the strict Assembly of God Church, were two forces that pulled him into very different attractions—and which would have torn other men up, but not so Jerry Lee Lewis. Even though living in poverty, Jerry's dad Elmo Lewis and his mother Mamie Lewis purchased a piano for their son, financed with a mortgage on their house. This piano is shown on Lewis 2010 album "Mean Old Man"!

Listening to gospel and a varied selection of musical styles on the radio, not caring about segregation, he absorbed the Americana music book of that time. His older cousin was Carl McAvoy and Mickey Gilley. Especially Gilley became a competitor at the dawn of Jerry Lee Lewis chart-driven Country Star period from the late 1960s until the late 1970s. His other cousin would become a well-known TV Evangelist—namely Jimmy Swaggart. Swaggart who preached almost his entire life against the music and the life of his cousin, fell from grace, when a scandal broke loose that the married TV evangelist and family father had visited more than once a street Prostitute and had actually had more than once had intercourse with her.

Sam Phillips was away on vacation, when Lewis auditioned for SUN Records. His father had sold eggs from the farm, to finance the trip for his SUN to go to Memphis to meet with Sam Phillips, and now Phillips was away. Lewis nevertheless persisted and ended up recording "Crazy Arms" at 706 Union Avenue.

"Crazy Arms" b/w "End Of The Road" would be his first SUN Single in 1956. Phillips employed young Jerry Lee also as Session pianist with artist like Carl Perkins and Billy Lee Riley. At one of the Perkins sessions not only Johnny Cash dropped by at Sun, before a shopping tour with his wife Vivian, but also the now RCA Star Elvis Presley. Somebody started to roll a tape, and a journalist and photographer from the Memphis Press Scimitar was ordered capturing the informal Jam Session as The Million Dollar Quartet!

A high profile engagement to the Big "D" Jamboree in Dallas/Texas and a tour with Johnny Cash and Carl Perkins through North America for five weeks profiled the young recording star, whose first SUN single hadn't set his career and the world on fire—yet!

The second release "Whole Lotta Shakin' Goin' On" b/w "It'll Be Me" made him a star, after appearing on the Steve Allen Show in New York. The A-side had been recorded by The Commodores as well as by Big Maybelle and Roy Hall. From Hall Lewis picked the song up, the b-side was written by Jack Clement.

Phillips put all at risk, stopped promoting all of his other stars including Billy Lee Riley, who just had promoted "Red Hot" as part of an Alan Freed Package Tour, costing Riley the hit. But launching Jerry Lee Lewis in as Elvis greatest rival for a short, but intense time! Follow up hits included the Otis Blackwell composed "Great Balls Of Fire", "Breathless" and "High School Confidential"—also the name of a Rock and Roll B-movie Lewis appeared in.

Jerry Lee Lewis meteoric rise was put down in ashes and dust, when in May 1958 the British press found out that Lewis had married the daughter of his bass player JW Brown, then aged 13 years young—Myra Gale (Brown) Lewis. Plus that his divorce to his second wife had not been legally divorced. Called a bigamist, baby snatcher and worse Lewis was sent home back to the US by British authorities, cancelling the British tour for him. The space left, was filled with British Rock and Roll Star Terry Wayne.

The now Last Man Standing of the Million Dollar Quartet would continue recording for SUN Records. With little, and in the early 1960s optimistic success when "What'd I Say" charted for him. A successful 1962 UK tour followed. He rose like Phoenix from the Ashes when in 1969 he started his Country career with the million seller "Another Place, Another Time". The 1990s seemed less successful recording wise, but in 2005 he returned with a strong album including duets with Little Richard, Ringo Starr, Mick Jagger, Rod Stewart ... becoming his bestselling album to date—"Last Man Standing". He followed two similar long plays with "Mean Old Man" and "Rock and Roll Time" in 2010 and 2014, and recently issued his autobiography with Pulitzer-Prize winning author Rick Bragg. Currently Jerry Lee Lewis continues to play his heart out on stage.

6 December 1956: Carl Perkins with his band, consisting of his brothers plus Jerry Lee Lewis as a hired session man, were most probably working on the songs "Matchbox" and "Put Your Cat Clothes On". As the session wound down, Elvis and his little entourage appeared. His girlfriend Marilyn Evans. The least known of Elvis girlfriends, she was a showgirl he had met in Las Vegas.

Elvis felt good at Sun, where he could escape the sarcasm and cruelty of big city media. If he sang, he would rather sing for the love of it, than for money— that's exactly what he did that day at Sun Records.

Elvis listened to the Carl Perkins recordings produced that day, and took a liking to them. Then he picked up a guitar and began to sing. Carl and the band, including Jerry Lee joined in. Sam Phillips realised an event was unfolding, calling Johnny Cash. Of course, also notifying The Memphis Press Scimitar, which sent Entertainment reporter Bob Johnson. He arrived with an UPI stringer Leo Seroka. Others dropped by, such as Sun artist, Smokey Joe Baugh. Sam Phillips placed one microphone on the centre of the studio floor and turned on the tape machine. With five later Rock and Roll Hall Of Fame members in the same room, some people today would consider a Rockabilly/Rock and Roll mayhem jam session. But except for a few Chuck Berry songs, a Pat Boone song and a few of the Elvis hits, the Memphis Million Dollar Quartet showed that much of Rock and Roll had its origins in the spirituals of the black people, formerly enslaved …

Rock and Roll was born of Gospel, Country, Street Corner Harmonies, Pop and Cowboy songs. That was this session was all about.

Still to debate is, if Johnny Cash can be heard on the tapes, or if he went shopping with his wife Vivian instead, as Nick Tosches told us in his Jerry Lee Lewis biography "Hellfire". Bob Johnson wrote about the impromptu concert the following day, also mentioning some songs that never made it to tape and spoke of Johnny Cash singing them, so it seems that the session, by now released, has a 750,000 Dollars Trio, rather than a Quartet.

On 7 December, the Memphis Press Scimitar reported: "If Sam Phillips had been on his toes, he'd have turned the recorder on … that quartet could sell a million."

"We thought you might like to read first-hand about our little shindig—it was a dilly!" a handwritten notice to the article sent out by SUN Records to DJs and Business associates.

Chapter Ten
On the Road

According to the 1981 documentary, "This is Elvis", plus some other sources, it was in the Army that Elvis learned about amphetamines. But it seems that he and Johnny Cash shared the same passion for it, early in their careers. It seemed to be a necessity for them to be able, being on the road. Driving for hours, the SUN Records roster, not in its entirety, but certainly the four most successful ones at that time: Elvis Presley, Carl Perkins, Jerry Lee Lewis and Johnny Cash were on amphetamines, just for being able to drive their cars on tour, as well as of driving their shows to ultimate heights.

"I don't sound like nobody." (Elvis Presley)

Elvis Presley's myth and in so also the second most visited home in the US, "Graceland" are built on many legends. One begins in July 1954:

Some think that Elvis Presley was just at the right time, at the right place. Not so, as you will probably be aware of—it was not an overnight success on a National Scale, but local fame spread, taking him out of a regional context, into the Nations mind, thanks to RCA Records and TV, later movie appearances. It is safe to say that it first came for him together in the Sun Studio, at 706 Union Avenue, Memphis/Tennessee in July 1954. Under supervision of Studio-Founder Sam Phillips, as well as the experimental approach by the musicians Sam had Elvis augmented with: Scotty Moore (lead guitar) and Bill Black (bass). Sessions commenced on 5 July 1954, resulting in a radio premiere of "That's Allright" on WHBQ on 8 July 1954, with a single ("That's Allright" b/w "Blue Moon Of Kentucky") being released on 19 July 1954.

While holding day jobs, the trio tried to capitalise on people's positive reaction towards the platter with live gigs in and around Memphis. Let's join Elvis, Scotty and Bill on their early touring maps, as outlined in Nic Hop's fanzine "At The Hop" by Nic himself. Nic being of great virtue and inspiration to this, my third book:

The Memphis Performances, 1954:

The possible first officially recognisable professional or semi-professional set by Elvis was set to occur at the Bon Air Club in Memphis: Scotty and Bill were regulars there with Doug Poindexter and The Starlite Wranglers. During an interval on 7 July 1954 Elvis Presley performed "That's Allright" and "Blue Moon Of Kentucky", which according to some there at the time, went rather unnoticed.

He returned on stage on 24 July and 31 July 1954 to the club located on Summer Avenue. While he wasn't settin' woods on fire live, record sales did considerably well. For that reason Sun secretary Marion Keisker set up an interview for Elvis with the Memphis Press Scimitar, for July 27th, for his first year as a recording artist. Another significant event was due to happen on July 30th, Elvis Presley and The Blue Moon Boys would open a show at the Memphis Overton Park, which included Slim Whitman, Webb Pierce, Marty Robbins, Carl Smith, Billy Walker, The Louvin' Brothers and Minnie Pearl.

Elvis was incorrectly named on the programme as Ellis Presley, misprinted. As it was the trio's turn the had decided for the songs of their, so far, only single. Elvis recalled later: "I was on a show in Memphis when I started doing it. I was an extra added attraction—and when I came out on stage I was scared stiff. I started doing 'That's Allright' and everybody was hollering and screaming. And when I came off stage my manager told me they were hollering because I was wiggling. Well when I went back for an encore, I did a little bit more. They more I did, they wilder, they went."

That's how Elvis laid his visual element to his music, certainly he had watched Rhythm and Blues singers at Memphis Beale Street in clubs, before.

In a single month, the three went from unsuccessful rehearsals in Scotty's living room, to a successful single and a frenzy opening for some big names of Country music. They found further engagements as intermission band at the Eagle's Nest. Their set for this music club, located at Lamar Avenue and Winchester Road, consisted of "That's Allright", "Blue Moon Of Kentucky", Blue Moon" and "Tiger Man". The first performances were held on August 7th 1954, with the Eagle's Nest welcoming them back on August 16th. This time they had incorporated "Ice Cold Love" within their set. They also played the Bel Air Motel, extending their small repertory with "Rag Mop". The month of August

'54 remained busy, with a Benefit appearance at a Baseball game at Bellevue Park on the 18th, another slot at the Eagle's Neston on the 27th and a benefit show at the Kennedy Hospital on 29 August 1954.

September 18th, 24th, and 25th, October 1st, 6th, 9th, 13th, 20th, 29th and 30th as well as dates in November were secured for the Eagle's Nest. By December 10th new songs to the bands repertory were added, namely "Shake, Rattle and Roll", "Money Honey" and "Hearts Of Stone". At that time hits, in order, for Bill Haley and His Comets, The Drifters and The Charms.

Around this time in the 1950s, the first shopping malls were installed, one was opening named Lamar. Incorporating a Katz Drugstore with Ice Cream Soda Fountains and a Jukebox. Elvis played with Scotty and Bill from a tuck, at the grand opening. The Memphis Press Scimitar ran a huge advertisement, Elvis surname was this time misspelled, written as Pressley. As of October 2nd 1954, the band had christened themselves as Elvis Presley and The Blue Moon Boys. After a one off at the Opry, first stints at the Hayride, they were already off for a gig in Atlanta/Georgia …

Contrary to all that rockin' cats like Carl Perkins, Johnny Cash, Jerry Lee Lewis or Roy Orbison that followed Elvis Presley's trailblazing trying to get to Memphis. It was time now for Elvis for getting out of Memphis. It was their first time on the road, their touring of 1954 that set the foundation for the world career of Elvis Presley. At the dawn of 1954, they played the Mint Club in Gladewater/Texas. (12 November '54). This followed by dates at the Lake Cliff Club in Shreveport/Louisiana (19 November '54), Cook's Hoedown at the Texarkana Auditorium (24 November '54), the Catholic Club in Helena/Arkansas on December 2nd. Covers in their repertory included "Fool, Fool, Fool", "Little Mama" (The Clovers), "I'm Gonna Sit Right Down And Cry" (Roy Hamilton), "Hearts Of Stone" (Otis Williams), "Shake, Rattle and Roll" (Big Joe Turner, Bill Haley).

As the Louisiana Hayride performances were such a success, as Scotty Moore handed over more responsibility for bookings to manager Bob Neal, who extended with Hayride booking talent representatives into Arkansas, Louisiana and Texas—the boys resigned from their day jobs. 1954 ended in an high for them … Travelling tirelessly the Highway 79 from Memphis to far away destinations, in between their hometown and Texarkana.

The year 1955 kicked off with an official new manager—Bob Neal, a local DJ from Memphis. Elvis third single on Sun 215 is also launched. Bob sets out to promote Elvis, Scotty and Bill in small towns all around the South: First they would visit some of the local newspapers and radio stations, then Elvis and band, would be part of Package Tours incorporating names like The Carter Sisters, Ed and Maxine Brown, Billy Walker or Jimmy and Johnny. Also Comedian Peach Seed Jones, was regularly part of this, at the time common touring, for music artists.

First tour in 1955 started on January 4th, ending already three days later on January 7th. The band travelling through Texas, with Bill Black's bass up on the car's roof. They would also play to strictly hillbilly audiences, for them Bill Black also included some comedy routines. They performed at the Odessa High School Auditorium, The San Angelo City Auditorium, as well as the Fair Park Auditorium in Lubbock/Texas, Buddy Holly's home town. Final show High School Auditorium in Midland/Texas.

The second tour billed as the "Louisiana Hayride Jamboree", lasting longer, with dates including in four different states. It commences on January 12th '54, supported by the Browns. An explosive show happens at the Clarksdale Auditorium in Mississippi. In the set, they incorporate the songs "That's Allright", "I Don't Care If The Sun Don't Shine", "Hearts Of Stone", Blue Moon Of Kentucky", "Good Rockin' Tonight" and "Milkcow Blues Boogie". Two dates in Arkansas follow: Helena—Catholic Club and Mariana on the 13th and 14th of January. Back in Mississippi with a date at the Booneville College on January 17th further songs are added to their repertoire: "Money Honey" (The Drifters) and "Tweedle Dee" (LaVern Baker).

The following day they appear for a performance at the Corinth Alcorn County Courthouse, then travelling to Sheffield/Alabama. Here they try Ray Charles' "I Got A Woman". The tour comes to a close in Leachville and Sikeston's National Guard Armoury in Missouri. Both concerts on 20 January 1955.

After an appearance at the Louisiana Hayride on 22 January 1955, it was time for a rare, but well-earned break in Memphis. "When I'm home" Elvis was later quoted "that's when I really eat. On the road, I hardly have any appetite." Elvis favourite cuisine included Burgers, Coconut Cake and Chocolate Milkshakes. Remembering these early days, he stated: "My mother worried constantly about me when I was on the road away from home. She didn't approve it really—she thought I wasn't taking care of myself. She was there at a few of my early concerts and saw the crowds screaming. She got very upset, but I told her it was going to keep on happening. At least I hope so, because it meant they liked me and would buy my records."

After this brief break, the trio swept once more through Texas: On 24 January 1955, they were in East Texas, once more with the Browns, plus singer Tom Perryman, a local who had regular slots on radio station KSIJ. The first show at the Recreation Hall in Hawkins saw the band adding "Nine Pound Hammer" to their set. Next gig was in Tyler/Texas (25th) and Longview (27th). The tour reached its end in Gaston, on January 28th, where they performed among other songs "Fireball Mail".

Then it was off to Shreveport for 29 January 1955. Elvis Presley had only been a recording artist and live performer for a few months, yet he was still short of repertoire, not a National star yet, but certainly on his way to either become one, or remain a regional phenomenon like some later Rockabilly artist—Ray Campi, Mac Curtis or Jackie Lee Cochran.

Guitarist Scotty Moore recalled: "There were all kinds of experiences in the early days. Fights sometimes, shows cancelled, not getting paid, it was fairly rough. Every time before we set out, Elvis' mother would call either Bill or myself and say 'you be sure to take care of my boy' and we'd assure her that we'd do. I suppose you could say Elvis was a typical wild kid to begin with. I don't mean wild in a dangerous way, but he loved pranks. We also had trouble getting him out of bed in the mornings, too. But actually I guess I wasn't that much older myself!"

"Unless we learn to keep up with him, that kid may put us all out of a job before it's over." (Webb Pierce)

2 October 1954: Elvis Presley appeared for his one and only appearance at the Grand Opry. A polite and lukewarm reception by the audience. Jim Denny, the presenter Jim Denny, advises Elvis to "stick to driving the truck." Why Jim Denny booked Elvis Presley remains unclear, probably it was the yellow Sun platters, especially "Good Rockin' Tonight" which did immensely well on the charts of Memphis. Two weeks after the Ryman Auditorium, another door opened. Far more promising, lucrative, rewarding and very influential to so many Southern Rockabilly artists following soon the trailblazers of young rocking Elvis!

Elvis Presley and The Blue Moon Boys landed their spot on the Louisiana Hayride, also broadcast live on the radio dials from Shreveport. Second chance and musical home to Hank Williams prior. Ignition for this deal commenced on

19 August 1954. Sam Phillips had come back from a promotional tour with some major news: An audition for the Trio had been negotiated for the Hayride show. Two days later young Elvis nervously sang two songs for the staff. Naturally the songs which had gotten the ball rolling in the first place: "That's Allright" and "Blue Moon Of Kentucky". (SUN Records 209) This led to the decision, that Elvis alternatively took a spot on 16 October 1954, held so far by Jimmy and Johnny.

The appearance of Elvis Presley, Scotty Moore and Bill Black was advertised in the Memphis Commercial Appeal on October 14th 1954. "Presley to sing on radio show Saturday night." The trio hit the road in the wee wee hours of the 15 October 1954. On that eight hour drive, they almost missed a turn at Greenville/Mississippi plus lead guitarist Scotty Moore almost hitting a team of mules. (Trying to make up for some lost time.)

Finally they arrived at their Sam Phillips booked hotel in Shreveport, the Captain Shreve Hotel. Sponsored by Lucky Strike Elvis, Scotty and Bill were set to perform in a special segment for new talent. Announced by Frank Page, airing from 9.00pm to 9.30pm, including Floyd Tilman with "Slipping Around" and "I'll Take You What I Can Get", Ginnie Wright ("Tell Me How To Get Married"), Dobber Johnson ("Black Mountain Rag"), Hoot and Curley ("Come Home With Me Today"), Tibby Edwards ("Love Me Now") and Betty Amos ("If Some Folks Would Leave Us Alone"). Elvis, Scotty and Bill performed "That's Allright" and "Blue Moon Of Kentucky" before Dobber Johnson's set.

There are surviving tapes of Elvis Presley's Louisiana Hayride sets, released on CD, including a conversation Elvis had on stage with Frank Page: "Just a few weeks ago, a young man from Memphis, Tennessee, recorded a song on the SUN label and in just a matter of weeks, that record has skyrocketed on the charts. He's only 19 years old; he has a distinctive style ... Elvis Presley. Let's give him a nice hand. We've been playing his songs for weeks. Elvis, how are you this evening? Elvis Presley: "Just fine, how are you, Sir?" Frank Page: "Are you geared up with your band there?" Elvis Presley: "Geared up." Frank Page: "To let us hear your songs?" Elvis Presley: "Well, I'd like to say how happy we are to be out there. It's a real honour for us to get a chance to appear on the Louisiana Hayride Show and we're gonna do a song for you. You got anything else to say, Sir?" Frank Page: "No, I'm ready." Elvis Presley: "We're gonna do a song for you we've got out on Sun Records and it goes something like this ..."

Logan was watching from the wings, noting that Elvis was even more intense than Hank Williams. Plus "young females in the audience exploded with excitement." The screams were deafening, sheer bedlam. Jimmy C. Newman, singer, who was present, was cited as saying: "It's got to be a fad." Elvis was immediately offered a spot for the week after, October 23rd 1954. At this third appearance, an offer with a contract followed: The one year agreement, signed by his parents Vernon and Gladys Presley, as Elvis was still a minor, asked for 48 Saturday night performances, paid Elvis 18$ for each, while Scotty and Bill received $12. The four hundred miles drive to Shreveport in Louisiana as well as food and lodging expenses were left to Elvis and the band, as reported by the Memphis Press Scimitar on 20 November 1954.

Elvis premiered on a personal level as a singer, in performing a jingle for Southern Maid Doughnuts: "You can get' em piping after four pm, you can get em piping hot. Southern Maid Doughnuts hit the spot, you can get 'em piping hot after four pm." Due to their popularity still increasing, they lengthened their set, adding the songs "Fool, Fool, Fool", "I'm Gonna Sit Right Down And Cry Over You" and "Sittin' On Top Of The World". On 13 November 1954, Elvis, Scotty and Bill performed on the CBS segment, for the first time. Performing "Blue Moon Of Kentucky", "Fool, Fool, Fool" and "Just Because".

As the sounds of audience, as the audience itself was increasing. As other Rock and Roll singers like Bill Haley also had a drummer: DJ Fontana joined Elvis, Scotty Moore and Bill Black on drums. He stayed with Elvis Presley until 1969, playing 46 recording sessions with him. Originally introduced to Elvis by Tilman Franks, DJ Fontana did not accompany Elvis on the SUN Records with drums. Johnny Bernero and Jimmy Lot did that. Elvis also met pianist Floyd Cramer at that time, he would work with him from 1956 onwards until 1968 on most Nashville sessions. Elvis popularity grew and grew, as Hayride Package Tours throughout the mid-south organised by booking agents Tillman Franks and Pappy Covington were in demand. For encores the repertoire extended, incorporating songs like "Hearts Of Stone", "Shake, Rattle and Roll" (18 December 1954), "Tweedle Dee" (5 January 1955) and in March "Little Mama".

Elvis 20th birthday was marked by a third single on Sun: "Milkcow Blues Boogie" b/w "You're A Heartbreaker" (SUN 215,1955). This being in sales, the weakest of all five Sun Records single releases, by Elvis. But the popularity of Elvis Presley grew and grew. Some appearances at the Louisiana Hayride had to be cancelled, due to more lucrative and promising offers: July 23rd appearing at the Dallas Big D Jamboree.

In May 1955 Elvis was added to his most ambiguous tour to that stage in his career: Three weeks touring twenty southern cities (including Baton Rouge/New Orleans, Mobile/Alabama, Birmingham/Alabama, Macon/Georgia, Daytona Beach/Florida and Orlando/Florida. The tour started, as Sun released Single 217 "Baby Let's Play House" b/w "I'm Left, You're Right, She's Gone" by Elvis Presley—kicking off in New Orleans/Louisiana on 1 May 1955.

The line-up boasted more than 30 artists including Slim Whitman and Faron Young. Elvis was scheduled to close each first half of the shows. The tour took it's audiences by storm and according to Logan's memoirs: "Elvis tore them up everywhere they went. There were near riots in several towns." On 13 May 1955, the climax skyrocketed in Jacksonville/Florida, at the Gator Bowl Stadium. Elvis addressed a frenzied audience, that did not let him go: "Girls, see y'all backstage."

Within the shortest time frame possible, a full blown crowd stormed stage and backstage areas. With Police protection, Elvis was escorted from the building. Faron Young recalled: "Elvis was scared. He'd climb up on top of a shower stall, trying to get away from them, but they were all jumping and grabbing at him. That was one time he had all the girls he wanted—and then some." Around this time good management was needed. A man naming himself Colonel Tom Parker soon introduced himself to the Elvis Presley business associations …

The manager of Elvis had been assumed by lead guitarist Scotty Moore, the oldest of the musicians surrounding Elvis Presley, in 1954. He was soon replaced by Disc Jockey Bob Neal, arranging tour dates nearby. The informal management deal turned hostile between the parties, when Bob Neal, tried to lure Elvis raw Rockabilly style to polished Country music. Tillman Franks and Horace Logan were approached as successors, but declined due to other commitments. By the outgoing year of 1954, Elvis was already a Southern superstar, without anyone properly taking care of business. When Jamboree Attractions approached Elvis in early 1955, a company tied to Tom Parker, the 22 year, almost lifelong business relationship between Elvis Presley and Colonel Tom Parker had commenced.

Elvis met Hank Snow who was made into a Country Star by Bill Haley Associate Jack Howard and Colonel Tom Parker, for a tour. Also Bill Haley and

Elvis Presley were on together, through Jamboree Productions. By January 1955, Parker was already handling all the bookings of young Elvis Presley's career. By August '55 Parker was already, due to legal papers, "Special Advisor" to his protege Elvis. The Contract read: "Special advisor (for a period of one year, for $2500) the aim to which is to assist in any way possible the build-up of Elvis Presley as an artist." In only a matter of time, Bob Neal's influence faded away. Now, the Louisiana Hayride was eager to renew its contract with Elvis.

A draft was presented to him of a final offer, in September 1955. 200$ for a show, one Saturday show allowed to be missed during each 60 day period, 400$ compensation to be paid by the artists for any additional show, to be missed. The on 8 September 1955 reported contract (Shreveport Times) went into effect, as of 5 November 1955. Only 16 days later the coupe was added on the icing, of the cake baked, with RCA purchasing Elvis Presley as a recording artist, including his entire Sun Records catalogue. In a deal engineered by Colonel Tom Parker, empowering himself as manager and employer. By the end of Summer 1955, Elvis was getting used being a headliner. He appeared on the Louisiana Hayride's New Year's Edition with Johnny Cash and Ferlin Husky, singing "Blue Suede Shoes", "Peace In The Valley" and "Heartbreak Hotel". (The ladder he picked up at a DJ Convention from songwriter, radio host and DJ Mae Axton).

His first Hayride appearance happened to be on 7 January 1956, for that new year, with cancellations increasing. The performance was in front of standing room. In February, three Louisiana Hayride Shows had to be cancelled. One thing became clear, Elvis Presley had outgrown the Louisiana Hayride and it's broadcasts. Elvis finally was bought out of his contract for $10,000 and a farewell performance. The Farewell Special was scheduled for 15 December 1956.

The last Louisiana Hayride Show: A triumphant return for a King, to be held at the Hirsh Coliseum, also known as the Youth Centre, at the Louisiana State Fair Grounds. The proceeds should go to the local YMCA charity. 13,000 attending, meant it to be record-breaking in attendance. The Shreveport Times reported: "Elvis' mere appearance on the Hayride stage last night set off a veritable atomic explosion of photographic flashbulbs and squeals from teenagers which ascended into pandemonium."

Elvis performed "Heartbreak Hotel", "Long Tall Sally", "I Was The One", "Love Me Tender", "Don't Be Cruel", "Love Me", "I Got A Woman", "When My Blue Moon Turns To Gold Again", "Paralysed" and "Hound Dog". By the end, the audience would not let go, so Mr Logan said the legendary words: "Elvis has left the building" for the first time ever, in order, to restore order.

Elvis had arrived in style, his first LP was Nr. 1 on the Billboard Charts, three of his singles had turned into gold, "Love Me Tender" was the box-office smash movie in the country. He still drove over himself in a white Lincoln, but a lot had happened in 26 months, he left Shreveport with a bang. "Elvis had left the building, The King had stepped in."

Elvis also had appeared on the Hayrides TV segment, yet a surviving recording is still to be found, from 5 March 1955.

By now, Colonel Tom Parker was fully in charge every career decision for Elvis Presley went over his desk. When on Sunday, 6 February 1955, Elvis had performed at the Memphis Ellis Auditorium—two shows, one at 3pm, another at 8pm: It was between these two shows that Parker and Presley had met. The dutchmen Parker, had shown interest in handling Elvis Presley's career as he had done with Eddie Arnold, and later would do with Tommy Sands. A meeting was arranged: The associates of the Colonel Tom Diskin and Oscar Davis met Scotty Moore, Bill Black and Sam Phillips to discuss options for an upcoming tour of Texas and New Mexico. This time the headliner would be Hank Snow.

The tour debuted in Alpine/Texas, on 10 February 1955, followed by two shows in Carlsbad/New Mexico the next day, at the Sports Arena and American Legion Hall. Moving further on the Route 180 hitting Lubbock on February 12th, at the Fair Park Coliseum. Then it was off to Roswell/New Mexico, which made headlines in the 1940s with a crashed spaceship supposedly with surviving extra-terrestrials on board.

In Abelene on February 15th Elvis, Scotty and Bill formally hooked up with Hank Snow's tour package. This at the Fair Park Auditorium. In Odessa/Texas they faced a 4000 attendance, 16th February, once more entertaining San Angelo the day after. Closing the tour in Monroe/Louisiana, where the trio added "Breakin' The Rules" to their set list.

Gaining momentum with Colonel Tom Parker's helping hand, things started to move: No less than 50 shows were played between the end of February and the end of April in 1955. Also an appearance north of the Mason Dixon Line occurred: Cleveland/Ohio. As well as a short trip to New York, securing a spot on television. A mini-tour of Arkansas and Louisiana at the end of February— the "WSM Grand Ole Opry". Elvis was third on the bill with the Duke of Paducah, Mother Maybelle and The Carter Sisters. "The kid from Memphis was no longer a total newcomer, he had gained in confidence and certainly knew about his audience."

The show's kick off happened in Little Rock/Arkansas on 20 February 1955 at the Robinson Auditorium. Followed by dates in Camden (21st), Hope (22nd), Pine Bluff (23rd) and a final engagement in Bastrop/Louisiana. Where the trio added "Gonna Paint The Town Red". Roy Orbison stated, after attending one of the shows that Elvis "was like a real raw cat, singing like a bird."

In early 1955, DJ Mike Michael of radio station KDNS, El Dorado (Arkansas) began promoting Elvis Presley: Not unlike Dewey Phillips in Memphis. Before long, he had to dedicate a 15 minute slot to Elvis, on listeners demand, three times a week. That with Elvis having only six songs on three singles on the market.

Elvis also performs at the Grand Prize Jamboree on KPRC TV in the Lone Star State performing "Good Rockin' Tonight", "Baby Let's Play House", "Blue Moon Of Kentucky", "I Got A Woman" and "That's Allright". The following day, the trio shows off at the Koral Club and the Magnolia Gardens. A show at the Parkin Auditorium in Arkansas follows.

Elvis Presley's bandwagon became unstoppable by Spring and Summer 1955. The Hillbilly Cat became the King of Rock and Roll: The music industry simply could no longer ignore him thereafter. He had become a money making licensed brand, Elvis Presley. His audience was set in mass hysteria. Culminating as early as 12 and 13 May 1955.

This first of the Colonel Tom Parker promoted tours, bringing his new protégée Elvis, together with Hank Snow, whom Parker had made a country music superstar. Other big names on the tour included Faron Young, Slim Whitman, Martha Carson, the Davis Sisters, Mother Maybelle and the Carter Sisters. Florida was like home ground for Parker.

Chapter Eleven
Bill Haley and Elvis Presley—
Their Reign as Kings of Rock and Roll

Elvis Presley and Bill Haley are the two most renowned rock and roll stars. Both were titled "King of Rock and Roll", and both created their own respective styles of rock and roll out of a fusion of white hillbilly music and black rhythm and blues. They first met in 1954 while touring Omaha, Nebraska; Kansas City; and Tulsa, Oklahoma. The tour was booked through Jamboree Attractions, owned by Hank Snow and Colonel Tom Parker, the latter becoming Elvis Presley's manager until the star's tragic and early death in 1977.

The star of the show back in 1954 was Bill Haley. Elvis was added as a last minute extra attraction, and his name was hardly visible on the show's posters. The show attracted eighty five thousand attendees. During that period, Colonel Tom Parker took over the Elvis Presley management from Bob Neal, a local DJ from Memphis and friend of Sam Phillips, founder of Sun Records. Colonel Tom Parker and Lord Jim Ferguson were old friends.

One day the Colonel inquired if a third artist could be added to the tour. Ferguson asked Bill Haley: "Parker says he's got this kid he wants to polish up a bit. His manager is a disc jockey in Memphis named Bob Neal, but Parker says he may want to take the kid over. The kid needs to go on the road with some real pros. He bombed out in Nashville, but they didn't understand him. I think he's got some real potential. Can we fit him in on the tour?"196 A tour poster: Elvis Presley was opening for Bill Haley and The Comets; also booked was Jimmie Rodgers Snow, who later became a Minister and preached against rock and roll!

In an interview over a decade later, Haley recalled Elvis coming to see him back stage in Oklahoma City: "He was just standing there … we were about to go on. He came up to me and said what a fan he was. He seemed like a nice kid to me. He said he wanted to learn the business and Colonel Parker had said I was one of the best to learn it from. He reminded me a little of myself, going up to Hank Williams and Red Foley with almost the same words. Several nights later, after his set, he asked me what I thought of his singing. I had watched him and so I told him that I thought he had a lot of natural rhythm. 'Show a little more of your feeling, son … don't look so scared. Let 'em know what you got. Let 'em feel your music!'

For a couple of days, we buddied around together. I was curious to see what the Colonel saw in him. I asked him how he got to meet the Colonel. He told me the Colonel knew a lot of the right people in the music business. He asked what I thought the best guitar was. I told him I always liked the Gibson L-7 myself. He loved my car, and I let him drive it for a while on our way to Tulsa. He said to me, 'One day I'm gonna buy me a Cadillac and I'm gonna' buy one for my momma, too!'

After about a week, he got lonesome, and would talk about his mother. Being on the road away from his family tended to get him low. He asked me if I was ever on the Grand Ole Opry … I said no, but I was once, almost … then I got into rock n' roll and ain't sang much hillbilly since! Now, with my drums and sax, man, I don't think they would even let me in town! He grinned with a funny kind of smile and said 'I don't need 'um, too …' He was only a nineteen-year-old kid then, and had a lot of spunk. His eagerness to learn reminded me of myself back when I was his age. He told me his favourite song was 'Crazy Man, Crazy', and after he heard it he knew he wanted to be a singer, too. I told him it was my first big hit. I wished him luck. He left us in Tulsa, and we finished the tour.

The thing I remember most about Elvis was the way he looked. At first, I thought he was just another starstruck youngster with a guitar. His long hair, it was kinda' sandy-blond 198 then; his clothes and the hulking way he carried himself, at first put me off. And if he hadn't been recommended by Parker, I probably would have never talked to him. But when you got to know him a little bit, he was really a very nice, polite young man. He always called me 'Sir', even after I told him to call me Bill. He had more than just talent. I think he was hungry to be 'somebody' to make it big, except he wanted it, it seemed, for his mother. At the time, I kinda thought that was unusual." Bill and Elvis met again in October 1955, both were due to perform in a film about the disc jockey Bill Randle. The filming started in Brooklyn High school in Cleveland, Ohio.

In the afternoon and early evening of 20 October 1955, the footage with Pat Boone and the group The Four Lads was shot. A picture of Elvis Presley and Bill Haley was taken by WERE Radio disc jockey Tommy Edwards. This picture was framed by Bill Haley and hung in his office in Chester, Pennsylvania. Another one of the same shot was placed on the wall of Bill's new house, Melody Manor. Bill Haley and Elvis Presley at their second meeting in 1955199 On October 1st 1958, GI Elvis Presley was shipped to Bremerhaven, Germany where he was greeted by 1,000 fans. Three weeks later, on October 23rd, Bill Haley and His Comets started their infamous 1958 tour through Germany. Elvis heard that Haley was due to perform on the 23rd and 29th of October in Frankfurt and Stuttgart.

Elvis came to both shows, and the meeting was a happy one when Elvis told the ten-year-older Haley, that without him, his help and advice, he would probably still be working as truck driver in Memphis! Comets drummer Ralph Jones remembered this meeting of the Founder and first King of Rock and Roll, Bill Haley, with the future King of Rock, Elvis Presley: "He was stationed at a nearby army base. He and a few friends would dance ... he loved our music. After the show, we took pictures of Elvis, in uniform with Rudy, Catfish, Johnny, Al (Pompilli) and myself. I remember him saying to us; 'You know, if it weren't for you boys, I'd be still driving a truck back in Memphis.'"

The Comets also traded stories from the years gone by, for instance recalling a shy and nervous Elvis Presley prior his first appearance on Bill Randle's "Rock and Roll Sock Hop Show" when Elvis told former bass player Al Rex "I hope these Yankees like my music!" or when young Comets roadie Catfish and Elvis played cards backstage when Elvis toured with Bill Haley for the first time. For the Stuttgart show, Elvis was invited to perform with Bill Haley and His Comets out on stage, but had to decline as the local authorities feared riots.

At the end of the Stuttgart visit, Elvis told reporters: "I was only able to watch Bill and the Comets from the back, but he was great! I owe him so much. Without him, I would probably never have discovered rock and roll." 200 A decade passed until Bill and Elvis met again; it wasn't until the 1970s, when both played the Las Vegas circuit with Haley and the band, now regulars on the 'Richard Nader's Rock and Roll Revival' touring road shows, and Elvis holding down his extended engagements at the International Hotel and the Hilton. It's also interesting to note that both recorded songs which were in each other's catalogue. For example, Elvis and Bill recorded versions of "Shake, Rattle and Roll", "Rip

It Up", "A Fool Such As I", "It's A Sin", "Yeah, She's Evil (The Meanest Girl In Town)", "Stop, Look and Listen", "Blue Suede Shoes", "Blueberry Hill", "C.C. Rider", "Flip, Flop and Fly", "Lawdy Miss Clawdy", and "Whole Lotta Shakin' Goin' On"… just to name a few.

In 1984, a commemorative picture disc was released with nine songs of each artist on each side, along with the 1955 colour photo of them, also on each side. The disc did predictably well on the strength of the recent resurgence of interest in rockabilly music and culture in Denmark. But it wasn't an official release, but a bootleg made in Hamburg, Germany, October 1958 in Frankfurt, Germany: Elvis listens to Bill Haley tune his guitar The record producer Kenny Denton, who worked with Bill Haley on his final album "Everyone Can Rock and Roll" is also a great admirer of Elvis Presley.

He brought the subject "Elvis" up in conversation with Bill: "Spending each evening with Bill and Martha at dinner. I would ask Bill a question about his early career, then sit back and enjoy the anecdotes. I could see he was reliving each and every moment of the story he was telling. One evening I mentioned to Bill that I had been to Graceland a few days before, which of course introduced Elvis into the conversation. I asked Bill about the last time he had been together with Elvis; he said it was in Germany in the late fifties. My memory of this story was that Bill was having a reasonably rough time with life in general. At this particular gig he had left instructions that no one was to come back stage for the usual meet and greet adulation."

"At one point Bill's road manager came into the dressing room to tell Bill there was someone outside who would like to say hello! Bill reacted angrily 'I said no one's to come back here'! 'You may wanna see this guy', said the road manager. Bill looked up to see the head of Elvis peaking around the door, 'Hi Bill I brought some friends who would love to meet you' Bill immediately invited them in. Bill told me how good he felt chatting, and reminiscing, and the other problems he had at that period in his life were forgotten for a while. I asked Bill about the rumours that he and Elvis had met in the early seventies, but he told me this never happened. Haley said when he heard that Elvis was having, as he put it, a very tough time, he wrote a letter to Elvis at Graceland's asking if he ever needed to talk to an old friend he was there for him, but he never received a reply." (From the book "There Ain't No Rules In Rock and Roll" by Kenny Denton.)

(Editor's note: Contrary to what Haley stated here, Elvis did indeed meet with him twice in the early 1970s. Rudy Pompilli kept a framed photo of Elvis standing with Bill Haley and the entire Comets band at a Richard Nader Rock and Roll Revival concert in Las Vegas, where Elvis had dropped in to visit them. Drummer Bill Nolte also recalls a Haley concert in Memphis, where Elvis showed up with some friends, and after the concert, Elvis and Bill both left in Elvis' car and went out together for the rest of the night!)

Chapter Twelve
The NBC Television Special—As
Remembered by Its Director Steve Binder

I had had a very passionate feeling about television and all it could do to educate America and the world. And I had gotten a break early in my life and had directed a show in New York called 'Hullabaloo'. And from there I decided to get into the specials business. And I did put together a lot of the team from 'Hullabaloo' behind the scenes to do a Leslie Uggams special. Then the next one we did was with Petula Clark and Harry Belafonte. And that became a shot heard around the world when it was the first incident of a black and a white person touching physically on prime time television. And it created a kind of a furore among very bigoted advertising representatives from Chrysler Motors. They wanted the scene taken out of the show and it became very controversial in Newsweek and Time Magazine.

And then I found out that through a phone call from a gentleman, I think Bob Finkel, who was somebody that :I only heard of in the past, cause of all the shows he had produced and directed. And he called me and said 'Listen we got this deal at NBC with Elvis Presley'. But the truth is, 'We got a deal but we're not getting the show made. We think maybe you'll be someone who Elvis can relate to because of your age and because of all that's gone on. And we'd love to set up a meeting if you're interested with Elvis and see if you guys could hit it off and do the show'. And, I was convinced after the Petula Clark Belafonte special that I would never work again in this town. I was told that by about 100 people, you know, you just crossed the line and anybody who does anything controversial is immediately gonna be sat on by the establishment. But it turned out to be the luckiest thing in my life.

To be honest with you I had no passion for Elvis Presley's music. I was amused by him being a west coast kid, and I was into the Beach Boys and all the

Jimmy Webb and 'McArthur Park' and so forth. And my partner at the time was a very prolific, well-established record producer. So we joined forces on the Petula Clark special as partners. And, Bones Howe did the recordings for the Fifth Dimension and the Association, Laura Nyro, etc. while we were a company. And Bones, when he heard I got the phone call said 'Hey, man, you got to meet him because you guys are gonna be great together. I used to engineer for Elvis. And I just know he's gonna like you a lot and vice versa'.

So I agreed to a meeting at our offices on Sunset Boulevard next to Tower Records. And I said okay but, if we're gonna have a meeting then, you know, I'm gonna tell him that he should come to our offices and we'll chat. And so sure enough we set up a meeting and Elvis came out with the gang. All these Lincoln Continentals drove into our garage. In those days, we were the only show business company in the building, so nobody ever knew it was Elvis or cared it was Elvis or even thought he was gonna be there. And he came upstairs with Colonel Parker and Joe Esposito and a group of his entourage. And we went into our office and we left everybody outside.

I think it was just the Colonel and myself, Bones, Allen Blye and Chris Beard who wrote the special. And we just talked. And I don't think we talked much about the special. We talked about life and, there was this commonality where Elvis walked in and said 'Hi Steve' and I said 'Hi Elvis'. And Bob Finkel told me that he never ever called him by his first name.

And, we talked about him going to Hawaii on vacation for a week, and so forth and so on. I remember asking him 'If I gave you 'McArthur Park' to record, would you have recorded it?' And he said, 'Absolutely'. And I knew that Elvis wasn't just a guy living in the past but he was up on things and really wanted to join the real world, the contemporary world. Cause I remember telling him that in my opinion if he didn't mind my bluntness, but to me he hadn't had a hit record in years. He wasn't makin' any movies so what was really making him this superstar was just Colonel Parker and his publicity machine. But television was a way to either instantly the next day become the biggest star in the world, or vice versa. You might do the television special and fall on your ass and that would be the end of your career other than the memory of what you used to do. And I think he respected my honesty and we just hit it off. Then Elvis said he was going to Hawaii and I said 'Okay we're all gonna work on the show and when you get back, we'll talk about the 68 special.' Which is exactly what he did. He left and we put the show together and he came back and heard what we had to say.

The first time I met Colonel Parker, Bones and I went out to MGM Studios and the Colonel was showing off his office space. And he was bragging about his contract with MGM that was one-page long. And, I remember him telling me that, if they had any dispute with the studio they could be packed and out in a moving van in about two hours. And, then he presented me with a Snowmans Club membership which was, for those that don't know, the Snowmans Club was a fictitious club that the Colonel was president of. And, he was strictly for anybody who was great at knowing how to BS, you became a member of Colonel Parker's Snowmans Club.

And I never considered myself much in that arena but it was fun to get the certificate and the little cards that went with it and the booklet and so forth. Colonel Parker had a lot of preconceived ideas but my experience from the very beginning of my career to the present is that, you know, let creative people create and let business people do their business. And it's business people are very creative but they should keep in the business world not the creative world. And Colonel Parker gave me an audio tape, the old-fashioned kind that used to play on reel to reel. And it was Elvis Christmas present to radio. And it was an hour of recorded Christmas songs. And then there was this fake DJ stuff where, you know, the local DJ could insert himself asking Elvis questions and Elvis would answer, even though the two were never in the studio at the same time. It goes on to this day. And I took it and I just heard all of the talk of this is going to be a Christmas special.

This is gonna have 26 Christmas songs in it. And to be really honest with you, it never phased me and it never entered my mind that that was what we were gonna do. It just wasn't part of my psyche. Well, when Elvis came back from vacation in Hawaii, and he was awesome looking. I mean, I'm heterosexual. I'm straight as an arrow and I got to tell ya, you stop, whether you're male or female, to look at him. He was that good looking. And if you never knew he was a superstar, it wouldn't make any difference if he'd walked in the room you'd know somebody special was in your presence. So he came back from Hawaii and he was all tanned and he was in great physical shape and he was in a real good mood. And, they came to our offices again.

And we took him into the back room. And Chris Beard, Allen Blye, myself, I think Bones might've been in the room. And basically speaking we had a whole stack of his albums, every movie he ever made, every recording he ever made, etc., which is how we basically tailor made the show. What I told Elvis when he went to Hawaii is that we would make him a show that nobody else could do. Only him. We would … it was like making a tailor made suit. It would be made for him. And that's the way that I like working and I like working with all the talented people that I've surrounded myself with. Where we'd go into a think tank, and we'd never had titles. There was no Mister anybody in the room. There was no director, producer, star, whatever. We just sat there and we just all pitched equally, and I love working that way.

And so we decided that what would be better than taking a theme, a main theme, which is here's this dirt poor basically country boy who's a singer, who starts in life with nothing. And he works his way to fame and fortune. And goes full cycle where after he's got all this fame and adulation, he realises that happiness is home. It's where he all—you know, he's a musician and it's all where he began. And with that thread through the show, we then weaved a lot of different segments. But they all related to music he had either recorded or he liked or whatever. It was a special that we could not have, if he dropped out, we couldn't have run to another artist and said do this show. It was impossible. It was Elvis show. And we ran into a great conflict with NBC, who wasn't used to having one star in prime time. It was unheard of. You had a star and a bunch of guest stars. I think NBC at one time asked if we'd put Milton Berle on the show or something.

And, it was a case of when Elvis came back and we pitched him the concept, and we had broken it all out in terms of, we're gonna do this sort of miniseries within a segment where you're gonna go to a pier. First thing was the bordello sequence where he leaves his hometown and he goes and the first encounter he has is he walks into a bordello. And then there's this virgin innocent girl who's never even worked one day and she looks Elvis and he looks at her, and just as they were about to get together the place gets raided and they jump out the window, and he's on the road again. And then he goes to an amusement park and he has a confrontation with Big Daddy, who's this mean carnival barker who breaks his guitar and so forth. And we just did this sequencing. He goes to a little tiny dive to sing. He goes to a more upscale club. And pretty soon he's a superstar in concert. And then it tags with, you know, where his real happiness is his roots, being home and being an artist. And that was one segment.

Then we knew how much Elvis loved the gospel. I was blown away with the fact that here's a man to this day that's never won a Grammy for rock 'n' roll. The only Grammys he picked up were in the gospel area. I think he won two in that category. So we put a gospel segment together. I wanted the whole show to be live Elvis, even though we had an orchestra. In some segments, I wanted him to sing live in everything. The only regret I have about the special is in the gospel segment, he did a lot of lip synching. And to this day I regret the fact that I caved in and let him lip-sync because I think his forte was live performance, even on television.

Well, the show was presold to Singer Sewing Centre and that was a deal before I walked in with Colonel Parker and NBC. And Singer was doing other specials at the time. I think they did a Don Ho special. They had a package deal at NBC. And, but they were thrown the Elvis special and they picked it up. And at the time, the phones were ringing off the hook when people realised Elvis Presley was gonna do a television special. I remember Colonel Sanders was dying to get involved and sponsor the show with their Kentucky Fried Chicken. It led to a really good experience after that because Mrs Paul's Fish Sticks was really wanting to sponsor the show and I'm sure NBC would've gotten a lot more money from these sponsors who really wanted to be involved with Elvis.

And instead, they said it was already a done deal. So when Singer was in a sense thrown into the pie, they were obviously concerned with little old ladies who would go to Singer Sewing Centres and buy sewing machines. So there was no real generic relationship with Elvis Presley and his music. But as long as they stayed out of the loop in the creative process, I was happy.

And they did for a long time until we reached this scene, which now is called for years the Bordello scene. It never was a bordello scene to begin with. It was all part of that, you know, life story of a musician trying to become famous. And, what happened is that we did scenically put a brass bed in the room of all these women. And somebody from NBC all of a sudden labelled it the bordello. And that's what started the ball rolling in terms of the negativity of shooting that scene. So when I got the buzz that, you know, the cleavage on the ladies was too low, I went to the costume department and I say 'Okay, let's have the NBC standards and practice person standing there,' and let's get some net and, you know, sort of work on their dresses and their cleavage to make sure it met NBC standards. And we went through that and everybody was happy.

And then the next thing that happened is I heard a rumour. Nobody came to me and said, 'We're gonna cut this out of the show.' So I went to the sponsors and I went to NBC and I said 'Look, I want to know before I shoot it, not after. Is it gonna stay in the show or is it going out?' And then somebody, even though I never said it, somebody said 'Binder's gonna walk out of the show if we tell him it's gonna be cut out of the show. So we better tell him it's okay.' So I got them to give their word of honour that this piece would not be taken out of the show. And then as soon as I shot it, word came down that they were gonna take it out of the show, and I threw a big tantrum I guess at the point.

And, nobody at NBC in the programming department wanted to confront me or face me on this issue. So they decided to bring somebody from New York who was making toasters for, you know, General Electric or somebody. It was probably before General Electric owned NBC. But whoever it was high up in the RCA world came down, and he had no knowledge of show business that I knew of. And, I met him down in the videotape editing room, and he was looking at the monitor at a Dean Martin Show. Dean Martin had this girl in a bikini who, you know, our girls were very conservative compared to what this girl looked like in prime time on NBC. And I think he had Phil Harris, the bandleader, and they were basically telling a dirty joke without the punch line. This guy was laughing his head off and I said 'This is gonna be a piece of cake'. He's gonna look at our thing and say 'Fine'. So I bring him over to our tape machine and I play the sequence. He looks up and I can see his face go from smile to frown. And, he looked at me and he said, 'Out'. So, that was a battle that I really fought and I lost it for a while. But years later, somebody said, 'Hey that was a really good scene. We got to put that back into the special', and they did.

I said, "What do you think would happen if you walked out on the street today?" And he said, "What do you mean?" I said, "Well what do you think would happen?" And he looked at me curiously and he said, "Well, I don't know; what do you think would happen?" And I said, "Nothing. This is 1968. You walk down the street on Sunset Boulevard, and I almost promise you, guarantee you, nobody's gonna tear your clothes off. Nobody's gonna hound you for autographs or whatever, you know, they're gonna just accept you. These are different times, you know. And that was the end of the conversation, and it was a few days later, we rehearsed the show at our offices in the piano room before we ever went to NBC with the full orchestra and the staff and so forth."

And every day Elvis would come to our office and we would rehearse the show on piano, and teach him the arrangements and so forth. And up until this time Elvis had never recorded in his life with anything bigger than a rhythm section. Drums, bass guitar, sometimes he'd even have a bass and that was it. And now we're asking him to, you know, appear before 50 musicians and sing. He was nervous about that. And then when I fired Billy Strange and brought in Billy Goldenberg, Elvis didn't even know who Billy Goldenberg was, to do all the arrangements and conduct the special. It truly changed his musical direction. After that he loved big bands and full orchestras and what have you.

Anyway, the story, I'm digressing. But the story on Sunset is a few days later while we were rehearsing, Elvis came to me and said "Let's go." I didn't even know what he was talking about and I said "Let's go where?" He said "Downstairs". So everybody grabbed their hats or coats or whatever and they said "Let's go" and Elvis said "No, no. Only Steve and I are going down there. You all, you can watch from the window," cause we were on like the third floor. And he said "But we're goin' down there, you know, to see what it's like on Sunset Boulevard." We went down at the peak of traffic, like 5:00 in the evening. And we got down in front of our building. And then, we stood out there for a few minutes, and we were chatting small talk. I don't even remember what we were talking about.

But what I was observing, and what he was observing, was that nobody was paying any attention to us. And after a while, it got uncomfortable. And Elvis pretty soon was trying to draw attention to himself. He was kinda waving at cars driving by and some kids were coming from Tower Records and they bumped into us and didn't even lift their heads up to see they had bumped into Elvis and so forth. And, we stood out there for like 10 almost embarrassing minutes, trying to draw attention to hey this is really Elvis Presley.

And after it was all over I could tell a real change of attitude in him. He was loose, he was really fun, and he really trusted me. And then, the irony of the thing is I was convinced if anybody had a sign out on Sunset Boulevard saying, this is Elvis Presley not some Hollywood impersonator or character or whatever, he would've been mobbed and they would've torn his clothes off and so forth but he never knew that and I never mentioned it to him.

Well when we finished the show and I had gone down into the catacombs of NBC. In those days we recorded the show on two-inch videotape. And then when you ever made edits you had to use a razor blade to cut the tape physically and so forth. So it was a very, very laborious system. And, because I was allowed to recreate. I never was allowed to do the real thing but I was allowed to recreate the improvisational acoustic session. I had tons of footage beyond the show that we originally prepared, which was a well organised written affair. But when I saw the improv I said, "This is what the world wants to see. This is Elvis with his hair mussed up and sweat under his arm pits," which NBC objected to when I showed 'em the show. They wanted that taken out of the show cause this is prime time.

And then, when Elvis passed away, some genius at NBC said, "Okay, we got to rush out a Elvis Presley tribute and we'll take the Hawaii special and we'll take the 68 special and we'll put 'em together and we'll make a big show out of this. We'll get Ann-Margret to host it." Well, whoever went down into the dungeon and into the library, not knowing anything, pulled the 90-minute tape out. And they ended up doing three hours as a tribute, and played the 90-minute special. Well there was technically no 90 minutes on tape. I thought they had erased it or destroyed it or whatever but they obviously didn't. And that ended up restoring and getting back the full 90 minutes, which had a lot of the improv segments in it.

And then eventually, the outtake reels became more important than the show itself. And HBO calling it 'One Night With You' aired the entire unedited improv sections which were, you know, which I had nothing to do with, I mean, is Elvis Presley and that proved he wasn't just a myth of the Colonels PR machine. And it even proved to Elvis himself that he was that special and that fantastic. Cause I think in the very beginning and the reason that Elvis bought that doing the special in the first place is because I thought he had lost confidence, which most artists do at one time in their life. And I thought he was afraid. In fact, I think he expressed it to me.

He didn't think he had it any more for the audience cause he had been taken away from that live audience for so many years making those movies. And I could visually see him gain his energy, excitement, confidence. You could just tell if you're behind the scenes, just by his facial expressions, the great thing about Elvis was his natural instinct and he never gave himself credit for being a great musician, though most musicians really feel he was. He was always sort of down playing himself, as strange as that may sound.

And, when we did the improv, you know, I think he really had so much curiosity and fear in him as to whether he really had it that when he walked out there and realised, you know, 'Hey. They not only are loving it but, you know, my guys are loving it and I'm loving it'. I mean, this is what it's all about. Well it was the Dean Martin stage. And, so Elvis had basically by moving in, he'd go get up and we'd start rehearsals early in the morning and, you know, there was a cast of hundreds. And, at the end of the day when everybody was wiped out and going home to rest up for the next day, Elvis went into the dressing room, and all the guys went in there, and they started to unwind. And how they unwound was to just jam.

These are those moments where'd you get to look through keyholes and see things that you're just in awe of because you're not supposed to be seeing this stuff. I said I got to get a camera in there and got to film this. This is better than anything we're doin out on the stage. And Colonel Parker said "No he wouldn't allow it, no cameras, no still photography." And so I was trying to figure out how to do it. And Colonel said "Okay I'll tell you what I'll do. Providing that I have total control and it won't go into the show unless I say it's okay to go into the show, I'll let you recreate it out on the stage," which is how the whole improv began. And, that's exactly what I did but it never was as great as it is, it never was the real thing that I saw in the dressing room.

At first, he didn't even want to go out there and do it. In fact, I was called into the dressing room. I think Joe Esposito came and got me. Said "We got a crisis." I said "What's the crisis?" He said "Elvis doesn't want to go out there and do this improv." So I had to go into the makeup room, and he cleared the makeup lady out of the room. He said "Steve I can't do it." I said "What do you mean you can't do it?" And he said, "I don't know what to say. I don't know what to do." And I said "Elvis, go out there. I mean, if you go out there and say hello and good bye, I'm happy. But you've got to go out there. You're not gonna cop out at this point. We got an audience waiting for you. And all your friends are here and you've got to go out."

And when he went out there, he was scared to death. And he went out there and the opening number he was shaky. His throat was dry. And you could see all these things. Then little by little, boy, this just, you know, amazing urge of confidence just flowed through his body and we had this cue at the end of the improvs, of playing Memories, which was a recorded track. And he sang live to the track. And the cue was, Elvis let me know when you've finished all the improv, and then I'll play the track. So we had this little hand signal between us. But the reality is when he did both of the improvs, both of them, he never gave me the cue. I kinda had to just sense the moment when I felt it was time to play the track.

I went to Colonel Parker and when I was told it was okay to do this and I decided we'd have two audiences and we were inviting 250, 300 people to come to each one of these sessions. And so I had NBC guest relations print up the Elvis Presley tickets. And believe me, we could've sold those tickets for $1000 apiece or something, even in those days. I mean, to see Elvis Presley for an hour or two, you know, improvisational singing and talking and everything was just unheard of. And so I went to the Colonel and I said, "How many tickets do you want for your friends or your family or RCA or whatever?" And he said, "Bindel said you don't understand how the Colonel works." He said, "I don't want any tickets. But, if you want all of Elvis fans with the bouffant hairdos and all the screaming and yelling and everything from Memphis," he said, "I want all the tickets. And if you give me all the tickets, that means all of 'em. You can't have any, NBC can't have any, Singer can't have 'em, nobody gets 'em."

So I went to NBC and I went to Bob Finkel, and I went to the sponsors and I said, "This is the deal. And for me there's no contest, let's give 'em to the Colonel and let's, get this, cull this audience." Not taking into consideration that my real feelings were, in all honesty, is I didn't trust what the Colonel said. I mean, I just didn't feel 100 percent confident when he said he was gonna do something it was really gonna happen. And I usually try and protect my backside all the time by anticipating whether things are gonna happen. In this case I didn't. I convinced everybody to give the Colonel all of the tickets for both shows, which I did. He got out his briefcase and all the tickets went into the briefcase. And I'm expecting these airplanes to fly in from Memphis, and all these screaming women coming out and all the Elvis hard core fans and so forth.

And about two days after the tickets were given to the Colonel, the guard at NBC while I was driving out one evening, said "Hey Steve, do you need any tickets for Elvis?" And I said "What are you talking about?" And there on his desk in the guard booth was a stack of Elvis Presley tickets. That was my first indication we're in trouble in River City, you know, we're in deep trouble if this doesn't come off. So the next morning I got there extra specially early, expecting to see the Johnny Carson, Jay Leno fans lined up outside of NBC but, you know, tenfold. I just expected there'd be fans taking over all of Burbank wanting to see Elvis Presley.

There was nobody and I drove into the gate and we're gettin ready to organise the staff and the stage to shoot this sequence and all of a sudden, the head of the guest relations comes to me and said "Steve we're in big trouble." There's just a few people standing outside. Those tickets weren't distributed. They didn't go to anybody. So we panicked. I mean, we called some friends of ours at some local radio stations and asked them to promote it on the air. We sent somebody over to Bob's Big Boy to ask customers eating hamburgers and malts to come over to see Elvis Presley and we somehow pulled together with enough people at NBC who were there, calling their friends and families and what have you to get these audiences in there.

I think I was doing another special at the time and was very involved in work and, I was very sad to hear that because my last conversation with Elvis, when we were alone at NBC just viewing the special, was that I had hoped—because he told me how much he passionately loved the special. He really did, which is very rare hearing an artist tell you to your face how much they love what they see of themselves on the screen.

A lot of artists don't even want to look at themselves after they finish a movie or a special. And he said how much he loved it, and he expressed to me that he was never ever going to record a song again that he didn't believe in and he wasn't gonna make a movie that he didn't passionately feel something about the script. And I said "I hear you and I hope you're strong enough to live up to that" because, the reality is having observed Elvis in his relationship with the Colonel, is that I didn't know if he had a lot of real close personal friends. I equated him to Hamlet, who was afraid to go out into the real world because he was sort of insulated and isolated.

And, I did go to see Elvis in Las Vegas when he performed the first time there and I was really excited about him exploring new worlds for himself. And then the next time I went to see him, he had his back to the audience and I knew he was bored. And I think that was the big danger of Elvis future was to prevent boredom. And I think he overstayed his welcome mat in Las Vegas as a Las Vegas entertainer. I would've loved to see him make movies, go around the world and do concerts and so forth and so on. For whatever reasons, he chose not to.

Chapter Thirteen
The Aloha Satellite TV Special

On 4 September 1972, the foundation was laid for the first ever, simultaneously satellite broadcast concert special of a singer, in over 40 countries. It was between Elvis Presley's dinner and evening show, on his 7th las Vegas engagement, that this historical press conference was held. On 20 November 1972, Elvis named on another press conference the date of this special concert: The 14th January 1973. He is scheduled to perform at 12.30 am at the International Convention Centre in Honolulu. Elvis Presley presents a cheque of 1000 Dollars for the Kui Lee Cancer fund. RCA Records and his manager Colonel Tom Parker hand in a cheque of $1000 also.

On 7 January 1973, the pre-ticket sale opens. 4000 of the available 6000 seats are already prebooked, while the remaining 2000 seats are sold on the very same day. There is no set ticket price, as it is a fundraiser, and each guest can set himself a price to enter the concert. The money goes to the Kui Lee Cancer Research Fund, named after the Hawaiian singer, his song "I'll Remember You" will become one of the new songs in Elvis' repertory.

Elvis arrives on 9 January 1973 in Hawaii. On 12 January 1973, a final rehearsing concert is held, which is fully recorded, this in case, there should be any difficulties at the grand show. 6000 tickets for this "rehearsal" are sold within a short time frame. Elvis in on another career height. January 13th is proclaimed as "Elvis Presley Day" in Hawaii, by its Governor. On 14 January 1973, the concert proceeds. Before Elvis enters on stage, his orchestra and band play an excerpt of "Also Sprach Zarathustra" by Richard Strauss, shortly before in the soundtrack to the Stanley Kubrick movie "2001: A Space Odyssey".

When the teaser of the band and orchestras fades in, a slim, well trained and tanned Elvis Presley enters the stage. He wears an "Aloha Eagle" jumpsuit with cape, designed for the show by Bill Belew. It was Elvis' own idea to feature the

American Eagle on it, a well displayed motive to the patriotism of Elvis Presley. Shortly after the show, after the audience had left, Elvis records five more songs on stage: "Early Morning Rain" and "Blue Hawaii" among them. The songs, are recorded for the US airing, which will feature the 14th January show, of 1 hour and four minutes, and extends it with this additional songs to 1 hour and 17 minutes.

Elvis chose mostly ballads for this show, songs like "What Now My Love" and "My Way". Additionally he performs Rock and Roll anthems like "Johnny B. Goode" and "Blue Suede Shoes". As well as older hits of his, like "A Big Hunk O'Love" and "Can't Help Falling In Love". Also the soft rock songs "Steamroller Blues" known by James Taylor and the Beatles song "Something" are added to the programme. The strength of the concert lie in the ballads, which also display Elvis private circumstances at the time, autobiographically: "You Gave Me A Mountain", "I'll Remember You" or "I'm So Lonesome I Could Cry". He receives strong rapport by the audience for "Burning Love" and "Suspicious Minds" two contemporary hits, for Elvis Presley at the time.

With over 2.5 million US dollars, "Aloha From Hawaii" breaks records, as to this date, being the most expensive TV production. For the first time, a show of a solo singer, was being transmitted in various countries. On the Philippines, more than 90 percent of the tv viewing audience was tuned in, in Hong Kong 70%, 80% in South Korea. The concert was also aired live in Europe, Africa and South America.

It wasn't until 4 April 1973 that the show aired in the States, with 51% viewers on NBC. Altogether 1.5 million people watched it on their TV sets. A double live LP was released, which made the Nr. 1 spot on the US charts. As well as peaking very high internationally. In later years, the show was released on video and DVD. In 2004, a Deluxe DVD Edition including both Hawaii shows was released. This DVD reached platinum status. Elvis was on top of his game at this concert, probably reaching his pinnacle as a live performer both nights in Hawaii.

Chapter Fourteen
Elvis, the Man

This chapter might be the one in which the life story of the superstar Elvis Presley, the image he had, and the reality in which he lived in—are so far apart. That it will be difficult to catch the man Elvis Aron Presley with words. He himself is famous for the quote "An image and a human being are two very different things. It is hard to live up to an image." Was there a destroying of his own persona through fame and fortune? Women, sex, sex-appeal all seem to fit well in one way the Presley image was created. Much of his fascination lies in his immense charisma, which appealed to both men and women. Colonel Parker might have said, at the beginning of their business venture: "Stay full of talent and sexy, while I make the business, to make us richer than the maharajas."

While in the mid-50s he appealed to teenagers and young ladies, it wasn't uncommon that women in their best age, lost all inhibitions when seeing him onstage. Some taking their underwear off and throwing it onstage. But that was one side of showbiz. His body movements in later years were much more choreographed, maybe a little more calculated, and had more of a macho-like gesture with the karate movements Elvis inserted. But regarding sex, he stayed clean-cut. The ideal son-in-law, the one southern mothers could see their daughters with.

Newspaper reports regarding affairs with his co-stars were always debunked by his management, film-companies and even RCA. Not only because he was living with young Priscilla Presley under one roof in Graceland ... After both married, he was the hard-working husband, relentlessly working the touring circuit, and a great father to his young daughter Lisa Marie, born exactly nine months after the couple had married. A fact. Graceland seemed like a monastery to some outsiders, and maybe after he and Priscilla divorced, like a castle, where a beautiful, lonesome Prince lived. Even his relationships with former Miss

Tennessee Linda Thompson, which did not lead to a wedding ceremony, which may could relate to, as he himself seemed not to recover from the separate ways he and Priscilla went, did not disturb his image as great American.

When he, at the age of 42, had a liaison with Ginger Alden, who was 21 at the time, no one doubted his sincere intentions with the young Lady. In the south, sex before marriage was unthinkable, maybe a reason why so many people in the region, married in their youth. Red West, the longest serving member of Elvis bodyguards the Memphis Mafia said "Elvis, in 1954, was a very shy boy." Red remembers that there was a relationship with June Carter, one of the beautiful daughters of Mother Maybelle, of the famous first family of Country music— The Carter Family, describing Elvis as a clumsy kid, whenever he was close to the young Country music goddess. When performing in Florida in the mid-1950s, Elvis lost consciousness backstage, tumbling into June Carter's arms— until emergency services arrived, June held him. At one am, Elvis appeared in Red's hotel room explaining that it was just an act, to get all the attention of June Carter.

Some sources claim that June did the same a few weeks later, to get the most of attention of Elvis. Red West explaining that it wasn't only Elvis who was a shy country boy, but also June a shy country girl. "He wasn't crazy about girls. He wanted to be a success as a singer. Partly for his mother, that was more important to him, than to bed different girls. He believed in himself and his talent, as well as in a clean life. It made him angry, when someone in his surroundings, dated married or divorced women."

In her novel, "Orion" Gail Brewer Giorgio describes the effect that her fictionalised Elvis Presley in the story called Orion Darnell had on women and men, through the eyes of the manager: "(he) moved his body because it was natural: the rest of the 'tight-assed' world moved their cheeks together as though their shit was gold and worth protecting. Thank god for the new generation …" According to Red West, as soon as Elvis found out, that women enjoyed sex as much as men, his idea towards the concept especially in his early years changed. Red said it was not uncommon, that Elvis slept with two or three different girls the same night. Despite of this one-night-stands, Elvis preferred Southern belles such as Dixie Locke, his first girlfriend. But Elvis' shyness did not dissolve, it was always the job of his boys in the Memphis Mafia to get the women close to him.

The King, in later years, in his self-chosen or outer world inflected isolation had no other choice. Regular dating had become impossible to him. Even after the King of Rock and Roll's reported death, the Southern Belles were still on hand to give out details about meeting Elvis Presley. For instance Diana Goodman, "Miss Georgia 1975", who sold her story to an editor of the National Tattler. The headliner proclaimed that it was a million females who dreamed about becoming Elvis Presley's love interest, and for one it became reality. It was fairy-tale like month for Diana Goodman, to spend in a world of glitter and gleam …

Diana Goodman tells about meeting the first time in June 1975, while she was contesting for the Miss USA title. She was in Memphis to pursue a modelling career. She also went to see Graceland, already then an attraction for tourists. Outside always a hundred or more fans waiting, she explains in the article further. "Like many Memphis travellers I decided to visit the house of Elvis, before leaving Memphis. At the front door gate, I engaged into a conversation with a man. It was one of Elvis' bodyguards. I asked him if Elvis was at home—"yes sure" was his reply. He wanted to check if I could see him, and asked me to come in. Inside Graceland I was told, that Elvis did not want to be disturbed. I should wait around little bit. I was in Elvis' house and he was in.

"On the very evening, I got to know him. He asked me if I wanted to see a movie. He was about to invite some of his friends to a private screening. In the cinema, were Elvis and his long-term relationship Linda Thompson, as well as members of the Memphis Mafia. Elvis had rented the theatre for a midnight screening. We were among us. We watched three movies. One with Peter Sellers, one with Charles Bronson, the third one I can't remember. Elvis had seen all movies beforehand. I learned that he often watched movies on his own, then invited his friends to watch them with him, pointing out certain aspects of the story to them. It was the same this very evening, he talked a lot, explained what would happen in the next scene and so on. Elvis was in a great mood the entire evening. He is really a movie-lover. It was about six am when we left the cinema, we drove back to Graceland. One of his employees brought me to my hotel."

"On the very same day I flew back to Los Angeles, to look for an agent, as I am an aspiring actress and model. Shortly after I arrived in LA, Elvis called me from Memphis. That was only two days after our six-hours rendezvous in the cinema. 'I am going on tour' he said, 'would you like to accompany me?' I tried to appear not to be too overwhelmed. But I, Diana Goodman from Forest

Park/Georgia was asked to go on tour with Elvis Presley? With the idol, of which 48 hours before I only dreamed of. I was very excited."

"Elvis sent his private plane, which picked me up from Los Angeles. We met in Connecticut. We toured Ohio, New York, Virginia, North- and South Carolina. We travelled in his private jet, accompanied by the ever present Memphis Mafia. The game 'who is the blonde girl' had begun. It was fun, both me and Elvis enjoyed it. I learned a lot about him, I saw aspects of his, that some people did not see or overlooked. He seems to prefer little town girls. It certainly fit me, I grew up on a farm. Sheila Ryan from Chicago is the only girl in his life which makes an exception of that rule. Maybe I should also comment on Linda Thompson, which was part of his life, through some of the recent years. They are good friends, have a friends relationship."

"Linda is always there, when he needs her—and vice versa. If there would be more, both of them would be married. When we three hung out, she was his friend, I his lover. Linda has other men, like Elvis has other women. We separated in Asheville. I travelled back to Georgia, and he returned home to Memphis. I called him a final time when he was in hospital, but we did not see each other again. Whatever will happen to me, I doubt that there will be a better time, than the dream summer I had when I was Elvis girl."

Linda Thompson shared her story in a one-hour Television interview with Stanley Siegel:

In the interview, Linda Thompson tells the interested TV viewer, that she met Elvis on a Thursday in 1972. Friends had invited her to one of Elvis common private screenings, after she was voted Miss Tennessee. Along with a female friend of hers. During the screening Elvis sat next to her, and told her that he was no longer married, which was news to Linda. Her reply was: "No, I didn't know, but you should look for a local girl for marriage." A day after the cinema visit, he invited both girls to his mansion Graceland. He showed them the entire house, but nothing more came off it.

The very next day, Linda and her parents went for a three week long vacation. As soon as she had returned to Memphis the phone rang, with an impatient Elvis on the other line, complaining that he could not find a trace of Linda. Following it with an invitation to Las Vegas. Linda agreed, to stay with him "for four years". Linda insisted that she was always faithful, throughout their relationship, while Elvis openly dated and slept with other women. She still saw him as a wonderful man, who shared openly his adoration to other women with her, but remained watchful that she did not date other men.

She also noted the close bond Elvis had to his father Vernon. The two came to a closeness only comparable to the relation Elvis shared with Priscilla, including baby talk, she was Mamy while he was baby buntyn. Elvis had some mood swings, and violent behaviour also towards his manager Colonel Tom Parker, according to Linda. A man full of contradictions. He cried and wept openly in her presence. She said that she had to make a decision between a life full of extravaganza or a normal, modest life, and she decided for the latter, which Elvis fully understood. Though in an afterthought, she thought she could have saved Elvis' life …

Linda Thompson: "Elvis needed more love than any other human being, that I met in my life. As long as I could, I lived up to his expectations." (In an interview with People magazine).

"How are people going to remember me when I'm gone? Will they soon forget me?" he asked in May 1977 in a hotel in the small city of Binghamton/New York his backup-singer and former lover Kathy Westmoreland. He was lying, lonely and depressed in his suite, temporarily abandoned after his latest girlfriend had become bored with the treadmill of touring. He had sent for Kathy Westmoreland to keep him company, as he couldn't bear to be alone, let alone sleep alone. His entourage didn't like him to be alone either. They worried when there was no one to watch over him. Kathy, who had been with him on stage for seven years, with him that night, listening as he talked about his mother, his weight, his health and his daughter, consoling him as he was fearing the release of a book, penned by former associates and members of the Memphis Mafia. "Elvis. What happened?"

He was only forty-two, but sick with a host of internal problems, addicted, exhausted and disappointed. He had started to talk about himself in the past tense. He joked that Kathy should wear something white for his funeral. She laughed and promised she would, holding his hand until he fell asleep. That was Elvis Presley, living his final months as an Entertainer, and the world's most loved entertainers. Had his life become a tragedy?

"I'm so tired of being Elvis Presley," he would repeatedly say during the year 1977, who was this man, and what had made him the King of Rock and Roll, maybe a few of this questions can be answered in this book.

"I don't sound like nobody," he had said to Marion Keisker of SUN Records, when he had made his first acetate pressing, in 1954. He had read about the Memphis Recording Service in a newspaper as being a place where you could walk into off the street and make a recording on a disc to take home. He had heard about Sam Phillips, the man who owned the company, a radio engineer from Alabama who had left his job to drive all over Memphis, making private recordings of weddings, funerals and rotary club speeches. Also Elvis knew that Sam's Memphis Recording Service was just a side business, something to help to pay the rent, while Sam Phillips was seeking to start his own record company.

The Memphis Recording Service was a single-storey shopfront building at 706 Union Avenue on the corner of Marshall Avenue. Elvis had driven past it many times, hoping to catch a glimpse of Phillips or Memphis DJ Rufus Thomas, who had cut an answer recording to Big Mama Thornton's "Hound Dog" there— "Bear Cat". A week after graduating from Humes High School, on a Saturday, in the afternoon he had walked up and down outside. His courage was failing him, when he noticed that a young lady in her mid-thirties was watching him from the inside.

Realising that it was not a good move now to leave, he entered the Memphis Recording Service with a little lie on his lips. He had asked to make a recording or his mother's birthday, but it was July, and his mum's birthday was in April. There were other young men waiting, maybe also hoping to be discovered, finally it was Elvis Presley's turn: "So, what kind of singer are you?" the secretary asked him. His reply was "I sing all kinds". "But who do you sound like?"

"I don't sound like nobody" was his reply. "So, who do you sound like in hillbilly?"

"I don't sound like nobody." He repeated. She led him into the small studio, of which he might even have been impressed, as it was his very first time in a recording studio. He cut two songs that day, "My Happiness" and "That's Where Your Heartaches Begin", the ladder he re-recorded professionally for RCA Records when he was already the most-promising Rock and Roll artist the country had to offer. Marion Keisker made a note, and recorded a tape of Elvis for Sam Phillips, she wrote down on a piece of paper "Sideburns Timothy" to not forget him, as she liked what he heard.

Elvis kept the acetate all his life, his mother Gladys loved it, and played it to the few neighbours she knew in Memphis. Elvis must have kept thinking about who he sounded, he loved the crooners like Bing Crosby, the pop balladeers like Dean Martin, the Country stars like Hank Williams, but also many of the Beale Street Rhythm and Blues artists, as well as Street Corner Harmonies known as Doo Wop. Was he sounding like an amalgam of all of this? Definitely he would record all aforementioned genres throughout his career.

In 1954, he began dating a girl named Dixie Locke. She was fifteen, and from a different school than he'd went to. He'd seen her at church with friends, overhearing the girls loudly talking about going to the Rainbow Roller-skating, the following day. Naturally, Elvis went there too. He and Dixie ended up talking, as both had hoped for. He even drove her home, in the fifty Dollar car, that Vernon had bought his son for his eighteenth birthday. At their date, planned for next week, her parents did not allow her to go. So Elvis stayed with them, playing monopoly. Despite of his loud clothes, he must have impressed them. As they soon went steady. They went to movies, and Diners, and spent most of their spare time together.

They did all the stuff that teenagers did, in a more innocent time, the 1950s.

Dixie was small with long, dark hair that came down to her shoulders. She wore bobby socks and seemingly was forever laughing. Loyal, she was too. She didn't mind if Elvis looked outlandish, compared to other teenagers in Memphis. She would go with him to listen to gospel singing, even sometimes to a black Baptist church on East Trigg Avenue in South Memphis. The pastor there, Reverend Herbert Brewster, was famous for his sermons. Also for having written for the Queen of Gospel Mahalia Jackson, the song "Move On Up A Little Higher". Elvis knew that, as he had some of Mahalia Jackson's records.

As Memphis, like many cities in Dixie, was still segregated, white people could not go inside a black church. Same for black people, they could not go into a diner and sit with white people side by side. Elvis and Dixie would stand as guests in a little porch behind a gate at the side of the church and would watch and listen. In Elvis Presley's opinion, it was "always something wonderful". He admired some of the soloists that Reverend Brewster had. He was also a fan of Clyde McPhatter, who sang with the Rhythm and Blues group "The Drifters". "I wouldn't want for nothing else," he would say to Dixie. She would laugh kindly and correct him on his grammar.

At that time, a career in a Gospel group was still possible. Elvis was thrilled when he was given a chance to audition for a young quartet who sang at the church he attended. They didn't think though, that he was the right candidate, and denied him the capability to sing harmony. He was upset, and never forgot. When he began making records a little later, he made albums with all of his favourite hymns, with a male quartet singing with him.

His first job after school had been on an assembly line, but he did not like it. He left a few weeks after to become an apprentice electrician at Crown Electric. It suited both Gladys and Vernon. Gladys especially had always wanted him to be an electrician. "I was serious about the job." Elvis would remember later. "It paid three dollars an hour." He wasn't learning too much on to do couplings and connections. Mostly he was driving a little black Chevrolet pick-up truck and would deliver equipment all through Memphis.

This was handy, because it gave him also the chance to call in at Sun Records a couple of times. To ask Marion Keisker if she knew anyone who wanted a singer. She never did, but as Marion was forever welcoming, he recorded another couple of tracks on an acetate for himself a few months later. To also remind her of where she could still reach him by phone. He always had a drive to launch himself a career in the music biz. Summing up his ambition later, he would describe it as "a dream with a V8 engine", his drive and ambition never lacked him, his entire career. He tried many other things as well, like working as a singer in several places, including a little nightclub called the Hi Hat, where he was told that he was never going to make it as a singer. Again he was upset. Gladys would shake her head at those who turned him down, but his father Vernon would shrug as if to say "well, what did you expect?"

Vernon had a good voice, and Elvis would at times wonder if there was a part of his father that really didn't want his son to succeed. Possibly, as he had envy himself, for never making it … Vernon would tell Elvis to concentrate on being an electrician, because that was a good job. Elvis wasn't so sure himself: "Electricians have to keep their minds on what they're doing. If they are at least bit absent minded, they're liable to blow up someone's house. I was always dreaming, my mind somewhere else."

For over twenty years, he would joke about the fact that he'd been "driving a truck" and had somehow fallen almost accidentally into "this crazy music business". He was very modest, about his beginnings. Certainly he was lucky, he came along just at the right time. But his plans never consisted of staying an electrician or driving a truck. He was doing it in the meantime, looking for a way to launch his musical career. According to Bill Haley, Elvis knew he wanted to break into the music business, since upon hearing Haley's 1953 pop hit "Crazy

Man Crazy", the first white Rock and Roll recording to crack the Billboard Pop Charts. On one hot Saturday morning at the end of June in 1954, a year to the day since he'd finished high school and first called in at Sun Records: Marion Keisker called him. She phoned him at work wanting to know if he could come over to 706 Union Avenue by three o'clock that afternoon. She later would joke, that he was faster there, than she could put the phone down, after her initial call.

It was their first professional meeting: Sam Phillips and Elvis Presley. Sam liked to tell how he'd been brought up on a farm in Alabama and had learned about the blues from a blind old man his father had employed there. It was Uncle Silas Payne. Uncle Silas had been born into slavery, and Phillips would soon see his mission in life as being able to "give the poor Negro a voice in a place where he didn't have one." At the same time, it has been said in almost any story or book about the life of Elvis Presley, that Sam Phillips was being famous for having said, that if he "could ever find a white boy who could sing with the passion of a Negro he'd make a million dollars."

One of the reasons why Marion Keisker wanted her boss to meet with the young Elvis Presley. Without her belief in him and her support none of what would happen would have been possible. At least, not in the way, as it would turn out. Sam Phillips had already released a few records, the new label though had only one small hit the previous year with a Doo Wop group called The Prisonaires. They had come together in the Tennessee State Penitentiary. Their lead singer Johnny Bragg, had been convicted of six rapes by the time he was seventeen, he had a beautiful voice, and after Sam Phillips had enquired about the group, which included three murderers. They all had been driven to Memphis under armed guard to record their single "Just Walkin' In The Rain".

Two years later the song turned out to become an international hit, when being recorded by white Johnnie Ray. On that Saturday in 1954, when Elvis was called into SUN, Phillips had just got back from Nashville with a new song— "Without You". The song had also been written by a prison inmate. Sam was looking for a singer to do it justice, and Marion recommended Elvis. Elvis spent that afternoon at 706 Union Avenue, doing "Without You" in all possible styles they could think of.

At the end of the session, Sam told Elvis: "Don't worry. It isn't you, Elvis. Maybe the song isn't what I thought it was. What else do you know? Just relax. Sing me something that that means something to you." Elvis Presley went through everything that had a meaning to him musically: Pop songs, spirituals, old all-time favourites, a few words of anything he remembered on that day. They spent approximately three hours, looking for something being worthwhile being recorded and possibly released. All the time Sam Phillips was watching him, concentrating. And that was it, at the end of what turned out to be a rather long rehearsal or audition instead of a recording session, Sam thanked him: "You did fine, Elvis, just fine. Let me think about it."

That was it, Elvis seemed to be discouraged, what was supposed to be his big break, didn't turn out to be what he thought it would. As it happened, his mind was taken off it, soon. Two members of the Blackwood Brothers Gospel quartet were killed in a plane crash in Alabama that week. It was the second time, Elvis knew of stars being taken out of life. In 1953, his mother had mourned for Country and Western Star Hank Williams. But Elvis was far more affected by the death of two of the Blackwood Brothers, it seemed. He even attended the funeral with Dixie and her family. Dixie went on to vacation with her parents to Florida the next morning.

Elvis was left behind, upset over the plane crash, and afraid that Dixie would meet someone else. He was the suspicious kind, always had been. He just couldn't help it. Without her, and with little else to do, he sat at the movies. He was sitting in the dark, when an usher pick him out. There was Gladys in the aisle beckoning to him. A guitarist named Scotty Moore had called the Presleys neighbour, she told him. Scotty said, that Elvis had been asked by Mr Sam Phillips to audition. He knew, he had to call Scotty back, quickly.

Sunday, 4 July 1954, was a humid holiday weekend. Elvis didn't go to church that morning. The Presleys had not been attending church as regularly as they did in Tupelo. When Elvis went now, it was usually in the evening. By the time, this weekend's Sunday came, he was busy changing his entire future. He was a mere 19 years old. Elvis had never had heard of Scotty Moore. Scotty had asked Elvis to come over to his place. Scotty was living in the north of Memphis. Elvis couldn't help but being impressed with how much Scotty had already managed to pack into his life.

At twenty-three, Scotty had already served in the US Navy on an aircraft carrier in Korea. He was now married for the second time, had two children by his previous wife, was leading a band by the name of the Starlite Wranglers and lived in an apartment in an attractive area of Memphis, at that time. Like most guitarists, he also had a day-job, fixing the hats at a dry cleaners. He was a busy man with a busy life. Yet he was the quietest, neatest, most unassumable person you could meet. As Elvis and Scotty chatted for a while, a friend of Scotty Moore from down the street had joined them. It was Bill Black, a double-bass player.

Elvis knew Bill Black's younger brother who also lived in the Lauderdale Courts. So he surely had heard of Bill Black. Bill didn't play that day. Instead he and Bobbie, Scotty's new wife just sat in silence, looking at the pink pants Elvis was wore with a white lacy shirt the young singer had put on, in hoping to impress. Scotty and Elvis went through a few songs. "How did it go?" his mother Gladys asked him, when Elvis got home. He didn't know how to answer that question. They had not thrown him out, but it could have been just another dead end. So he must have been relieved the following day, when Marion Keisker called in at work asking him to come over to the studio.

Together with Scotty Moore and Bill Black. It seemed that Sam, Scotty and Bill all agreed that young Elvis could sing. Elvis discovered later, they didn't think him as being too special either. As Elvis, until that day, had never sung with any musical accompaniment, Sam Phillips was curious if indeed he was capable of doing so. Sam would later say, that he could hear something in Elvis' voice, but at that time did not know what it was. It was the same for Elvis. So they started work that night. No drums, just Bill Black on bass, Scotty Moore on lead guitar, and Elvis Presley on the rhythm guitar. Sam Phillips used every trick he could think off, to make it a worthwhile effort in finding out what he could do with the three young men.

Air conditioning wasn't possible at the tiny Sun Records studio, so it was sticky when they all went to work that night. All three, as Scotty would admit "below average musicians". Phillips' wasn't paying them per hour, as the major record studios did, as Elvis would learn later, after signing with one—RCA Records. Sam didn't care about union rules, neither about mistakes or even a wrong note, he was looking for the right feel and in so the right sound. Elvis made his way through "Harbour Lights" and "I Love You Because", Sam encouraged him—"That's fine Elvis."

Soon though, it became evident, that whatever Elvis was trying, wasn't "fine" enough. Late in the evening, they were allowed a break. Elvis was half expecting that Sam Phillips would call it a night, as they were all up early called, the next day, for their day jobs. Elvis kept looking around the little studio imagining B.B. King and Howlin' Wolf right there with him. Had he got it wrong, had they got it wrong, then they were recorded here? His mind must have been wandering around the blues.

As he waited for Scotty and Bill to come back, who had gotten themselves a drink to cool down, he began messing with an old blues song. He knew dozens of blues songs, but this one had been on the radio mainly, when he had arrived in Memphis. It was by an artist called "Big Boy" Arthur Crudup. So Elvis went into "Well, that's all right, Mama, that's all right for you …" to break some of the evening's tensions. Bill got up, grabbed his bass, which was nearly as tall as he was, and began to slap it, Scotty joined in. It would be the first jam session Elvis Presley was ever in. Then Sam's voice came through, breaking it up: "He, what the hell y'all doin' in there?"

"I don't know. Just foolin' around." Scotty Moore told him. "Well, it don't sound too bad", Sam replied. "Find out what you're doing, find a place to start, and let me get it balanced right." That's what they did, and the definitive Rockabilly blend was born that night, on the blue-print of Bill Haley and Hank Williams.

"Don't complicate it, Scotty. Keep it honest. If we'd wanted Chet Atkins, we'd have brought him over from Nashville. I want it fresh. And Elvis, sing it plaintive and needy. That's what you're good at." They did six takes, three or four broke down as a result of them not knowing their parts. Sam chose one or two to keep and that was it.

"So, what the hell we got here?" Scotty asked, as they prepared to leave, that night. Bill was amused, jokingly saying "Damn, if we ever get that played they'll run us out of town." They all knew what it meant, what they had recorded wasn't black nor white, it wasn't pop as it wasn't Country, Blues or Rhythm and Blues. They had fused a blues song with country. The people who demanded white singers to do pure country wouldn't like it. As for the radio stations, who were also segregated in their playlists between race music and pop music, nobody was sure how they would react.

It was a very different song achieved that night, probably only Bill Haley and Hardrock Gunther, had come close to a sound like that, before.

But the job was half done, they would need a flip side for the record of "That's Allright (Mama)". So, they very next night, they attempted it.

By this time, Sam Phillips, had already tested the song "That's Allright (Mama)" over Dewey Phillip's "Red, Hot and Blue Show" on WHBQ. Elvis always listened to Dewey Phillips, who had not relation to Sam Phillips, but was a good friend of Sam's. Marion Keisker called him and told him that Dewey would play "That's Allright" on the radio. Elvis turned the radio to the right spot for his parents, and went himself to the cinema. Once again Gladys came looking for him. "Did Dewey Phillips play my record?" he asked, as she hurried him out of the cinema.

Her reply was: "Play it? He's been playing it for over an hour and people are ringing in. They just called from the station to say Dewey wants you down there so he can talk to you on the radio." Quite a challenge for Elvis, who hardly even ever spoke in class. "I don't know nothing about being interviewed", he said, as Dewey sat him down in the little WHBQ studio in the Hotel Chisca. "Don't worry about that, Elvis. Just don't say anything dirty, all right. Now, for information, first off ... tell me a little bit about yourself. Where are you from, Elvis?"

Elvis told him about Tupelo/Mississippi. "And where did you go to school?" Elvis telling him about Humes High School. After a while, Dewey just said, "Thank you, Elvis." Disappointed, Elvis asked him about being interviewed. Dewey said: "I already did. You were going out live all the time you were talking. If I'd told you that you were on the air, you'd have been tongue-tied with nerves. The reason I asked you about the school you'd been to was because a lot of callers who like your record think you best be coloured, singing the way you do."

That day, Elvis learned about the colour of music.

The following day, with Marion Keisker already taking orders from Memphis records stores for "That's Allright", their task was to come up with a b-side for the upcoming single. Again that night, they threw in songs and ideas, with Sam Phillips never being satisfied. It was only when Bill Black started singing the Bill Monroe Bluegrass hit "Blue Moon Of Kentucky", that things were getting off the ground again. Sam's response was: "That's an idea. Let's try that." At first, they tried it slow, similar to Bill Monroe's own approach. "No, no. That isn't different enough. You could be any hillbilly singing like that, Elvis." Sam was heard saying over the speakers.

They tried it again, also adding a new front to the song. They came up with another Rockabilly platter, and as Bill Black already suspected when he jokingly said: "Just don't nobody tell Bill Monroe what we've done with his song", Monroe hated the Elvis version complaining "that Elvis ruined my damn song." When Elvis came home late that night, Gladys as always was still waiting for him, he played her both sides, with the echo put on his voice he sounded clearer, sharper, somehow more free than he'd heard himself any time before. Sitting there with his mother it was likely that he was amused that finally he was becoming the Elvis, he himself imagined to be, for the past three years.

His world had changed, as soon as the record was pressed it was played on every station in Memphis. While the Rhythm and Blues Disc jockeys went for "That's Allright", the country ones turned onto "Blue Moon Of Kentucky". The band still wondering where to fit in, hitting on both markets, with their very first release. For Elvis, one of the biggest thrills must have been walking down North Main and hanging around Charlie's until he saw someone buy a copy, or play both sides on the jukebox there. With six thousand copies being sold, within a few days of the release, the record was soon up to Nr. 3 on the local chart.

That didn't mean much to the world, of which Elvis was aware of, but he would discover it was as sweet as having a worldwide hit like "Don't Be Cruel". International fame might have been out of his scope, but local success was easy to comprehend, the way celebrity was treated in Memphis was: Everyone was glad for you, except for the folks who couldn't abide you or who were just plain jealous. Dixie first heard "Blue Moon Of Kentucky" on the radio in her father's car as they drew near to Memphis on their way home from Florida. Elvis had sent her a telegram telling what had happened, asking her to hurry home. She didn't fully understand. But that changed of course, when her boyfriend came out of the car radio!

So much had happened in the two weeks she had been away. She missed it all. She would tell him over and over again that she'd never known anyone who made a record. But she also began to realise, that the plans they had already made, would either get an halt, or might not work out, at all. Though she was only 15, both already had talked about marriage, Dixie more than Elvis, as he would later recall …

Sam Phillips' office at Sun was small, so when Sam wanted to discuss things with more than one person they would all meet in, at Taylor's café next door. It was there one day, that Same showed Elvis, Scotty and Bill musicians' union forms and insisted that they should all join. Scotty, Sam thought should be the Manager of the band, the deal was that Scotty would get 10% of all bookings he would get for them. As musicians both Bill Black and Scotty Moore would get what was left, after Elvis the had his 50%. As Elvis was only 19, Vernon Presley had to countersign on his son's behalf. Scotty and Bill were both working musicians, while Elvis himself hadn't even sung in public yet, though having a local hit on his name.

Nevertheless, Scotty reckoned the front man should be given more. That's how the deal would work out. Throughout his entire career Elvis never took much notice of contracts or payments. It was complicated and he didn't have the time and interest. But, years later, he did know that although he'd earned a mountain of money, he had also been ripped off many times—for millions of dollars. He didn't really care, but it should be said that Scotty Moore nor Bill Black, in all fairness, did steal from him. Not one penny.

Strangely, Elvis had made a record that was all over on the radio in Memphis, but he still had to go to work, driving all over town in his pick-up truck, and attending rehearsals with Scotty Moore and Bill Black at the same time. It wasn't any glamour, but it was surely exciting. One lunchtime Marion Keisker introduced him to a journalist, a reporter on the Memphis Press Scimitar. As Elvis couldn't think of what to say, she answered all the questions for him—of course it didn't look that way, then the newspaper came out. A picture was taken, Elvis being thin as a rail, wearing a Western-style jacket and a bow tie. From what Elvis could see from the actors in magazines, they all wore eye make up on screen. So he began sneaking some of Gladys' eye shadow on to his eyelids. Other boys in Memphis would have seen that as being weird, but Elvis had been seeing things differently for most of his adolescence.

A few weeks later, Sam Phillips managed to get Elvis, Scotty and Bill on the bill at a concert at the Memphis Overton Par Shell amphitheatre. It would be their major public debut. Opening for Slim Whitman, who had just the million selling hit "Indian Love Call". Elvis nerves played up as he was about to face hundreds of people for the first time. The advertisements also had gotten his name wrong, billing him as Ellis Presley.

As the three walked out on stage for the afternoon show, Elvis could see his parents sitting with Dixie. For a moment, it seemed as if the trio of Elvis, Scotty and Bill froze. The place looked big and wide. Then Bill Black began thumping a rhythm on his bass fiddle, Elvis joined in on the guitar and they went into "That's Allright". At first Elvis concentrated so hard, that he did not notice, but there seemed to be a lot of shouting and yelling going on from some of the girls in the audience. It just got louder and louder, then he went onto sing "Blue Moon Of Kentucky". Elvis was confused, it was a wild sound. Were they laughing at him? "What happened, what happened?" he asked Sam Phillips as he came off. Sam was smiling: "I don't know, Elvis, but whatever it was you were doing, get back out there and do it again."

So they went back again and sang the songs again, the only ones they could do together: "That's Allright" and "Blue Moon Of Kentucky". The girls went even wilder. After the show, Scotty Moore explained what he thought the whole matter was. Most singers in those days stood flat-footed and still by the stand-up microphone. As Elvis and the Blue Moon Boys did not have a drummer, Elvis used his body to keep the rhythm, plus he wore very-loose fitting pants.

So when he moved his body, leaning forward out to the balls of his feet and shaking his leg to keep time with the music, it looked provocative. The girls went crazy for it. They got very excited. Elvis had seen preachers and singers at revival meetings moving around like that, but later he promised the first time he did it on stage, the reaction caused was unintentional. But after that he learned quickly, he had appeared with Slim Whitman and stole the show. Elvis would quickly grow to expect that kind of reaction to his music and stage show.

All through the summer of 1954 Elvis was either seeing Dixie or trying out new songs at Scotty's place. Sam arranged a regular spot several times a week at the Eagle's Nest. They also played on the back of a flat-bed truck, the same way later staged in the music movie "Loving You" starring young Elvis Presley. As they were in a public parking lot, it wasn't a segregated show, so it was the first time that Elvis saw the black folks get excited to his music, also. He was paid $32.50 for a short appearance, which was nearly as much he earned all week at Crown Electrics. Johnny Cash was also in the audience, stating later, that seeing Elvis Presley on stage had pushed him to start his own career.

Other bookings were coming along—clubs, school gymnasiums and even a free show in a hospital ward for paralysed people. It was mostly small, local stuff, but at the time it was a great thrill, sales of the first single now spreading also to Arkansas. Elvis saw his record in the Mid-South country chart in Billboard Magazine. He was excited—"Blue Moon Of Kentucky" being the bigger hit, outside of Memphis. But he would mostly refer to "That's Allright" in later stage shows, when referring to his start in music, and perform that song even at his last concert tour in 1977.

Probably if Elvis Presley would have been asked which time in his life he would like to live over again, he would have chosen the summer of 1954. What can you ask for, but for your parents to be proud of you, for a girl that loves you, and a hit in your own hometown. Surely the gold records, the money, the fame … he would soon enjoy it all, but he would be a prisoner of his fame soon …

With a little more money coming in from the stage shows he even bought himself a new guitar. Scotty and Sam had never been impressed with the cheap one he had called his own: So he went into a place just up the street from Sun Records and got a Martin D-18. Scotty helped him to choose it. It would cost him $175, being the most expensive thing, he ever owned. He even had the shop to engrave his name on it. She shopkeeper took his old guitar for eight dollars in and said he would trash it. He should have kept it. Everyday something new was happening for Elvis. Now he was often seen shopping sharp clothes at Lansky Brothers on Beale Street, admiring the bright colours and styles that normally black singers would buy.

Rufus Thomas was a regular disc jockey character around Sun Records for years before he recorded even "Walking The Dog", a big friend of Sam's. Teasing Sam forever that Elvis should record his "Tiger Man", which eventually did many years later. Sam also introduced young Elvis to B.B. King. What a summer!

In September 1954, a follow-up record was needed. They decided to cover "Good Rockin' Tonight" which had been both a Rhythm and Blues hit for Roy Brown and Wynonie Harris. The b-side was "I Don't Care If The Sun Don't Shine". A member of the Starlite Wranglers was asked to sit in on the drums. Sun Records was also a laboratory for the young Elvis Presley, most of his experience he would gain there, before becoming a household name in the music industry when singing with the major label RCA Records.

On the way to RCA in becoming the undisputed King of Rock and Roll, there were a couple of failures to conquer: The Grand Ole Opry (after the first of which an Opry manager advised Elvis to go back to truck driving), an unsuccessful audition for the national television program Arthur Godfrey's Talent Scouts. But there were many triumphs, far more than failures; As Elvis, Scotty and Bill made news and fans wherever they played throughout the South. Before long, the other established country acts Elvis often shared the bill with were requesting that he should close the show, no one could follow him.

For the next year or so, Elvis was primarily a country phenomenon, riding Country and Blues charts with a series of rockabilly-style Sun releases ("Good Rockin' Tonight", "Baby Let's Play House), culminating in September 1955 when "Mystery Train" b/w "I Forgot To Remember To Forget" hit number one on Billboard's national country chart. The constant travel from show to show kept Elvis away from home much of the time. The Presleys left the Lauderdale Courts in early '953 and had moved four times since.

Gladys worried about Elvis whenever he was out of her sight, and had premonitions of disasters. That she had correctly envisioned a car fire as it occurred near Texarkana/Texas (Elvis told her of it when he called sometime later), only increased her worries. She knew that Elvis made girls scream, which incited more than a few young men to challenge him. In May 1955, fans at concert in Jacksonville/Florida rioted. It was the first time the emotions Elvis inspired in his audience reached such a dangerous level. Soon these demonstrations of uncontrollable fans became the new normal to him. He would be threatened, chased, hounded, clothes would be torn from his body.

But Elvis' dream came true, and there was no stopping him, a fact not missed by the ex-carny turned music-biz manager Colonel Tom Parker. Elvis had been managed until then for several months by Scotty Moore, then by the local disc jockey Bob Neal. Parker connected with Neal when he helped him procure a booking for Elvis, and within a short time Parker was managing Elvis Presley. Gladys never liked Parker. As Elvis was a minor, Parker had to convince not only his future protegee but also Vernon and Gladys, with the promise that he would protect their son and make him rich at the same time.

On 15 August 1955, with his father co-signing as his legal guardian, Elvis signed his management agreement with the Colonel. Through Elvis' career will certainly go down in show-business history as one of the worst-managed ever, Parker started off with a bang, convincing the major RCA label to give the young singer the richest contract ever granted to a new talent. For just $40,000 RCA bought Elvis Presley's contract from Sun and the publishing rights to his records. Elvis received $5000 of it, for which he bought his mum a pink Ford.

In January 1956, Elvis released the first of a long line of hits and made his national television debut on The Dorsey Brothers Stage Show, a normal sedate variety program. Over the next two months he would make six appearances, each more exciting than the one before. Watching old tapes of Elvis then, one is struck by not only his talent and presence, but his pure joy. A playful sneer, a flirtatious glance, a shrug, a bump—each little gesture was tested, incorporated, expanded, refined, until by early 1958, his mastery style was complete.

From early 1956 until March 1958, when he entered the Army, Elvis could do no wrong. Except for a miscalculated attempt to conquer Las Vegas, everything he turned his had to was big success. His records sold in the millions, his television appearances guaranteed the highest ratings, his movies drew crowds all across the country. He was a star and, to fans and critics alike, sex personified. The public was surprised to learn the he was a soft-spoken, well-mannered young man. He played with his image just as he had tinkered with is performance, still trying things out.

To one female interviewer who asked what he did with all the girls who threw themselves at him, he replied, "I usually take them." Elvis was a great bundle of contradictions, and yet all of it was true. That is part of the Elvis Presley mystique. It all happened so quickly that Elvis didn't always absorb it all, but some things stuck in his mind. One event he described was his first appearance on the Ed Sullivan Show. "I didn't even know where I was," he confided to friend and spiritual adviser Larry Geller. "I knew that going to New York meant that I was in the major leagues, but I was so scared I didn't know what I was doing. My shaking wasn't even natural, but thank God I moved, because that rid of some of my nervousness. When I went on, I heard people screaming, but it all happened so fat. I just went with hit. All I knew was, the only way to do it, the only way to make it, what got me to this point, was to just be natural and let it happen. And don't stop. Don't stop anything, don't think. The minute I started thinking, it would turn off. So, you don't think. Just do. Just be it."

Whatever it was, it inspired girls to carve his name into their skin with penknives and demolish cars with their bare hands. It changed the way millions of kids viewed themselves and their world. It made Elvis a millionaire within nine months. Elvis was it!

In February 1957, he went to Hollywood to make his second film, Loving You, and took along his parents (who can be seen in the audience during one scene). The next month he bought Graceland, a twenty-three-room mansion, though it was not even twenty years old, had fallen into disrepair. Originally Elvis and his parents talked about getting a farm, but Gladys and Vernon had fallen in love with Graceland. It wasn't a farm, though it did sit on more than thirteen acres in Whitehaven, a suburb of Memphis that was still open and somewhat rural.

It should have been the happiest time in Gladys' life, but ill health, abuse of prescription diet pills, and tremendous anxiety over Elvis, who now couldn't venture out of the house without being besieged by fans, were wearing her down. According to family testimony, Gladys had refused medical treatment for gallstones, and by the time the family moved to Graceland that May she was depressed, apathic and tired. Public criticism of Elvis she took personal. She resented his success for giving the family everything they wanted except him. Of his time, Elvis remarked that he felt he was working to give his mother everything, all she deserved, to make up for all she had suffered. Some people also said that Gladys drank then, but if Elvis knew, it was his secret. He occasionally remarked about drinkers in his extended family, and he detested drunks. Elvis did mention that Gladys had an occasional beer, but that was all.

In late 1957, Elvis' draft notice arrived. He was inducted into the Army in late March 1958, allowed to finish the movie King Creole. Following his basic training at Fort Hood/Texas, in late March 1958. Following basic training he rented a house where he could live off base with his parents, his grandmother and his friend Lamar Fike. Weeks after the move to Texas Gladys became very ill, and on August 8th 1958 she and Vernon returned to Memphis, where she was admitted to a hospital. Doctors found that she had hepatitis, but despite the fact they weren't sure what had caused it, their initial prognosis was promising. She began failing next day, though, and by the twelfth she was on the critical list. Elvis rushed home, and two days later, very early on 14 August 1958, Gladys died of a heart attack. Her body was returned to Graceland, where she lay in state until Colone Parker decided to move Gladys' body to a funeral home so that Elvis' fans could pay their last respects.

With Parker in control, the national press had full access to Elvis and Vernon during the days before the funeral. Somehow one must feel like an intruder when reading Elvis' statements from these days of mourning. His private grief was crassly laid out for public consumption. Understandably from then on Elvis held a long distance to the press. To friends, like Larry Geller, he confided over the years that he preferred dealing with the press as infrequently as he did, and usually in press conferences—which he and Parker could easily control, rather than one-on-one interviews, because he felt it heightened his mystique. But one reason must also the events surrounding Gladys' death and not see another reason.

At her gravesite, Elvis cried: "I love you so much. I lived my whole life for you. Oh, God, everything I have is gone." Elvis returned to Graceland, shut himself in his room until he had to return to Texas. In the fall he travelled with is unit to West Germany and there served out his term of duty. When he turned to civilian life in the spring of 1960, he was twenty-five. RCA had continued releasing new singles, so he had had hits in his absence, plus Colonel Tom Parker had some new movie deals cooking. But it wasn't as though he had never gone away.

Many of the other early rockers who had come up with him were either dead or tamed. Their replacements, the so-called teen idols, were made of softer stuff. They were cuddly, shorn of sideburns, and gutless. Elvis wasn't so sure that the fans would want him again, and in the back of his mind was the fear that, like most pop stars, he had had his moment of fame. Maybe it was all over? For fans, he would have had cemented his name in Rock and Roll history, and would remain the King, always.

In his personal life, things were also different. He was going back to Memphis, where he'd be surrounded by a smaller, close-knit group of friends and family. He had a girlfriend, fourteen-year-old Priscilla Beaulieu, whom he had met in Germany. Vernon was in love with his wife-to-be Davada "Dee" Stanley, a divorced mother of three boys, Graceland was there, but, while it always should be home, it would never be the same. And neither would Elvis.

In the 1960s, Elvis would also set out trying to conquer the spiritual world, his aid and helper in this would prove to be Larry Geller, who was also The King's hairstylist. Larry, as he went to work full-time and pretty much exclusively for Elvis, introduced the King of Rock and Roll to many books, which Elvis would keep in his personal library. And which had a profound effect on Elvis, including "The Impersonal Life, Autobiography of a Yogi, The Initiation of the World and Beyond The Himalayas". As soon as Elvis finished one of the books which Larry selected for him, he asked for another. This pattern would continue for years.

Larry Geller recalled: "Although it hardly fit his public image as the King of Rock and Roll, Elvis was a voracious and careful reader. The books we shared offered ideas about religion, God and man vastly different from anything Elvis might encounter in Tupelo or Memphis, areas where such books were denounced as evil, even satanic. Almost all of the works dealt with abstract metaphysical concepts, and some were written in archaic, convoluted style that can be difficult to follow. He impressed me with his diligence and determination to understand each word he read. Before long you rarely saw Elvis when he wasn't carrying his newest book and dictionary. Inquisitive by nature and eager to learn, he displayed no compunction about interrupting someone in midsentence to ask the meaning of an unfamiliar word."

"For someone like Elvis, who was desperately self-conscious about appearing ignorant, this was a big concession. The first work Elvis read was The Impersonal Life, a very small, pocket-sized book of less than two hundred pages. A man named Joseph Benner, acting as channel, 'received' the book's message sometime around 1914 from his higher divine self, or God. The Impersonal Life appealed to Elvis for several reasons: it speaks of purpose, of an intelligence—God, if you will—guiding seekers to the knowledge of the god within us all. An early passage reads: 'In one of My other Revelations, called the Bible, you are told much about 'The Word', but very few, even the most learned Bible students, comprehend My meaning." (…)

Elvis Presley grew up in the First Assembly of God Church, an evangelical, fundamentalist Pentecostal denomination. The small wooden First Assembly of God church Elvis attended as a child had been built by a preacher, named Gains Mansell, Elvis' Great-Uncle, the husband of Glady's Aunt Ada. In church Elvis learned the basic tenets of the faith, that the bible was infallible, that Jesus would return and the good would be rewarded and the evil punished. Ture believers were commanded to live in the world but not be of it. When Vernon, who was never a religious person, took Elvis to see his first motion picture at the age of thirteen, warned his son not let know his mother Gladys. In Elvis' church all movies, were forbidden. It was the movies that made Elvis stray away from his church at the end.

There is a tendency to think of all Protestants, particularly Sothern Protestants, as the same, but they are clearly not. The point where the First Assembly of God parts company with many other denominations in in its recognition of the supernatural and its acceptance of such phenomena as speaking in tongues and divine healing as the work of God. Though Elvis loved many things about church—the singing and dancing, the stories and sermons, the ceremony, the community—he often said what the church taught about God ("hellfire and brimstone," Elvis called it) was wrong, because it inspired fear for rather than love for God.

Elvis felt, even at an early age, that there had to be more to spirituality than what organised religion presented. Rather than taking the Bible literally, as many of his fellow parishioners did, Elvis sensed that the words and stories were mere symbols and myths that held deeper significance and meaning for those who thought to discover them. In the 1960s for the first time, he came to believe in the universal Christ, or the light of Jesus and his teachings, which some believe is embodied with everyone. This idea goes deeper than what Elvis had been taught as a youngster: basically, believe in Jesus and you will be saved. "I always knew there was truth to my religion," he often said. "Somehow I never lost faith in God, despite those old preachers tryin' to make people feel guilty for things they never done. I always knew that deep inside me there were answers that went beyond rigid old closed minds."

As his spiritual mentor recalled in his book "If I Can Dream": "Guided by the readings, Elvis made that truth a foundation onto which he added ideas from other teachings. The process was progressive, and Elvis moved from one level of study to the next just as a child graduates through consecutive grades in school. The widespread misconception about Elvis' spiritual life is that he was some kind of faddist, jumping from one philosophy to the next on whim, embracing anything and everything just because it was "weird". While it is true that Elvis lacked the patience and discipline to stick to certain practices, it wasn't out of fickleness. In fact, he remained a Christian his whole life, but not a Christian to the exclusion of anything else. He was open to other beliefs and teachings, and even then realised that no one has all the answers."

Elvis himself said: "What was Jesus doing, where was he during the 'missing years'. What's so strange about the idea that he might have been travelling to Egypt or India? Didn't Jesus himself say, 'Ye are gods'? And what about reincarnation? It sure does explain a lot of things. And even if it isn't true, why shouldn't we be able to read and talk about it, and decide for ourselves?"

Particularly in Hollywood, Elvis Presley realised that he needed something more substantial and nourishing in his life. He turned to the spiritual, because he was a deeply spiritual person. He lived in constant pursuit of that elusive "something else" that gives life real, true meaning. The paradoxical nature of his past never lost its power to confound him. The years of poverty suddenly ending in a grand flush of fame and wealth; Gladys dying and leaving her son at the most frightening, vulnerable moment in his life. There was an inability in Elvis to see the nature of a personal God who blessed his parents with only two children, yet took one away at birth; one who gave Elvis riches beyond his wildest dreams but stole away his mother.

In a fundamentalist mindset, Elvis' life could be seen as a series of blessings and punishments in which one hand gave while another took away. Elvis wanted to know about life, what other people had taught, written and said through the ages. He hungered for understanding. The Impersonal Life offered an interpretation of God and His purpose different from any Elvis had encountered before, one that struck a chord in him, articulating things he had long felt but could barely conceive of, let alone express. The Impersonal Life spoke of a man and the universe as manifestation, or reflections, of a Creator's idea, and all part of a single entity.

"The Key is

To Think is to Create, or

As You Think In Your Heart, so it is with you …

You have within you all possibilities.

Elvis had to go beyond his childhood teachings to begin to understand his own life. Among his relatives were people who believed than any book but the bible was sinful, so it's easy to see that without the guidance Larry Geller gave him, he might never ever have discovered the words that changed his life. It must have been comforting for him to read in The Impersonal Life: "When you have found The Kingdom, you will likewise find your place in It, realising … that your work was all laid out for you from the beginning, and that all that has gone before has been but a preparation and a fitting of your human personality for that work."

In the years to come, Elvis always kept a copy of *The Impersonal Life* with him wherever he went and gave away hundreds of copies to others.

Elvis the man, wouldn't have been without this entourage—The Memphis Mafia. Some people assume that tall that the guys did was hang around Elvis Presley, but in fact Elvis was a demanding boss, and there was a lot to do. Though a guy's job description could change over the years, or he might be called on to do anything, in fact he had only one job, and that was to "take care of business"— which meant taking care of Elvis. Driving him, arranging for a private movie screening, procuring a favourite type of fireworks, attending to his wardrobe, making sure that the stranger whose plight moved Elvis got the money or the new car.

Over time some of the guys showed to be less than loyal, but that was all years ahead. In the early and middle sixties, the guys were just the guys. They wanted to work for Elvis and Elvis wanted them to work for him. His reasons for hiring them ran from having been close friends at Humes High School (Red West, Marty Lacker), being cousins (Billy Smith, Gene Smith), army buddies (Joe Esposito, Charlie Hodge), or people who he met on the way, that he liked also. (Lamar Fike, Alan Fortas.)

The Memphis Mafia's configuration changed many times through the years, as some left as being tired of living the upside-down, hurry-up-and-wait lifestyle or struck out to make a living with a less demanding boss.

Most public figures maintain something of an entourage, but few have or had anything like the Memphis Mafia. There was something about them that Hollywood people found off-putting, to say the least ... The group was all decked out in variations of the styles Elvis wore: flashy suits, brightly collared shirts from Fred Segal's, black Continental boots. Between takes movie sets became the scenes of water balloon fights and other juvenile practical jokes. Even Hollywood regulars who believed they had seen everything were taken aback by the Mafia's behaviour, and were more than a little surprised that Elvis—who was generally considered a polite, soft-spoken, dedicated young man—seemed oblivious of the impression his guys made. The Memphis Mafia soon had earned themselves a reputation of some of the wildest guys in town. Those who worked with Elvis knew that the entourage was part of the deal and had to be tolerated. Early on, it was hard to tell if Elvis was aware of how the Mafia was perceived, or whether or not he even cared.

To outsiders, a twenty-four-hour, seven-days-a-week job was anything but glamorous. But for many of the boys, working for Elvis was fun and exciting. And to each of them in his own way, Elvis was a friend and always accessible; he never set himself apart. If your wanted to be with him, you could. Many believed to be the best friend of Elvis, because Elvis made people feel that way. He was gracious and gave you his full attention, whether you were the President or his gardener. With Elvis, people travelled to places they would have never seen otherwise and met people the folks back home only read about in the papers. If your wife wanted plastic surgery, or you needed a down payment on a new house, you counted on Elvis. To guys whose alternatives ran from pumping gas to holding down a white-collar-job, there was no reason to leave Elvis.

Larry Geller noted on the Memphis Mafia: "Contrary to the Mafia's image, some of the guys were bright and sensitive, such as Jerry Schilling and Charlie Hodge, two I liked especially. For the most part, though, regardless of Elvis' efforts of good intentions, the battle to reform some of the group's lesser lights was going to be uphill all the way."

In 1964, Larry Geller met Priscilla for the first time, in his book with Joels Spector and Patricia Romanowski on Elvis—"If I Can Dream", he gives an interesting account of Elvis' relation to Priscilla at that time:

"After shooting four Roustabout ended, Elvis invited me to come back with him to Memphis. Like most fans, up until then I knew nothing of Elvis' personal life except what I'd read. Gossip columnists dutifully reported the studio publicity mills' rumours linking Elvis with his female co-star of the moment. And he was the country's most famous bachelor. Probably the most scandalous rumour circulating then was that Elvis kept a young girl back at Graceland. Less than six years before, another Memphis rocker, Sun Records star Jerry Lee Lewis, saw his career ruined within days of the press exposing his marriage to his thirteen-year-old second cousin, Myra. Suggestions that Elvis had something equally unsavoury cooking back in Memphis raised a few eyebrows, even in Hollywood, where someone in his position was expected to be promiscuous. While people in showbusiness might be allowed their eccentrics, they very idea of Elvis living in sin with such a young woman was shocking. Only Elvis' all-American image, extremely private lifestyle, and the fact that Priscilla rarely left Memphis explain the story's staying so tightly under the wraps.

So I knew of Priscilla, as did practically anyone who could read a newspaper in March 1960 when Elvis completed his tour of duty and headed home from West Germany. Priscilla was "the girl he left behind", or so the stories went. Despite the fact that Priscilla didn't meet Elvis until August 1959, approximately six months before he returned to the States, and that, at fourteen, she was ten years his junior, the press served up a fairy-tale romance, and the American public gobbled it down. Between the time Elvis left the service and May 1962, when Priscilla moved to Memphis, they communicated sporadically; sometimes several months elapsed between transatlantic phone calls.

But in the end, true love, and, more to the point, Elvis, won out. Following their daughter's extended visits to see Elvis in Los Angeles and Graceland, Priscilla's parents finally capitulated to Elvis' and Vernon's pleas and permitted Priscilla to move to Memphis. As Vernon and Elvis promised Mr and Mrs Beaulieu, she did complete her schooling and, as far as the public knew, lived with Vernon, Dee and Dee's three little boys, Rick, David and Billy Stanley, in a separate house on a lot adjoining Graceland."

Larry Geller also talks about Elvis' habit of taking amphetamines: "One evening in late May 1964 we set out for Memphis: Elvis, I, his bodyguards Alan Fortas, Red West and Sonny West, his cousin Billy Smith, the Mafia foreman Joe Esposito, Jim Kingsley, a general assistant, and Richard Davis, who was also a general assistant as well as Elvis' valet. We boarded Elvis' large customised bus. Elvis loved to drive anything, and, because he still feared flying, during the sixties, we travelled between Memphis and the West Coast by bus."

"The routine was to drive from Los Angeles after completing a film, then drive back a few days before Elvis was needed for the next movie. The bus was accompanied by a caravan of cars and station wagons, all packed with luggage. If we were lucky enough to leave on schedule, the trip stretched over four or five days, because we'd stop for sleep in motels during the day and travel only at night. Elvis' bus was quite luxurious by the day's standards, equipped with stereo, television and eight-track tape deck."

"This being my first trip back to Memphis, Elvis took it upon himself to stick by me and show me the ropes, so to speak. We sat together during the whole journey, talking and getting to know each other. Less than an hour after we left Beverly Hills, we were approaching San Bernadino. Suddenly Elvis extended his hand towards me. 'Here,' he said, opening his palm to reveal a couple of triangular-shaped tablets that I later learned were Dexedrine, a potent amphetamine commonly prescribed for weight reduction, narcolepsy and, in children, abnormal behaviour syndrome. To the general public amphetamines seemed a wonder drug: they kept you slim and awake. General knowledge of their adverse effects and potential for abuse were years away."

"Elvis had been using amphetamines in various amounts since his army days. They were legal, they came from a doctor, so how could they not be good for you? He honestly could not see any danger. "Take these," Elvis implored, "because we're going to be up and we'll be driving. We want to be alert." I'd been smoking marijuana since the early sixties, but had never ingested pills of any kind. For some reason, though, the hundred miles that lay ahead and the fact that Elvis and I had so much to talk about weakened my resistance. I popped the pills into my mouth and settled back for the long ride ahead. And what a trip it was.

"As Elvis sat listening intently, I talked, and talked, and talked, and talked. I literally could not shut up, and while Elvis enjoyed hearing me ramble on and on about every spiritual book I've ever read, every idea I'd investigated, but the next day my jaw was killing me. Only later did I learn that Elvis didn't want me to "loose up" as he so delicately put it, for his benefit alone, but for the guys'. From the moment Elvis embarked on his spiritual studies, he never totally relinquished the idea he could teach others by his example. He believed that everyone had the potential to improve one's life, one's attitude, one's disposition, and cold do so by taking time each day to read and meditate. That he had some inkling of the guys' reactions was obvious.

"And just as Elvis set me up as the mouthpiece, to say to the guys things he wanted to say himself, many of them answered him by making me a sort of walking effigy of the spiritual Elvis, they guys didn't like. The wisecracks and insults they didn't dare hurl at their boss were aimed squarely at me. The next day we stopped in Williams/Arizona, to get some food, stretch our legs and gas up. The speed had worn off, leaving me exhausted. I found myself chatting with Richard Davis. He too had stayed up the night before, listening to Elvis and me talk.

All he had to say about it was, "I'll bet you took psychology in college, didn't you?" I paused for a minute. Psychology. Who had mentioned psychology. "No," I replied naively. "I went to college for a while, but I didn't take psychology." What a strange thing to say, I thought. Only later did it dawn on me that to many around Elvis the spiritual studies weren't about God, or religion, or faith, or philosophy as they understood them. Rather, this was strange, foreign and somehow sinister. In Richard's mind—and he wasn't alone—it was inconceivable that Elvis would eschew football magazines and water-balloon fights willingly to read The initiation of the World or The Prophet. Something— or someone—must have "influenced" him, they reasoned. This wouldn't be the last time I'd be accused of using "psychology" with Elvis."

In Graceland, Larry Geller introduced Elvis to numerology. They had countless discussions about the different teachings and traditions. Elvis loved discovering connections, no matter what subject. He wanted to know how beliefs, ideas, words, symbols, names and concepts originated and how they were interrelated. Elvis himself would have been a perfect 8 in numerology, someone concerned with the material and the spiritual, intense, ambitious, lonely and misunderstood. "Good Lord! I probably would never have left my church if they taught this material." He was heard saying more than once.

He and Geller traced numerology back to antiquity and to the Biblical Hebrews, the Chinese, the Egyptians and other early cultures. They read various accounts on the life of the Greed philosopher Pythagoras, whose CV include mathematics, astronomy, philosophy and music, all derived from the esoteric wisdom of numbers. They found similarities among Islamic art, Gothic architecture, complex Oriental mandala patterns and the Chinese I Ching. It was also words that Elvis was fascinated by.

Though he knew that his name had been given to him because it was his father's middle name, he still wondered where it originally came from. "How does anyone name their kid Elvis?" he remarked one day, scratching his head, while in conversation with Larry Geller. "There had to be an Elvis, and there's a definite reason for that name." El is synonymous with El-Ohim., God as he is referred to by the Jews. And Vis is spoken of as power, as the force of God. El was used in a number of faiths when referring to the Divine in the highest aspect. It meant the sun, the preserver and saviour. For example, Beth-El means "house of the sun", the name of many Jewish temples. Elvis was also aware that "Aaron", was the name of Moses' brother, a high priest of Israel. And, of course, Elvis is an anagram for "lives".

One day Larry Geller explained to him: "In Judaism rabbis change people's names according to numerological principles. The science of numerology comes from the Cabala, the ancient Jewish mystical work, and specifically from a part of the Cabala called the Gematria. The Gematria deals with numbers and uses the twenty-two characters of the Hebrew alphabet and their corresponding numbers to obtain information about a person's character and fate. Today, if you were to go to a numerologist, he or she would first assign a numerical value to each letter of your name, add and/or reduce these, and then interpret the resulting numbers or combination of numbers."

Larry also told Elvis a story about his childhood: "When I was just a few days old, I started coughing up my food and turning blue. Frightened, my parents rushed me back to the hospital, where the doctors determined that I had a closed valve in my digestive tract. In those days, my chances of surviving were somewhere around fifty-fifty. My mother refused to accept that her baby might die, and so she ran to the rabbi and told him what was happening. He replied, "Don't worry. We'll change his name from Laib to Chaim." My parents had given me the Hebrew name Laib, but on the rabbi's advice they renamed me Chaim, from chai, which means life. And I lived."

Elvis loved this story. When I told him that a chai symbolised life, that it had a specific numerical value, and drew it for him on a piece of paper, he recognised it immediately. "Wow!" he exclaimed. "I've got to get one of those. I've noticed that a lot of guys in Hollywood wear that." Shortly afterwards, he purchased a chai made of gold and wore it always. He's been widely quoted as saying that he wore both the chai and the cross so that he wouldn't be kept out of heaven "on a technicality", a remark that suggests that Elvis took Judaism lightly. Nothing could be further from the truth. Though he wouldn't reveal it to me until 1977, Elvis was part Jewish and viewed his Jewishness as something precious and sacred, another thing that set him apart from other people and accounted for his being different and misunderstood …"

When Elvis was quite young, Gladys Presley told him that her maternal grandmother, Martha Tackett Mansell, was Jewish. But Gladys also warned Elvis: "Don't you tell. Don't you mention this to the relatives or our daddy." It was never clear how Vernon felt about there being Jewish blood on the Smith side, he did not talk about it, and that may have said as much …

Elvis himself was fascinated by it and confided to Larry Geller: "You know, when you think about it, our whole modern civilisation is built on Jewish thinkers. Look at the Jewish religion. Jesus was a Jewish boy. In psychology, there was Sigmund Freud. All or our science is Albert Einstein, And look what's going on in Communist Russia. That was all started by Karl Marx's writings. Listen, man, if we went back into everyone's family tree, if we went back one hundred, five hundred years, a thousand years, if we would do that. I'll bet we'd find that everybody living today has some Jewish blood and that we all come from the same place."

Elvis' ambivalence towards Judaism was founded, Gladys' fears also: Three men in Elvis' entourage, Alan Fortas, Marty Lacker and George Klein, were Jewish, "But most of the other guys understood it in terms of their not attending church, celebrating different holidays and not being Christians. Some of them still believed that Jews had horns. This was the atmosphere in which Elvis kept his secret." As Larry Geller recalled.

Larry Geller: "Through the sixties Elvis made at least three movies a year, so the time spent away from Hollywood was precious. A routine of sorts had been established. Following each long drive back from Hollywood, Elvis holed up in his room for a few days to sleep and eat. His appetite was tremendous, and only youth, regular karate workouts, crash diets and amphetamines kept him in shape for the cameras. Many of his later health problems surely began with his diet: multiple helpings of the few foods that he loved, most of them high in sugar, salt, fat, cholesterol and spices, low in fibre, complex carbohydrates and vitamins.

"In fact, Elvis' daily diet was a textbook example of how not to eat. An extremely health-conscious eater since 1960, I couldn't imagine eating some of the things Elvis consumed. The first few times we ate together I had to remind myself not to stare as he coated his dishes with what looked like ounces of black pepper or gorged himself on multiple helpings of lardy fried meats, greasy French fries and sugary pies. Given how physically beautiful Elvis was and the pride he took in his appearance, it's surprising that vanity didn't arouse a greater awareness of and respect for his body.

"Many of his books (including the Bible) said, in so many words, that the body is a temple, to be nourished and cared for, but Elvis overlooked those parts. Intellectually, he knew it was correct, but he figured, what the hell. Anything concerning health invariably fell into one of Elvis' blind spots, and it's easy to understand why. For all the abuse his mortal being endured, for the most part Elvis remained an incredibly good-looking man. Part of this was certainly genetic. Vernon was a dashing guy, even in his last years, and photographs of Elvis' forefathers, especially on his mother's side, show them to have been beautiful in a timeless, almost unearthly way. Whether the cause lay in his family's having wanted for food in the past or in Elvis simply doing what he wanted to do, or some deeper reason, Elvis love to eat. And like anything that Elvis enjoyed—with the exception of promiscuous sex—he did it to excess."

Wherever the man Elvis Presley travelled, he always carried his Bible and Cheiro's Book of Numbers, two books that were always on his nightstand and were found missing from his nightstand only hours after his death. Numerology, the science of numbers as related to the occult, or secret patterns involving the universe, nature's calculations—frequently relate to the spiritual side of things. This ancient study, was used by Egyptians, who were absolute masters of the hidden meaning of numbers, their application to time and their relationship to human life. The number seven always relates to God, for instance: The Seven days per cycles of Genesis' Creation; the seven heavens; the seven thrones; the seven seals; the seven churches; the seventh day. The Bible speaks of the seven generations from David to the birth of Christ. Revelations speak of the seven spirits of God sent forth into all the earth, while Ezekiel speaks of the seven angels of the Lord that go to and fro though the whole earth ...

For Elvis, his spiritual studies were part of his spiritual evolution. He believed in reincarnation as part of that evolution, a series of steps into one's continuous development. But on the contrary he did not subscribe to the Buddhist theory of transmigration—that is, that if you do evil things, for example, you come back in the next life as a lizard. While he did not believe in contacting the dead, he did feel the presence of deceased loved ones, as many of us do. He held to the Christian belief that he would be reunited with his mother in death. Often he spoke of her waiting for him after his death, when they and everyone else dear to him would all meet again. When Elvis Presley read that ancient manuscripts on the true nature of Jesus' life and teaching were locked away in the Vatican archives, along with other controversial, secret materials, he said to Larry Geller: "I'm not a prophet, but I'll tell you, someday that information they're hiding from the masses will become known, and it will be a new ballgame."

Among his favourite boos in this area were those by Very Stanley Alder, such as The initiation of the World and The Fifth Dimension, works whose focus is the application of ancient knowledge to modern life. Elvis had an interest for the supernatural, he believed in the noncorporeal aspect of living. He was interested in telepathy, healing through touch and a number of phenomena that are only recently being scientifically studied. His mother had healed him through touch and prayer … According to Larry Geller, Elvis also had the gift of healing people: "Jerry Schilling, accepted that Elvis did have the ability. Even Red West and Sonny West, and Priscilla, have admitted as much, though they present it in a negative way. Then there were those who refused to believe that Elvis could heal.

One of the bodyguards, for example, writes of allowing Elvis to heal his child, then "playing along" with Elvis by humouring him, pretending he believed it, too. Someone else wrote Elvis knew that he had helped someone but sensed he was being laughed at, it hurt his feelings very deeply. He thought he was doing something good for people, their snide comments cut him to the quick. I once saw Elvis heal a man who was having a heart attack. Another time Elvis treated Jerry Schilling after he had taken a nasty spill on his motorcycle and was unable to move. "The next thing I knew," Jerry said later, "I woke up the following morning healed." Several times we healed Grandma Minnie Mae at Graceland, and she loved it. Of course, having lived with it all her life, Minnie Mae had no problem with healing. For her it was completely normal, and her grandson just happened to be one of those God had blessed with that power. Several times, after we'd given Minnie Mae a healing, Elvis would say, "I'll bet she outlives all of us."

Even though the healing process was kept quiet, even among the Memphis Mafia, Larry Geller witnessed hundreds of concertgoers carrying their crippled children to the stage and crying out, "Elvis, please touch my baby," or "Elvis, just hold her for a minute." Few fans knew of his studies then, yet thousands apparently sensed that he had some ability to heal.

Elvis was fascinated by Jesus, not just the image of Elvis but who he was. He didn't think that Jesus was the only begotten son of God. He thought that all people had Christ in them and had the same potential. Knowing the Scriptures as well as he did, Elvis would pose questions like "Didn't Jesus say that you could do greater things?" Elvis favourite book of the bible was the mystical book of John. Elvis Presley had a different conception of Jesus Christ than modern Christianity. Elvis felt that while on earth Christ revealed very deep, profound secrets, but that what we read today of what Jesus supposedly said is a watered-down version. Elvis thought that Jesus experienced everything that all people experienced, that he was the flower of humanity, that he suffered, and his suffering was ecstasy. Later in Elvis life, when he was truly suffering, Elvis would say: "This is the way Jesus was. Did you ever see Jesus mentioned in the Bible laughing? Never. Not once does it say that Jesus smiled or laughed. That's because he had this compassion for other people. He knew where other people were at. He knew the sufferings of humanity. I understand that, and that's why I am who I am. That's why God put me on earth. That's part of my mission. Only today things are different. Today, everything is technical."

He had an altered vision of Christ. In Alder's The initiation of the World, she speaks of a group of spiritual masters called the White Brotherhood, whose job it is to oversee human affairs. Elvis believed that he was working under the aegis of these masters, including Jesus. He was not into channelling or messaging, but felt that they guided him through life, he also saw potential in himself to take the cross upon himself, and follow Jesus.

Elvis was a Christian in that his belief in Jesus was steadfast, yet he never closed his mind to the belief that God could work and might work through any others of us or at least those who took the time to find enlightenment. Religion, soul-searching, or rather finding the "God-Within", was never a fad for Elvis Presley but rather a search that began from infancy, a search that proved to him how much there was to know and to be explored. His deep faith did not outlaw studies and questions.

Elvis noted, early on, the "Missing years of Jesus"—those years, some say sixteen, when Jesus was supposedly involved in spiritual studies, perhaps travelling to discover the truth in various other teachings and philosophies. (There is evidence, that Jesus was also influenced by age-old teachings such as

Buddhism or Taoism, that the God Is Love principle ... Do unto others ... Whatsoever you sow, so shall you reap ... the law of Karma ... the law of sequence and consequence.) When Jesus said, "Ye are gods ...."

Elvis knew it meant that Jesus was talking about the god-love within all of us, that presence we are taught to bring to the surface, so that we can act in a "godly" way. Elvis also remarked that to believe one has been born many times (reincarnation) was no more ridiculous than to believe that man was born once. Above all, Elvis Presley believed the relationship between man and God was a personal journey travelled at one's own speed. His quest to understand the God-Within was total and sincere; he knew he was chosen, yet he tried to define for himself for what?

When Larry Geller talked about how hard it was for Elvis to reconcile how God could both bless and punish with the same hand, like also found in Gail Brewer-Giorgio's fictional but on Elvis based character of the novel Orion was the "blessings/punishment" thesis, something Orion had to work through. (One twin lives, one dies ... fortune/fame=poor/pain ... height of joy/loss of mother and so on.) Realising—via only a brief view—Elvis connection to Jesus, the fact that The Passover Plot is prominently on display in Graceland's museum is worthy of examination, particularly because the book The Passover Plot deals with the possibility of Jesus hoaxing his death. Was Elvis truly looking for a way out of being Elvis Presley?

Elvis told many around him: "This life I am leading cannot go on much longer ..." He also spoke in a low voice, these words during his last concert: "I am, and I was." As with all his favourite books, Elvis read The Passover Plot many times over. It seemed he saw something of himself in it. There are two further horoscopes featured on Elvis Aron Presley in this book, here is another one by Debbie C. of Jackson/Tennessee, focusing and pointing out, like Larry Geller, that Elvis was numerology wise speaking, a perfect eight: "deep and very intense nature, much misunderstood in life and intensely lonely at heart, great strength of individuality, generally play some important role on life's stage but on that is fatalistic, fanatic in their zeal, warm hearts towards the oppressed of all classes, no happy medium, they are either great successes or great failures, if ambitious they generally aim for public life—which involves great sacrifice, are often called on to face the very greatest sorrows, losses and humiliations, represent two worlds, spiritual and material, after their death, their work is praised and lasting tributes are offered to their memory.

Elvis entered his career in the month of the sun and left it in the month of the sun. Elvis Presley often changed directions in life, when his song "If I Can Dream" charted in 1968 he told a reporter around this time: "I'm planning a lot of changes, you can't go on doing the same thing year after year." Shortly after completing the "live" segment of his NBC Television Special, Elvis made up his mind that he wanted, needed, to be onstage again. How and why he ended up returning to the stage in Las Vegas, or "Sin City", as Elvis called it, had never been clear.

Elvis always hated Vegas, and he longed to travel, not just across America but around the world. The response from the television special indicated that he was welcome anywhere. But Colonel Tom Parker devised another scheme and arranged for Elvis to make his Las Vegas debut at the International Hotel—the longest in the city—on 26 July 1969. Elvis' Vegas shows inspired the same high praise and enthusiasm as the special. He stood at another pint, from which a hundred different opportunities would have been to go to.

Instead, his career fell into three phases. The first, the Fifties. The Sixties, the movie years so to say, followed by the Seventies. Looking back, the seventies were a reprise of the sixties. Elvis was performing before live audiences, and not making film after film, and while the product might have been superior, the routine that evolved in each phase was beginning to wear on Elvis.

And 16 August 1977, was only a few years ahead of Elvis' most triumphant nights onstage ...

Shortly before his death, Elvis rebelled a last time, confiding to Larry Geller: "What I'm about to tell you is top secret. And I don't want you to tell anyone. But I'm going to get rid of the ol' Colonel. I need a change, new blood. I've always been loyal to the Colonel, and I appreciate what he's done. But nothing can last forever. The times are changin' and I don't think the Colonel is up-to-date with what's going on like Tom Hulett is. I've had it with him. And I also want a different lifestyle. I don't want the Memphis Mafia anymore. I don't need the scene anymore. I've had it with all the little jealousies, the infighting. I know who my real friends are. I want to live a different kind of life; this one has gone on long enough. After the next tour, or the one after that—I'm not sure yet, but by the end of summer—it will happen. A drastic cut. Daddy's been on me a long time about it. This will make him very happy. He feels too many people have taken advantage of me for too long ..."

When Colonel Tom Parker had made a deal with CBS to tape several shows from Elvis' tour in summer of 1977, a ten-day swing through the Midwest, there was already a couple of psychics in the news, who predicted Elvis' death. The press had also picked up a few leaks from the fired bodyguards book to be entitled "Elvis? What Happened?"

On 15 August 1977, after nine o'clock, Larry Geller saw Elvis for the final time, he dutifully reported it in his book "If I Can Dream":

"I hadn't seen Elvis in six weeks, and when I saw him I was horrified. He walked through the front door and stopped in the foyer, about fifteen feet from where I was standing in the dining-room in the doorway. He removed his glasses and shook his head from side to side. He never said a word, but the look he gave me spoke volumes. I saw fear and pain. He put his sunglasses back on, then with Ginger at his side slowly ascended the staircase to his room. I'd seen him in bad shape before but nothing like this. Charlie and Billy said hello; I didn't hear them or anyone else. I sat down on a sofa and for the next forty-five minutes tried to absorb what was happening. I snapped out of it only after I heard my name and had a telephone receiver pushed into my hands. "Hello?"

"Lawrence," Elvis said very softly, "did you bring that book on the Holy Shroud of Jesus?"

"Do Angels have wings?"

"Yeah, and don't: Angels fly because they take themselves so lightly." We both laughed longer than we should have; it must have been nerves. When we finally settled down, I said, "Wait until you feast your eyes on the other books I brought you also. You'll love 'em."

In his Inspector Clouseau voice, Elvis replied, "I know that already," sending us back on another giggling jag. "Well, what do you think we should do, Larry? Do you wanna come up here and talk, or do you think we should wait until tomorrow?" I was struck by the tone and texture of his voice. It sounded so light and pure, the way I imagined he spoke when he was a very small child. I had never heard him sound so peaceful.

"Well, E," I said slowly, still trying to figure out what he wanted, "it's really good hearing you like this. Maybe we should wait until tomorrow. It's already past one-thirty in the morning. This way you can get some rest for the tour, and I'll come up when you wake up tomorrow, do your hair, give you the books. And we have the rest of the tour. I'm sure we have a lot to talk about. How does that sound?"

"Well, whatever's right." I hesitated for a moment. Elvis was many things, but never so passive. It was unusual for him not to ask to see me or at least get his new books right away. "All right," I answered, "I'll see you later, E. I'm going back to my room at Howard Johnson's. I'll be there if you need me."

"I knew that," Elvis quipped a la Clouseau. Laughing, we both hung up, never bothering to say goodbye ..."

It was not the only time he was weary when he got home to Graceland. Mostly he spent time recuperating and rarely leaving his room. Another tour had been planned for the second half of August 1977. Elvis himself preferred to rest in bed, talk occasionally to Charlie Hodge who still lived in the basement, or to Billy and Jo, watch television and read. He would also call Priscilla to plan Lisa Marie's next stay, and to while away the loneliness. He called Kathy Westmoreland, too, and of course, Larry Geller ... His family was there also, Grandma in her room at the back of the house watching "Hee-Haw", Aunt Delta marching around shouting at her dog, and naturally, his father Vernon would call in.

But when old friends, like George Klein or Lamar Fike, stopped by, they weren't encouraged to come upstairs to Elvis' chambers. "I'm just so tired of being Elvis Presley", he had said to Felton Jarvis one night. He didn't feel that way all the time, on other days he just loved being Elvis. But when blackness overtook him it was difficult to find consolation. His swollen body, hands, face and ankles would upset him. They did not belong to the look he had in mind. Hours were spent wondering where Ginger Alden was, when she wasn't around. He wondered also if the new Triumph sportscar he had bought for his fiancé, wound endear him to her.

There were also fearful, sleepless nights as he was very worried about the reaction of his fans to the upcoming book "Elvis: What Happened?". Lurid articles in tabloid newspapers would be dismissed as gossip without foundation, but he thought that people would took a book more seriously, especially written by insiders. It was only on a few occasions that he summoned up the energy to go out through the gates of Graceland. Mostly at night, when they were less besieged by fans. But there was really nowhere he had to go any more.

Years earlier, he'd been able to call in at Sun Records at 706 Union Avenue once in a while. On Sam Phillips, to talk about his career, and get friendly advice. Though Elvis would still glare at the building as he drove by, the studio was no more, the microphones and mixing equipped had been ripped out when the place had been turned into a motorcycle repair shop. Only Taylor's Café, next door, remained ... Lansky was still on Beale Street, but he wouldn't be able to go there without drawing a mob ...

On 16 August 1977 D.J. Fontana, Elvis' former drummer happened to be working for SUN Records. D.J. Fontana explained: "It's like from the beginning to the end" sort of story. I just happened to be recording for the same record company we had started with. I forget who I was with, but Shelby Singleton who was the owner of Sun Records came into the studio at about 4.30pm and said, "D.J., maybe you wanna go home."

I said, "Why, am I fired?" And Shelby said, "We just got it on the radio, Elvis is dead." We had about 30 minutes left in the session so we finished it. You know news on radio and TV isn't always accurate. So I tried anybody I could, the Colonel, his assistant Tom Diskin, Elvis' friend George Klein, but I couldn't get through. Finally, I got hold of Alan Fortas, another friends, and he said, "D.J., I'm afraid it's true." It was so strange that—from Sun to Sun, the same recording company. It freaked me out. It scared the heck out of me—it really did."

Chapter Fifteen
Taking Care of Business

Ronnie Tutt, drummer for Elvis TCB Band, said in an interview with journalist Stuart Coupe, how Elvis had envisioned his return to the stage:

"Elvis told me that one night he woke in the middle of the night and he'd had a dream. He said: 'In my dream, I saw myself onstage. I saw myself in front of a hard, driving rock band that was really kicking. On one side I saw a white male gospel quartet and on the other side a black female soul group, and then I saw this big orchestra as the background to it, and we were doing a live concert."

Elvis' manager Colonel Tom Parker had other plans, he had visioned Elvis in a slight extension of the 1968 NBC TV "Comeback Special". In other words, Elvis would be a stage version of the bland films that had stunted his career for the previous years. But Elvis was so excited about the dream, that he did something that he never did. He called the Colonel in the middle of the night and told him, about his dream. The Colonel, maybe also as Las Vegas, was at that time not known for full time rock concerts, was less enthusiastic. But Elvis was convinced: "I'll tell you what Colonel, out of all due respect, we're just going to do it this way or we're not going to do it all."

Instead of another Las Vegas musical, Elvis and Rock and Roll would arrive in Vegas big time. Being much more, than the production numbers of his movies.

Having now convinced the Colonel or at least agreeing, Elvis now needed a good band, a male white gospel outfit, black soul singers and an orchestra.

The first person for the band to be called was James Burton. James had begun his career aged 14, playing guitar for the house band of Shreveport's famous "Louisiana Hayride Show". Also playing in Dale Hawkins band in 1955, writing the music for the hit song of Dale Hawkins—"Susie-Q". In 1957, he worked on recording sessions, weekly performances on the classic television show "The Adventures of Ozzie and Harriett", as well as live concerts with young Ricky

Nelson. By the mid-sixties he was an in-demand session player and also made recordings on his own.

Over the years James Burton recorded with artists such as: Elvis Presley, Ricky Nelson, Jerry Lee Lewis, Roy Orbison, John Denver, Johnny Cash, George Harrison, Rosanne Cash, Frank Sinatra, Henry Mancini, The Everly Brothers, The Byrds, Tina Turner, Elvis Costello, Andy Williams, Dolly Parton, Linda Ronstadt, Hank Williams Jr., Emmylou Harris, Willie Nelson, Dean Martin, Glen Campbell, Merle Haggard, Waylon Jennings, Arlo Guthrie, Johnny Mathis, The Mamas and The Papas, The Mills Brothers, Herb Alpert and many more.

It was Elvis himself who called James Burton personally and asked him to put together a band for his 1969 engagement in Las Vegas. James would be Elvis lead guitarist and band leader for concerts in Vegas, as well as on a national scale and on many recordings, from 1969 until the singers death in 1977.

In 1969, James Burton received a phone call at home, which is wife took. He actually was in the shower "getting ready to go to work". Explaining: "I was very busy with studio work, doing five or six sessions a day, seven days a week. It was an unbelievable time. My wife came in and said you have a phone call from a Mr Joe Esposito. That name didn't ring a bell so I said to my wife ask him if I can call him back, and my wife said well, I think maybe you should take this call. So, I went in and got on the phone and Joe Esposito said, "Hi James, very nice to talk to you. I'm Joe Esposito and I have someone here who'd like to speak with you."

Elvis got on the phone. Oh man. We started talking and Elvis was very gentlemanly and told me how he'd followed my entire career and watched me on television on the Ozzie and Harriet Show with Ricky (Nelson). He said I watched the Ozzie and Harriet Show just to watch you play guitar at the end of the show. I thought that was pretty interesting coming from the King of Rock and Roll. When Elvis called, we talked for about three hours, and he asked me to put a band together. He said he was tired of doing movies and he wanted to get back into doing rock shows for a live audience, and that was where his heart was at. That is where he wanted to be.

My telephone conversation with Elvis was quite interesting. It appeared that he had been listening to me for a while. It was through the Ricky Nelson records, but also, he'd heard about me from some people that worked with him. His record producer, Felton Jarvis, said that he had recommended me very highly to Elvis.

And of course, Red West was taking credit for it. And then Charlie Hodge said it was his idea. Elvis said later, all you guys are wrong, but I've always assumed Felton Jarvis played a big part in it."

Interestingly, Elvis Presley and James Burton had never met on a personal level, until 1969, though travelling similar paths. James Burton, further as quoted in a wonderful back about the TCB Band and Elvis written by Stuart Coupe: "Back in the early days I knew Scotty Moore and DJ Fontana who is from my hometown of Shreveport/Louisiana. It was strange that Elvis and I didn't meet earlier because I was on the Louisiana Hayride when I was 14 years old playing guitar with the staff band playing behind George Jones, Johnny Horton and a whole bunch of other country artists. Then there was a chance that we could have met when I was playing guitar with Bob Luman.

Bob was a pretty good guitar player and did a lot of Rockabilly. We did tours with Gene Vincent and The Blue Caps, Eddie Cochran and I used to go motorcycle riding together. But for whatever reason I didn't meet Elvis until 1969 even though I knew all the Memphis Mafia. I knew Red West, Sonny and all these guys. As a matter of fact, I was offered a job with Elvis when I was working with Ricky. Red West asked me in the '60s if I'd be interested in working with Elvis right after he got out of the army. I told Red that I was very happy playing with Ricky and that I didn't have a real good reason to change.

Bob Luman actually did a lot of Elvis's songs because I played guitar like Scotty did. It was interesting the sound that Scotty got, the way he used an echo amp. I had no idea how he was getting that sound, but I found out later. We were playing a club one night in Louisiana with Bob, and Elvis's boys showed up—Scotty, D.J. and Bill. They all came into this club and we asked them if they'd like to get up and play. Scotty got up onstage, but he wouldn't play any solos on Elvis tunes even though Bob did a lot of them. That seemed pretty strange to me. He'd played on all these records, but he was making me play the solos. When we took a break, Scotty told me he'd be right back. He went out to his car and brought in his amp and that was how he got that sound, using the echo amp. I thought that was pretty interesting because I was doing it all with my fingers. I'd learnt to play that way with my fingers but with Scotty I realised that his amp was doing all the work."

Ronnie Tutt, the drummer of the TCB Band, is originally from Dallas/Texas. He studied music at the University of North Texas, playing gigs in the Dallas/Fort Worth area, holding staff positions (drums and vocals) at two "jingle" studios. In 1963, he moved to Memphis and played with some of the city's finest rhythm sections while there was an exciting time in the music history of Memphis. In 1969, he auditioned for Elvis, landing the job. What got him into that spot, was that despite of being an excellent drummer, he and Elvis connected in a special way: Watching him, making eye contact, anticipating where Elvis was going with a song. Their musical connection was part of the great shows that Elvis and the TCB Band were capable of putting on. He was the drummer for Elvis from 1969 until 1977, on stage, as well as on a number of recordings. He was a studio musician in Los Angles for a long time, later relocating to Nashville. For years, he was part of the Jerry Garcia Band, from 1981 being part of Neil Diamond's band, recording and touring the world.

James Burton on the audition of a capable drummer for Elvis Presley: "I has some drummers in mind as well. The drummer who played with Ricky Nelson, Ritchie Frost, was a superb player who played on all of Nelson's hit records. He was just a great player, so he came in and played the show great. We played a couple of songs with Elvis and when we took a break he came over and said I love this music and I really enjoy playing it, but I don't want to work this hard. I really appreciate you keeping me in mind, but I'm pretty close to retiring from the stage. Larry and I were talking after this and he told me he knew a guy in Dallas, a great guy and a great drummer who wanted to move to L.A. I said he should give him a call and see if he was interested, so he did, and it was Ronnie Tutt. Larry and Ronnie had worked together in the Memphis area and the Texas area, so they were quite good friends. He called Ronnie who came out to do a little audition. We also had a couple of other drummers to come in and audition."

One of those drummers was Gene Pollo, who looked like of getting the job in the rehearsal studio, plus he wanted to be very much be a part of the band, telling that also to James Burton. Jerry Scheff (bass) recalls the audition as follows: "Gene Pollo was an LA session player originally from New York. He had played on some Motown hits and was a very strong drummer with lots of chops. Pollo was the only one out of the bunch of drummers that came down there to audition that had the power and the energy so when he played, all of Elvis guys—including Red West—were going, this is it, this is it. And Pollo was picking up on all this and the idea that he was getting the gig. It was an amazing scene.

When we finished playing, all of Elvis' guys were over there shaking his hand. All the gophers were giving their approval. Elvis liked him okay because he had the power and the chops to do it. Then Larry Muhoberac (piano) stood up and said "wait, hold it, hold it, my friend Ronnie Tutt just flew all the way out here with his drums to audition and he's been sitting over there all night." I looked over and there in the corner was this guy I hadn't noticed earlier. Elvis was cool and said okay, go and set up Ronnie. Gene Pollo is watching on. Ronnie set his drums up and we started playing. Two bars into the song and as if like magic happened everybody knew that Ronnie was it.

I remember it was very poignant because you could see Gene Pollo's face dropping. He knew. He had all the strength, but he didn't have the feel that Ronnie did. I felt so bad for him." Ronnie Tutt remembered his audition: "Everyone was looking around in the so-called stage at that time and obviously thinking well, we finally got a guy. They'd been rehearsing for a couple of weeks by then and had gone through a lot of drummers. I guess they were getting a bit tired of it, so after Pollo played they were thinking oh, I think we've got a drummer. So when the last note of the song was hit, they started putting their instruments away in cases and everyone was getting ready to leave. Then Larry goes over to Colonel Parker and says, his friend that you just flew in … and hit him in the purse strings and reminded him that he'd paid for Ronnie's ticket.

"So, the Colonel went over to Elvis and calls the guys. I could see a bit of head-to-head going on. They were all reluctant to get playing again but then they looked at each other and accepted that they had to do it. The minute we started playing Elvis looked around me and was transfixed by the situation we were creating. We held that connection until the last note we hit together. The rapport that we had was the reason Elvis was so taken by me. He said later on, 'you know Ronnie, that other drummer was good'—but he really didn't know how to speak in sophisticated musical terms, he just spoke from the heart—'you know that other drummer is good, but you watched everything I did. I could look up at any time and I could see your eyes and I knew you were with me.'" Ronnie Tutt added: "Some people have it. I don't know how you really describe his charisma, but he definitely had it. He had that presence. He was striking physically, and he also had a smile and a sense of warmth, and you could see the little twinkle in his eye. It was that sense of humour and look that said, 'I'm here and I'm laughing at the whole thing'."

Glen D. Hardin (piano) grew up in Texas and made his way to LA in the autumn of 1961, leaving the U.S. Navy. In early 1962 he was playing piano at the Palomino Club, soon touring with Buddy Holly's former band The Crickets.

Over the years he would work as an arranger and recording session pianist with artists such as: Elvis Presley, Emmylou Harris, John Denver, Merle Haggard, Marty Robbins, George Jones, Dolly Parton, Tanya Tucker, The Everly Brothers, Ricky Nelson, Travis Tritt, Trisha Yearwood, Alan Jackson, Vince Gill, Willie Nelson, Kenny Rogers and The First Edition, Bing Crosby, Andy Williams, Jim Nabors, Dean Martin, Sammy Davis Junior, Sonny and Cher, KD Lang, Roy Orbison, Linda Ronstadt, Ike and Tina Turner, Cass Elliott, Ricky Skaggs, Marty Stuart, Tammy Wynette and many others.

He toured with Emmylou Harris for three, The Crickets for eleven and John Denver for sixteen years. His work with Elvis was from 1970 to 1976, playing live concerts with him, creating some arrangements and being a part on numerous Elvis recordings.

Glen D. Hardin joined the TCB Band in 1970 for the second season in Las Vegas. In August 1969, Larry Muhoberac had played piano but then decided that he didn't want to do it anymore, preferring to stay in LA to work on other projects. "The boys had tried to get me to play with Elvis the first time as we'd worked together before, but I was tied up with other projects and just couldn't do it. When Larry decided he didn't want to do it again, I decided I would. I was arranging music at that time and that was about all I was doing. I didn't play the piano at all anymore and I really wanted to get back to it. I was sick of being behind schedule with the music arranging. I love arranging music but the easiest thing I ever stumbled into was playing piano, so I decided I wanted to get back to doing that and it worked out real good because I not only played for Elvis, but I started arranging music for him. I arranged a lot of the things that were on the show."

Glen D. Hardin saw three of Elvis Presley's shows in Lubbock/Texas in the 1950s: "I remember that people said that the first time he played there he was paid something like $75. I believe the gig was on a flatbed truck at a car dealership. The second time he played there I think he was paid around $600 and then the third time, which was just a short time later, he got $3000—so things were changing and happening for him really quickly."

When they first met face to face, so to speak in person Glen described Elvis as "he was just great and very friendly. He was real trim and just looked great. I had to audition. They had a list of people they wanted to audition, and I was on the list, I knew the boys wanted me to do it, but I still had to impress Elvis. He was just so easy to get on with at the audition. We sat down and started playing.

He started doing some of his old songs and couldn't remember some of the words. Maybe he was just thinking about something else. I was just sitting there playing and singing the words to him, so he obviously thought I was okay and knew my stuff. When we started first rehearsing with him, we spent a bit of time together. He booked long rehearsals. I think he liked to rehearse, and he also liked to hang out with the boys. We spent a lot of time at rehearsals just taking breaks and arm wrestling and sending out for cheeseburgers and all that sort of thing, but we'd also get a lot of work done. And one time or another we ran through every song he had ever done, at least touched on it briefly, so that if it ever came up, we would know it."

Jerry Scheff (bass) grew up in the Bay area of San Francisco. He started to play tuba in grammar school, by the seventh grade, also having gotten into playing string bass. He leaned towards Jazz and Rhythm and Blues. At the relatively young age of fifteen he was playing clubs in his new hometown of Sacramento and also back in San Francisco. As a high school senior Jerry Scheff joined the U.S. Navy and wound up in the Navy's school of music in Washington, D.C. absolving a nine-month course studying theory and harmony, as well as getting to play with some great musicians. After the classes, he stayed on to teach, also moonlighting to play jazz clubs.

Later, he was transferred by the Navy to San Diego. After his discharge he moved to Los Angeles, playing regularly at The Sands, a club in Watts, where a teenager named Billy Preston appeared, at that time still doing James Brown covers. As a session player in LA, he found work on the trombone firstly. Over the years he recorded with Bobby Sherman, Tiny Tim, Johnny Mathis, Nancy Sinatra, Sammy Davis Jr., Bobby Vinton, The Everly Brothers, The Nitty Gritty Dirt Band, Dionne Warwick, Barbra Streisand, Linda Ronstadt, Judy Collins and many others. In the late 1960s he crossed paths with guitarist James Burton, who remembered Scheff's work and called him when given the responsibility by Elvis to compose a band, for Elvis' first live engagement for ten years.

Jerry Scheff worked with Elvis from 1969 to 1973 and from 1975 until 1977, on stage and on a number of recordings. He says: "Elvis had a big impact on my career. It was like going to school". He continues to work as a session musician, another passion of his in the past years, is songwriting. Though his career was more in the Pop and Rock field, he still plays a little Jazz now and then, as he says "to keep the cobwebs clear". Both of his sons, Darin and Jason, are musicians. Jason Scheff playing in the band Chicago.

James Burton and Jerry Scheff had worked together on many sessions. "We'd done several projects and I just love the way Jerry plays. He had that little bite that you get when you pop the strings. He was just a wonderful player, so I definitely had him on the top of my list." Said James Burton. Jerry Scheff was mostly driven by curiosity into the TCB Band, working for Elvis: "James called me up and said he was putting together a band for Elvis, so I thought I'd just go down and check it out, Jerry remembers. I was thinking that I probably wasn't going to do it, but I wanted to see what was going on.

"Anyway, I went down and did it and then I went home and told my wife you've got to come down tomorrow and hear this. She thought I was kidding but she came down the next day. Being there made me feel like I was going to school. It really opened up my mind to things other than my usual narrow scope. All the players were great, but I hadn't played that type of music before at all. At the rehearsal Larry Muhoberac was there with James. I was the only bass player. I asked James about it later and he said they never auditioned anyone else. So, I guess when he said we'll get Jerry Scheff, then that was cool."

Elvis Presley's and Jerry Scheff's paths had crossed before: "I think it was around 1966 and I was working with Billy Preston in Watts three nights a week. I wasn't making very much money. Then Red West called me up and said, 'are you Jerry Scheff, the trumpet player?' And I said yep. Actually, I played tuba, but I thought what the heck. He told me that they were doing an Elvis Presley movie and wanted a five-piece horn section, so I said this is me. I borrowed this old silver trumpet which didn't even have a case and took it down there. I didn't play anything over a middle C for two days, collected my money and went home." He also, according to his Union checks tell him, worked on another Elvis move.

Meeting Elvis seemed not like a big deal to him: "I remember thinking he was a good-looking-guy. He wasn't dressed real flashy. I wasn't in awe of him at all. For me, it was like okay he's a good-looking-guy, but let's play and see what's going on. Elvis was a natural entertainer. He liked to entertain everybody. We'd be rehearsing and he'd do songs that we loved, especially in the first few days. He did things that he thought we would like, and we'd play them and it was fun. But then, say two ladies would walk into the room and all of a sudden, he'd be into love songs, literally. Whoever was there he'd play for them. He wanted everyone to enjoy what he was doing so he would divide it up and do something for everybody."

Jerry's wife was also impressed by Elvis Presley. "The thing that she liked about him, and that I liked about him as well, and the reason I continued to like him, was that he was a natural, pure singer. It was the same thing that Frank Sinatra had. There are people like Bruce Springsteen and Garth Brooks who are entertainers in that sense that they're thinking about how they look, what clothes they're wearing and every moment they make onstage and more often than not it comes across the way, whereas with Elvis, he just did it, effortlessly, unselfconsciously, without thinking about it. Above everything, the lyrics always travelled through is brain and then back out through his mouth. He always sang the lyrics of the song."

JD Summer and The Stamps led by J.D. Summer, who is recorded by the Guinness Book Of Records, as holding the lowest bass note ever recorded, show one of a long list of great moments in the life of a musical legend.

Most of his career J.D. had led the Stamps Quartet, one of the most successful groups in Gospel music history. The group was nominated for Grammy, Dove and TNN awards, touring the world in concert.

J.D. Sumner is also credited with being a major force in forming the Gospel Music Association, the Dove Awards and the National Quartet Convention. Also being significant in leading the gospel world to even greater levels of professionalism and organisation. His direction and management of The Stamps became a role model for other groups of that musical niche. The Stamps worked with Elvis Presley from 1971 until 1977 as the male back up group for his shows in Las Vegas and on national tours, also working with him on numerous recordings. J.D. Sumner (bass), Ed Enoch (lead) and Ed Hill (baritone), the latter singing with the Stamps in the years 1976 and 1977. They were joined at various times by Bill Baize, Donnie Sumner, Larry Strickland and Richard Sturban, currently with the Oak Ridge Boys. J.D. Sumner died in 1998.

The Imperials—Elvis loved Gospel music, particularly male gospel harmony, which was not only so much of a part in his own Gospel recordings, but also an element in so much of his pop, rock and country recordings.

The Imperials first worked with Elvis doing some of the great backing vocals on the 1966 recordings for the album "How Great Thou Art", which won Elvis Presley his first Grammy award for Best Sacred Performance for 1967. The Imperials worked on a regular basis with Elvis on stage and in the recording studio from 1969 until the latter half of 1971, beginning with the first triumphant Las Vegas engagement of '69. A major highpoint of their collaborating with

Elvis was the 1972 released album "He Touched Me", earning Elvis Presley his second Grammy award, Best Inspirational Performance for 1972.

Founded in 1964 by former Statesman member Jake Hess, The Imperials became somewhat of a super group of Gospel music. The group prevailed, even though some criticism, selling a lot of records, enjoying a long series of major TV guest spots, having toured with Country singer Jimmy Dean plus appearing regularly on his Television show. The group had regular bookings in Las Vegas, Reno and Lake Tahoe. Of course not to forget the special connection they had to Elvis Presley. Over the years, the group in various incarnations released forty albums with fourteen of their songs hitting number one. Receiving twelve Grammy awards and thirteen of Gospel's Dove Awards.

As the first Christian group, they played the Grammy Award Telecast. Their catalogue of songs is most enduring, many of them landmark recordings in Gospel music. Like Elvis Presley's other male backing groups they are inductees into the Gospel Music association's Hall of Fame—with namely The Jordanaires and The Stamps. Members included are: Armond Morales, Jim Murray, Joe Moscheo, Terry Blackwood and Sherman Andrus.

The Sweet Inspirations and their soulful harmonies have created music with Aretha Franklin, Wilson Pickett and other legends. They have collaborated with writers and producers such as Carol King, Burt Bacharach and Hal David.

They had success with Rhythm and Blues, Gospel and Pop recordings. Their first hit single "Sweet Inspiration" giving the group it's final name and winning them a Grammy nomination. It was that song, which caught the attention of Elvis Presley. He signed them to provide backing vocals for his first Las Vegas engagement in 1969. No audition was required. The Sweet Inspirations meeting him for the first time at the rehearsals for his triumphant stage comeback in Vegas. The Sweets worked with Elvis in Las Vegas, on his national concert tours and on recordings from 1969 until 1977.

Myrna Smith, Sylvia Shemwell, Estelle Brown and Cissy Houston (mother of Whitney Houston) made up the original line-up. Cissy Houston pursuing a solo-career after the initial Elvis Las Vegas show. In the nineties Myrna Smith, Sylvia Shemwell and Estelle Brown reunited, after they had gone their separate ways. Performing also for several projects connected with Elvis—including Graceland. In the mid-1990s, Portia Griffin joined the group, and later Kelley Jones. Myrna Smith recalls the first meeting with Elvis as follows:

"He walked in and had on a chocolate coloured suit. He had a tan, and he looked absolutely gorgeous. He walked over to us and introduced himself—like we didn't know who he was: 'Hi, I'm Elvis Presley.' (Cissy literally fell off her stool.) From then on, whenever he'd see us, it was always a kiss. He had so much energy. His voice was a lot more remarkable than it ever came off on record … He was just a much better singer than could ever be captured … Some great singers' voices are just too big. Elvis' was like that."

Joe Guercio despite his prolific career is probably best remembered and admired for his work with Elvis Presley. He was the musical director and conductor for Elvis' concert shows from the summer of 1970 to August 1977 when Elvis made his last concert performance.

Elvis was known for his spontaneity and improvisation, the cast had to be ready for everything: "He'd just turn around and start a tune. The rhythm section knew him backwards and forwards, but when you're up there conducting a twenty-six-piece orchestra, what are you going to do?" Joe Guercio remembered for the book "On Stage with Elvis Presley".

Joe Guercio was the musical director for the International Hilton in Las Vegas at the time when Elvis began performing there. Along with the contributions he made to Elvis' live shows was the triumphs of Elvis' concert era, as well as creating the shows now most almost iconic six-note theme for Elvis Presley's stage entrances and bows. He also suggested that Elvis uses the theme from 2001—A Space Odyssey. The inspiration came when Joe and his wife saw the movie in a theatre, for the first time. His late wife whispered to him: "You'd think Elvis was about to enter."

Joe Guercio first left his hometown Buffalo/New York as an accompanist for singer Patti Page. He has lived in Las Vegas since 1967, having been musical director for Diana Ross, Jim Nabors, Florence Henderson, Diahann Carroll, Steve Lawrence and Eddy Gorme, among others. His arrangement for the medley Sweet Inspiration/Where You Lead was a 1972 hit for Barbra Streisand, another arrangement of The Way We Were/Try To Remember hit for Gladys Knight in 1975. He also worked on the Natalie Cole/Nat King Cole Medley bringing her on stage with her late father, pre-dating the famous 1990s duet. He also accompanied blues legend BB King to Rome to meet Pope John Paul II, for performing in the Vatican's fifth Christmas concert. He also served as musical director for the Elvis In Concert '97 event in Memphis and reprised this role in the touring production Elvis—The Concert.

Charlie Hodge met Elvis Presley in 1956. He was a singer, guitarist and assistant to Elvis, living in a converted apartment behind Graceland for seventeen years. With five feet three inches tall, Charlie Hodge was one of the shortest members of Elvis inner circle, the so called Memphis Mafia. He tried to compensate with lifts in his shoes. Charlie and Elvis recorded a duet of the song "I Will Be Home Again" in 1960. Charlie Hodge's responsibility was to look after Elvis Presley's personal life, as well as his music schedule. It was him who drove Priscilla and Elvis to the hospital on the day Lisa Marie Presley was born. Charlie Hodge, Red West and Elvis wrote "You'll Be Gone". He had cameo parts in the Elvis Presley movies Charro!, Clambake appearing as himself in the 1979 Kurt Russell starring biopic on Elvis. He was also a featured character in the 1988 TV drama "Elvis and Me". Through the 1970s he performed with the TCB Band.

Other members of the TCB Band included Hal Blaine, who played drums on occasion, Jerry Shook on bass, when Jerry Scheff was not available. Duke Bardwell a bass player of Elvis in the studio and on the stage in the 1970s. Tony Brown was the piano player to replace Glen D. Hardin in 1974, and again in 1977. Joe Osborne was an occasional bass player with the band, Larry Muhoberac preceded Glen D. Hardin on the piano, and had also recommended Ronnie Tutt on drums. Jimmy Mulidore played the flute solo on "American Trilogy" in February 1972.

Of course, there was also Kathy Westmoreland.

She was often introduced by Elvis Presley as the girl "with the beautiful high voice". She sang soprano with Elvis Presley from 1970 until 1977 replacing Millie Kirkham who had left to have surgery.

Kathy Westmoreland who had classical training later wrote a book on Elvis, debunking some of the myths and facts concerning Elvis Presley. Partly also to defence to some other books already being published such as "Elvis—What Happened" penned by three former bodyguards—Red West, Sonny West and Dave Hebler with journalist Steve Dunleavy, and probably also as response to the Albert Goldman published biography on Elvis, as well as the Albert Goldman written "Elvis—The Last 24 Hours". Kathy Westmoreland and Elvis Presley shared the bed for some time, but for a long time without having intercourse. Elvis who did not like to be alone at night, not only having often nightmares, but also suffering insomnia and sleep-walking benefitted from it.

There were good times and bad times: On one incident Elvis insulted Kathy and the Sweet Inspirations on stage in 1975. All of them with the exception of Myrna Smith walking off-stage as a matter of protest. Kathy had decided after that, to leave the entourage, but was asked by Colonel Tom Parker's assistant Tom Diskin to stay, which she eventually did.

Elvis Presley opened in Las Vegas on 31 July 1969. He had flown in from recording sessions in Memphis to sign the as yet incomplete contract for an engagement to be held in February 1970. Doing this for publicity reasons during the construction work of the International Hotel. The first act to appear at what, at that time was hailed, as the world's largest showroom was Barbra Streisand. She opened in July. It had not been until April 15th 1969 that Elvis had actually signed his contract. The Colonel continued his trademark publicity campaign which included posters, banners, balloons, 8x10 glossy photos, colour portraits of Elvis and many other promotional items.

As the opening night came closer, Colonel Tom Parker's publicity machinery became more intense even: Even though that the season was an 80% sell-out Parker did not take any risks, and had the showroom, after Barbra Streisand's final night, transformed into Elvis showroom, overnight. The opening night was an invitation-only affair. The owner of the International Kirk Kerkorian flew in actor Gary Grant who would join the likes of Fats Domino, Paul Anka, Pat Boone, Phil Ochs, Carol Channing, Shirley Bassey and Dick Clark in the audience. Parker flying in loads of critics and rock-journalists from New York, while Elvis himself sent an invitation to his early-days mentor Sam Phillips.

It was an obviously important night for Elvis Presley, one of the most important performances of his career. If it worked, it could be a triumphant rejuvenation of his career, but what if it flopped?

Elvis was very nervous, as drummer Ronnie Tutt remembered: "The only time I ever saw him get really nervous and moody about performing and saw how it obviously affected us around him was opening night. A few things hadn't gone right in the rehearsals and that added to that tension."

Showtime was at 8:15pm as the curtain rolled up for The Sweet Inspirations and comedian Sammy Shore, the reception was okay, but nothing compared to what would follow when Elvis Presley would hit the stage. Elvis entered and opened with a rendition of Carl Perkins' "Blue Suede Shoes"—the entire showroom exploded. This was Elvis, augmented by a great band, despite, the audience had been there for just one performer—Elvis Presley.

The set continued with "I Got A Woman", "Love Me Tender", "Jailhouse Rock" and "Don't Be Cruel" before Elvis addressed the audience in words: "Good evening, Ladies and Gentlemen. Welcome to the big, freaky International Hotel, with those weirdo dolls on the walls and those little funky angels on the ceiling and, many, you ain't seen nothing until you've seen a funky angel. Before the evening's out I'm sure I will have made a complete and utter fool of myself— but I hope you get a kick out of watching."

The show continued relentless, Gary Grant was on his feet applauding, whereas the comedienne Tootie Fields was dancing on a table, with a wine bottle in her hand, all of the waiters and waitresses staring wide-eyed at Elvis Presley. Ronnie Tutt remembered: "Besides all the hoopla, or whatever you want to call it, that was made out of it the first show, there was also this excitement of what we were doing. My image of Elvis at that particular time was that physically he was in the best shape I ever saw him. He looked like a black panther out there, almost like an animal. He was so sleek, and the way he moved and that we moved with him and the music moved us in time together was just amazing."

Bass player Jerry Scheff sees the opening night still as one of the highlights of his career: "You have to understand that one of the things with Elvis prior to that night is that he hadn't really done much performing in front of people for a long time. He'd just done patches here and there and he really didn't know how people were going to react, especially in Las Vegas as he'd had funny experience there before and hadn't done so well. We were with him in the dressing room before the show started and Elvis was extremely nervous. I think one of the most poignant moments I ever saw on stage was when he went out on that stage that night. I ever saw onstage was when we went out on that stage that night. We were just standing there, and the audience went wild."

"Through the first and second number of the show, the transformation in Elvis was just astonishing. You could see the change in his facial expression and muscle tone. It was a very physical thing. Essentially it was the transformation of someone going out there not knowing what to expect. By the third song, it was amazing. It was simply Elvis realising that this was where he wanted to be and that this was what he wanted to do. This was it for him."

Technically, the T.C.B. Band had little rely on, the band depended on its musical skills, as Jerry Scheff recalled: "We had very little in the way of proper equipment in those days." Ronnie Tutt: "We never even had a band stand on the stage. We set up right on the stage with the drums flat on the floor. Jerry was on

369

one side of me, James on the other and Elvis in front. We might have had a small drum riser in Las Vegas, but certainly not when we were touring." Jerry Scheff, when reflecting on those days with music journalist Jerry Coupe: "Am I just looking through rose-coloured glasses or was it nice playing without monitors? We stood close together and we didn't rely on something artificial to know what we were doing and to hear each other." Ronnie Tutt: "The only thing that was hard to hear at times was the keyboards. But we all listened to each other in close proximity. Elvis stood right in front of us because he was digging it too. He loved to stand right in the front."

Difficult was the lights, Ronnie Tutt: "They were brutal. A lot of the arenas had low sightlines. I know that because I stood behind him (Elvis) and there would be four or five spotlights blaring directly at him. That's why he had to have such glittery jumpsuits—there was no real lighting." Remembering the stage wear, James Burton says: "We would go to places and have someone bring us all these patterns. We didn't have a lot of time to pick and choose. It was pretty much a case of selecting a colour and style we liked and getting the shop to make them up for us." Ronnie Tutt: "In a way the stage costumes were embarrassing, but you've got to remember that it was Las Vegas. The whole idea of the look we were going for was a combination of something showy, something that would look good, something that would fit well, something that was practical—but at the same time it had a look that I think the music itself spoke for. It spoke of a little bit of gospel, a little bit of country and a little bit of rock and roll. We played a bit of everything and I think we tried to get our wardrobe to mirror that."

Joe Guercio pointed out: "My guys in the orchestra used to call the band The Polyesters. There was no way there were the TCB Band. They were the Wash-n-Wears." Jerry Scheff: "I was in charge of selecting the colours each night. Charlie Hodge would come down and tell me what Elvis was wearing that night and I'd get the word to the guys that we were wearing dark blue or whatever it was. We all had quite a few suits. We had two whites, two blacks, and turquoise. We had a lot of rhinestones. We must have had ten rhinestone outfits made. We even had a one-piece suit."

Glen D. Hardin: "That was the jumpsuit. I remember saying to one of the guys one night 'excuse me while I go and slip into something less comfortable'. The first wardrobe we got was Segal's. I was down there, and found these shirts that had a fringe. We had them in black, and white, and wore them with a pair of black or white pants. Then we all went out and got Italian boots." Joe Guercio:

"I went out and brought the band vests the second day so we wouldn't sit back there in those Las Vegas tuxedos. We had purple busts instead."

James Burton: "You know, the stage costumes didn't worry me. It did bother some of the other guys, what with the rhinestones and flares. For me, it was interesting and pleasing that Elvis wanted us to look like a group, his group. It was Elvis and All The King's Men, The T.C.B. Band. And TLC—Tender Loving Care—for the Ladies."

The content of the Las Vegas Shows was as follows:

The Sweet Inspirations would appear with their own band and do a set of 45 minutes. They would be followed by a Comedian, after an intermission it was showtime for Elvis Presley and the TCB Band. The shows weren't overly long, ranging from 45 minutes to a more typical one-hour set. However, sometimes a lucky audience would be also treated to a 75 minute show by Elvis and the TCB Band. Encores were not given. Once Elvis had left the stage that was it. He then was already in a limousine on his way to the hotel or the airport within minutes of the show finishing.

Ronnie Tutt explains why: "For security reasons he didn't want to hang around. He had told me stories of the early days and he'd learnt his lessons well. If he got out late to the limousine or was delayed for some reason the fans would literally tear his clothing off and patches of his hair away from his head. These were the '60s and '70s, not the '50s, but at the same time you never know with an audience exactly what a crowd is capable of under those particular circumstances. I know, for example, that he had to tape his rings so that people wouldn't tear them off. He had fingernail marks and claw marks all over him if he'd been caught after a show."

Jerry Scheff: "The show was just one solid hour and goodbye. There were no encores, no nothing. He'd disappear immediately after he came offstage, which is where that thing about 'Elvis has left the building' came from. People would rush the stage the moment he finished. I remember one show we had a temporary stage and people got underneath it and started rocking it so hard that we had to get off quickly before it collapsed. Elvis had already left the building, but they thought he was backstage. It was frightening."

Elvis Presley and the T.C.B. Band were something that Las Vegas had never experienced before, as James Burton pointed out: "It was always intense. There was the excitement of the show and the audience building up to an explosion. It was like that every night. Every night when we walked onstage, we really didn't know what was going to happen. There was always lots of energy coming from the audience. They were always brilliant and loved everything. They screamed so hard that often we couldn't hear Elvis. Basically, we always knew where we were in the song, but it got to a point sometimes where the actual noise from the audience overpowered the stage sound."

Jerry Scheff recalls those for the TCB Band early shows as well: "Well, we didn't use monitors. It wasn't like stacks of Marshalls. James was using pretty much what he uses now. When we started with Elvis, I had this bass amp and that sat over by itself between Ronnie and the piano. Sometimes on solos I cranked it up but during the main part of the show we had a pretty good balance. Back then I could hear just about everything going onstage."

Joe Guercio: "This was Elvis' second time in Las Vegas. On the first season I wasn't with the group, but I'm pretty sure they weren't happy with the conductor they had then. I'd taken over the band at the International Hotel and had brought in a lot of new players, including some really hot guys from New York. Originally, I was offered a job at the International, but I had other clients that I was working with at the time like Florence Henderson and Diahann Carroll. Later I got a call from Tom Diskin in the Entertainment Department. He called me at home and asked if I'd like to conduct for Elvis and I told him that would be part of my gig because I was now working for the hotel. I was not an Elvis fan by any stretch of imagination.

"Tom Diskin said that I should go to Los Angeles and meet him and the Colonel and that's what I did. I was certainly capable of doing what they needed doing. Let's face it, for me doing 'Hound Dog' was not exactly a musical experience! I came out of a whole different world and this was totally different musically. The first thing we worked on was the motion picture 'That's The Way It Is'. Glen D. and I got along from the moment we said "hello". Anyway, Joe Esposito came over at the first rehearsal and said Elvis was coming in and that I should meet him. It was no big deal for me at all.

"But, you know, from the time I said hello there was an electricity there. I could see exactly where he was coming from. We rehearsed a few things, and everything was precise and happening. The eye contact with Elvis gave me a feeling of confidence that it was all going to happen the way it should. There was something special about Elvis. I'd worked with a lot of so-called headliners and stars, but he was something very different. His charisma went to the back row at any place he was playing.

"At that point the International Hotel was the largest showroom in Las Vegas. It sat 1200 people, but it wasn't so much the size of the audience, but the reaction. I've sat on that stage with a lot of people, but I've never seen a reaction like it outside of Gladys Knight and The Pips on a Saturday night for the Black Schoolteachers Convention. When Elvis was onstage the power would just vibrate through the back wall of that room."

James Burton added for the book "On Stage with Elvis Presley": "It was so much more than just another gig for us because Elvis was such an icon and a huge idol around the world and in the music industry. It was really an honour for me and I'm sure everyone else felt the same way. He was such a wonderful entertainer and a great artist. The energy you felt when he was around was just incredible. He just had so much charisma. The chemistry in the band worked right from the start. Ronnie's such a great player and all the band are superb musicians. It had a lot to do with the fact that we all worked so well together. Our background in music was very similar to Elvis' background, so it was like a marriage in that respect as well. The thing about Elvis' show was the intensity and the energy that he projected along with the band and the singers. Everything was just so perfectly tight."

Joe also tells this very amusing story: "After the first show in Vegas, one of Elvis' guys asked me how I enjoyed working with Elvis and I told him it was like following a marble falling down concrete steps. That obviously got back to Elvis because the next day when I came to work and opened the door of my dressing room—there were marbles all over the floor. The sink was full of marbles; there were marbles in my clothes pockets. Written on the mirror was, 'follow the marbles—EP'."

Audiences both in Las Vegas and concerts around the States were not completely cray from the moment Elvis came onstage until the moment he departed an hour later. But stages pretty soon became littered with all matter of objects hurled by the audience. "There were lots of knickers and hotel room keys and notes," Jerry Scheff recalled and pointed out: "I remember a couple of un-used Tampax. I believe they were unused. None of us examined them that closely. Then there was stuff like teddy bears.

"I have a photo of Elvis standing right in front of my amplifier and we're both laughing because there's this little teddy bear peeking out from behind my amplifier. It had been thrown onstage and someone had walked back, and stuck it on my amplifier." Guitarist James Burton points out: "The thing for us was just the excitement, the energy and the reaction of the audiences. We had tourists coming from Japan, sometimes two 747's a week, maybe four. The Japanese fans were just unbelievable. There was one little girl who came over to Elvis front of the stage. She hugged him and whispered in his ear and he started laughing. The band were looking at each other and wondering what was going to happen next. And then she jumped onstage and ran over and grabbed me and kissed me and hugged me. Elvis got the biggest kick out of that. He thought it was so great and we talked about it for a week. Little things like that which you didn't an expect to happened all the time and that was part of what kept it so interesting for us."

Regarding security on stage, James Burton added:

"There was no way of knowing what Elvis' reaction would be to someone from the audience. Occasionally he'd get mad at someone in the audience who'd start calling out for songs he hadn't got to, but not very often. He liked to surprise people with the songs he did. There were few times when female fans made it onto the stage, the majority of times they just rushed to the front of the stage and waited—and hoped—Elvis would come over in their direction. That was mainly a security thing, they tried to keep it from happening as much as possible.

There were some incidents that happened over the years. Some guys jumped onstage one time and the security people had to tackle them. It got to the point after so many different things happened onstage that everybody started to get a little gun shy. It got real scary in act, after the death threat the hotel told Elvis that they would understand if he didn't want to go out and perform the show that night. They had F.B.I. men and Memphis Mafia and police all planted in the audience.

The main worry was when Elvis sang 'You've Lost That Lovin' Feeling'. What he would do in that song was turn his back to the audience and there'd be a little pin spot on the back of his head. The room would be dark except for that little spotlight on his head and everyone figured if someone was going to try to shoot him it'd be during that song. So that night we started doing the song, but it had been decided that they wouldn't take the lights all the way down. Elvis had refused the suggestion to not do the show. He said, 'I can't worry about that stuff, I can't let this bother me and I must do the show.' He was certainly wary but was adamant that he had to perform."

Jerry Scheff: "They had trained people, FBI people, watching at the show. It was quite heavy. From what I recall someone sent a threatening letter that was written on a really cheesy black and white Xerox photo of Elvis and it had a knife, childishly drawn sticking out of his face. The experts looked at it and decided that it could be serious. At the show that night … I think it might have been Sammy Shore the comedian. After he'd done his bit onstage he went and sat with friends in the audience and when Elvis came out Sammy stood up and put his hand out to shake Elvis' but it looked, particularly in the semi-darkness, as though someone was pointing a gun at Elvis and at least twenty guns clicked on him from security in the room."

"That wasn't the only tense moment or time over the years when Elvis received threats. One time there was a doctor backstage waiting with oxygen. Everything was set up just in case something happened. They had everything covered. There were often some weird times with guys in the audience too. There were guys that got off on watching the reaction between Elvis and the women in the audience and I suspect they would have liked to have watched Elvis in bed given half the chance. And on the other hand, there were guys sitting there who just had poison in their eyes because they were so jealous of the way women, often those who were with them, responded to Elvis."

Soon after the TCB Band had started their first Las Vegas season, James Burton would introduce a new guitar of his own: "That guitar was an incredible thing. When Fender called me and told me they had this new guitar for me I asked them to send it. They said there was no way they'd do that—I had to come down and get it. I saw this guitar and, wow, it was flashy. I couldn't see myself playing it because I'd never played what you'd call a real flashy guitar like that. I took the guitar to Las Vegas, but it took me two weeks before I got the nerve to bring it out and play it onstage. Until that point, I was playing an original 1952 Telecaster guitar that my Mum and Dad bought me."

"In Vegas, Red West had kept telling me that I should play the new guitar, so finally one night I decided to go for it. Elvis was singing Johnny B. Goode and was joking around with one liners, so he wasn't paying any attention to the guitar. Then it was time for the solo on that song and he looked around did a double take when he saw the guitar. I almost stopped playing waiting for his reaction. I didn't know what he was going to say. In fact, he didn't say anything during the show, but afterwards he called me to his dressing room and asked where I'd gotten the guitar from, so I told him that Fender had sent it to me. I went on to tell him how I was afraid to pull it out, that I didn't want him to embarrass me onstage by saying something about it being a terrible colour, but he loved it, so I stayed with it and he was happy."

Elvis Presley and The TCB Band carried and on to bring ecstatic shows throughout the 1970s, to some maybe reaching its pinnacle when being televised with the 1973 "Aloha From Hawaii" TV Special. But it was all over on 16 August 1977, actually a date for Elvis in Portland/Oregon. The start of new tour ... But it was over, before it had begun. Drummer Ronnie Tutt remembered being at home the day he heard the news, that Elvis had died. He hadn't seen Elvis for some time, having been busy playing and recording with Jerry Garcia.

"My mother-in-law called and said, 'You're not going to believe what I've heard,' so I immediately called Graceland and Felton Jarvis picked up the phone and I asked him if it was true and he told me yes, Elvis had died. We talked briefly and he told me it was a zoo at Graceland and not to come out unless I felt I had to. I didn't want to make my association with Elvis seem more than what it was and use it for any publicity purposes. I just went out in my garden and said my little piece with him.

"It's weird to think about it now. There had been a drought in California for several months and the minute I had it confirmed that Elvis had died and went into my garden, a little misty rain started coming down, so it was quite a moving time."

Bibliography
Sources for the Book "Elvis Presley"

Books:

Elvis Presley—Wo waren Sie, als Elvis starb? Schirmer/Mosel ISBN 978-3-8296-0827-5—Lester Bangs

Elvis—Die letzten 24 Stunden—Die Wahrheit über den Tod des King of Rock and Roll Bastei Lübbe ISBN3-404-61258-2 Albert Goldman 1993

Mein bester Freund Elvis von George Klein Hannibal Verlag ISBN 978-3-85445-328-4

Elvis—His Life from A-Z Fred L. Worth and Steve D. Tamerius Contemporary Books ISBN 0-8092-4528-0s

Elvis Presley Report Henno Lohmeyer Ullstein ISBN 3 548 27504 4

ELVIS Collection Rolf Heyne—Tara McAdams ISBN 978-3899103281

Elvis by the Presley's Edited by David Ritz Arrow Books ISBN 978-0-09-949797-4

Orion by Gail Brewer-Giorgio Tudor Books ISBN 0-944276-39-3

Is Elvis Alive? By Gail Brewer Giorgio Tudor Books ISBN 0-944276-31-8

The Elvis Files by Gail Brewer Giorgio Shapolsky Publishers ISBN 1-56171-000-8

Elvis Undercover by Gail Giorgio Bright Books ISBN 1-880092-49-2

On Stage with Elvis Presley by Stuart Coupe SEG Publishing ISBN 9780578777467

Bill Haley—The Father of Rock and Roll, The Rise of Bill Haley and Rock 'n' Roll by Otto Fuchs Books On Demand ISBN 978-3-7412-4856-6

Bill Haley—The Father of Rock and Roll, The Rock and Roll Revival Years and Bill Haley's Legacy by Otto Fuchs Books On Demand ISBN 978-3741248740

Hollywood Rock—A Guide to Rock 'n' Roll in the Movies—Marshall Crenshaw—Plexus ISBN 0 85965 218 1

Being Elvis A Lonely Life—Ray Connolly—Orion books ISBN 978-1-4746-0457-4

Elvis—The Music Lives On—Richard Peters—Pop Universal Souvenir Press—ISBN 0-2850-63099-7

Magazines:

Rock and Roll Musik Magazin, Edition 68—"Was mir auffiel?" by Claus D. Roeglin, Oldenburg/Germany (1989)

Rock and Roll Musik Magazin, Edition 69—"Post Box—Readers opinion on who is The King of Rock and Roll", Oldenburg/Germany (1989)

At The Hop Fanzine—"History of the Teddy Boys" by Otto Fuchs, UK (2018)

At The Hop Fanzine—"Elvis Series" by Nic Hop

Vintage Rock—Elvis In The Movies—Anthem Publishing

Newspapers:

The Guardian

The Independent

Internet:

www.elvis.com.au